Modern American Drama: Playwriting in the 1990s

DECADES OF MODERN AMERICAN DRAMA: PLAYWRITING FROM THE 1930s TO 2009

Modern American Drama: Playwriting in the 1930s
by Anne Fletcher
Modern American Drama: Playwriting in the 1940s
by Felicia Hardison Londré
Modern American Drama: Playwriting in the 1950s
by Susan C. W. Abbotson
Modern American Drama: Playwriting in the 1960s
by Mike Sell
Modern American Drama: Playwriting in the 1970s
by Mike Vanden Heuvel
Modern American Drama: Playwriting in the 1980s
by Sandra G. Shannon
Modern American Drama: Playwriting in the 1990s
by Cheryl Black and Sharon Friedman
Modern American Drama: Playwriting 2000–2009
by Julia Listengarten and Cindy Rosenthal

Modern American Drama: Playwriting in the 1990s

Voices, Documents, New Interpretations

Cheryl Black and Sharon Friedman

Series Editors: Brenda Murphy and Julia Listengarten

methuen | drama
LONDON • NEW YORK • OXFORD • NEW DELHI • SYDNEY

METHUEN DRAMA
Bloomsbury Publishing Plc
50 Bedford Square, London, WC1B 3DP, UK
1385 Broadway, New York, NY 10018, USA
29 Earlsfort Terrace, Dublin 2, Ireland

BLOOMSBURY, METHUEN DRAMA and the Methuen Drama logo
are trademarks of Bloomsbury Publishing Plc

First published in Great Britain 2018
Paperback edition first published 2021

Copyright © Cheryl Black, Sharon Friedman and contributors, 2018

Cheryl Black and Sharon Friedman have asserted their right under the Copyright,
Designs and Patents Act, 1988, to be identified as authors of this work.

For legal purposes the Acknowledgements on p. x constitute
an extension of this copyright page.

Cover design by Louise Dugdale
Cover image: Rally to Save the National Endowment of the Arts in Union Square
Park, New York City (1990). Photo © Images Press/Getty Images

All rights reserved. No part of this publication may be reproduced or
transmitted in any form or by any means, electronic or mechanical,
including photocopying, recording, or any information storage or retrieval
system, without prior permission in writing from the publishers.

Bloomsbury Publishing Plc does not have any control over, or responsibility for,
any third-party websites referred to or in this book. All internet addresses given
in this book were correct at the time of going to press. The author and publisher
regret any inconvenience caused if addresses have changed or sites have
ceased to exist, but can accept no responsibility for any such changes.

A catalogue record for this book is available from the British Library.

A catalog record for this book is available from the Library of Congress.

ISBN: HB: 978-1-472-57247-9
PB: 978-1-3502-1546-7
ePDF: 978-1-3501-5365-3
eBook: 978-1-3501-5366-0
Pack: 978-1-4725-7264-6

Series: Decades of Modern American Drama: Playwriting from the 1930s to 2009

Typeset by Fakenham Prepress Solutions, Fakenham, Norfolk NR21 8NN

To find out more about our authors and books visit
www.bloomsbury.com and sign up for our newsletters.

CONTENTS

Acknowledgements x
Biographical Note and Notes on Contributors xi
General Preface Julia Listengarten and Brenda Murphy xiii

1 Introduction to the 1990s *Cheryl Black* 1
  Politics 2
    The Clinton presidency 2
    International relations 4
  Society 5
    Terror on the home front 5
    AIDS 6
    Identity politics 7
  Science and technology 13
    Silicon Valley 13
    Genetics 14
    Space 15
  Everyday life 15
    Population and demographics 15
    Religion 15
    Domestic economy 16
    Fads 16
    Education 17
    Media 18
  Culture 18
    Music 18
    Film 21

Television 23
Sport 25
Literature 26
Art 28
Fashion 29
Food 29
The millennium approaches 30

2 American Theatre in the 1990s *Sharon Friedman* 33

The economic climate and funding sources in the 1990s 38
Censorship and the National Endowment for the Humanities: The 'NEA Four' 41
New business models for the theatre 43
The 'Broadway' theatre in the 1990s 44
Musical theatre 48
    The megamusical: British and French imports and the Americanization of the genre 50
    Disney on Broadway 53
    Lower-budget musical productions in the non-profit theatre 54
    Images of the nation in musical theatre 55
Drama and dramatists Off-, Off-Off-Broadway and beyond 60
Canonical playwrights 61
Themes of White male heteronormativity in the theatre of the 1990s 64
African American ethnic and feminist theatrical visions as genres and cultural practice 68
    African American theatre 69
    Asian American theatre 75
    Latina/o theatre 78
    Feminist theatre and the under-representation of women playwrights 81
    Lesbian/gay/queer theatre 87

Performance art 89
Conclusion: A theatre of diversity in form and intention 93

3 Terrence McNally *John M. Clum* 97
Introduction 97
Lips Together, Teeth Apart (1991) 101
A Perfect Ganesh (1993) 105
Love! Valour! Compassion! (1994–5) 108
Master Class (1995) 112
Corpus Christi (1998) 114
Conclusion 118

4 Paula Vogel *Joanna Mansbridge* 121
Introduction 121
The Baltimore Waltz (1992) 124
Hot 'n' Throbbing (1995) 128
The Mineola Twins (1997) 134
How I Learned to Drive (1997) 139
Conclusion 147

5 Tony Kushner *James Fisher* 149
Introduction 149
Angels in America (1991–2) 154
Codas to Angels: *Slavs!* (1994) and *G. David Schine in Hell* (1996) 162
Adaptations: *The Good Person of Setzuan* (1994) 163
Adaptations: *A Dybbuk; or, Between Two Worlds* (1997) 165
Homebody/Kabul (1999–2001) 168
Conclusion 172

6 Suzan-Lori Parks *Kevin J. Wetmore, Jr* 175
Introduction 175
Imperceptible Mutabilities in the Third Kingdom (1989) 184

The Death of the Last Black Man in the Whole Entire World (1989–92) 186
The America Play (1993) 188
Venus (1996) 191
In the Blood (1999) 193
Conclusion 196

Afterword *Cheryl Black and Sharon Friedman* 199
Introduction 199
Terrence McNally 205
Paula Vogel 208
Tony Kushner 211
Suzan-Lori Parks 213

Documents 217
Terrence McNally 217
    Nathan Lane, *Playbill*, 2015 217
    Interview by Mervyn Rothstein 218
    Interview by Charlie Rose 219
    Opera and Maria Callas 220
    On the evolution of *Master Class* 221
    Zoe Caldwell on McNally 221
    In protest against *Corpus Christi* 223
    McNally on *Corpus Christi* 223
Paula Vogel 224
    Interview with Arthur Holmberg on *How I Learned to Drive* 224
    Miriam Chirico on *A Civil War Christmas* 228
    On teaching 229
    On collaboration 230
Tony Kushner 231
    Interview with Zeljko Djukic by Cheryl Black regarding the Serbian premiere of *Homebody/Kabul* 231

Suzan-Lori Parks 239
    Liz Diamond 239
    Richard Foreman 241
    'An Equation for Black People Onstage' 241
    Interview with Han Ong 242
    Commencement Address at Mount Holyoke 243

Notes 245
Bibliography 277
Index 285

ACKNOWLEDGEMENTS

The authors would like to thank series editors Julia Listengarten and Brenda Murphy, and commissioning editor Mark Dudgeon from Bloomsbury Methuen Drama, for their knowledgeable, thoughtful and meticulous guidance throughout this process. We are deeply grateful to authors John M. Clum, Joanna Mansbridge, James Fisher and Kevin J. Wetmore, Jr. for their authoritative and insightful contributions. We would like to thank Syma Mohammed, LR Hults, Zeljko Djukic, Natasha Djukic, Kim Storry, Ronnie Hanna, Ian Buck and the staff at Bloomsbury Methuen Drama for their invaluable assistance. Special thanks to the University of Missouri Research Council for granting Cheryl Black a research leave to work on this project and to Dean Susanne Wofford and the faculty at the Gallatin School of New York University for granting Sharon Friedman a Faculty Research Fellowship.

BIOGRAPHICAL NOTE AND NOTES ON CONTRIBUTORS

Cheryl Black is Curators Distinguished Professor Emerita from the University of Missouri, a Fellow of the College of Fellows of the American Theatre and a Fellow of the Mid-America Theatre Conference. Her publications include *The Women of Provincetown, 1915–1922*, co-editor of *Experiments in Democracy: Inter-racial and Cross-Cultural Exchange in American Theatre, 1912–1945* (with Jonathan Shandell), editor of Volume 1 of Bloomsbury's forthcoming series on *Great North American Stage Directors*, and numerous journal articles and book chapters. She is also an actress (member AEA-SAG-AFTRA), stage director (30+ productions), and dramaturg.

Sharon Friedman is Associate Professor of Modern Literature and Drama in the Gallatin School of New York University. She is the editor of *Feminist Theatrical Revisions of Classic Works* and has authored numerous essays in publications such as *Theatre Journal, American Studies, New Theatre Quarterly, Women and Performance, New England Theatre Journal, Text and Presentation, Codifying the National Self: Spectators, Actors and the American Text* and *Intertextuality in American Drama*. She is currently working on a book project titled *The Gendered Terrain in the Theatre of War*.

John Clum (PhD, Princeton) is Professor Emeritus of Theater Studies and English at Duke University. He is the author of a number of books including *Still Acting Gay: Male Homosexuality in Modern Drama* (2001), *Something for the Boys: Musical Theater and Gay Culture* (2000), *The Drama of Marriage: Gay Playwrights/Straight Unions from Oscar Wilde to the Present* (2012), and *The Works of Arthur Laurents: Politics, Love and Betrayal* (2014), as well as numerous essays on twentieth- and twenty-first century playwrights, musical theatre, film, and opera. He has also edited three anthologies of contemporary gay drama. He is the librettist of two operas (composer George Lam) that have been produced in New York: *Heartbreak Express* (2015), and *Rumpelstiltskin* (2018).

James Fisher is Professor Emeritus in Theatre at the University of North Carolina at Greensboro, where he received the Mary Settle Sharp Teaching Excellence Award in 2017 and the Outstanding Teacher Award from the School of Music, Theatre and Dance in 2016. He was also the recipient of the 2007 Betty Jean Jones Award for Excellence in Teaching American Theatre from the American Theatre and Drama Society and is a Fellow of the College of Fellows of the American Theatre. He has acted in and/or directed over 150 theatre productions and his many publications include the forthcoming second editions of *The Theater of Tony Kushner: Living Past Hope (Routledge)* and *The Historical Dictionary of Contemporary American Theater* (Rowman & Littlefield), both to be published in 2021. Other publications include *The Historical Dictionary of American Theater: Modernism*, co-authored by Felicia Hardison Londré, and *The Historical Dictionary of American Theater: Beginnings*.

Joanna Mansbridge is Assistant Professor in the Department of English at City University of Hong Kong. Her teaching and research interests include theatre and performance studies, film, gender studies, and ecocriticism. Her work appears in *Theatre Journal, Genre, Theatre Research International, International Journal of Performance Arts and Digital Media, Modern Drama,* and *Theatre Topics,* as well as in edited collections. She is the author of *Paula Vogel* (University of Michigan Press, 2014), which is the first book-length study of the Pulitzer-winning playwright. She is on the international advisory board for the open source journal, *Performance Matters*.

Kevin J. Wetmore, Jr is Professor and Chair of Theatre Arts at Loyola Marymount University. He is the author of eight books, including *Athenian Sun in an African Sky: Modern African Adaptation of Classical Greek Tragedy, Black Dionysus: Greek Tragedy and African American Theatre* and *Modern Asian Theatre and Performance 1900–2000* (with Siyuan Liu and Erin B. Mee). He is also the editor or co-editor of 11 books, including *Suzan-Lori Parks: A Casebook, Portrayals of Americans on the World Stage, Black Medea* and the *Methuen Drama Anthology of Modern Asian Plays* (with Siyuan Liu).

GENERAL PREFACE

Decades of Modern American Drama: Playwriting from the 1930s to 2009 is a series of eight volumes about American theatre and drama, each focusing on a particular decade during the period between 1930 and 2010. It begins with the 1930s, the decade when Eugene O'Neill was awarded the Nobel Prize for Literature and American theatre came of age. This is followed by the decade of the country's most acclaimed theatre, when O'Neill, Tennessee Williams and Arthur Miller were writing their most distinguished work and a theatrical idiom known as 'the American style' was seen in theatres throughout the world. Its place in the world repertoire established, American playwriting has taken many turns since 1950.

The aim of this series of volumes is to focus attention on individual playwrights or collaborative teams who together reflect the variety and range of American drama during the 80-year period it covers. In each volume, contributing experts offer detailed critical essays on four playwrights or collaborators and the significant work they produced during the decade. The essays on playwrights are presented in a rich interpretive context, which provides a contemporary perspective on both the theatre and American life and culture during the decade. The careers of the playwrights before and after the decade are summarized as well, and a section of documents, including interviews, manuscripts, reviews, brief essays and other items, sheds further light on the playwrights and their plays.

The process of choosing such a limited number of playwrights to represent the American theatre of this period has been a difficult but revealing one. In selecting them, the series editors and volume authors have been guided by several principles: highlighting the most significant playwrights, in terms both historical and aesthetic, who contributed at least two interesting and important plays during the decade; providing a wide-ranging view of the decade's theatre, including both Broadway and alternative venues; examining many historical trends in playwriting and theatrical production during the decade; and reflecting the theatre's diversity in gender and ethnicity, both across the decade and across the period as a whole. In some decades, the choices are obvious. It is hard to argue with O'Neill, Williams, Miller and Wilder in the 1940s. Other decades required a good deal of thought and discussion. Readers will inevitably regret that favourite playwrights are left out. We can only respond that we regret it too, but we believe that the playwrights who are included reflect a representative sample of the best and most interesting American playwriting during the period.

While each of the books has the same fundamental elements – an overview of life and culture during the decade, an overview of the decade's theatre and drama, the four essays on the playwrights, a section of documents, an Afterword bringing the playwrights' careers up to date, and a Bibliography of works both on the individual playwrights and on the decade in general – there are differences among the books depending on each individual volume author's decisions about how to represent and treat the decade. The various formats chosen by the volume authors for the overview essays, the wide variety of playwrights, from the canonical to the contemporary avant-garde, and the varied perspectives of the contributors' essays make for very different individual volumes. Each of the volumes stands on its own as a history of theatre in the decade and a critical study of the four individual playwrights or collaborative teams included. Taken together, however, the eight volumes offer a broadly representative critical and historical treatment of eighty years of American theatre and drama that is both accessible to a student first encountering the subject and informative and provocative for a seasoned expert.

Brenda Murphy (Board of Trustees Distinguished Professor Emeritus, University of Connecticut, USA)
Julia Listengarten (Professor of Theatre at the University of Central Florida, USA)
Series Editors

1

Introduction to the 1990s

Cheryl Black

The last decade of the twentieth century is framed by two world-changing events: the fall of the Berlin Wall in 1989, heralding the end of the Cold War between America (Western democracy) and the Soviet Union (Eastern European communism), and the destruction of the World Trade Center Towers by the militant organization al-Qaeda on 11 September 2001, an event that triggered America's 'war on terrorism' now entering its fifteenth year.[1]

From the vantage point of the second decade of the twenty-first century, the 1990s, before 9/11 and before the fiscal debacle of 2007–8, was an era of relative peace and prosperity, dominated (for most of the decade) by a charismatic and moderately liberal president whose approval rating peaked at 73 per cent during his final year in office despite a steady stream of sexual and other scandals that led to his impeachment for perjury and obstruction of justice. It is a decade that has recently evoked a wave of nostalgia. In 2015, *New York Times* writer Kurt Anderson proclaimed the 1990s the 'best decade ever', citing economic prosperity; dramatic reductions in violent crime and in deaths from HIV/AIDS; an international 'tide of progress' marked by the fall of the Soviet Union, the end of South African apartheid and the normalizing of relations with China; vibrant cultural expression in music, literature and film; and *'just the right amount* of technology'.[2]

Like Clinton's presidency, however, the decade was marked by profound contradictions and has also been characterized as a 'best of times, worst of times' historical moment,[3] when the scientific and technological advances that created dot.com billionaires, cloned mammals and genetically modified crops inspired awe and anxiety in roughly equal proportions. It was a decade when the increased visibility and audibility of cultural minorities cracked the surface of mainstream complacency, revealing troubling undercurrents of sexism, racism and homophobia. It was a decade when the term 'media frenzy' entered the lexicon to describe the excessive zeal on the part of the media to satisfy public obsession with the decade's sensationally (in)famous events that rocked the nation, harbingers of even worse disasters (natural, political, military and economic) to come.

Politics

The Clinton presidency

The media feeding frenzy found much to relish during the presidential election of 1992. The Republicans had held the White House for twelve years, and the Republican candidate, incumbent President George H. W. Bush, who had also served for eight years as vice president during the administration of his party's revered Ronald Reagan, must have thought a second term would be a slam dunk. Bush was also a decorated veteran of the Second World War and had waged his own military 'operation' in Iraq in 1991, after which his approval rating rocketed to 90 per cent. His Democratic challenger was the largely unknown Arkansas governor Bill Clinton, whose campaign was plagued by accusations of draft-dodging and sexual indiscretions. Clinton was also the first presidential candidate to admit to having experimented with smoking pot, although he notably denied inhaling. In April 1992, *New York Times* reporter Wick Allison proclaimed that Clinton did not have a prayer and urged Democrats to snag the third party candidate, eccentric Texas billionaire Ross Perot, as their nominee.[4]

The tide began to turn, however, as the economic recession (begun in summer 1990) worsened and unemployment continued to rise.

In August 1992, the nation was devastated by the most destructive hurricane in US history, Hurricane Andrew, which caused sixty-five deaths and over $65 billion in damage.[5] Bush's approval dropped to 30 per cent. Meanwhile his running mate, incumbent Vice President Dan Quayle, was widely ridiculed for his inability to spell 'potato' on national TV. Although Clinton was criticized for choosing Tennessee senator Al Gore (a fellow Southerner) as his running mate, the 'Baby Boomer' ticket (at ages forty-five and forty-four, respectively, the youngest White House team in history) appealed to MTV's 'Rock the Vote' generation,[6] and Clinton's saxophone solo on the *Arsenio Hall* show in June 1992 sealed the deal. Clinton's crackerjack campaign team focused on the recession, and 'it's the economy stupid' became the iconic slogan of his winning campaign. In November 1992, Clinton won a decisive election, garnering 370 electoral votes (to Bush's 168) and 43 per cent of the popular vote (to Bush's 37.5 per cent and Perot's 18.9 per cent).[7] In true 1990s paradoxical fashion, Clinton's lead strategist James Carville and Republican campaign director Mary Matalin, who had alluded to Clinton in a 1992 *New York Times* article as a 'philandering, pot-smoking draft dodger',[8] were married in 1993.

As soon as Clinton took office, a fierce counter-attack was launched by conservative Republicans, spearheaded by Congressman Newt Gingrich. Gingrich and Congressman Richard Armey authored a 'Contract With America' that promised smaller government, lower taxes and other conservative reforms. As a result, the Republicans swept the 1994 elections, winning majorities in both houses of Congress for the first time in forty years, and Gingrich became Speaker of the House in 1995. Despite this setback, and an increasingly polarized political climate, Clinton, for the most part, fulfilled his campaign promises to generate economic growth, expand world trade, tackle crime and drug use, cut taxes on the middle class and move people from welfare to work.[9] Economic prosperity was his greatest achievement. Inheriting a budget deficit of 3.8 per cent, he left office with a budget surplus of 2.3 per cent.[10] The unemployment rate dropped from 7.5 per cent in 1992 to 4 per cent in 2000.[11] According to historian Mark White, Clinton can claim to have been 'the most successful economic president' of all time in terms of performance on these issues.[12] Along with Clinton, Federal Reserve Chairman Alan Greenspan was lauded as author of the economic boom. The 'boom', however, did not significantly reverse income inequality. By the end of the decade, Greenspan admitted that 'the gains have not been as widely spread across households as I would like'.[13] Writing in the early twenty-first century, historians compared the economic boom of Clinton's administration to other, unstable 'boom' and 'bust' eras, labelling the 1990s 'the roaring nineties', 'the new Gilded Age' and 'the greediest decade in history'.[14]

International relations

In 1992, Francis Fukuyama's bestselling *The End of History and the Last Man* posited Western liberal democracy as the last and best form of human government.[15] Colin Harrison has argued, however, that Fukuyama revealed a 'hubristic' complacency following the collapse of apartheid and communism that may have encouraged America's subsequent 'regime-change' interventions.[16] Although America avoided prolonged military engagement during the 1990s, several interventions that hovered somewhere between peace-keeping and nation-building laid the foundation for increasingly tense international relations. In 1991, President George H. W. Bush authorized 'Operation Desert Storm', which, in ten days, effected the liberation of Kuwait from invading Iraqi forces and elicited an agreement from Iraq to end support of international terrorism. During Clinton's administration, 'Operation Restore Hope', an effort to intervene in Somalia's Civil War, led to a disastrous attempted raid in Mogadishu in October 1993. Somali militia shot down two US Blackhawk helicopters, and the subsequent attempt to rescue the helicopter crews resulted in the deaths of twelve US soldiers and seventy-eight injured. After the battle, the bodies of two American soldiers were dragged through the streets.[17] Stung by the Somalian debacle, the US largely ignored the genocidal wars that raged in Rwanda (1990–4) and the military and ethnic conflicts following the dissolution of Yugoslavia that spanned the decade (1991–2001).[18]

At about the same time the Berlin Wall came tumbling down, two militant extremist organizations were formed, Hezbollah al-Hejaz and al-Qaeda, determined to end Western (especially American) influence in the Middle East. In 1992, al-Qaeda operatives bombed two hotels in Yemen where US troops were lodged en route to Somalia. No US personnel were harmed, but two tourists were killed.[19] In 1993, bombs exploded in the World Trade Center parking lot, killing six people and injuring a thousand. Six conspirators associated with al-Qaeda were captured, convicted and imprisoned. In 1996, Hezbollah operatives bombed the Kobar Towers in Saudi Arabia, which housed foreign military personnel. Nineteen USAF servicemen were killed and nearly 500 persons from various nations were injured.[20] In August 1998, al-Qaeda bombed US embassies in Nairobi, Kenya, and Dar es Salaam, Tanzania, killing more than 200 people and injuring more than 5,000 others.[21]

Society

Terror on the home front

As chilling as international acts of terror seem from a post-9/11 perspective, during the 1990s, terror on the home front garnered even more attention. Domestic terrorism included the 1996 bombing of the summer Olympic Games in Atlanta, Georgia, resulting in one death and over a hundred injuries. In 1997, two subsequent bombings in the Atlanta area (of an abortion clinic and a lesbian nightclub) led to the arrest and conviction of Eric Robert Rudolph for all three bombings. In 1995, the 'Unabomber', Theodore Kaczynski, was convicted and sentenced to eight life sentences; his mail bombs, delivered between 1978 and 1995, had killed three and injured eleven. In 1992, a stand-off between federal agents and anti-government separatist Randy Weaver (wanted on a weapons charge) in Ruby Ridge, Idaho, resulted in the deaths of Weaver's wife and son and a deputy US marshal. In 1993, a bloodier encounter between federal agents and an anti-government religious group called Branch Davidians in Waco, Texas, resulted in the loss of nearly ninety lives. Heated debate surrounded these tragic events; some blamed the Davidians as a 'doomsday cult' bent on self-destruction; others considered Waco and Ruby Ridge unwarranted abuses of federal power.

Among the tragic consequences of these events was the 1995 bombing of the Alfred P. Murrah Federal Building in Oklahoma

City, masterminded by Gulf War veteran Timothy McVeigh in retaliation for what he perceived as federal abuse of power. The blast killed 168 people, including nineteen children, and injured nearly 700 others. The destruction also included more than $600 million in damage. McVeigh was convicted of murder and conspiracy in 1997 and executed in 2001. His partner Terry Nichols was sentenced to life imprisonment without parole.[22]

The decade of shocking acts of domestic terror was brought to a heartbreaking conclusion with the deadliest high school shooting in US history.[23] In April 1999, two teenage boys, seniors at Columbine High School in Littleton, Colorado, shot and killed twelve students and a teacher, injured twenty-one others and then committed suicide. Documents left by the shooters indicate their wish to emulate the Oklahoma City bombing. The 'massacre' sparked heated debate throughout the nation regarding gun control, mental health, high school culture, Goth subculture, popular music, and violence in movies and video games. Rocker Marilyn Manson was particularly targeted as a harmful influence, a charge he rebutted in an interview with *Rolling Stone*.[24]

AIDS

The AIDS epidemic, which had erupted during the 1980s, continued to ravage the nation. The decade's casualties (over 300,000) included artist Keith Haring, dancer Rudolf Nureyev, designer Halston, actor Anthony Perkins, Queen's lead singer Freddie Mercury, tennis star Arthur Ashe, model Tina Chow, activist Elizabeth Glaser and eighteen-year-old Ryan White, who had been expelled from middle school when diagnosed at the age of twelve. In 1991, the Center for Disease Control reported that one million Americans were HIV-positive; by 1995, AIDS had become the leading cause of death among all Americans aged twenty-five to forty-four.[25] Awareness and activism, however, increased throughout the decade. In 1990, Congress passed the Americans with Disabilities Act, which protected individuals, including people with HIV/AIDS, from discrimination. In 1991, HIV-positive basketball legend Earvin 'Magic' Johnson became an advocate for HIV/AIDS research. In 1992, HIV-positive tennis star Arthur Ashe founded the Arthur Ashe Foundation for the Defeat of AIDS, and President Clinton established a new White House Office of National AIDS Policy.[26] In 1993, Tom Hanks won an Oscar for his role as a gay man with AIDS in the film *Philadelphia*. In 1995, Clinton formed the President's Advisory Council on HIV/AIDS. Beginning in 1996, new combination therapies led to a dramatic decline in AIDS-related deaths, which continued to drop throughout the remainder of the decade.[27]

Identity politics

'Identity politics' (an awareness of differential treatment within a society based on identity categories of race, class, gender, sexuality, religion, ability, etc.) had a major impact on American society in the 1990s. The renewed fervour with which the politics of identity dominated public discourse was partially attributable to shifting demographics.[28] A wave of immigration from Mexico significantly expanded the Hispanic and Latina/o population; by the end of the decade, three states had majority 'minority' populations, and one out of four Americans was of a race other than White.[29] Meanwhile, globalism challenged prevailing perceptions about national identity, and gender and sexual identities became similarly destabilized. All categories of identity were increasingly called into question, a condition that many found liberating and many found alarming. Race and racial conflicts dominated headlines for much of the decade, conflicts frequently complicated by gender, class and religious identities.

The case of Rodney King

In March 1991, George Holiday looked out of the balcony of his Los Angeles apartment and saw four White police officers brutally beating a Black man. It was not, as history suggests, an unusual event, but most likely no one would ever have heard about it if Holiday had not just purchased a Sony Camcorder (introduced to consumers in the 1980s). His videotaping of the beating of Rodney King 'went viral', sparking public outrage around the globe. Within a week, the LA district attorney dropped all charges against King (who suffered nine skull fractures, a crushed eye socket, a broken leg and nerve damage in the attack) and the LA County Grand

Jury charged the four officers with felony assault. When a mostly White jury in East Ventura County acquitted all four officers of the charges in April 1992, LA exploded. Six days of rioting, looting, arson and violence devastated the city and shook the nation. Fifty-five people were killed, 2,000 injured and property damage was estimated at over a billion dollars. These acts of violence reflected and brought into the public consciousness decades of disenfranchisement, poverty, oppression and racial conflict.

Crown Heights

Just a few months after the Rodney King incident, in the Crown Heights neighbourhood of Brooklyn, New York, a seven-year-old Guyanese American child named Gavin Cato was struck and killed by a station wagon bearing Lubavicher Grand Rebbe Menachem Schneerson, a Jewish spiritual leader in the community. The incident inflamed already-smouldering racial tensions; Black residents rioted, and a group of young Black men attacked and killed a Hasidic student from Melbourne, Australia, Yankel Rosenbaum. After three days of rioting, resulting in nearly 200 injuries, New York police finally restored order. Before he died, Rosenbaum was able to identify one of his assailants, who was tried and acquitted in 1992, but eventually served a ten-year sentence for violating Rosenbaum's civil rights.[30]

Anita Hill vs Clarence Thomas

In 1991, President George H. W. Bush nominated African American federal circuit judge Clarence Thomas to replace retiring Supreme Court Justice Thurgood Marshall. The nomination was somewhat controversial, as Thomas was known to hold conservative views on affirmative action and abortion rights, but his confirmation seemed assured until a young law professor named Anita Hill (also African American) accused Thomas of sexual harassment that occurred years earlier when she worked for him at the Equal Employment Opportunities Commission. Hill's televised testimony of Thomas's lewd conversation and conduct, and Thomas's dismissal of the hearings as a 'high-tech lynching', fed the media frenzy and threw the current state of racial and gender relations into sharp relief.

Thomas was eventually confirmed by a narrow margin. Feminists rallied in support of Hill, however; six Democratic congresswomen marched on the Senate to urge greater consideration of Anita Hill's charges, scrutinized by a Judiciary Committee composed entirely of men. The case brought increased attention to workplace sexual harassment, and the number of claims of sexual harassment filed with the federal Equal Employment Opportunity Commission more than doubled between 1991 and 1998.[31]

Susan Smith: Sex, lies, race and infanticide

In October 1994, a tearful, 23-year-old Susan Smith, from Union, South Carolina, claimed that her car, with her two small children inside, had been carjacked by a Black man. Days later, Smith admitted that she had deliberately drowned her children, strapping them into her car and then pushing it into a lake. Her apparent motive was her involvement with a man who did not want children. During her sensational trial, it was revealed that she had been sexually abused in her teens by her stepfather and had attempted suicide twice. The case attracted worldwide attention, and her false accusation exacerbated racial tensions in America. In 1995, Smith was sentenced to life imprisonment. By the end of the decade, two correctional officers had been convicted of having sex with her while in prison.[32]

O. J. Simpson's 'Trial of the Century'

Race, gender and technology converged in the highly publicized, televised trial of former professional football star O. J. Simpson for the murder of his ex-wife Nicole Simpson and her friend Ron Goldman in 1994. Both Nicole and Ron Goldman were White. For eight months, America obsessively tuned in to this real-life drama, beginning with the televised car chase in which Simpson, driving a white Ford Bronco, evaded LA police, with 95 million viewers watching. All the major players, including the judge, detectives, attorneys and witnesses, became overnight celebrities. The public fixation continued unabated for the duration of the trial, during which Simpson's history of physical abuse of Nicole was revealed, and *Time* magazine incurred public outrage by digitally darkening a cover photo of Simpson. Public opinion regarding Simpson's guilt was sharply divided along racial lines, and as the jury (composed of ten women and two men, with a racial/ethnic make-up of nine Black, two white and one Latino) deliberated, the nation braced itself for riots. On 3 October 1995, 100 million people stopped what they were doing to hear the verdict announcement. Cameras across the nation recorded the racial and gendered responses to the 'not guilty' verdict, as Black supporters cheered and White doubters shook their heads in shocked disbelief. According to a CBS poll, 78 per cent of Black Americans thought O. J. was innocent, and 75 per cent of White Americans thought he was guilty.[33] In 1997 the families of Ron Goldman and Nicole Simpson won a wrongful death lawsuit against Simpson. Like the Rodney King case, this trial exposed racial conflicts and racism within the US justice system, but Simpson's trial also brought increased attention to domestic abuse in America.

The status of women

Women in the 1990s were still feeling the effects of the conservative backlash of the 1980s, documented by journalist Susan Faludi's bestselling *Backlash: The Undeclared War Against American Women*, published in 1991. The decade saw the popularization of the term 'postfeminism', coined to suggest a 'third wave' in feminist activism, more inclusive than the 1970s 'second wave' of feminist activism, which third wave feminists critiqued as too focused on White, middle-class women and issues. More commonly, however, the prefix 'post' was used to dismiss any form of feminist activism as irrelevant and passé.

Yet women made substantial advances during the decade. Cultural icons of powerful womanhood included First Lady Hillary Clinton, media impresario Oprah Winfrey and domestic mogul Martha Stewart. Indeed, 1992 was dubbed 'the year of the woman' following the election of a record number of female senators. Clinton's administration saw the first 'Take Our Daughters to Work Day' in 1993 and the passage, in 1994, of the Violence Against Women Act. Hillary Clinton redefined the image of the 'First Lady', acting as a powerful political partner throughout her husband's presidency. On the other side of the political spectrum, in 1992 televangelist Pat Robertson demonized feminism as a 'socialist, anti-family political movement that encourages women to leave their husbands, kill their children, practice witchcraft, destroy capitalism, and become lesbians'.[34]

It is indicative of America's conflicted views of women and feminism that the era's most notable male figure, Bill Clinton, is equally remembered for sexual harassment and for record appointments of female cabinet members. Clinton appointed America's first female Attorney General (Janet Reno), first female Secretary of State (Madeleine Albright) and added a second female Supreme Court justice (Ruth Bader Ginsberg). Clinton's record as an advocate for women, however, was forever marred by recurring accusations of sexual harassment, beginning with allegations of a past affair between Clinton and Gennifer Flowers that surfaced during the 1992 election campaign. Clinton vehemently denied the affair at the time but later admitted to a sexual 'encounter' with Flowers. In 1994, Paula Jones, a former Arkansas state employee, sued the President for sexual harassment, eventually receiving an out-of-court settlement of $850,000. During the Jones hearing, former White House volunteer Kathleen Willey accused Clinton of sexually assaulting her in 1993. Foremost among Clinton's sexual scandals, however, was 'Monicagate', the gradual revelation of a sexual relationship with 22-year-old White House intern Monica Lewinsky, which spanned 1995–7 and eventually led to Clinton's impeachment for perjury and obstruction of justice. Special prosecutor Kenneth Starr's zealous pursuit of Clinton made him a controversial figure, and Clinton's infamous televised statement (later recanted), 'I did not have sexual relations with that woman', remains a YouTube favourite.[35]

Women struck back against sexual abuse with a vengeance in the 1990s. In 1991, eighty women who worked for the US Navy alleged sexual assault by nearly 100 men attending the Tailhook convention at the Las Vegas Hilton. Several women sued the Tailhook Association, a fraternal organization founded to support sea-based aviation, and the Hilton; defendant Navy Lieutenant Paula Coughlin settled with the Tailhook Association and won over $5 million in her suit against the Las Vegas Hilton.[36] In June 1993, a young woman named Lorena Bobbitt took drastic measures to end domestic abuse, cutting off her husband's penis with a knife while he slept (the penis was later surgically reattached). At the trial, Mrs Bobbitt claimed that her husband had repeatedly raped and abused her, and after seven hours of deliberation, the jury found her not guilty due to insanity. Although the case became fodder for late night comedians, it also brought increased attention to the issue of domestic violence, and 'bobbittize' entered the medical lexicon.

LGBTQ (lesbian, gay, bisexual, transgender, queer) rights and wrongs

As with women and ethnic minorities, identity politics of the 1990s encouraged gay Americans to 'come out' as a politically oppressed community seeking redress. In March 1990, AIDS activists in NYC founded Queer Nation to increase LGBTQ visibility and to combat homophobia. Their defiant chant, 'We're here! We're Queer! Get used to it!' became a rallying cry.

In 1997, comedienne Ellen DeGeneres made television history by coming out herself on *The Oprah Winfrey Show* and as her character on her popular sitcom, *Ellen*, becoming the first lesbian lead in television history. The episode attracted 42 million viewers and garnered DeGeneres an Emmy, a Peabody, a GLAAD award and a *Time* magazine cover.[37] The following year, NBC premiered *Will and Grace*, featuring a gay lawyer and straight interior designer as roommates, which ran for eight seasons, earning 16 Emmy Awards.

Despite increased visibility of gay Americans in popular culture, Gay Rights were forcefully opposed by the Christian Coalition (founded in 1989 by Pat Robertson) and an increasingly conservative Republican 'right wing'. The decade saw the implementation of both the 'don't ask, don't tell' policy for US military service (1994), which prohibited military personnel from discriminating against or harassing homosexual or bisexual service members, as long as they remained 'closeted', and the passage of the Defense of Marriage Act (1996), which defined marriage for federal purposes as the union of one man and one woman and allowed states to refuse to recognize same-sex marriages granted under the laws of other states.[38] What *New York Times* columnist Frank Rich labelled the 'homophobic epidemic' of 1998 culminated in October of that year with the brutal murder of a young gay man, Matthew Shepard, in Laramie, Wyoming.[39] This murder, along with the horrific murder of African American James Byrd, Jr by White supremacists in Jasper, Texas, also in 1998, led to the passage in 2009 of the Matthew Shepard and James Byrd, Jr. Hate Crimes Prevention Act, which expanded the 1969 United States federal hate-crime law to include crimes motivated by a victim's actual or perceived gender, race, sexual orientation or disability.

Science and technology

Silicon Valley

The 1990s saw the rise of the internet, a mechanism for connecting computers anywhere in the world, allowing unprecedented dissemination of information among individuals and heralding a worldwide technological and cultural transformation comparable to that following Gutenberg's invention of moveable type in the fifteenth century.[40] America entered the 'information age', personal computers became ubiquitous, a globally linked network of resources that could be accessed via the internet called the World Wide Web debuted and internet use increased from 14 per cent in 1995 to 46 per cent by 2000.[41] In 1993 the computer services company Mosaic, followed by Netscape, offered the public a quick and easy way to 'browse' the web. Netscape went public in 1995, was overtaken by Internet Explorer and eventually was acquired by the global media corporation AOL. By the mid-1990s, pocket-sized 'mobile phones' and affordable digital cameras appeared. The online auction site now known as eBay debuted in 1995 as AuctionWeb. Google, which offered users a method for searching the internet, was founded in 1998. By the late 1990s, 10,000 websites were being created daily, and billion-dollar, internet-inspired deals transpired at a rate of thirty per day.[42] By the end of the decade, movies recorded on DVDs replaced those recorded on videotape, and portable devices played music in MP3 (digital audio) format.

The technology boom was born in the southern San Francisco Bay Area, thereafter known as 'Silicon Valley', the land of high-tech innovation and dot.com tycoons. The giant among the new techno-billionaires was Microsoft mogul Bill Gates. Founded in 1975 by Gates and Paul Allen, Microsoft was a computer software company that developed and sold computer operating systems. In 1998, the

US Justice Department filed an antitrust suit against Microsoft, involving a plan to divide it into two companies. After years of legal battle, Microsoft avoided a break-up order by modifying some of its business practices.[43]

One of the major Silicon Valley stories of the decade was the return of tech entrepreneur Steve Jobs as CEO of Apple Inc., a company he had co-founded in 1976 to sell the Apple II, a personal computer primarily designed by Jobs's partner Steve Wozniak. In 1985, a power struggle within the company led to Jobs's resignation. After leaving Apple, Jobs founded NeXT, which developed computers for higher education and business markets, and helped fund and develop the animation studio Pixar. His triumphant return to Apple in 1996 brought the corporation from the verge of bankruptcy to the height of economic and cultural influence. It would become the world's largest and most profitable IT corporation in the twenty-first century, introducing the iMac, iTunes, the iPod, the iPhone, the iPad, Apple Stores and the iTunes Store.

Genetics

In 1997, scientists in Scotland introduced the world's first cloned mammal, a domestic sheep named Dolly. A year later, scientists in Hawaii announced the creation of dozens of cloned mice, and Japanese scientists reported the cloning of eight calves from the cells of a single cow. In 1998, maverick geneticist J. Craig Venter, impatient with the slow progress of the US government's Human Genome Project, announced his own plan to map and publish the entire human genetic code within three years, founding Celera Genomics to do so.[44]

Biotechnologists at the multinational, agrochemical corporation Monsanto made headlines in the development of genetically engineered crops; 'GMO' (genetically modified organisms) entered the vocabulary, and GMO foods appeared in American grocery stores in 1994. By 1999, over 100 million acres worldwide had been planted with genetically engineered seeds, and in 2000 *Time* magazine introduced the GMO controversy that would heat up in the twenty-first century. Were GMOs a miracle that would solve world hunger – or a toxic time bomb (fuelled by capitalist greed) that would destroy the eco-system?[45]

Space

Even as Americans heralded cyberspace as the 'new frontier', the launching of the Hubble Space Telescope in 1990 ushered in a 'new chapter of humanity's exploration of the universe',[46] sending back to earth high-resolution images from undreamed-of depths in space, leading to breakthroughs in astrophysics and astronomy. Other developments in the realm of astrophysics included the discovery of 'dark matter' (invisible, inferred from gravitational effects and generally believed to comprise 27 per cent of the total mass-energy of the universe), the discovery of the comets Hayakutake (by Yuji Hayakutake) and Hale-Bopp (by Alan Hale and Thomas Bopp, independently) and, in 1998, the landing of the robotic spacecraft Mars Pathfinder on Mars.

Everyday life

Population and demographics

In the 1990s, an ever-expanding US population grew older, more ethnically diverse and more urban. The population grew from 248.4 million in 1990 to 281.4 million by 2000, a 13.2 per cent increase, the largest in US history.[47] By the end of the decade, the median age in the US was 35.3, the highest median age on record, with a population of 35 million who were 65 or over.[48] The Latina/o population increased from 22.4 to 35.3 million. By 2000, three states (California, Hawaii and New Mexico), and the District of Columbia, had majority 'minority' (i.e. non-White) populations. Throughout the decade, approximately 80 per cent of Americans lived in metropolitan areas.[49]

Religion

Although, according to a Gallup poll, 82 per cent of Americans identified as Christian throughout the decade,[50] a Pew Research study discovered a 'reversal of increased religiosity observed in the mid-1990s' and 'declines in traditional social attitudes' including 'greater public acceptance of homosexuality and less desire for women to play traditional roles in society',[51] trends that had begun in the previous decade and would continue into the twenty-first century. According to Gallup, religious identifications for other groups also remained relatively stable throughout the decade (with 8–11 per cent identifying as unaffiliated and 7–8 per cent as Jewish, Muslim or 'other').[52]

Domestic economy

Median income grew from $52,623 in 1990 to $57,843 in 2000. In 1990, the median price of a house was $125,000; a new car, $16,950; a gallon of petrol, $1.34; a dozen eggs, $1.09; a loaf of bread, $0.70.[53] The average ticket price for a movie varied from about $4.25 at the start of the decade to around $5 by the close of the decade.[54] The high-tech boom, however, had its socio-economic downside, factoring into America's increasingly expanding expectations for 'the good life'. In 1998, sociology professor Juliet B. Schor reported that technological advances had vastly expanded the list of things Americans 'absolutely have to have', including home computers, answering machines, microwaves and car and home air conditioning. For the more affluent, sport utility vehicles, urban spas, personal trainers, limousine rides, computer equipment and 'McMansions' (large, showy homes) were becoming de rigueur. Schor cites a 1994 poll revealing that the 'dreams-fulfilling' income for Americans had doubled since 1986 (from $50,000 to $102,000).[55] By the end of the decade, the number of American households with a net income of more than $10 million had quadrupled, and the ultimate mark of material success in America was elevated from *millionaire* to *billionaire* status.[56]

Fads

Increasingly, high-tech 'toys' and equipment were popular with teens and adults, including personal computers and printers, mobile phones, pagers, discman players, home video games (Nintendo, Sega, Gameboy) and the file-sharing programme Napster. Fads for children included Pogs, Beanie Babies, Pokémon, Power Rangers, American Girl Dolls, Tamagotchi 'virtual' pets (a high-tech version of the pet rock), Furbies, Tickle-Me Elmo, troll dolls, My Little

Pony, Koosh Balls, Supersoakers, rollerblading, McDonalds Happy Meals, Ring Pops and Pop Rocks.[57]

Education

Public school enrolment at the elementary level (pre-kindergarten through to grade eight) rose from 29.9 million in autumn 1990 to 34.2 million in autumn 2003. Public school enrolment at the secondary level (grades nine through to twelve) rose from 11.3 million in 1990 to 15.1 million in 2007.[58] Maths and reading scores for US students improved slightly over the decade (after a dip in the previous decade), drop-out rates declined and, in 1992, 69 per cent of seniors planned to attend college, compared with 39 per cent a decade earlier. In 1990, 40 per cent of graduating seniors enrolled in four-year colleges or institutions (42 per cent by 2000). It was the decade in which college students joined the technological revolution, as computer labs and internet research became the norm.

The decade also witnessed a number of troubling trends: US seniors tested on general mathematics and science scored well below the international average;[59] the debate over teaching 'creation' as well as evolution to explain human origins continued throughout the decade; and metal detectors, police presence and routine locker searches became common in schools across the country as threats and acts of violence increased.[60] Despite efforts throughout the decade to increase diversity in US schools (for example, the Immigration and Nationality Act of 1990), schools became increasingly more separated by race in the 1990s.[61] Another disturbing development among undergraduates was the steadily increasing number seeking help for mental health concerns, including substance abuse, eating disorders, anxiety, depression and thoughts of suicide.[62] Meanwhile, college tuition costs rose steadily; in 1990, tuition for full-time undergraduates averaged $2,900 at public four-year institutions and $12,000 at private not-for-profit institutions. By 2000, the averages had risen to $4,300 and $15,900, respectively.[63]

Media

It would be impossible to overstate the pervasive impact of print and electronic media on everyday life in the 1990s. According to a government report, the average American worker devoted about nine hours a day to media: four hours and nine minutes for television; three hours listening to radio, mainly in a car; 36 minutes for recorded music; and 28 minutes for print reading (daily newspaper). In 1991, adult consumers spent $108.8 billion – about $353 per person – to receive news and entertainment via these means, and advertisers spent $80 billion to advertise their products through the media.[64]

Culture

Cultural expression in the 1990s both reflected and shaped the prevailing social context – race, class, sexuality and shifting gender roles infused the form and content of all cultural genres. Culture was also significantly characterized by an increased blurring between 'low' and 'high' categories of cultural forms and by the increased transference of the marginal into the mainstream, from 'subculture' to 'mass culture', as theatres, art galleries, museums and other performance spaces across the nation opened their doors to ever more diverse producers and consumers of cultural products. The decade witnessed such an increased blurring of former distinctions between 'popular' and 'elite' cultural expression that such categories, by the end of the decade, were virtually meaningless.

Music

The 1990s was a golden age for music in America. Traditional genres, like pop-rock and country, enjoyed a renaissance, new subgenres emerged and independent record labels and artists commanded attention. *Rolling Stone* writer Brian Hiatt has described the 1990s as

> richer, funnier and weirder than [previously considered] ... [with] fake grunge bands writing better songs than some of the

real ones, Eighties holdovers U2 and R.E.M. reaching creative peaks with *Achtung Baby* and *Automatic for the People*, Metallica and the Black Crowes co-existing on MTV, Phish tending to the Deadhead nation after Jerry's passing – and Vanilla Ice and MC Hammer ceding their pop thrones in a few short years to Dr. Dre, Snoop and Eminem.[65]

The first multi-musical-genre Lollapalooza was held in 1991 featuring alt-rock, metal and mixed-genre bands Jane's Addiction, Siouxsie and the Banshees, Living Colour, Nine Inch Nails, Fishbone, Ice T and Body Count, Butthole Surfers, Rollins Band, EBN and Violent Femmes.

Women enjoyed unprecedented success in all genres, including pop stars Britney Spears, Mariah Carey, Celine Dion, Whitney Houston and the Spice Girls; country stars Dixie Chicks, Faith Hill and Reba McEntire; rappers Sister Souljah, Lil' Kim, Lauryn Hill and Queen Latifah; and genre-defying folk/blues/rock blenders Liz Phair, Sheryl Crow, Tracy Chapman, Sinead O'Connor and the Indigo Girls. The pop-rock/singer-songwriter movement was linked to third wave feminism and was perhaps best represented by Alanis Morissette's multi-platinum 1995 album *Jagged Little Pill*.

Country music continued to build on the 1980s momentum, increasingly blurring lines between country, rock, pop and folk genres. *Country Weekly* magazine debuted in 1994. The CMT cable music video series, begun in the 1980s, grew in popularity and in its resemblance to MTV and VH1. Garth Brooks dominated country music, becoming one of the bestselling recording artists of all time. Billy Ray Cyrus's 'Achy Breaky Heart' started a dance craze in 1992. Tim McGraw shot to the top of the charts with his debut album, *Not a Moment Too Soon* (1994), and his marriage in 1996 to country music singer Faith Hill, whose hit single 'This Kiss' went platinum in 1998, created a country music power couple. Other popular country artists of the decade included Reba McEntire, The Judds, Alan Jackson, Shania Twain and Toby Keith.

The movement from subculture to mass culture was particularly pronounced in the rise of gangsta rap and grunge as the most influential genres of the era. Grunge emerged in the 1980s as part of Seattle's underground, alternative rock scene. Described by a local producer as 'Seventies-influenced, slowed-down punk music',[66] grunge was developed by young and vaguely rebellious White guys sporting longish, unkempt hair, flannel shirts, wool sweaters, worn jeans and combat boots and became a national phenomenon when Nirvana's *Nevermind* debuted in 1991. By January 1992, *Nevermind* had replaced pop star Michael Jackson's *Dangerous* at number one on the Billboard chart. *Nevermind*'s single 'Smells Like Teen Spirit' became an anthem for America's 'Generation X', and Nirvana's frontman Kurt Cobain was the rock icon of the day. In 1994, however, the brilliant and troubled new superstar committed suicide. The grunge sound (and look) remained popular throughout the decade, manifested in bands like Foo Fighters, Pearl Jam, Alice in Chains, Smashing Pumpkins and Soundgarden.

Gangsta rap, as a sub-genre of hip-hop music and culture, gave artistic expression to the reality of life in the inner city for young Black men, including gang violence, police brutality, crime, drug use and sex. Influential albums of the 1990s include Body Count's *OG: Original Gangster*, with the provocative single 'Cop Killer' (1991), and Snoop Doggy Dogg's *DoggyStyle* (1993), featuring the single 'For All My Niggaz and Bitches'. The founding of Death Row Records (1991) by Dr. Dre, D.O.C., and Suge Knight was another milestone. Among their roster of artists was Tupac Shakur, whose *Me Against the World* (1995) is considered one of the most influential hip-hop albums of all time.

Despite the enormous commercial success of gangsta rap, it was widely condemned by religious leaders, politicians (from Left and Right) and some Black celebrities, including Bill Cosby (whose successful sit-com, *The Cosby Show*, was portraying a distinctly different, upper middle-class Black experience) and film director Spike Lee. Critics perceived gangsta rap as promoting violence, crime, misogyny, profanity, homophobia and drug use, and perpetuating racist stereotypes. Gangsta rap, however, struck a responsive chord in young Americans, making it into the mainstream with later artists whose themes and lyrics were somewhat less raw, including MC Hammer, Prince (Will Smith), Puff Daddy and female rappers Lil' Kim and Queen Latifah. Toward the end of the decade White rapper Eminem caused a sensation with his second album, *Slim Shady LP* (1999). During the next decade, Eminen became one of the bestselling rappers in the world and would be dubbed 'the King of Hip Hop' by *Rolling Stone* in 2011.

Near the end of the decade, a *Wall Street Journal* article reported similar surges in classical music forms since 1980: 110

new American symphonies founded; opera attendance up 34 per cent ('spurred by the use of computerized 'supertitles' that translate lyrics'); and a threefold increase in public radio stations broadcasting 'a once-exotic blend of classical music and introspective news'. According to sources cited in this article, the percentage of Americans who reported listening to classical music on the radio had increased from 19 per cent in 1982 to 41 per cent in 1997.[67]

Film

Filmmaking in the 1990s saw the ascent of 'underground' cinema, with many major studios developing independent branches that produced some of the decade's most memorable films. As the average film budget continued to climb, reaching over $50 million by 1998, the industry witnessed a surge of surprisingly successful low-budget efforts. The phenomenal success of Miramax's *Sex, Lies, and Videotape* (directed by Steven Soderbergh on a $1.2 million budget), which won the Palme d'Or at Cannes in 1989 and realized over $24 million, was a harbinger of things to come. In 1992, Quentin Tarantino made a historic screen debut in what would become his signature non-linear, 'neo-noir' style with *Reservoir Dogs*. Film critic David Edelstein has compiled a list of seminal, independent films that appeared in the watershed year of 1993: 'Richard Linklater's *Dazed and Confused*, Ben Stiller's zeitgeist-defining *Reality Bites*, Larry Clark's grungy *Kids*, and Kevin Smith's scrappy *Clerks*.'[68] In 1994, Tarantino's *Pulp Fiction*, a campy, meta-cinematic blend of homages to other movies (especially film noir), which Edelstein considers the most influential film of the decade, won the Palme d'Or and seven Oscar nominations.[69] In 1994, the Independent Film Channel was created by the Bravo cable network as an outlet for independent films, and in 1995, the Sundance Channel was created as a similar outlet by the Showtime cable TV network. A new Hollywood studio, DreamWorks, was formed in 1994 by director Steven Spielberg, former Disney executive producer Jeffrey Katzenberg and film and music producer David Geffen. In 1996, four of the five films nominated for Best Picture Academy Awards were from independent studios. By the decade's end, DreamWorks had two Best Picture winners: Sam Mendes's *American Beauty* (1999) and Ridley Scott's *Gladiator* (2000), and the distinction between 'independent' and 'major studio' films had irrevocably blurred.

Notable cinematic innovations made possible by new digital and computer technology included digital soundtracks (*Dick Tracy* was the first in 1990) and digital photography. In 1994, *Forrest Gump* used digital photography to insert Tom Hanks into historical footage, to erase the legs of amputee Gary Sinese and to enhance the ping-pong game, and in 1999, *Star Wars Episode I: The Phantom Menace* included characters that were entirely digitally rendered.

Another notable development in film during the decade was the renaissance in commercially and critically successful animated features (including computer-animated films), beginning with Disney's 1989 *The Little Mermaid* and including *Beauty and the Beast* (1991) *Aladdin* (1992), *The Lion King* (1994) and Pixar/Disney's *Toy Story* (1995) and *Toy Story 2* (1999).

Although noted for innovation and independent entrepreneurship, the 1990s was also a decade in which record numbers of media mergers transformed even the mainstreams into a sea of concentrated power. In 1990, Matsushita Industrial, Inc. acquired the entertainment conglomerate MCA/Universal; in 1992, Warner Communications and Time Inc. merged to form Time/Warner. In 1994, Viacom bought Paramount Pictures. In 1995, Seagram bought MCA/Universal (renamed Universal Studios), and Disney (which had become, in 1994, the first studio to gross $1 billion at the box office) bought the ABC network. In 1996, Time/Warner bought Ted Turner's Turner Broadcasting System (TBS) and in 1997 MGM acquired Orion.

The decade's top ten box-office hits were *Titanic* (1997); *Star Wars Episode I: The Phantom Menace* (1999); *Jurassic Park* (1993); *Forrest Gump* and *The Lion King* (a tie in 1994); *Independence Day* (1996); *The Sixth Sense* (1999); *Home Alone* (1990); *Men in Black* (1997); *Toy Story 2* (1999); and *Twister* (1996).[70] The decade's Oscar-winners for Best Picture were *Dances with Wolves* (1990), *The Silence of the Lambs* (1991), *Unforgiven* (1992), *Schindler's List* (1993), *Forrest Gump* (1994), *Braveheart* (1995), *The English Patient* (1996), *Titanic* (1997), *Shakespeare in Love* (1998) and *American Beauty* (1999).

Television

In the 1990s, MTV gained increasing influence as a cultural ambassador for America's youth, profoundly influencing television programming, the film industry, sport, race, teen sexuality and politics.[71] In 1992, MTV premiered *The Real World*, launching reality TV as we know it by filming the daily, unscripted interactions among seven strangers who agreed to live together in a Soho loft. The following year, MTV introduced the animated, adult cartoon *Beavis and Butthead*, featuring semi-literate cartoon teens whose crude language and attitudes ('That sucks!' was their mantra) delighted actual teens and horrified the conservative.

Animation had won a prime-time network television audience with the 1989 premiere of *The Simpsons*, which remained enormously popular throughout the 1990s. Ostensibly a parody of American family sit-coms, *The Simpsons* addressed current social issues, like the environment and the economy, in a subtly subversive way. Edgy enough to arouse indignation among conservatives and applause from the hip, *The Simpsons* achieved iconic status, contributing popular catchphrases such as Bart Simpson's 'Eat my shorts' and 'Don't have a cow, man.' Other adult-themed, animated shows that attracted large audiences included *South Park* and *King of the Hill* (premiering in 1997) and *Family Guy* and *Futurama* (premiering in 1999).

Some of the decade's prime-time, network sit-coms reflected changing perceptions of gender, sexual and ethnic identities. New images of womanhood were presented in *Murphy Brown* (Candice Bergen's powerful, professional, broadcast journalist) and *Roseanne* (Roseanne Barr's strong-willed, working-class mother). Representations of women grew increasingly ambiguous, however, toward the end of the decade. In their later seasons, Murphy Brown's decision to have a baby as a single mother outraged conservatives but disappointed some women who saw this choice as prescribing motherhood as a 'natural' expression of womanhood,[72] and Roseanne Barr was 'rescued' from her socio-economic status by winning the lottery. In 1997, Ally McBeal was a single, professional woman (a lawyer) who wore mini-skirts and was haunted by visions of a dancing baby, while 1998's *Sex and the City* featured thirty-something, single women who prioritized female friendships over wayward boyfriends yet displayed dismayingly superficial dependence on high fashion and expensive footwear.

The popular sitcom *Frasier* presented a new image of American masculinity – Kelsey Grammer and David Hyde Pierce as sophisticated, witty and well-groomed siblings, quintessential 'metrosexuals' (a term coined in 1994 to describe an urban male who pays careful attention to appearance and lifestyle). *Ellen* and *Will and Grace* mainstreamed gay characters and lifestyles. *The Fresh Prince of Bel-Air* offered a reassuring image of hip-hop culture in its relocation of a street-smart yet affable young Black man (Will Smith) from the streets of Philadelphia to a wealthy Los Angeles suburb.

Popular dramas like *Murder She Wrote*, *Law and Order*, *The X Files* and *ER* featured women and ethnic minorities in leading roles. *Freaks and Geeks*, *My So-Called Life* and *Beverly Hills 90210* presented teens confronting real-life issues: substance abuse, sexuality, homophobia, AIDS, racism, eating disorders, violence and homelessness.

NBC's 'Must See TV' Thursday night line-up included two of the most popular sit-coms in television history. *Friends*, which premiered in 1994, touched a chord with its romantically ambiguous relationships among six (three of each sex) twenty-something New Yorkers with indefinite professional and personal futures. Its finale was watched by 52.5 million viewers after a decade-long run.[73] *Seinfeld*, which ran from 1989 to 1998, depicted the personal and professional misadventures of four self-absorbed, cynical, yet highly entertaining characters, starring comedian Jerry Seinfeld essentially playing himself. The show introduced popular catchphrases like 'yadda, yadda, yadda', 'spongeworthy' and 're-gifting', and imbued familiar terms or phrases like 'double-dipping', 'shrinkage' and 'Not that there's anything wrong with that' with new meanings. Their finale in 1998 was watched by 76.3 million viewers.[74]

As in film, entrepreneurial mavericks and mergers made news in television during the 1990s. In 1991, TBS network founder Ted Turner became the first media figure to be named *Time* magazine's Man of the Year; in 1992, the Cartoon Network debuted; in 1995, two additional national broadcast networks were formed, Warner Brothers (WB) and Paramount (UPN), and the Fox News Channel premiered; in 1996, Warner Cable and Time Inc.'s American Television and Communications Corp. merged to form Time Warner Cable.

Sport

Throughout the 1990s, football remained America's most popular sport. The decade's Superbowl winners included the San Francisco 49ers (1990 and 1995), the New York Giants (1991), the Washington Redskins (1992), the Dallas Cowboys (1993, 1994, 1996), the Green Bay Packers (1997) and the Denver Broncos (1998 and 1999). Significant milestones of the decade included Don Shula becoming the most successful coach in NFL history (with 325 victories); Miami's Dan Marino surpassing Pro Football Hall of Famer Fran Tarkenton in four major passing categories to become the NFL's all-time career leader; San Francisco's Jerry Rice becoming the all-time reception and receiving-yardage leader; and Dallas's Emmitt Smith scoring twenty-five touchdowns, breaking the season record of twenty-four set by Washington's John Riggins in 1983.

The Chicago Bulls dominated basketball in the 1990s, winning six championships with superstar players like Scottie Pippen, Dennis Rodman and the man many consider the greatest basketball player of all time, Michael Jordan. The Bulls' Michael Jordan and Scottie Pippen helped America win a worldwide fan base in 1992, when the US sent its first Olympic team that included NBA players to Barcelona. The legendary 'Dream Team', still considered by many the greatest team ever assembled, in any sport, also included Magic Johnson, Larry Bird, Charles Barkley and Patrick Ewing. They dominated the Olympic competition, winning the gold medal with a 117–85 victory over Croatia.

Baseball made headlines in the 1990s with its 1994 Major League Baseball strike, the eighth (and longest) in baseball history. Motivated by financial disputes between owners and players, the strike began in August 1994 and continued for a year, including, for the first time since 1904, the cancellation of the World Series. Other notable events in the game included Baltimore Orioles' Cal Ripken Jr's 1995 breaking of Lou Gehrig's record for consecutive games played (Ripken Jr's 2,632 to Gehrig's 2,130) and the race in 1998 between St Louis Cardinals' Mark McGwire and Chicago Cubs' Sammy Sosa that resulted in both beating Roger Maris's home-run record (61) with seventy and sixty-six runs, respectively. World Series championships went to the Cincinnati Reds (1990), Minnesota Twins (1991), Toronto Blue Jays (1992 and 1993), Atlanta Braves (1995), Florida Marlins (1997) and the New York Yankees (1996, 1998, 1999).

Sport in the 1990s included memorable feats of heroism and notorious acts of infamy. In 1994, figure skater Nancy Kerrigan won the silver medal in the 1994 Lillehammer Winter Olympics just seven weeks after an attack by a hired assailant that seriously injured her right knee. In 1996, Olympic gymnast Kerri Strug won the gold medal in Atlanta despite an ankle injury. That same year, 25-year-old champion professional cyclist Lance Armstrong was diagnosed with testicular cancer. When Armstrong returned to cycling in 1998, winning the 1999 Tour de France, he became an international sports hero. One of the greatest hockey players of all time, Wayne Gretzsky, retired in 1999 holding 61 NHL records. Twenty-one-year-old professional golfer Tiger Woods won the 1997 Masters Tournament and became the number one ranked golfer in the world, finishing the decade by winning the PGA Championship in 1999. In 1994, America hosted the World Cup, creating a new fan base for soccer in America. In July 1999, *Sports Illustrated*'s cover image of Women's World Cup soccer champion Brandi Chastain became iconic. Pete Sampras dominated tennis, achieving number one ranking in 1998. Women's tennis star Monica Seles recovered from a nearly fatal assault by an obsessed fan in 1993 to win the 1996 Australian Open. Fallen heroes included heavyweight champion Mike Tyson, who was convicted of rape in 1992, served three years, regained the title in 1996 and lost it to Evander Holyfield in the same year. A 1997 rematch ended when Tyson was disqualified for biting part of Holyfield's ear off. In June 1994, champion figure skater Tonya Harding was banned for life from the US Figure Skating Association after pleading guilty to hindering the prosecution following the January 1994 attack on Nancy Kerrigan, one of Harding's competitors, an attack arranged by Harding's ex-husband and bodyguard.[75]

Literature

In the 1990s, bookselling became a very big business, heralded by the creation and national proliferation of superstores Barnes & Noble and Borders, and online book sales pioneered by Amazon.com in 1995. The term 'postliterate' appeared, suggesting that the internet age had rendered literature passé, but whether or not people were *reading* books, they were definitely *buying* them. Both superstores and online shopping boosted sales, which climbed to $25 billion by 2000.[76]

Another boost for literacy came through the creation of Oprah Winfrey's Book Club in 1996, for which Oprah selected a new book for viewers to read and discuss each month. The 'Oprah Effect' significantly boosted sales for its selections, which included *The Deep End of the Ocean* by Jacquelyn Mitchard (1996), *Paradise* by Toni Morrison (1997), *A Lesson Before Dying* by Ernest J. Gaines (1997), *I Know This Much is True* by Wally Lamb (1998) and *A Map of the World* by Jane Hamilton (1999).

Mergers also affected publishing, as Bertelsmann AG acquired the largest US trade publisher, Random House, Inc., and merged with Bantam Doubleday Dell. Further consolidation of adult trade book publishing occurred in mid-1999, when News Corporation acquired William Morrow and Avon Books from the Hearst Corporation.[77]

Stephen King and John Grisham were two of the decade's bestselling authors of fiction: King's bestsellers included *Dolores Claiborne* and *The Stand*; Grisham's included *The Firm*, *The Pelican Brief* and *The Client*. Other bestselling fiction included Jean Auel's *The Plains of Passage*, Robert Ludlum's *The Bourne Ultimatum*, Tom Clancy's *The Sum of All Fears*, Terry McMillan's *Waiting to Exhale*, Robert James Waller's *The Bridges of Madison County*, Laura Esquevel's *Like Water for Chocolate*, Michael Crichton's *The Lost World*, Charles Frazier's *Cold Mountain*, Thomas Harris's *Hannibal* (sequel to *Silence of the Lambs*) and Terry Brook's *Star Wars Episode I: The Phantom Menace*. The end of the decade brought a sensation from an unexpected source, as a children's book by an unknown British author, J. K. Rowling's *Harry Potter and the Sorcerer's Stone*, soared to the *New York Times* bestselling list in 1999. Other popular children's books included R. L. Stein's *Goosebumps* series and Louis Sachar's *Holes*. It is worth noting that almost all of these books were made into films, as film and other media became increasingly important as a conveyor of literature (as well as music).

Influential non-fiction works addressing topical issues such as race, shifting gender roles, LGBTQ experience, the environment, poverty and international politics included Camille Paglia's *Sexual Personae*, Judith Butler's *Gender Trouble*, Eve Kosofsky Sedgwick's *The Epistemology of the Closet*, Christina Hoff Sommers's *Who*

Stole Feminism? How Women Have Betrayed Women, Naomi Wolf's *The Beauty Myth*, Ellen Fein and Sherrie Schneider's *All the Rules: Time-Tested Secrets for Capturing the Heart of Mr. Right*, Dinesh D'Souza's *Illiberal Education: The Politics of Race and Sex on Campus*, Al Gore's *Earth in the Balance*, Cornel West's *Race Matters*, Homi Bhabha's *The Location of Culture*, Richard J. Herrnstein and Charles Murray's *The Bell Curve*, Nelson Mandela's *Long Walk to Freedom* and Barack Obama's *Dreams from My Father*.

Art

As with other forms of cultural expression during the decade, visual art in America reflected an increasingly diverse and heterogeneous culture as artists from marginalized communities gained prominence. They produced art that blurred genres, multi-media art, installation art, performance art, site-specific art and art that more and more overtly functioned as cultural criticism. As art critic Allex Allenchey declared (in retrospect), 'paintings are dead! Subcultures rule!'[78]

Representative artists include Nari Ward, whose sculptural installations used found materials from his Jamaica Queens neighbourhood to comment on race, poverty and consumerism; Kara Walker, whose 1994 silhouette mural *Gone, An Historical Romance of a Civil War as It Occurred Between the Dusky Thighs of One Young Negress and Her Heart* exposed and critiqued the relationship between sexuality and slavery (and American culture's romanticization of such); and Cindy Sherman, whose *Sex Pictures* series (using prosthetic limbs and mannequins) critiqued the sexual exploitation of women and women's bodies.

Critic Jerry Saltz has pinpointed the 1993 Whitney Biennial as a watershed moment, featuring admission buttons designed by artist Daniel J. Martinez that read 'I Can't Imagine Ever Wanting to Be White', artist Coco Fusco costumed as a Native American in a cage in the courtyard, and a video of artist Matthew Barney as a satyr sans genitals. According to Saltz, 'people went batshit', clamouring that politics had replaced pleasure in art. For many, however, including Saltz, it was 'the moment when today's art world was born ... these artists were against not beauty but complacency; they were for pleasure through meaning, personal meaning.'[79]

Fashion

Music, politics and sport influenced fashion in the 1990s. Fashion accessories tied to political causes included the yellow ribbon that appeared in support of the first Gulf War and the red ribbon to foster AIDS awareness (1991). The grunge look included overalls, flannel shirts, faded jeans, bulky sweaters and hiking boots. Hip-hop inspired urban streetwear and sportswear: unlaced trainers, oversized baseball jackets, baggy jeans, bomber jackets, tracksuits, All Stars and Air Jordans. Later in the decade, the British girl group All Saints popularized baggy jeans, cargo pants, T-shirts, sweatshirts, tanktops and crop tops among young girls. Young women also wore sports bras, hoodies, leotards, tights, leggings, slouch socks, Nikes and Reeboks. Piercings (not only ears, but tongues, navels, nipples, lips and noses) and tattoos were favoured by both sexes. Among women, the 'Rachel', a layered brown shag with blonde highlights worn by Jennifer Aniston's character in *Friends*, became the iconic hairstyle of the decade. Men in the 1990s wore long hair, cornrows, as well as short, spiky looks. Bandannas and baseball caps worn backward were popular headgear.

Other fashion trends included solid tees under blazers, Timberland boots, Doc Martens, high platform shoes, jelly shoes, the colours of Benetton, Guess jeans and Calvin Klein jeans and underwear (CK's sexy ad campaign in 1995 featuring scantily clad and provocatively posed young models led to accusations of child pornography and eventually caused CK to withdraw the adverts). The 1990s also ushered in a more informal trend in corporate fashion. In 1992, Levi's published *A Guide to Casual Businesswear*, prominently featuring Levi's Dockers. What began as 'Casual Fridays' (suits and ties optional) would become the new normal in professional attire by the twenty-first century.

Food

During the 1990s, an increasingly anxious yet self-indulgent population, worried about weight and cholesterol levels, struggled to have its cake and eat it too, consuming low-fat versions of ice cream, cookies, beverages, chips, salad dressing, bacon and hamburgers, some containing a new fat substitute called 'olestra'. Given the pervasive two-career household, speed and convenience were also paramount. Microwaves were ubiquitous. Groceries super-sized into gigantic emporiums featuring chemists, banking services, coffee and fast-food bars, and food-to-go counters. Meanwhile, Martha Stewart encouraged women to return to the kitchen with style, Barbara Bush and Hillary Clinton published rival cookie recipes, and the 24-hour Food TV Network premiered.

Popular trends included organic farming, 'Fusion' cooking, which combined ingredients from diverse cuisines and cultures, and 'alternative beverages': bottled water, smoothies, Jamba Juice, sports drinks, flavoured water, designer sodas and flavoured bottled teas.[80] Southwest and Mexican cuisine grew increasingly popular, and salsa replaced ketchup as America's favourite condiment. Coffee shops, following the Starbucks model, proliferated, becoming the new trendy meeting place (as portrayed in popular television shows like *Frasier*, *Seinfeld* and *Friends*).

The millennium approaches

Americans in 1999 faced not only the usual *fin de siècle* mixture of hope and dread that marks the end of a century, they faced the end of a *millennium*. Certainly the decade's extremes of advance and upheaval, prosperity and deprivation, heroism and terrorism, were enough to arouse *fin de millénaire* consternation. Throughout the decade, surveys indicated a steady expansion of desire and expectation, along with an increasing doubt of their fulfilment. In July 1999, 'America's Prince', John F. Kennedy Jr, died in a plane crash, a profoundly symbolic bereavement for Americans who remembered his charismatic father's assassination in November 1963 as the defining moment of their generation, and the image of three-year-old John-John solemnly saluting his father's coffin as the quintessential symbol of mourning and loss.

In March 1999, a blockbuster movie exploiting America's fear of technology appeared, reminding Americans, 'The Matrix "is everywhere," yet "nowhere," because it is not "real."'[81] *Fin de millénaire* anxieties finally coalesced into the 'Y2K' problem. When computers were first developed, storage space was at a premium;

to save space, programmers wrote dates with two digits rather than four. Panic set in as people confronted the possibility that computers might not be able to distinguish '2000' (coded '00') from '1900', thereby causing 'worldwide failures in computer systems leading to severe economic damage, and in more apocalyptic accounts, The End of The World As We Know It'.[82] Nations across the globe spent billions of dollars in efforts to address the crisis, an undertaking that involved the 'rewriting of millions of lines of computer code and the scrapping and replacement of equipment worth billions of dollars ... [T]he leading nation in responding to Y2K, and in promoting international action, was the United States.'[83] In 1998, President Clinton created a Council on Year 2000 Conversion and appointed John Koskinen chairman. Koskinen (aka the Y2K 'czar') worked with twenty-five task forces and a staff that grew to 200 to prevent or deal with the catastrophe, creating a consumer hotline and a website to allay public anxiety.[84]

And then everyone held their breath, as the millennium approached.

2

American Theatre in the 1990s

Sharon Friedman

Theatre historians writing in the early years of the twenty-first century look back on the developing American theatre as a powerful cultural force in the construction and performance of American identity. The liveness of theatre, with performers as our proxies interacting with audiences that function at times like a public forum, enables us to play out conflicts in national values, structural inequalities and the personal ramifications of these tensions. In *Performing America*, co-edited by Jeffrey D. Mason and J. Ellen Gainor, Mason speaks of America as a 'formulation' or concept rather than its physical boundaries and institutions, 'an unfolding, proliferating narrative that is the product of generations of contributing authors'.[1] The idea of 'America' or 'American' emerges from competing discourses as much as from key events or crisis moments in our histories when 'American values' are cited for opposing or defending particular positions and policies. If, as Mason argues, the 'hallmark of "America" is its broad capacity for self-invention and subsequent self-contemplation', the stage gives us the 'creative freedom ... to explore, test, and dispute conceptions of national character'.[2]

A recurrent discourse in conceptions of the nation and a thematic concern in its literature is the promise or failure of the 'American

Dream', the attainment of self-determination, equality under the law and financial security. America, in this discourse, is seen as a beacon of hope and freedom for various groups embarking on its shores, escaping poverty and persecution and seeking a better life for the next generation, perhaps even wealth and power. However, for those struggling for civil rights and economic opportunity within a nation that promises equality, the contradictions in ideology and practice have been brutally apparent.

It is not surprising that Mason and Gainor published *Performing America* in 1999 precisely because they heard at the end of the millennium a 'growing chorus of resentful, accusatory, and critical voices' frustrated by their inability to access the 'halo of freedom and righteousness' that America has symbolized for more than two centuries.[3] Almost all theatre histories of the 1990s focus on the discourse of 'identity politics' woven into the dramas. Many plays of this period rendered the interests and perspectives of those organizing around a range of collective identities to demand recognition as well as political rights. After years of civil rights struggles and calls for anti-discrimination laws by African Americans, Latina/os, Asian Americans, Native Americans, women, and the LGBTQ community – and the pleas to address the scourge of AIDS and the political backlash against the populations who suffered most – the politics of race, ethnicity, gender and sexual identity often 'took center stage' in the 1990s. The concerns of these various groups informed playwriting as well as the mission of many theatre companies.[4]

The decade of the 1990s is also associated with the 'culture wars' – the polarization between conservative and liberal groups that disagreed about what constitutes American values in relation to such issues as same-sex relationships, family values, sexual harassment, abortion, race relations, gun laws, drug use and the role of the government concerning private life and control over one's body – issues that continue to inform national politics well into the twenty-first century. In 1991, James Davison Hunter published *Culture Wars: The Struggle to Define America*, in which he observed an underlying conflict between what he termed 'orthodoxy and progressivism' in setting standards for the family, art, education, law and politics in the nation.[5] These lines of conflict were manifested in public discussion of major events, such as the televised Supreme Court hearings of nominee Clarence Thomas accused of sexual harassment by former aide and law professor Anita Hill; the police beating of an unarmed African-American man Rodney King, which set off riots in Los Angeles; the student killings at Columbine High School outside Denver, Colorado; and the 1995 bombing of a federal building in Oklahoma City, which took 168 lives (see Chapter 1).

The theatre responded to these issues and their manifestation in current events with plays such as Anna Deavere Smith's *Twilight: Los Angeles* (1992), which addressed racial and ethnic conflicts; David Mamet's *Oleanna* (1992), which depicted the relationship between power dynamics and accusations of sexual harassment; *The Laramie Project* (2000) by Moisés Kaufman and the Tectonic Theater Project about the 1998 murder of University of Wyoming gay student Matthew Shepard; and Paula Vogel's *Baltimore Waltz* (1992), Terrence McNally's *Love! Valour! Compassion!* (1994) and Tony Kushner's two-play epic *Angels in America* (1993), which took up intimacy and homophobia, among other issues, in the age of AIDS.

Even in the midst of cultural and political divisions, the buzzword of 'multiculturalism' was in the air as identity politics morphed into a discourse of inclusion. Rather than the stress on 'separatist' discourse, each group advocating for itself, multiculturalists celebrated 'diversity' and a kind of 'rainbow coalition' (activist Jesse Jackson's 1986 attempt to unite various groups for social change), and many theatres included 'multicultural theatre' in their mission statements (e.g. Mixed Blood Theatre in Minneapolis, Minnesota; Borderlands Theater Company in Tucson, Arizona; and Cornerstone Theater in Los Angeles, California). Social theorist Kimberle Crenshaw, in her groundbreaking essay 'Mapping the Margins', written for the *Stanford Law Review* in 1991, argued for the concept of 'intersectionality', the overlapping or intersecting social identities (e.g. working-class Black women) that subjugated individuals within related systems of oppression, domination and discrimination.[6] All of these perspectives – identity politics, the culture wars, multiculturalism, intersectionality – found their way to the stage.

In another vein, S. E. Wilmer observes several attitudes and approaches taken by dramatists that questioned, or perhaps yearned for, the idea of a unified nation. He points to Anna Deavere Smith's polymonologic dramas on urban riots (*Fires in the Mirror* and *Twilight: Los Angeles*) and to what he sees as Tony Kushner's ultimately 'utopian vision [in *Angels in America*] that represents the tapestry of American multicultural society moving toward a harmonious future' and that 'enables the disenfranchised and marginalized gay community to become fully integrated into society as equal "citizens".'[7] Wilmer notes other playwrights such as Guillermo Gómez-Peña who address hybridity and transnational identities in their depiction of characters who transgress 'cultural and national borders', and confront the complexities of border culture for individuals and two nations.[8]

Further challenges to American hegemony were manifest in the questioning of the nation's position on the world's stage of the past half-century – the Cold War and its thaw, movements for national liberation from colonial powers, increasing concerns over American military intervention in international and internecine conflicts in Africa, Eastern Europe and the Middle East, the questioning of America's moral as well as political responsibilities, and US power in global corporate interests. Not surprisingly, theatre artists responded with war-themed plays that spoke to the wages of armed conflict: Sam Shepard's *States of Shock* (1991), Shirley Lauro's *A Piece of My Heart* (1991) and Naomi Wallace's *In the Heart of America* (1994). In 1993, the San Francisco Mime Troupe collaborated with theatre directors from Asian nations to create *Offshore*, which addressed free trade and the Pacific Rim marketplace to question the price of economic integration.

Concerns about Western cultural hegemony, the representation of marginalized groups on stage, as well as greater access for actors from various ethnic groups to choice roles, fuelled heated debates about casting actors. In this context, a major controversy emerged during the enormously successful Broadway production of Alain Bublil and Claude-Michel Schönberg's musical *Miss Saigon*, brought over from London in 1991. The musical adapts the opera *Madama Butterfly* and transposes the story from Japan to 1970s Saigon during the Vietnamese War. Many in the theatre community were incensed that the role of the French-Vietnamese engineer/brothel owner had been given to Jonathan Pryce, a Caucasian actor who had created the role in its London premiere, comparing this choice to the practice of blackface.[9] The following year, a similar controversy arose when Actors Equity and the Hispanic Organization of Latin Actors protested against the absence of

Hispanic actors in Chilean playwright Ariel Dorfman's *Death and the Maiden*. The story depicts a former political prisoner in an unnamed Latin American country who had been raped by her captors and, years later, confronts the man that she believes abused her. In the end, the producers agreed to search for Hispanic actors as replacements and understudies.[10] The issue of cross-racial and 'non-traditional casting' received national attention in the 1997 legendary debate between Pulitzer Prize-winning playwright August Wilson and Robert Brustein, Artistic Director of the American Repertory Theatre (see pages 70–1).

The structure of American theatre production in the 1990s enabled theatre artists to explore themes of identity politics, multi-culturalism, racism, sexism, homophobia and many other concerns in a range of plays and venues, especially in the not-for-profit theatres that gained momentum across the country. The 1990s represented the culmination of a gradually decentralized theatre that included Off- and Off-Off-Broadway, residential and regional theatres across the nation, as well as academic theatres. Many of these not-for-profit theatres developed experimental forms and often dramatized personal and political concerns about exclusion and subjugation.

The theatre provided an arena for expressing these conflicts, offering an alternate reality for envisioning transformation and projecting a more humane and equitable democratic polity. Writing just before the 2000 national elections, theatre theorist Jill Dolan implored readers to consider civic engagement – to 'perform democracy' – through theatre. In her impassioned essay, she argues that 'just the act of going to the theatre, of demonstrating a willingness to see and hear stories that might not otherwise be accessible, models a hopeful openness to the diverse possibilities of democracy'.[11] Eschewing what she sees as the 'binary of aesthetics versus politics', she maintains that 'art is not outside history' and that theatre has the potential to create citizen-spectators who 'rehearse democracy' through productions that air differences and antagonisms, and to represent 'contradictions in our various pleasures'.[12]

It is important to note that Jill Dolan was president of the Association for Theatre in Higher Education (ATHE) in the late 1990s, and her essay responds to a political climate of government censorship and massive federal cuts to arts funding during the 'culture wars', and especially to the notoriety surrounding grants given and then challenged by the National Endowment for the Arts in the early 1990s to performers whose works were seen as 'morally unacceptable'. Issues such as censorship of the arts by federal institutions, the arts and public policy, and the relationship between art and morality continued to be debated and negotiated throughout the decade as theatres sought to engage and negotiate cultural currents from multiple perspectives and yet bring in large enough audiences to sustain its enterprise and of course to retain its funders.

The economic climate and funding sources in the 1990s

As we move into the discussions of the plays produced during the decade, it is also important to consider the economic climate as well as private and public funding patterns, crucial considerations for surveying theatre production at any point in time. In his history of American drama of the twentieth century, Gerald M. Berkowitz maintains that 'by its very nature the drama – the literature of the theatre – is more closely bound to the marketplace than any other literary form' because it is intended to be staged and staging is expensive.[13] Furthermore, the economy and various funding sources for the theatre have influenced the number and types of plays performed and the venues that produce them. Berkowitz identifies changes in the structure of American theatre that began in the mid-twentieth century and developed in ways that shaped theatre production in the 1990s: (1) the 'alternative theatre environment' – Off- and Off-Off-Broadway was to some extent freed from some of the intense commercial constraints of theatres that depend upon investors looking for lucrative yields, large audiences and high ticket prices to sustain its ventures; alternative theatres operated with lower budgets and fewer resources, and created opportunities to produce more experimental work for audiences eager to see intellectually and emotionally challenging drama; (2) the development of regional theatres made theatre available to many more people and also created opportunities for new theatre artists; (3) the changes in the financial basis of the American theatre enabled the development of Off-Broadway, Off-Off-Broadway and residential theatres across the country that were not-for-profit. Changes in income tax laws over the century motivated wealthy individuals and charitable foundations to make large gifts to non-profit theatres.[14]

In *Angels in the American Theater*, Robert A. Schanke traces the history of arts philanthropy and the significant 'angels' – theatre investors and backers with money – who have made a significant impact on the theatre. These 'angels' include charitable individuals and philanthropic institutions. Some support individual artists and companies with a specific artistic or political focus. One motivation for these backers was the tax advantage – a deduction for gifts to non-profits that could substantially reduce the taxable portion of their income. These gifts ensured that non-profit theatres would not be dependent only upon ticket sales and low production costs, and therefore could support new writers through commissions and grants. In addition, in the second half of the century, corporations increasingly donated gifts to the arts for visibility (to build their brand) and public relations benefits.[15]

Not surprisingly, then, the fourth development cited by Berkowitz is the decline of Broadway in the last third of the century, which by the 1990s was producing few new American plays and had become home to extravagant musicals, star vehicles and revivals, often with noted film stars, to ensure ticket sales.[16] Although ticket prices were at record highs, the plays often needed long runs to full houses to pay off investors and also realize a profit. Artistic choices were made with financial requirements in mind. Furthermore, most of its popular offerings had been produced elsewhere first. The many imports from London became known as the 'British Musical Invasion'. In her comprehensive essay 'American Drama of the 1990s On and Off-Broadway', June Schlueter concludes that 'Broadway in the 1990s was not the place for serious drama but for the musical with popular appeal.'[17]

Of course the economic climate and the development of various forms of entertainment modes using new technologies affected attendance as well as investments, funding and new play development. The economic recession of 1990–1, during President George H. W. Bush's term, certainly took its toll on both private investment and public funding, and while the public continued to pay high ticket prices, they were given fewer choices and overall attendance declined.[18] Even in later years, when the stock market was bullish, the economy strengthening under the Clinton administration and Broadway benefiting from this upturn and increased tourist trade, there were fewer new musicals or new plays by Americans on the Broadway stage.[19] Theatre also competed for audiences with film, television and the creation of virtual reality spectacles and performance pieces on the World Wide Web – all enhanced by the development of innovative technologies.

At the same time that commercial theatre confronted economic constraints and vied for audiences with other mediums, the Off- and Off-Off-Broadway theatre continued to develop significant theatrical works. Schlueter notes that 'if the challenges to Broadway had any positive effect, it was to secure the transition already in place for decades, to Off-Broadway, that group of theatres outside New York's entertainment district'.[20] Among the theatres that she cites are the Manhattan Theatre Club, Playwrights Horizons, the Circle Repertory Theater, the Joseph Papp Public Theater, the Vineyard Theatre, the Roundabout Theatre Company, Circle in the Square and Lincoln Center, though, as she says, some of these theatres are technically classified as Broadway because of size and funding. Increasingly, mixed funding has come to characterize even alternative theatre venues.[21]

It is worth noting that in 1998, *Playbill Magazine* defined these distinctions between Broadway, Off-Broadway and Off-Off-Broadway by contracts, involving unions and wages as well as the number of tickets that needed to be sold. Theatres with up to ninety-nine seats were considered Off-Off; 99–499 seats generally denoted Off-Broadway; and those with 499 and larger indicated Broadway, though there were many exceptions and a few overlaps. Unsurprisingly, ticket prices are higher for Broadway productions, and in 1998 were as high as $75 ($100 for the popular musical *Miss Saigon*) versus a high of $45 for Off-Broadway, and $20 or lower for Off-Off-Broadway.[22] Many theatres in the latter category functioned in lofts, garages, basements, unused theatres or converted spaces.

To be sure, Schlueter acknowledges the 'primacy of New York Theatre' across its venues, but she also makes the important point that many plays produced in Manhattan venues of all types 'neither originate nor end there' and that New York theatre is 'reciprocal'. Many plays developed by regional theatres transfer to New York, and Broadway shows often have touring productions that travel to theatres across the nation. As she says, 'The story of American drama in New York in the 1990s, then, is the story of theatre in America.' She goes on to list an array of regional theatres across the country that have contributed to what we might be proud to call a 'thriving national theatre'. This list includes Cambridge's American Repertory Theatre, Boston's Huntington Theatre Company, the Williamstown Theatre Festival, New Haven's Yale Repertory and Long Wharf Theatre, Providence's Trinity Repertory Company, Princeton's McCarter Theatre, Chicago's Goodman Theatre, Minneapolis's Guthrie Theatre, Actors Theatre of Louisville, Houston's Alley Theatre, Seattle's Intiman Theatre, the Seattle Repertory Theatre, San Francisco's Eureka Theatre Company and ACT, Los Angeles's Mark Taper Forum, Costa Mesa's South Coast Repertory, San Diego's Old Globe Theatre and many more.[23] These theatres not only made theatre available to more people but also offered opportunities for new play development. Most regional theatres produced full seasons of several plays a year, which meant that audiences buying a full subscription would experience plays with a range of styles and themes.

Censorship and the National Endowment for the Humanities: The 'NEA Four'

One of the most prominent issues regarding funding for the theatre in the 1990s was the controversy surrounding the National Endowment for the Arts and its censorship of what at the time the selection committees considered 'obscene art'. As Marshall W. Mason, Founding Director of the Circle Repertory Company, proclaimed in his keynote address to the East Central Theatre Conference in 1993, 'Under [President] George H. W. Bush, the arts became a bitter political battleground with the rights of free speech severely curbed.' Religious right-wing groups and their influence on conservative members of Congress deemed federal funding 'dangerous', and 'grants were slashed, withdrawn, or withheld'.[24] Throughout the decade, even as the market and the economy recovered from the recession, the cuts to federal funding and the challenges faced by artists during this decade were daunting. Schanke recounts the original mission of the NEA, founded in 1965 following the assassination of President John F. Kennedy whose arts commission paved the way for this federal endowment: 'Rather than supervising programs themselves as the government had with the Federal Theatre [during the Great Depression], the NEA established peer-review advisory panels that channelled funds to nonprofit organizations ... establishing grants and matching grants with a principle of decentralization.' A large part of this mission was to make the arts 'accessible and available outside major cities', and to act as a 'catalyst to spark nonfederal support'. Schanke provides this background to his succinct description of the debacle of the 1990 NEA controversy and quotes historian Arthur Schlesinger proclaiming that the 1990s marked a '"time of crisis in the state of the arts"'.[25]

In May of 1989, Senator Jesse Helms condemned Andres Serrano's performance art work 'Piss Christ' in an NEA-funded exhibition at the Southeastern Center for Contemporary Art in Winston-Salem, North Carolina. Similar objections were raised in response to photographer Robert Mapplethorpe's exhibit in 1990. In the summer of 1990, performance artists Karen Finley, Holly Hughes, Tim Miller and John Fleck (referred to as the 'NEA Four') had NEA grants amounting to $23,000 rescinded. The immediate consequence was a congressional action banning federal funds for art that 'may be considered obscene', and artists awarded grants were required to sign an anti-obscenity clause. In protest, the Theatre Communications Group, along with 69 artists and individuals, accused the NEA of becoming an 'art cop', proclaiming that 'the Constitution does not permit the government to manipulate a federal arts subsidy program into a vehicle for suppressing controversial speech'. In late 1990, the NEA no longer required the anti-obscenity pledges, but it articulated the need for 'general standards of decency and respect for diverse beliefs and values of the American public'. Schanke maintains that by 1996, as a result of these 'art wars', the NEA budget was slashed by almost 40 per cent, and the cutback lasted five years. Citing Robert Brustein, he also explains that although the NEA's financial contribution is minimal, this federal agency set a tone for national philanthropy during this period, which had a 'demoralizing effect on artists, organizations, and donors'.[26]

New business models for the theatre

In response to these cutbacks to public and private investment in the arts after the recession of the early 1990s and the NEA debacle, Marshall W. Mason's 1993 address to the East Central Theatre Conference expressed concern about the place of theatre among social institutions in America. Mason extended a rallying cry for the specific potential of the stage to 'celebrate common human values ... learn to be more divine in our humanity ... recognize, tolerate, forgive'. Echoing many theatre theorists, Mason spoke of the 'social communion of the theatre' that might 'see' and 'change the world, to make it a better place'. In this context, he put forth the challenge to theatres of all stripes to do more with less – that is, 'use our resources more fully, more imaginatively' – indeed to be 'dangerous'. Citing many of the issues preoccupying the public, such as AIDS awareness, sexual discrimination and harassment and the recognition of a 'history of black America', Mason advocated the production of more plays such as Paula Vogel's *The Baltimore Waltz*, David Stevens's *The Sum of Us*, August Wilson's *The Piano Lesson* and many others.[27]

At the end of the decade, the prognosis for American theatre improved. Transfers from Off-Broadway and regional theatres to Broadway, as well as new business models, including not-for-profit and commercial partnerships, 'redefined' these categories to some extent. This was especially true for the four largest not-for-profit Broadway-designated theatres – the Public Theater, Lincoln Center, the Roundabout Theatre and Manhattan Theatre Club – due to size and other considerations. In 2000, the Theatre Congress convened a conference, ACT II, to discuss the ramifications of these new partnerships and the challenges for the identities of non-profits.[28] Reflecting on the decade leading into the 2000s, the National Endowment for the Arts report, entitled *All America's a Stage: Growth and Challenges in Nonprofit Theatre*, chronicled the 'enormous growth and general financial stability' of the US non-profit theatre, not only in traditional cultural centres but also in every section of the country. Although still vulnerable to large economic downturns and the resulting reduced funding from donors and foundations, the number of non-profit theatres grew by approximately 50 per cent between 1990 and 2000, and these theatres 'maintained a healthy balance sheet' in terms of assets and liabilities and earned and contributed income. The NEA also asserted that individuals and foundations – the 'angels' referred to by Schanke – remained the biggest contributors to non-profit theatre, which has come to depend upon their support. The report offers interesting data on audience attendance and preferences; for example, from 1992 to 2002, there is a slight decrease in attendance for non-musical theatre (13.5 per cent to 12.3 per cent). Whatever the genre or 'whether or not they improve box-office sales', the report concludes that 'programs with a clear civic interest can be key to raising public and private contributions'.[29]

The 'Broadway' theatre in the 1990s

During the first half of the twentieth century, the term 'Broadway' signified American theatre, and its serious dramas as well as musicals were internationally acknowledged and influential. As Arnold Aronson describes it, 'At the start of the twentieth century, American theatre was centred in a group of magnificent rococo buildings on 42nd Street near Times Square in New York City, and most cities of any size had at least one theatre that housed either road companies emanating from Broadway or resident companies that would provide the context for productions by touring stars.'[30] However, 'Broadway' is a business, and even the numerous successful productions by major theatre owner the Shubert Organization could not stem the tide of radical changes in the American cultural landscape affecting the constituency of audiences and the configuration of theatre producers. Beginning with the decade following the Second World War, the centrality of what was known as 'Broadway' theatre began to decline. Many converging factors – demographic, economic and political – help to explain this shift. Gradually many people left the city for the suburbs and in addition to the erosion of audiences, the business of theatre entailed higher costs, more spectacular productions to entice audiences not necessarily drawn to drama, and the parallel growth of alternative theatres, some more experimental, in New York and across the nation to reflect the interests of next generation audiences. 'Broadway' experienced a decline. By the 1970s, the 42nd Street area was in decline as well, evidenced by the proliferation of x-rated movie houses and peep shows.

Theatre-goers might look back nostalgically to the 1940s as a kind of golden age when plays by such renowned dramatists as Arthur Miller, Tennessee Williams and Lillian Hellman addressed social and psychological concerns – generational conflicts, challenges to social norms, the problematic pursuit of the American Dream, and the ramifications of the war against fascism – and developed the genre of domestic realism to address these issues. However, beginning in the post-war period, the centrality of what was known as 'Broadway' gave way to alternative theatre venues and organizations already mentioned. The Off- and Off-Off-New York theatre and regional and residential theatres shifted the landscape of American theatrical production and offered new American plays to the theatre-going public. Gerald M. Berkowitz maintains that 'from 1970 on, each Broadway season featured several transfer productions from regional theatres, and by the 1980s transfers from Off and Off Off-Broadway and imports from London'[31] – even for musical theatre, formerly known as a specifically American genre. Citing the 1989–90 season, Aronson reports that there were only forty new productions on Broadway, and of those only ten were new American plays, three of which had originated either Off-Broadway or in a regional theatre, and only eight were new musicals. Others were solo shows or revivals.[32] Schlueter says that in the decade of the 1990s about five plays each year were new American plays and about five were revivals of American plays.[33]

Although Broadway's record of originating new plays was increasingly sparse in the 1990s, many productions had already been developed and vetted in the non-profits. The high cost of producing a play in New York was a factor in working through the process of play production in less expensive venues outside of the city, and many of these venues belonged to their own support organization – the League of Resident Theaters (LORT). The 'transfers' to Broadway drew attention from critics and certain audience niches, though not always for long runs (e.g. August Wilson's Pulitzer Prize-winning play *The Piano Lesson* (1990) and *Two Trains Running* (1992), and Kushner's Pulitzer Prize-winning *Angels in America* in 1993). If 'Broadway' theatre was no longer seen as the creative force behind serious American drama, however, it would continue to play an important role in showcasing its theatre. Broadway was still 'the ultimate destination', as C. W. E. Bigsby tells us, 'no matter how perilous and costly productions there might be, no matter that its audience was increasingly defined by price and not always receptive to work which challenged their assumptions'.[34] The pattern of production might be seen as a two-step process: a successful play in a regional theatre might then be staged in a not-for-profit Off-Broadway company, or staged Off-Broadway by a commercial producer as a low-cost try-out before moving to Broadway.[35]

To be sure, 'Broadway' was resilient in its continuing efforts to attract theatre audiences. In addition to the Shubert Organization, the largest single theatre owner in the country (and its Shubert Foundation, the largest single supporter of not-for-profit theatre), other players attempted to revitalize the theatre district. The now-defunct Canadian producing company Livent, originally helmed by Garth Drabinsky, who had faith in financially independent theatres for offering huge spectacles for large audiences, developed a series of 1,500 to 2,000-seat theatres, including renovations of two of the 42nd Street houses – parts of the old Lyric and Apollo theatres – transformed in 1998 into the Ford Center for the Performing Arts to bring in large-scale touring shows. In addition, the Disney Corporation embarked on transforming musicals from its animated films, such as *Beauty and the Beast* (1994) and *The Lion King* (1997). The latter production opened at the newly refurbished Amsterdam Theatre. In 1990, Governor Mario Cuomo and Mayor David Dinkins announced the formation of the New 42nd Street, a non-profit partner to find uses for seven of the historic theatres that had fallen into decay.

The 'corporate musical' was, as John Kendrick articulates it, 'invented' by Disney Theatrical Productions and ushered in shows that were developed, produced and managed by multifunctional entertainment corporations. The consequence for these entertainment models was that key artistic decisions were often made in boardrooms, giving them the quality of a streamlined product that could be easily reproduced for distribution with 'matching sets and anonymous casts', diminishing the 'spontaneity and vitality' that Kendrick fears has been lost, particularly in the megamusicals that carried over from the 1980s into the 1990s.[36] Between 1989 and 2001, PACE theatrical group participated in 20 Broadway musicals and partnered with JuJamcyn Theaters in 1997 to both create and distribute shows. Nathan Hurwitz mentions other companies that created subsidiaries to develop Broadway musical entertainments, and explains that this increasing number of entertainment companies constituted 'vertical theater empires' that financed multimillion-dollar plays and musicals from inception to full-scale production, producing them in their own theatres and on tour. Clearly these kinds of productions eclipsed the role of the 'visionary producer' with a 'personal aesthetic', such as David Merrick, Stuart Ostrow and the legendary Joseph Papp.[37]

Other organizations, however, emerged not only to revitalize New York City as a hub of theatrical entertainment, but also to build new and younger audiences. In 1990, the Broadway Alliance was formed to address rising ticket costs and promote the production of plays in three Broadway theatres by lowering production costs. The organization involved as many players as possible from theatre owners to artists to backstage unions. *Theater Yearbook 1990–1991* cited the plan that unions and guilds would cut about 25 per cent in minimums and royalties for shows that would be capitalized for under $400,000 and would charge no higher than $24 for tickets. If the show earned profits, then those who cut their wages would share in 10 per cent of the profits.[38] After a disappointing track record, the Alliance scored a success in 1994 with Terrence McNally's *Love! Valor! Compassion!* and in 1995 with McNally's *Master Class*. Both plays had transferred from successful productions Off-Broadway.

Another organization, the League of American Theatres and Producers, a trade organization that promotes Broadway theatre, negotiates contracts with theatrical unions and agreements with the guilds, and co-administers the Tony Awards with the American Theatre Wing, was active in the 1990s to improve the climate for purchasing tickets through various sources. In 1992, the League joined the Times Square Alliance to entertain delegates to the Democratic Dramatic Convention, featuring performances from the current roster of productions. This effort resulted in a free outdoor party that was reprised the following year and for decades after as 'Broadway on Broadway'.[39]

In addition to organizations that promoted attendance at Broadway theatres, two initiatives by theatre artists enhanced play offerings in New York City On-and Off-Broadway in the 1990s, and these enterprises included revivals of classics to draw audiences that craved serious drama. Tony Randall, renowned film and television actor, founded his own company in 1991, the National Actors Theatre, which produced classic plays such as Arthur Miller's *The Crucible*, Henrik Ibsen's *The Master Builder*, Anton Chekhov's *The Seagull*, George Bernard Shaw's *Saint Joan* and many others. Although productions did not always receive laudatory reviews, the company brought major stage and screen stars (Lynn Redgrave, Earl Hyman, Jon Voight, Tyne Daly, Julie Harris) to Broadway's Lyceum and the Belasco Theatre, which became its home. Also in 1991, James Houghton founded the Signature Theatre, a non-profit, Off-Broadway theatre company that was the first to devote an entire season to the work of a single playwright, including reconsidered productions of past works as well as world premieres of new plays. The company spearheaded the idea of an extended commitment to a playwright's body of work, inviting audiences to see the trajectory of a dramatist's work over time. The 1990s Signature Theatre offered seasons devoted to the works of Romulus Linney, Lee Blessing, Edward Albee, Horton Foote, Adrienne Kennedy, Sam Shepard, Arthur Miller, John Guare and Maria Irene Fornés.

Musical theatre

In a period of rising production costs, higher ticket prices and competing forms of entertainment, Broadway theatre producers continued to attract large audiences for musical theatre in all its incarnations, though some shows were more successful than others in sustaining long runs. Because the musical is a collaborative art form that brings together many entertainment elements at once – book/story/libretto, music and lyrics, choreography and stage movement, inventive scenic design, costumes, and technical stage apparatus to enhance spectacle – it appeals to a range of tastes and sensibilities. Furthermore, as Stacy Wolf argues, the Broadway musical theatre is a 'social event and a commercial product', bolstered by 'mammoth marketing machines' as well as tourists and locals bearing souvenirs and T-shirts, and sharing their experiences of the event on fan-sites and blogs.[40] Rather than 'apologize' for its commercialism, Wolf values the audience's attachment to the genre and analyses the ideas expressed in musicals in relationship to its historical moment. Indeed, as a home-grown entertainment, one of three distinctively American widely influential art forms (along with jazz and American film),[41] the musical has been sensitive to cultural discourses and of course entertainment trends of the period in which it is produced.

Although various forms of musical theatre developed throughout the twentieth century and productions did not necessarily adhere to any one definition attached to any one decade, critics often distinguish between the 'book show', with its emphasis on plot or story developed at mid-century, and the 'concept musical', a contested term that alludes to a 'stage idea', developed in the late 1960s and 1970s. Rather than a strictly linear-structured story, the 'concept' or 'fragmented' musical combined subject, songs, dances, visual presentation to communicate idea, theme or metaphor.[42] In the 1980s into the 1990s, Broadway saw the rise of the megamusical, also referred to as the 'technomusical', that featured spectacular sets and special effects intended to dazzle audiences by sheer design/technological ingenuity. In the late 1990s, the musical as genre continued to be redefined, though not without controversy. Some plays featured just enough music and musical staging to be considered 'musical works', for example Claudia Shear's *Dirty Blonde* and Julie Taymor's adaptation of Carlo Gozzi's *The Green Bird* (both in 1999–2000), and Susan Stroman and John Weidman's dance play without singing, *Contact* (1999–2000), which was nominated for a Tony as best musical.

The 1990s saw several trends in musical theatre from previous decades continue to define productions, and new musicals included stories transposed or recontextualized from other mediums, such as biography, film and popular music. In addition, the lucrative revivals were often given new interpretations by inventive directors.[43] John Degen catalogues these trends as follows: new book shows recycling old songs, such as the 'new Gershwin musical' *Crazy for You* (1992); new revues recycling old pop-hits, like *Smokey Joe's Café* (1995); and sequels to old musicals like *The Best Little Whorehouse Goes Public*. He also notes the turn to stage versions of familiar movie musicals, such as Disney's *Beauty and the Beast* (1994), Henry Mancini's *Victor/Victoria* (1995) and Rodgers and Hammerstein's *State Fair* (1996). Even familiar non-musical movies were musicalized, such as Jule Styne's *The Red Shoes* with lyrics by playwright Marsha Norman, and Neil Simon's adaptation of his own film *The Goodbye Girl* (1993). Transpositions across mediums included the staging of Pete Townshend's 1960s 'rock opera' *Tommy* (1993), already recognizable from the Who's 1969 double album rock opera *The Who's Tommy* (1969) and the Ken Russell film. Although Degen, writing at the close of the decade, declared that 'American musical theatre stands at a crossroads, having only rarely produced original material', he cites several new productions in 1997 and 1998 (e.g. *Titanic*, *The Lion King* and *Ragtime*) that gave him encouragement.[44]

Looking back over the decade with the hindsight of the twenty-first century, we can see the developments in production and innovative staging that continued to lure audiences both young and old, and particularly aficionados of the musical who wanted to see the next best thing: the continuation of British and European imports, the megamusical in new configurations, the 'Disneyfication' of Broadway, and productions from Off- and Off-Off-Broadway that challenged conventional scenarios, introduced contemporary themes and brought in new theatre artists who stretched the parameters of the musical theatre genre. To be sure, the megamusical, a spectacle-driven production, continued to exert its influence, if not dominance, on the American stage, but it also diversified and informed productions that mixed various styles.

The megamusical: British and French imports and the Americanization of the genre

The megamusical is 'mega' in several respects. As Jessica Sternfeld defines this form, it often features 'epic, sweeping tales of romance, war, religion, redemption, life and death, or some combination of these lofty sentiments' that tend to be set in some previous historical era. In addition to the epic plot, megamuscials share several features: they are often sung-through, with 'recitative-like singing' or musical motifs, with little or no spoken dialogue; the sets and staging are spectacular and expensive; and the production depends upon large-scale marketing through advertisements, the production of merchandise sold with logos, theme songs, advance release of a recording to induce anticipation for the event that is

about to appear on Broadway, and advance ticket sales to rev up
the excitement. And, finally, the musical must be exportable to
other parts of the globe, replicated without regard to star or even
language. The extravaganza is all important.[45]

Riding high on 1980s megamusicals, such as Andrew Lloyd
Webber's *Cats* (1982) and *The Phantom of the Opera* (1986)
and Claude-Michel Schönberg and Alain Boublil's *Les Misérables*
(1987), producer Cameron Mackintosh reunited the *Les Misérables*
creative team, including the English lyricist Richard Malby Jr and
the revered scenic designer John Napier, for the megamusical *Miss
Saigon* (1991). Transposing the scenario of Puccini's opera *Madama
Butterfly* (itself adapted from the play *Madame Butterfly* by
American theatrical impresario David Belasco) to the American war
in Vietnam, the creators tell the love story of an American soldier
Chris and a seventeen-year-old bar-girl Kim, who are separated in
the days before the fall of Saigon in 1975. The production's most
notable use of technology and spectacle, the military helicopter
that landed and took off onstage, has become legendary in musical
theatre lore. Furthermore, the uproar over retaining Englishman
Jonathan Pryce in the role of a bi-racial (Vietnamese French)
'engineer'/pimp was debated in the *New York Times* throughout
the summer of 1990 as the London production was preparing
for its Broadway opening (see page 36). This story takes on epic
proportions with a spectacular score and stage machinery. In one
fantasy sequence, the exploitative 'engineer' imagines a larger than
life 'American dream' in the form of a pink Cadillac convertible
carrying the young Kim in a Statue of Liberty costume.[46]

In 1994, Andrew Lloyd Webber, the British composer most
associated with the megamusical, returned to Broadway with
Sunset Boulevard, after a less successful production, *Aspects of
Love* (1990). Along with designer John Napier and director Trevor
Nunn, Webber staged a version of the Billy Wilder Hollywood
film about Hollywood. The story of a young screenwriter's
fraught relationship with a fictionalized, deluded and dangerous
ex-movie star from the silent film era brought several accomplished
performers to the role of Norma Desmond: Glenn Close (who won
a Tony Award), Betty Buckley and Elaine Paige, among others.
This time Webber's compositional technique invoked elements of
the book musical, inserting dialogue leading to set numbers – songs
that express the emotions or ideas of the spoken words. Again, the

stage mechanics of the megamusical were noteworthy, in this case the cavernous mansion with grand staircase descending from a back wall, the set at one point rising off the stage floor to show the more modest dwelling of the screenwriter. This staging no doubt rendered the young man's yearning to escape the mundane that gave way to his gradual absorption by the bizarre but mesmerizing former movie queen and the era she evokes.

Sternfeld underscores the point that although the megamusical did not 'dominate' Broadway in the 1990s as it had in the 1980s, it certainly influenced several American productions.[47] In the mid-1990s, composer Frank Wildhorne emerged with *Jekyll and Hyde* (1997), lyrics by Leslie Bricusse, that told the story adapted from Robert Louis Stevenson's novel of the split-personality doctor and his gruesome experiments. Wildhorne generated a great deal of excitement for the show, relying on a more pop-heavy style than the lush, opera-like songs of the British megamusicals, but he employed the large-scale spectacle element and the appeal to escapist fantasy. This show also notably garnered a fan group, known as 'Jekkies'. Two other Wildhorne shows followed quickly. *The Scarlet Pimpernel* (1997), based on a novel written in the early twentieth century and depicting a spy intrigue among the English aristocracy during the French Revolution, was yet another melodramatic production set in the past. And in 1999, he created the less successful *The Civil War*.

Toward the end of the decade, two musicals also revisited events of the past. Maury Yeston's *Titanic* (1997) took as its subject the well-known tragedy of the sinking of the famed cruise liner and the stories of the persons on board representing the class hierarchy central to the story. Indeed, its Tony Award-winning book was seen by one reviewer as a critique of the greed-driven but failed technology that led to disaster.[48] The production received several Tony Awards, including one for scenic design that, like other megamusicals, intended to awe audiences (e.g. furniture sliding offstage as the ocean liner tilted at an angular level). In 1998, the composer/lyricist team of Stephen Flaherty and Lynn Ahrens created *Ragtime*, awarded a Tony for best book by the noted playwright Terrence McNally, adapted from the 1975 novel by E. L. Doctorow (see Chapter 3 on McNally). Emblematic of the shift from British imports to the American megamusical, *Ragtime* signalled a new kind of music – a syncopated or 'ragged' rhythm originating in African American communities in the nineteenth and early twentieth centuries. The musical focused on the social, economic and cultural changes in American society.

Disney on Broadway

One of the major developments in the production of musical theatre of the 1990s is the Disneyfication of Broadway. Using marketing strategies of the megamusical, but bearing the Disney imprint, these musicals staged widely known animated films – *Beauty and the Beast* and *The Lion King* – that would appeal to families and tourists. Both musicals had record-breaking long runs lasting more than a decade. *Beauty* (1994), with music by Alan Menken, lyrics by Howard Ashman and Tim Rice and a book by Linda Woolverton, retells the story of Belle, the heroine who transforms the frightening but soft-hearted Beast back into his princely human form by the miracle of her love. Of course, his castle in which the imprisoned Belle must effect this transformation is presented in a lavish rotating stage set that simulates in some respects the movement of film, replete with humans in object costumes, such as the candelabrum Lumière.

In 1997, the artistically innovative production *The Lion King* achieved fame with the celebrated talents of director, puppet creator and costume designer Julie Taymor, who became the first woman to be awarded the Tony for directing a musical and also received a Tony for original costume design. The coming-of-age story alludes to Hamlet in the plight of the young lion Simba who must avenge his father's death and claim the throne as King of the Pridelands' animal universe. With songs composed by Elton John and lyrics by Tim Rice as well as Mark Mancina, Jay Rifkin, Hans Zimmer and Taymor, the score incorporated African-inspired music in addition to other melodies shaping the varying moods of mourning and joy. At one point, Taymor's impressive staging includes what appears to be a stampede of animals (human performers in masks and suggestive animal costumes) moving toward the audience in increasingly larger groups. Most importantly, Taymor's human–puppet combinations achieved a depth of personality to reveal both public and private selves and a range of moods.[49] *The Lion King* is the top-earning title in box-office history for both stage and film productions.[50]

The decade ended with Disney's third production, *Aida* (1999), based on Verdi's opera, with music by Elton John and lyrics by Tim Rice. Although far less successful than the previous Disney productions, its pop-diva Heather Headley as well as the acclaimed lighting and scenery were all recognized by the Tonys.

Not surprisingly, Disney productions as well as other variations on the mega- or technomusical were enormously popular with audiences, but often received harsh comments by theatre critics and theatre artists who saw the spectacle element eclipsing the potential for a more substantial story and more nuanced characters. John Bush Jones calls attention to the metaphor of Broadway as 'theme park' rather than theatre in David Richards's review of *Beauty and the Beast*, also referred to by the prolific musical theatre composer Stephen Sondheim interviewed by Frank Rich.[51]

Lower-budget musical productions in the non-profit theatre

Musical theatre demonstrated greater variation and innovation in several productions during the 1990s, including those emerging from the non-profit sector. For example, in 1990, *Assassins*, composed by the prolific, award-winning composer and lyricist Stephen Sondheim with a book by John Weidman, was produced at Playwrights Horizons. Sondheim, long associated with the 'concept musical', created a non-chronological narrative about presidential assassins during the century between Lincoln's and Kennedy's assassinations, bringing together historical melodies of each period with original music. Raymond Knapp interprets the show's perspective as a 'counter-mythology' to the 'hopeful American dream' narrative that he sees in many Broadway musicals, instead focusing on 'the shadow' that accompanies that discourse, 'a disturbing presence that has always been there' in our history. *Assassins* brings together these 'outsiders' into a 'cohort' that has at least in 'the popular imagination ... formed itself into the semblance of a community, located outside temporality'.[52]

Perhaps the prime example of the influence of Off-Broadway is the 1996 Pulitzer Prize-winning *Rent*, a rock musical originating in the New York Theatre Workshop before its Broadway production. The production presented another kind of community onstage, countering the hopeful American Dream trope – the struggling young artists in New York's East Village, confronting poverty and AIDS. This book-driven musical by young artistic creator Jonathan Larson adapted the storyline of Puccini's 1896 opera *La Boheme* about a group of bohemians in the Latin Quarter of Paris. At the centre of the youth-inspired *Rent* is Mark, a middle-class filmmaker who brings the audience into this milieu replete with cross-dressing characters and performance artists. Larson's unexpected death on the evening of the dress rehearsal brought publicity to the show that was produced at far less cost than most musicals of the period, and brought in the youth audience for its long run in something of a cult phenomenon that made the show seem heir to the counter-culture musical *Hair* of the 1960s.

Images of the nation in musical theatre

Several studies of American musical theatre situate productions in the context of cultural history. John Bush Jones examines the musical stage as 'both *in* history and *as* history', and he argues that musicals 'variously dramatized, mirrored or challenged our deeply held cultural attitudes and beliefs'.[53] Similarly Raymond Knapp argues that the American musical has played a role in 'shaping' American identity by addressing 'both the ideals of America and its realities, and helping us deal with the frequent disparity between them'.[54] In her feminist history of the Broadway musical, Wolf maintains that the musical explores social issues and changing roles in American culture, 'sometimes directly and sometimes obliquely'.[55]

Bush Jones identifies a series of national troubles that he sees as a 'prime precondition' for a 'nostalgia epidemic' beginning in the 1970s, but intensifying in the 1980s and 1990s.[56] The financial woes stemming from 'Wall Street greed', the first President Bush's broken promises not to raise taxes, the Gulf War and the wars in Bosnia and Kosovo, the World Trade Center bombing in 1993, the Oklahoma City Federal Building bombing in 1995 and the Columbine high school massacre in Littleton, Colorado, he argues, produced a yearning among audiences for 'nostalgia based' productions that evoked an imaginary simpler and happier time in America. The decade began with *The Will Rogers Follies* (1991), a musical with a book by Peter Stone, lyrics by the famed team of Betty Comden and Adolph Green and music by Cy Coleman, that chronicled the life of the legendary humorist-philosopher through large production numbers. Rogers, who began his career in vaudeville, went on to films and also became a newspaper columnist, was seen as the political wit of his time, a larger than life American figure who, for many, symbolized the common man, the individual, who, though he often targeted the foils of politicians and government, realized the American Dream.

Fuelling nostalgia, a yearning for better times envisioned in a mythical past, 1990s revivals garnered large audiences. Several revivals mined productions from the golden age of the 1940s and 1950s, such as *Damn Yankees* (1994), *Guys and Dolls* (1994), *Annie Get your Gun* (1999), and retrospective revues of the music of previous eras, such as *Forever Plaid* (1990) or the already mentioned *Smokey Joe's Cafe* (1995), the former about the guy-groups of the late 1940s–1960s and the latter reviving the 1950s and 1960s rock and roll music of Jerry Leiber and Mike Stoller. Bush Jones also observes 'manufactured nostalgias' such as the 1970s *Grease*, a parody of 1950s adolescent culture and early rock and roll, revived in 1994.[57]

In addition to musical theatre that relied on nostalgia, productions continued to render themes related to nation formation past and future. Knapp identifies American musicals with themes related to a range of American 'mythologies', providing 'reassuring accounts of who "we" are as our nation', rooted not only in a 'valuable past' of nation-building, but also a belief system (if not practice) of inclusion, the idea of equality among 'men', and reconciliation between those considered Americans and those deemed outsiders.[58] The aforementioned *Miss Saigon* revisits America's troubled history during and after the Vietnam War, the destruction of the land and its people, and the ramifications for both Vietnamese civilians and traumatized American soldiers in the years to come. Ultimately, the young Vietnamese woman, Kim, commits suicide to insure that her son, the result of her affair with Chris, is adopted by him and his American wife. Viewers might see the ending as a form of reconciliation or making amends to the Vietnamese orphans (the Bui Doi) left behind by American servicemen. However, as Knapp also makes clear, myths of inclusion offer comfort to Americans troubled by their history. Musicals that stage the representation of other cultures do so for audiences who see them 'in relation to some sense of who *they* are as Americans'.[59]

Other musicals of the 1990s offered the mythology of an inclusive America even in the presence of intense racial and ethnic strife. The aforementioned *Ragtime*, set in the early twentieth century, juxtaposes fictional and historical figures to tell the story of a nation steeped in class, ethnic and racial conflicts amid a machine-age economy that often pitted groups against each other. The scenario works allegorically as it juxtaposes and then mixes three different families whose lives not only intersect but represent the historical changes and values of a nation coming to terms with group tensions but also its potential for coalitions among groups that insured the rights of citizenship. Historical figures, such as J. P. Morgan, Henry Ford, the socialist activist Emma Goldman, the architect Stanford White and his scandalous affair with the entertainer Evelyn Nesbit, contribute to the symbolic rendering of industrial growth, wealth, the emergence of American cultural hegemony as well as the seething conflicts of groups exploited or participating in the social mobility of this turbulent era.

Yet another historically oriented musical, *Parade* (1998), lyrics and book by Alfred Uhry, music by the relative newcomer Jason Robert Brown and direction by the veteran Harold Prince, rendered an actual event in America's history driven by ethnic and racial hatred and institutional power. Although its conclusion was far less hopeful than *Ragtime*, the staging of this tragic story of a Jewish man first imprisoned and then lynched for a crime that he did not commit addresses the need at the end of the twentieth century to revisit this fraught history rather than ignore it. In 1913, Leo Frank, a Jewish businessman and manager in a pencil factory in Atlanta, Georgia, was found guilty by a court of law for killing Mary Phagan, a fourteen-year-old White girl who worked in the factory. His case relied on the testimony of an African American employee who was also a suspect in the murder. In her fully developed analysis of the dramatic, musical and cultural dimensions of this production (including its stereotyped African American characters), Wolf notes that 'Brown and Uhry infused their representation of the South with ambivalence at once critical of the forces that scapegoated Leo Frank – crooked politics, a rabid Christian right, limitless racism, a bored media, and a mob easily stirred into a frenzy – and also sympathetic to the South, which suffered its own losses of men and pride'.[60] Wolf's feminist lens, however, illuminates the role of Leo's wife, Lucille, who eventually comes into her own as she assumes responsibility for her husband's fate in the courts and, in the process, transforms her marriage into a meaningful union.

The strengthened union between Leo and Lucille in *Parade* adheres to what Knapp calls the 'marriage trope' in the American musical – the crisis and resolution in personal relationships that signal the larger-scale political issues presented in the production.[61] We see this symbolism in *Ragtime* as well when at the conclusion of the play a new family is constructed by the remarriage of the former suburban housewife with the newly successful immigrant and their adoption of a Black child that had been orphaned during a racist episode.

Alongside these conflict-ridden historical narratives produced in the late twentieth century and pointing to the American mythology of progress in achieving the American Dream and realizing greater inclusion and recognition, other musical productions gave voice to formerly marginalized voices and perspectives. For example, musical productions paid homage to the contributions of African American music and dance to American culture and performance history. In 1992, *Jelly's Last Jam*, with a book by George C. Wolfe, depicted the life of the jazz composer and musician known as Jelly Roll Morton, a prime mover in the development of jazz in the early twentieth century though not without personal conflicts involving racial attitudes. In 1995–6, *Bring in 'Da Noise, Bring in 'Da Funk*, which utilized contemporary tap numbers to trace the history of Africans in America, premiered at the New York Shakespeare Festival/Public Theater. The acclaimed dancer Savion Glover received a Tony Award for his choreography.

Under the heading of 'the gay '90s', Bush Jones discusses musicals that focused on or incorporated homosexual relationships and issues over twenty years after the Greenwich Village Stonewall riots sparked national recognition for the gay and lesbian movements.[62] When *Rent* appeared on Broadway in 1996, depicting same-sex couples and straight and gay characters either HIV-positive or with AIDS, the public was already primed by several non-musical plays in the 1980s and 1990s that addressed homophobia, same-sex relationships and the AIDS crisis. However, two other noteworthy musicals addressed these issues as well.

In 1992, composer/lyricist William Finn brought to fruition his 'Marvin musicals' with *The Falsettos*, the culmination of two earlier Off-Broadway one-act musicals about a gay man enmeshed in a constellation of relationships with a former wife, their son and several other characters, including his male lover and his wife's new husband. Bush Jones cites the earlier one-act *March of the Falsettos* (1981), produced at Playwrights Horizons and then Chelsea Westside Theatre, as the first successful musical to depict a gay male relationship. *The Falsettos*, in which Finn collaborated with James Lapine, combined two one-acts into one two-act production that foregrounded several themes emerging from these concentric relationships with Marvin at its core: the ramifications of individual flaws in relationships regardless of gender and sexuality; the costs of egocentricity; and the plight of children of divorce. *Falsettos* also depicted a loving lesbian couple, one a doctor who recognizes AIDS even before it had a name.

A more politically driven musical portraying a same-sex love relationship, *The Kiss of the Spider Woman* (1993), was set in a prison cell in an unnamed Latin American country. Adapted from a novel by Manuel Puig into a script by the prolific dramatist Terrence McNally, with music and lyrics by the famed team of John Kander and Fred Ebb, the scenario focused on the developing love between an initially homophobic Vantin, imprisoned for aiding political fugitives, and Valentine, a homosexual imprisoned for 'corrupting a minor'. As Bush Jones notes, the 'pairing of prisoners immediately sets up the political focus of the musical – the worldwide parallels between human rights violations against political dissidents and hate crimes against gays'.[63]

As the decade came to an end, two megamusicals announced that they would close – *Cats*, after a run of almost nineteen years, and then *Miss Saigon* after almost ten. In his essay *The Best Plays of 1999–2000*, Jeffrey Eric Jenkins refers to a frequently discussed topic in 'millennium' media coverage of Broadway theatre: spectacle theatre closings. Was this indeed the 'end of an era'? Jenkins suggests that with Disney's *Aida* in play, the 'end' was highly unlikely. Furthermore, he argues that theatre is an art form that constantly changes in order to survive, and that these musical productions are part of a 'theatrical mosaic'.[64] The figures in this mosaic also take shape in the recurring themes concerning national identity and disenfranchised groups that emerged across genres, and most pointedly in the drama of the decade.

Drama and dramatists Off-, Off-Off-Broadway and beyond

The *Theater Yearbook* essay for the 1991–2 season began with news of the 'shock' that ran through the theatre community with the passing of Joseph Papp, famed artistic director of the New York Shakespeare Festival and the Public Theater. The essay's author, Jeffrey Sweet, offered this encomium:

> How ... will those of us who came of age in the 1960s and the 1970s be able to summon up for our children and grandchildren the importance of Joseph Papp ... He was indeed one of that small handful of figures who define an era ... By the end of Papp's reign, and largely under his leadership, as a matter of course we came to expect that virtually all new work of consequence would originate in such non-commercial houses.[65]

Theatre historians in the 1990s underscored the decentralization of American theatre, and most playwrights of the last two decades of the twentieth century premiered their work either in regional theatres, Off- and Off-Off-Broadway or abroad.

The Pulitzer Prize-winning epic drama *The Kentucky Cycle* (1991) provides an example of the production history of many serious plays during this period as well as the prevailing thematic concerns with American identity, the problems inherent in the nation's history and its mythology. It also marked the first time in its history that the Pulitzer Prize for drama had been awarded prior to a New York City production. The Pulitzer privileges plays dealing with American life, and Robert Schenkkan's series of nine plays – a six-hour, two-part saga – presents the story of three intersecting families in a small area of eastern Kentucky from the Revolutionary period to 1975. From the perspective of the late twentieth century, this history incorporates key conflicts between Native Americans and White settlers, the North and the South, racial conflict, labour union battles and capitalist exploitation, particularly by the oil industry. True to the critique of American greed during the 1980s and 1990s, the representation of these bloody battles not only asks audiences to view the 'corruption and despoilment' of America, but also the aspirations and failures of what theatre critic Frank Rich characterized as 'its author's passionately held vision of an American paradise lost'.[66] Before its Broadway opening in 1993, the play had been through several years of development, premiering in 1991 at the Intiman Theatre in Seattle, Washington, produced at the Mark Taper Forum and then produced at the John F. Kennedy Center in Washington, DC.

Canonical playwrights

Further indication of the changing landscape of play production in the later decades of the twentieth century can be seen in the later works of Arthur Miller, writing well into his eighties and still lauded as one of America's most accomplished living playwrights in the 1990s. Miller was revered for his plays of the 1940s and 1950s, with such productions as the Pulitzer Prize-winning *Death of a Salesman*, *The Crucible*, *All My Sons*, *A View From the Bridge*, and in the 1960s, *The Incident at Vichy* (1964) and *The Price* (1968). Although Miller was a multiple award-winning playwright (the Drama Critics' Circle Award, an Obie and three Tonys as well as the John F. Kennedy Lifetime Achievement Award), he had not had success in his home country during the 1970s and 1980s. During this period his plays were considered overly 'realistic' or in some cases didactic in intention, no doubt because some of his characters are remembered for their lofty speeches, moral in tone. Or perhaps because the moral concerns of his plays were associated in the public imagination with Miller's appearance before the House Un-American Activities Committee during the McCarthy years when he refused to name names. Annette J. Saddik argues that along with Tennessee Williams, Miller's canon of plays illustrates the 'contradictions of the American dream, as late capitalism's ideological failures left behind those betrayed by the promise of self-determination, wealth and power'. He also responded to the 'social anxieties' of the McCarthy era regarding 'private and public identity'.[67]

In the 1990s, Miller enjoyed a resurgence on the American stage with four productions and several revivals, including the 1999 50th anniversary revival of *Death of a Salesman*, with Brian Dennehy as Miller's modern tragic hero – Willy Loman. In 1997–8, the Off-Broadway Signature Theatre devoted its season to Miller's past works as well as a new play (the fourth that decade), *Mr. Peters' Connections*. Although Miller opened his 1991 play *The Ride Down Mt. Morgan* in London's West End, he brought the revised play seven years later to the Joseph Papp Public Theater. Originally written in the 1970s, again in 1980s and then in the 1990s, the spectre of the Nixon and Reagan years hovers over this comedy/drama that, as Christopher Bigsby recounts, 'seemed to many to be based on a denial of the social contract and a legitimizing of a self detached from personal and public responsibility'.[68] In 1993, Miller's *The Last Yankee* premiered Off-Broadway at the Manhattan Theatre Club. The focus in this play is on two wives under treatment for depression in a state mental hospital, both experiencing the constraints on their lives by their husbands' aspirations. Ironically, the carpenter, the 'last Yankee' of the title and descendant of Alexander Hamilton, is viewed from his wife's perspective as sacrificing their family's welfare for his vision of the 'dream'.

Miller's most successful play of the 1990s, *Broken Glass* (1994), premiered at the Long Wharf Theatre in New Haven, Connecticut, before transferring to Broadway. In this play, set in Brooklyn in 1938, during the same period as *Kristallnacht*, the night of the broken glass – when Hitler's Brownshirts launched a nationwide pogrom against Jewish synagogues, businesses, homes and people in Germany. At the heart of the play are the Gellburgs, a couple who respond to these events abroad in very different ways that manifest both viscerally and symbolically. Sylvia is not only increasingly agitated by the reports and the complaisance of those around her, notably her husband's indifference and repression of his Jewish identity, but she also experiences paralysis of the legs. In this play, Miller once again integrates the personal and the political, and in critiquing inertia in the face of oppression, the theme of anti-Semitism and fascism resurface in his work. Although the play is set in 1938, it asks us to remember the risks of denial and indifference in the presence of contemporary oppression. *Broken Glass* was produced in 1994, when the world gaped in horror at the atrocities of ethnic cleansing in the former Yugoslavia and in Rwanda.[69]

Although Tennessee Williams, another of American theatre's most revered playwrights of mid-century, died in 1983, his early 'lost' play *Not About Nightingales* was found by actor Vanessa Redgrave and produced in 1998 by the National Theatre in London in collaboration with Corin and Vanessa Redgrave's Moving Theatre. Later that year it was produced in America by the Alley Theatre in Houston, and in 1999 at Circle in the Square on Broadway, winning Tony Awards for Best Play and Best Performance by Corin Redgrave. Williams is known as a poetic playwright and remembered for his portraits of failed lives, particularly the Southern gentlewoman, and those suffering delusions of grandeur and sexual repression. However, the social context of these lives is always apparent in the transformation of the South in an increasingly industrialized economy, the war and the Depression. Uncharacteristically for Williams, *Nightingales* is a prison drama about inmates who resort to a hunger strike for better conditions. Originally conceived for the Group Theatre, the 1930s ensemble theatre group associated with the politically charged drama of Clifford Odets, *Nightingales* was never produced. However, the play's poetic language and psychologically drawn characters reminded audiences in the 1990s of Williams's most well-known plays – *The Glass Menagerie* (1944), *A Streetcar Named Desire* (1947), *Cat on a Hot Tin Roof* (1955) and *Sweet Bird of Youth* (1959) – which had been revived for decades in theatres around the world. *Nightingales* explicitly revealed the political dimension of Williams's work.

Miller and Williams were not the only revered playwrights of earlier decades to reclaim their stature on the American stage of the 1990s. Edward Albee, best known for his works in the late 1950s and 1960s, such as *The Zoo Story*, *The Sandbox*, *The American Dream*, *Who's Afraid of Virginia Woolf* and *A Delicate Balance*, was less successful in the 1970s and 1980s, but received acclaim for his 1994 play *Three Tall Women*. Associated with the post-war European absurdist theatre of Beckett, Ionesco and Genet, Albee combined absurdist and realistic styles to form 'accumulated images of a dreadful, absent, or imaginary history'.[70] Saddik maintains that Albee 'attacked the hypocrisies of America's national identity embedded in the notions of progress and optimism', the failure of communication in bourgeois conformist culture and, in *The American Dream*, 'the worship of the superficial ... explored through the presentation of a family who, after having lost the adopted child they mutilated for failing to live up to expectations, are confronted with a Young Man at the end of the play ... emotionally dead' and now suitable for the 'sanitized American family'.[71]

The figures of the lost child, the young man and the dysfunctional family make an appearance in Albee's plays of the 1990s. *Three Tall Women*, which had its American premiere Off-Broadway at the Vineyard Theatre (awarded the Pulitzer Prize for Drama, his third, as well as the Drama Critics' Circle award, the Lucille Lortel and the Outer Critics' award), is often said to be based on the life of his wealthy, conservative and disapproving adoptive mother with whom he had a troubled relationship. The three women of the play emerge after the first act as the dying woman and her earlier selves in dialogue with each other, forming what critic Steven Price calls 'a cubist portrait' in which he inserted a silent young man, presumably the son.[72] The 'foundling' appears in his 1998 *The Play about the Baby*, reminiscent of the fictional child in *Who's Afraid*, that, as Bigsby argues, represents the 'illusions and evasions of his characters'.[73] In 1993–4, the Signature Theatre devoted its season to Albee's plays, revitalizing his career and introducing new audiences to his work.

Themes of White male heteronormativity in the theatre of the 1990s

In many ways, the Postmodern male triumvirate lauded in the 1970s and 1980s – Sam Shepard, David Mamet and David Rabe – took on the mantle of questioning the American Dream and the ramifications of this multifaceted mythology of success particularly for men. Although they were not nearly as prolific in the 1990s, some of their plays responded to the political and cultural issues of the decade that revolved around sexual politics and constructed gender identities. Saddik maintains that whether it is in real estate, gambling, street crime or Hollywood films, 'success in the con game of American enterprise rests on the ability to convince others that our cultural fantasies are tangible and available for purchase'.[74] The performance of masculinity in these plays becomes a desperate attempt to wield power and gain autonomy in relationships with women or between men. They also dramatize the quest for a stable American identity in a capitalistic system as hollow and limiting.

Shepard, playwright, actor and director, achieved an international reputation Off- and Off-Off-Broadway. Brenda Murphy sees in his early work the depiction of the 'culture heroes' of his Southern California youth – 'the cowboy, the rock star, the gangster, and the movie mogul'. He then shifted his lens to the dysfunctional family in *The Curse of the Starving Class* (1977), *Buried Child* (1978) and *True West* (1980), winning the Pulitzer Prize for *Buried Child* in 1979. Murphy notes that his style has been described as 'hyper-realism', particularly in his sets, costumes and colloquial dialogue, but she also observes his use of poetic monologues, symbolist allusions and hallucinatory episodes.[75] Shepard had been prolific early on, but in the 1990s he only wrote three new stage plays: *States of Shock* (1991), *Simpatico* (1994) and *Eyes for Consuela* (1998). However, in 1996, Shepard's reputation as a significant American playwright received a boost. His revised version of *Buried Child* was brought to Broadway and nominated for a Tony, and the Signature Theatre devoted its 1996–7 season to his work. Although Shepard has been criticized by feminists for a 'masculinist aversion to emotional intimacy', among other attitudes, such as the marginalization and objectification of women characters and a 'high-octane machismo', Leslie A. Wade also sees a more 'meditative, even ethical element to Shepard's dramatic vision' in the 1990s.[76]

With *States of Shock*, which premiered at the American Place Theatre in 1991, Shepard responded to America's involvement in the Gulf War of the early 1990s with an anti-war play, and he turned once again to the performance of masculinity, the concomitant need to assert power, and a more critical stance to this 'masculinist posture' in relation to war. As in earlier plays, he pits two men against each other. The Colonel, dressed in a conglomeration of military styles and spouting heroic platitudes, cannot accept the maimed and presumably impotent war veteran and perhaps son Stubbs, or confront the challenges to war that Stubbs presents. As Wade interprets the scenario, 'the play is forthright in its indictment of militaristic enterprise and nationalist allegiance

... [and] the Colonel serves as the perverse embodiment of this viewpoint ... In the name of the nation, he justifies the bloodshed of history and argues the necessity of aggression.'[77]

Shepard wrote two other plays in the 1990s with male characters involved in a struggle for power: *Sympatico*, which premiered at the Joseph Papp Public Theater in 1994, and *Eyes for Consuela*, produced by the Manhattan Theatre Club in 1998. In *Sympatico*, Vinnie and Carter confront the ramifications of their past crime, a blackmail scheme in which they had ensnared a Kentucky Derby racing official. In *Eyes for Consuela*, Shepard places his businessman in a boarding house in the Mexican jungle, where he confronts his inner demons, his failed marriage and the choices that he has made to accrue success.

Sexual politics are also central to Mamet, whose works in the 1970s and 1980s invoked the 'masculine' mythology that shapes men's identities as they battle with each other in the world of American business, reminiscent of Miller's *Salesman*. Feminist critic Carla J. McDonough observes that several critics in the 1980s addressed only Mamet's rendering of the loss of morality in a critique of capitalism, the exploitation and betrayal suffered by these characters in a world where human connection is commodified.[78] McDonough, however, has focused on the gender and sexual politics in Mamet's works from this era:

> the rules of acquiring masculinity ... are made dependent on the destruction or exclusion of female subjectivity in order to glorify male independence or strength ... [A] feminine presence is continually evoked by Mamet's characters as they attempt aggressively to deny, attack or degrade what they perceive as feminine qualities in themselves and others.[79]

The sexual politics of the 1990s, particularly in relation to workplace inequities and sexual harassment, made it impossible for critics to ignore Mamet's rendering of a gendered and class-based struggle for power in his provocative 1992 play *Oleanna*. Set in academia, this two-actor play depicts a college professor John and his female student Carol locked in an increasingly hostile verbal battle, shaped by the power dynamic between teacher and student that turns abusive when John is accused of sexual harassment by the formerly insecure and vulnerable young woman.

Oleanna was produced shortly after the nation watched the televised Senate hearings for Justice Clarence Thomas's appointment to the Supreme Court and the accusations of sexual harassment brought against Thomas by former aide and law professor Anita Hill (see Chapter 1). The issue of sexual harassment clearly informed the divided responses of audiences and critics to Mamet's play and its film adaptation. Mamet resisted these interpretations, however, declaring that the play was not about sexual harassment but rather a 'tragedy about power'.[80]

Challenges to White male privilege took many forms in the 1990s, addressing gender, sexuality, race and class conflicts often from the point of view of White, male heterosexual playwrights rendering their observations of a society coming to terms with conscious and unconscious bias. John Guare's 1990 play *Six Degrees of Separation* depicts a well-to-do Upper East New York couple, the Kittredges, liberal-minded art dealers who buy and sell art among the rich and famous, who are 'conned' by a charming young African American man, Paul, who arrives at their door seeking shelter after his escape from a Central Park mugging. Initially attracted to the young man who says that he is Sidney Poitier's son and friend of their Harvard-educated children, they alternately feel titillation, betrayal (he is gay and brings a 'hustler' into their home when they are out) and ultimately sympathy, which comes too late. The phrase 'six degrees of separation' is ironically about relatedness, the theory that everyone is six or fewer steps away, by introduction, from any other person in the world. Gene A. Plunka argues that the play 'documents the pathology' of upper-class modern urban life in the desire for 'radical chic'.[81] David Roman offers a searing interpretation of the play in terms of its 'racialized sexual discourse' represented by Paul as a 'spectacle of difference, if not chaos' offered for Ouisa's 'spiritual epiphany'. This interpretation eluded most theatre critics, pointing to the 'limited discourses available within liberalism [in the early 1990s] for discussing race and sexuality'.[82] The play was first produced at the Mitzi E. Newhouse Theater at Lincoln Center and then transferred to Broadway, testament perhaps that the audience saw aspects of their own desires in the Kittredges.

African American, ethnic and feminist theatrical visions as genres and cultural practice

Although several of the playwrights discussed thus far query and critique the concept of American identity, the mythology of the American Dream linked to the exercise of power, the performance of masculinity and the acquisition of money and fame, they do so, according to Saddik, 'from within the system'. She argues, however, that their plays have been 'crucial to opening up a space for marginalized and culturally diverse voices in their exposure of identity as a performance or "act" within dominant structures of commodity capitalism'.[83] We might debate the various conditions that paved the way for alternative depictions of nationhood, the definition of American identity and the pursuit of the American Dream represented in the theatre, but the sea change in the last three decades of the century, culminating in the 1990s, was transformative. A panoply of race-, ethnic-, gender- and sexuality-based companies and theatre artists who identified with and addressed the issues current in these theatrical communities were making their voices heard.

Several prominent dramatists and theatre groups of the decade challenged White, male heteronormativity as well as prevailing American narratives of success and the discourse of 'universality' (interpreted as white, male, heterosexual and middle class). The theatrical trajectories of these groups and individual artists that identified with them, which some consider as constituting a genre of American theatre,[84] will be the subject of this next section.

As we highlight artists, plays, performances and companies, it is important to keep in mind that theatre with roots in specific communities or gender/sexual identities is always in process, responsive to larger cultural movements, geopolitical and sociohistorical interests and ideologies, as well as aesthetic strategies and forms.[85] Definitions of 'Black', 'Asian American', Latina/o, feminist, lesbian, gay and queer theatre have changed significantly since the 1960s, when many of these theatrical groups began.[86] Gradually a less 'essentialist' – immutable, monolithic – construction of culture has morphed into a notion of self and community as hybrid, continually changing and socially constructed. Some playwrights mix genres and sources, drawing on contemporary life experience, autobiography, realistic drama, avant-garde non-illusionist theatre, ancient folklore and contemporary source material from the country of origin. More recently, artists have adapted solo performance and comedic monologue that satirize family dynamics, stereotypes and the culture that has created them.

African American theatre

African American theatre is by no means a monolithic concept. Harvey Young has given careful attention to the question of what constitutes 'Black Theatre', citing artists and critics from different historical eras, such as W. E. B. Du Bois's championing of the creation of African American theatre in the 1920s that Young describes as a 'bold and powerful act of self-determination', a 'tool to engage black communities' and a space where 'audiences could gather to see themselves, their stories, their culture, and their lives represented on stage'.[87] In the Black Arts Movement of the 1960s, building on Du Bois's 'about/by/for/near formulation', Amiri Baraka called for a 'black theatre' that must be 'liberating' and empowering as well. Various conceptions of a Black aesthetic, distinct from Anglo-Euro traditions, were articulated by artists and political activists in the Black Power movement. From the mid-1960s through to the mid-1970s, hundreds of short-lived theatre companies emerged to take up the political and social issues that preoccupied the Black community. Young observes a generational shift toward the end of the twentieth century into the new millennium in which artists and scholars complicated the commonly accepted definitions of 'blackness' and considered the intersecting experiences (e.g. race, class, gender and sexuality) and political and cultural identities that construct the self.[88] Most importantly, Black Theatre is seen, not as a subset of American theatre but as integral to American theatre. Furthermore, the rise of critical studies of 'whiteness' in the 1990s – the 'invisibility' of whiteness in a raced culture and the idea of whiteness as a social construct – has led to studies of 'iterations of *whiteness* in African American performance'.[89]

In 1996, Pulitzer Prize-winning dramatist August Wilson, a

pre-eminent voice in American theatre, presented the keynote address at the biennial conference sponsored by the Theatre Communications Group (TCG), an organization of theatre artists and scholars. In what has become a canonical essay, 'The Ground on Which I Stand', Wilson addressed the continuing need for artists of colour to create work that represents their respective experiences and cultural history, and he called for theatres dedicated to producing their work. Developing his position, he noted that the largest professional association of non-profit and not-for-profit theatre organizations in the United States, the League of Resident Theatres (LORT), identified only one of their 67 theatres as 'African American'. Young underscores the significance of these remarks because the success of Pulitzer Prize-winning Wilson's own cycle of history plays – seven by 1996 and ten in all prior to his death in 2004 – suggested that 'racial diversity' as well as 'racial syncretism' had been achieved. This, of course, was far from the case. Young notes that Wilson's speech prompted a 'national conversation, within the arts, about race, multiculturalism, and cultural separatism'.[90] Wilson was careful to state that 'we are not "separatists" but artists who seek to develop our talents and give expression to our personalities. We bring advantage to the common ground that is American Theatre.'[91]

In addition to encouraging Black theatre artists and companies of colour, the issue of cross-racial or 'non-traditional' casting was given more attention in the now famous debate on 27 January 1997 between August Wilson and Robert Brustein, professor of drama at Harvard and artistic director of the American Repertory Theatre. This event, titled 'On Cultural Power', staged at the Town Hall, New York City, was moderated by playwright and performer Anna Deveare Smith and sponsored by the Theatre Communications Group as 'an exploration of the political and aesthetic underpinnings of that mélange we call American culture'.[92] Once again, Wilson, whose plays represented the lives of African Americans across the decades of the twentieth century, argued for the development of Black theatres as a drama of, by and for Black Americans. He discouraged Black actors from playing characters that were not explicitly Black and called for a theatre that would sustain the values of their ancestors, including their African origins. Anything less would be a capitulation to the notion of universalism that belied the equation of universalism with whiteness. Brustein countered these arguments with a defence of colour-blind casting and the need for presenting Black experience in white institutions, calling Wilson's argument separatist. Ultimately Brustein argued that 'art does not change social consciousness' and resisted what he called 'ideological art'. Wilson retorted that 'art changes individuals, and individuals change society'. The fact that this debate has become legendary reflects the high stakes of representing the various strands of racial politics in American society then and now.[93]

Wilson had accumulated several playwriting awards by the time he premiered three new plays in the 1990s: *The Piano Lesson* (1990), *Two Trains Running* (1992) and *Seven Guitars* (1996). Working closely with Lloyd Richards, the first Black director on Broadway as well as Director of the O'Neill Playwrights Workshop and the Artistic Director of Yale Drama School, Wilson premiered his works at Yale Repertory Theatre and then transferred them to Broadway. He won his second Pulitzer Prize in 1990 for *The Piano Lesson*; in 1992 he won the American Theatre Critics' Association Award for *Two Trains Running*, and in 1996 the New York Drama Critics' Circle Award for *Seven Guitars*. *Jitney* was produced in 2000, winning the Outer Critics' Circle Award. In 1999, Wilson was awarded the National Humanities Medal.

These dramas are part of his ambitious ten-play cycle – a play for each decade of the twentieth century – that focused on ordinary lives, almost exclusively set in the Hill District of Pittsburgh, Pennsylvania, where he spent his childhood and formative years. As Harry J. Elam, Jr explains, each play is situated at 'critical junctures' in African American history and 'explores the pain and perseverance, the determination and dignity in these black lives'.[94] Wilson incorporated the language and style of the people into a dramatic structure informed by the blues as well as supernatural elements that signify profound and often haunting elements of the past. As Elam articulates it, Wilson's '"bluesology" acts as an aesthetic and cultural intervention disrupting the conventional frame of realism. Rather than plot or action, character and the lyrical music of the dialogue drive the plays.'[95] Sandra Shannon perceives Wilson as 'medium, storyteller, culture bearer or as an African-in-America ... but can best be described as an autoethnographer ... His stories about separation, migrations, and reunions at once reflect the plight of thousands of African Americans subjected to the lingering traumatic splintering effects of slavery and mass migration and their ongoing quests to reconnect.'[96]

Throughout the 1990s, Wilson continued to develop his history cycle plays and in the process retell American history from an African American perspective. In *The Piano Lesson* (1990), Wilson addresses the issues of inheritance and legacy through his depiction of a conflict between a brother and sister over the destiny of a family heirloom, a carved piano. *Two Trains Running* revisited the late 1960s from the perspective of the 1990s. The 1960s had been a 'liminal' moment in African American history, when Martin Luther King's call for non-violence in the civil rights movement of the 1950s and 1960s was challenged by the more militant Black Power movement, and these voices and discourses are woven into the play. The plot is centred on the character Memphis and his struggle to gain fair compensation for his restaurant – his 'American Dream' in the midst of an urban renewal project in Pittsburgh. Set immediately after the Civil Rights Act of 1968 that prohibited discrimination in renting and selling property as well as the Fair Housing Act of 1968, African American property owners confronted a white dominated housing market and discriminatory practices against Blacks.[97] In 1996, Wilson's *Seven Guitars*, set in 1948, portrays the aftermath of the funeral of a local blues guitarist, Floyd 'Schoolboy' Barton, and seven of his circle tell stories from their lives in relation to Floyd. However, the play also works as a flashback not only to the days before Floyd's death but to the Second World War and earlier, to depict the racism and the broken promises that devastated Blacks during this period.

Among the most enduring dramatists of the past four decades, Adrienne Kennedy changed the theatrical landscape in terms of rendering the psychic states of Black characters, more often women than men. In her break-out play *Funnyhouse of a Negro* (1964), her protagonist experiences a crisis of identity, seeing herself through the lens of White culture and at the same time projecting herself onto cultural icons who speak her story, figures as disparate as Queen Victoria, Patrice Lumumba (the first premier of Zaire, now the Democratic Republic of Congo) and Jesus Christ. Derangement and distortion emerge from the sights and sounds of a consciousness frantically attempting to sort out the multiplicity of images and voices that have shaped her even as they reject her.[98] Kennedy has staged her plays Off-Broadway at La MaMa Experimental Theatre Company, the Theatre Company of Boston, the Goodman Theatre in Chicago, the Julliard School in New York and the Mark Taper Forum in Los Angeles, in addition to her success abroad, having produced works at the Royal Court Theatre, the National Theatre, the Petit Odean in Paris and San Saba in Rome. She has won Obie awards for *Funnyhouse*, *June and Jean in Concert* (1995) and *Sleep Deprivation Chamber* (1996). In 1995, the Signature Theatre Company devoted a season to her work.

In the 1990s, Kennedy continued to write non-linear plays that rendered surrealistic, dreamlike and often nightmarish states that dealt with the trauma of miscegenation, rape and racial profiling. Her *Alexander Plays*, published in 1992, are named for the alter-ego protagonist Suzanne Alexander constructed by Kennedy to render her experiences. The most well known of these plays, *The Ohio State Murders*, premiered in 1992 at the Great Lakes Theater Festival in Cleveland, and moves between the younger Suzanne, a student at the racially divided Ohio State University between 1949 and 1953 (when Kennedy had been a student there), and the older Suzanne, a fictive version of herself – an alum who became an established Black playwright and whose work represents the history of racism, often violent. Philip Kolin, who has written extensively about Kennedy's theatrical project, maintains that 'she has been on the cutting edge of experimental theatre, bringing a unique voice to the African American experience'. Caroline Jackson Smith notes that she is one of 'the first playwrights to represent the self in multiple characters'.[99] In *Sleep Deprivation Chamber* (1996), co-authored with her son Adam, she presents a 'surrealistic documentary' on Adam's victimization by the police. The play resonated with the widely publicized 1991 case of police brutality toward Rodney King in Los Angeles. In her characteristic approach and style, Kennedy places her audience in a nightmare that Kolin compares to a 'macabre film noir, [in which] deprived of sleep, we are up all night like the characters, battling hallucinations' as 'Teddy relives the horrors of his arrest, and his mother accompanies him in her own surrealistic fantasies and fears'.[100]

Versatile actor/performance artist/playwright Anna Deavere Smith created a theatrical genre that transforms documentary theatre into a solo performance of multiple characters to address two major events in the decade that involved ethnic and racial conflict. The Obie Award-winning *Fires in the Mirror* (1992) explored the crisis between Caribbean immigrants, the police and Lubavitcher Jews in Crown Heights, Brooklyn, when a car carrying a Hasidic spiritual leader struck a boy from Guyana. The subsequent reaction of the district's Black community against the police and the Lubavitchers resulted in the killing of a young Hasidic scholar from Australia and heated discourse about the exercise of political power in the community and in the city. Later that year, Smith created *Twilight: Los Angeles, 1992* (1993), which treated the Rodney King riots following the acquittal in 1992 of four police officers who had brutally beaten an unarmed African American motorist. She conceived both productions from interviews that she conducted with community members and notable commentators or scholars in relation to the events. In tour-de-force performances, aided by video clips, music, slide projections and changes in hairstyle or articles of clothing, she inhabited her subjects, speaking their words, rendering their speech rhythms and physical gestures. As she has written, 'if I said a word often enough it would *become* me, the reenactment, or the reiteration of a person's words would also teach me about that person'.[101] Above all, her aim in this project had been to create a dialogue among these disparate voices embroiled in an ongoing 'negotiation of identity', sometimes brought to explosive conflicts triggered by horrific events. Joan Wylie Hall has written that Smith 'expands notions of race and gender far beyond the typical Black–White, male–female binaries'.[102] Kimberly Rae Connor sees Smith as 'facilitating a radical empathy' in the audience that enables them to share in 'a transformative slipping across socially produced identities of race, nation, gender, and class'.[103]

Suzan-Lori Parks, the inventive and most produced new dramatist of the 1990s, was acclaimed by critics for her groundbreaking theatrical styles, influenced by African American writers (Kennedy and Ntozake Shange among them) as well as White Modernists such as Gertrude Stein and Samuel Beckett. In 2002, she became the first African American woman playwright to win the Pulitzer Prize for her play *Topdog/Underdog*. Her plays and her essays about drama often use the metaphor of 'digging' to excavate the buried objects and most pointedly the unrecorded or 'forgotten' aspects of African American history to resurrect and retell this history through parodying painful practices, stereotypes and debasing images, and then burying them repeatedly. We see this scenario in *Death of the Last Black Man in the Whole Entire World* (1990) and *The America Play* (1994).

Parks also draws on historical and literary sources to render hegemonic discourses around Black women's sexuality as deviant in such plays as her 1996 *Venus* and her 'red-letter plays' that reimagine American literary history's most outcast mother, Hester Prynne of Hawthorne's *The Scarlet Letter*, as an impoverished Black welfare mother. Clearly the image of the welfare mother would have been salient to audiences attuned to the welfare reform debates in the 1990s during the Clinton administration and the movement from welfare to 'workfare' with a five-year limit on benefits, despite few opportunities for jobs with a living wage or childcare.[104] Parks's works are discussed in depth in Chapter 6 of this book.

Asian American theatre

Like other theatre artists and companies that identify with a particular ethnic or racial group, Asian American theatre has generated many debates about the definition of an Asian American play and what constitutes Asian American identity (or 'Asianness') in terms of grouping dramatists and theatrical productions. These debates emerge from the changing attitudes and circumstances of generations of Americans of Asian ancestry, some recently arrived and others with American-born parents and grandparents. Daphne Lei points out that although many Asian American plays render a 'binary confrontation' – the 'either/or' choice ('having to choose being either Asian or American, having to position oneself on either side of the binary system', or adopt an attitude of 'us versus them') – several plays of the last decades of the twentieth century 'appear to embrace a different representation of identity, establishing an alternative '"neither/nor" situation and implying an avoidance of ethnic positioning – whether by choice or by force'. These plays consider the complexity of the designation 'Asian American', the representations of both terms in the binary and the assumption of a 'pan-Asian overarching ethnicity'. Furthermore, within the context of globalization, borders are traversed and cultural influences 'exchanged, consolidated, and recreated'.[105]

The origin of 'Asian American theatre' is often rooted in the 1960s with the establishment of the first Asian American theatre company, the East West Players in Los Angeles, followed by the Asian American Theater Company in San Francisco, Northwest Asian American Theatre in Seattle and Pan Asian Repertory Theatre in New York City.[106] Although these companies had distinct aims, they shared the goal of creating a place for the 'development and expression of Asian American theatre'. They were comprised of theatre artists who addressed culturally specific themes and adapted forms with the specific goals of providing more work for Asian American actors, including playing non-Asian characters; protesting against stereotypes of the 'oriental'; and telling stories that dealt with personal and group experience. In her history of Asian American theatre, Esther Kim Lee states emphatically that Asian American theatre became 'established as an institution' because of the first four companies.[107] However, she begins her study by designating David Henry Hwang's 1988 Tony Award-winning play *M. Butterfly* (Hwang was the first Asian American to be produced on Broadway) as the 'single event that put Asian American theatre on the national and international cultural map'.[108]

In the 1980s, Hwang, Philip Kan Gotanda and Velina Hasu Houston became well-known playwrights of what Lee and Hasu Houston call the 'second wave' writers working in mainstream theatre. Each dramatist had worked with Asian American companies early in their careers, and Gotanda had his works co-produced by Asian American theatre companies and various regional theatre companies (including his 1999 *Yohen*, co-produced by East West Players and Roby Theater, an African American theatre company). Gotanda's 1990 play *The Wash* depicts the tension and eventual separation of a second generation Japanese American couple when the wife seeks autonomy and new love, and the husband must grapple with issues related to his sense of masculinity in the context of the Japanese American community. Other plays by Gotanda in the 1990s include *Day Standing on its Head* (1994) and *Sisters Matsumoto* (1998). Velina Hasu Houston is of Japanese, African American and Blackfoot Pikuni heritage, and even with her success, she has confronted resistance both from Asian American and African American groups. Known nationally and internationally especially for her trilogy of plays, *Asa Ga Kimashita* (1981), *American Dreams* (1984) and *Tea* (1987), based in part on her parents' personal history, she also published two groundbreaking anthologies of plays by Asian Americans in the 1990s: *Politics of Life* (1993), which included only women writers, and *But Still, Like Air, I'll Rise* (1997). *Tea*, based on interviews with Japanese war brides in an army base in Kansas, brings a feminist lens to her rendering of Asian American narratives, as is true of her other plays as well. [109]

Hwang, the most well known of these playwrights, has achieved fame for debunking 'orientalism', cultural representations of Asians as 'others' and 'oriental' stereotypes. He involved himself in the protest against White actors playing Asians in the *Miss Saigon* controversy in 1991 (see page 36) and wrote two plays that addressed 'yellowface' casting. His 2007 play *Yellow Face* renders a complex view of his own position in the controversy, cast as the representative of Asian American theatre following the success of his award-winning *M. Butterfly* (1988), especially given that his 1990 plays, specifically *Bondage* (1992) and *Face Value* (1993), trouble the label 'Asian American playwright' and represent race as an 'artificial' societal construction. Esther Kim Lee observes that 'all of the plays he wrote during the decade [of the 1990s] question assumptions he held during the 1980s', and his work engaged different forms and styles.[110] In *Golden Child* (1996), Hwang revisits his family history, and the story of his great-grandfather's conversion to Christianity, among other themes. Lee notes that in this play, Hwang gives 'validity to both traditional Chinese ancestor worship and Christianity by allowing the possibility of both belief systems exerting real power in people's spiritual lives'.[111]

In the 1990s, companies emerged with a wide range of mission statements – some more ethnically specific, others more interested in the Asian diaspora and therefore intercultural, or refusing any labelling.[112] Anthologies of Asian American plays were published and scholarly works emerged on Asian American theatre from historical, analytical and theoretical perspectives. Like Lei, Lee observes that many 'third wave' writers transcended the boundaries felt by earlier Asian American writers, ignoring or resisting the 'binary choice' to represent a particular group or not. As she notes, 'Instead they began to tell their individual stories in which Asian American identity is only a part of their complex experiences', rejecting any essentialist construction of identity. Lee gives many examples: Sung Rno's *Cleveland Raining* (1995) renders the feeling of detachment from ancestry and group belonging. In *A Language of their Own* (1995), by Chay Yew, a couple discover that it is not their 'being Chinese' that links them or even divides them when they discuss the implications of being 'Asian' for their relationship. They discover, instead, that the demise of their relationship has all to do with communication, the ability to speak and be heard. Diana Son's *Stop Kiss*, successfully produced by the Public Theater in 1998, told the story of two women who discover their desire for each other, and neither character was described in racial or ethnic terms. Lee includes Naomi Iizuka in her discussion of theatre in the 1990s by Asian American playwrights who do not address cultural identities directly. Perhaps mirroring her personal experiences as a daughter of a Japanese father and a Latina mother, Iizuka's play *36 Views* (1999–2001) deals with 'perception and illusion in art and human relationships'. For these artists, cultural identity is not only socially constructed but also fluid and fragmented.[113]

Latina/o theatre

Historically, Latina/os have also been an under-represented population in American theatre and in histories of American theatre. However, with increasing visibility in the 1980s and 1990s, playwrights and theatre companies with a designated mission (though not always exclusively) to convey a sense of culture, history and shared aesthetic forms have brought Latina/o productions to wider theatre audiences and collaborations with 'mainstream' theatres. The terminology has evolved to specify the particular groups assembled or represented: Latina/o (the 'a/o' designating gender) refers to a heterogeneous group in the United States with origins in Mexico (Chicana/o), Cuba, Puerto Rico, and/or the Puerto Rican diaspora in New York City (Nuyorican), the Dominican Republic, El Salvador and many other cultures, all linked to the Spanish language. Yvonne Yarbro-Bejarano describes the Chicana/o theatre movement as political and oppositional from the start, an 'arm of the Chicano movement to resist cultural and economic domination'.[114] Virtually every history of the Latina/o theatre movement begins with Luis Valdez's El Teatro Campesino (ETC), founded in 1965 during the grape strike of the United Farmworkers Union at Delano, California, and known as the farmworker's theatre. Its primary form was the 'actos' – short scenes originally devised through improvisation, usually comic, encouraging audiences to take social action. Valdez was also a trained playwright, and his play *Zoot Suit* appeared in Los Angeles and then on Broadway in 1979. Valdez's work and before him Miguel Piñero's *Short Eyes*, a prison drama, produced at the New York Public Theater in 1974, are credited with putting Latina/o theatre on the map. At the same time, Valdez's theatrical success in mainstream theatre was also seen as shifting the political focus of his theatre – by and for the Chicana/o community. ETC continues to thrive into the twenty-first century with new goals and theatre strategies.

Theatre artist Maria Irene Fornés (Cuban-born) was another formative influence on playwrights of the 1990s. In the early 1980s, she founded the Hispanic Playwrights Lab at INTAR (International Arts Relations) in New York City to encourage a new generation of writers. Her own plays, including her 1977 *Fefu and Her Friends* (also famous in the developing feminist theatre), made a major contribution to Latina/o as well as the avant-garde American theatre, though she has not used ethnic or gender labels to identify her own work. The many playwrights that emerged from her theatre workshops and produced work in the 1990s include Cherríe Moraga, Migdalia Cruz, Octavio Solis, Luis Alfaro, Caridad Svich, Oliver Mayer, Nilo Cruz and many others.[115] The following discussion includes only a few of the playwrights who have contributed to diverse productions related to Latina/o theatre in the 1990s, some of them rooted in the exclusive concerns of Latina/o communities, and others working across cultural boundaries to take up issues of sexism, sexuality and violence.

Cherríe Moraga worked with Fornés and credits Valdez as an influence in the development of Chicana/o theatre. However, she has transformed the cultural nationalism in these early plays to include women, and she adopts a feminist lens to challenge race, culture and class oppression. In *Shadow of a Man* (1990) she reveals the adverse effects of gender politics in the traditional Chicano household, and her later plays depict subjugation and gender conflicts in intimate relationships and in communities. In *Heroes and Saints* (1992) she addresses the subject of children dying of pesticides in the fields and the agribusiness that ignores them, specifically depicting a young Chicana born deformed.

Openly gay, Moraga wrote *The Hungry Woman: A Mexican Medea* (1995) to transpose and transform the Aztec creation myth of the Hungry Woman and incorporates this figure into a critique of 'Chicanismo's failure to acknowledge the intra-cultural diversity of Chicana/o identities (differences based on region, gender, class, language, and sexuality)'.[116]

Addressing works by Valdez, Moraga and others in 1997, W. B. Worthen observes that they use 'history to provide an empowering body of imagery, a narrative that locates Chicana/o agency in history as a way to support and enable Chicano/a identity – and identity politics – in the present. At the same time, however, many of these plays are also reflexively preoccupied with the indeterminacies of *staging* history.'[117] Worthen asks how these representations resist commodification by the dominant culture. And how do they resist the idea of a fixed, unchanging, totalizing representation that elides the hybridized and multivalent nature of identity? Of course, these questions might be posed to any of the ethnically identified theatres discussed in this section.

Two Nuyorican playwrights who won acclaim in the 1990s are José Rivera and Migdalia Cruz. Alberto Sandoval-Sanchez situates Rivera as part of a new generation of Nuyorican dramatists who 'revisit, re-vision and reimagine the history of Latino diaspora, exile, and nostalgia, as new hybrid identities articulated and constructed on the stage'.[118] Incorporating the use of fantastic or mythical elements in what appears to be a realistic scenario, Rivera's 1992 Obie Award-winning play *Marisol* depicts a young Latina copy-editor in New York City, isolated and detached from any semblance of cultural identity, who becomes lost in a threatening 'post-apocalyptic' urban landscape, searching for herself and salvation in this 'nightmare journey'.[119] Migdalia Cruz (who also studied with Fornés at INTAR) brings a feminist perspective to her rendering of the difficult lives of women (often living in the Bronx) who survive poverty, abandonment and abuse. In *Miriam's Flowers* (1990), she portrays a sixteen-year-old Puerto Rican girl in the south Bronx in 1975 who must cope with the demise of her family following her young brother's tragic death. *The Have-Little* (1991) tells another woman's story in the south Bronx. She has experienced a series of abandonments, alcoholism in her family, death and a pregnancy that results in single impoverished motherhood.

Feminist theatre and the under-representation of women playwrights

Feminist theatre, like the culturally and politically based theatres related to race and ethnicity, has been analysed in terms of its origins, its defining attributes, ideological predilections, aesthetic practices, political goals and the material conditions undergirding productions and theatre companies. A body of theory has produced several critical categories informed by an array of feminisms – various approaches to interpreting the role and status of women, the qualities ascribed to the constructed category of 'woman' and strategies for social change in a patriarchal-, raced- and class-based society. Although this scholarship has been crucial to thinking through the issues raised by feminist theatre, theories also emerge from the process of creating theatrical works.[120]

In their 2013 study of contemporary women playwrights, Penny Farfan and Lesley Ferris cite Lynda Hart's 1989 book, *Making a Spectacle: Feminist Essays on Contemporary Women's Theatre*, to recall the 'ground-swell' of women's writing for the theatre that seemed to promise more productions by women in the years to come, and to acknowledge the extraordinary work by women playwrights since 1990.[121] However, they also underscore the limited access for women in theatre even in the twenty-first century, identifying studies that point to the lack of parity between men and women playwrights and directors. In their examination of dramatic texts by women, the essays build on, complement and enhance the developments in feminist theatre studies and of feminism within the larger culture in the past twenty-five years: 'the shift from women's studies to gender studies, from gay and lesbian studies to queer theory; the emergence of third wave feminism concerned with sexuality, race, and class, as well as popular culture ... and the increased attention to international, transnational, and intercultural feminisms and their articulations in and through performance'.[122]

In the 1990s, many American women playwrights incorporated a range of feminist concerns into their works that addressed marginalization and exclusion, and interfaced with poverty, violence and the intersections of race, class, ethnicity and sexuality in systems of domination. Playwrights such as Kennedy, Parks, Fornés, Moraga, Cruz and Hasu Houston, discussed in previous sections of this chapter, represented these interrelated problems in their works. In 1996, Kathy A. Perkins and Roberta Uno edited an anthology titled *Contemporary Plays by Women of Color* that enabled readers/viewers to see commonalities amid difference. In their 'Introduction' they observe:

> Although these works can be viewed in many different ways, we were struck by the recurrence of certain themes: violence against women, response to media and historical stereotypical images, identity formation, the impact of poverty on individuals, families, and communities; the relationship of woman to her body, the relationship of women to each other, the response of a given community to crisis. The plays present varying approaches to playmaking, including solo performance and collective creation.[123]

Theatre historians situate the emergence of feminist theatre in the 1970s, developing out of the radical theatre of the 1960s that was committed to addressing political issues such as civil rights, ethnic and class hierarchies and inequalities, as well as the Vietnam War. These issues continued to preoccupy playwrights into the 1990s, including war, this time in the Middle East. For some groups, radical theatre meant the creation of new theatrical forms and a new relationship with audiences, devising works collaboratively to resist the hierarchal structure within organizations, including theatre companies, and performing for women-only audiences. Although most of these groups no longer exist, Women's Project and Productions continues to flourish, serving many women theatre artists over its thirty-seven-year history.

Feminist theatre criticism burgeoned in the 1980s and 1990s, attracting the attention of mainstream media. Feminist critics theorized that texts and productions were coalescing into a distinct cultural form. In 1996, Helene Keyssar described feminist theatre as

> [p]roductions and scripts characterized by consciousness of women as women; dramaturgy in which art is inseparable from the condition of women as women; performance (written and acted) that deconstructs sexual difference and thus undermines patriarchal power ... and the creation of women characters in the 'subject position.'[124]

Susan Steadman's comprehensive 1991 review-essay on the theoretical and historical background of feminism and/in theatre identified two other practices associated with feminist theatrical production: breaking 'sexual taboos' in the foregrounding of women's sexuality, and challenging the assumption of heterosexuality as the norm. She also discusses the feminist concern with spectatorship and the need to subvert the 'male gaze' – the objectification of women's bodies onstage as a mechanism by which the patriarchy exerts authority and power over women through the processes of looking and shaping women's aspirations to be 'looked at'.[125]

Many of the plays included in Perkins and Uno's anthology of plays by women playwrights of colour were produced in the early 1990s: Kia Corthron's *Come Down Burning* (1993) depicts the dependency and support between two sisters, one a paraplegic and the other a mother who wants to be self-sufficient; Hortensia and Elvira Colorado's *1992 Blood* speaks about the 'mythical' discovery of the Americas as the turning point for native people; Breena Clarke and Glenda Dickerson deconstruct the figure of Aunt Jemima, 'simultaneously dismembering and reconstructing this icon' while subverting many other racist myths about Black women; and solo performer Marga Gomez's trilogy, including *Marga Gomez is Pretty Witty & Gay*, is a comic rendering of her lesbian identity.

Among the playwrights who placed women characters centre stage and who achieved recognition in mainstream theatre, Marsha Norman, Beth Henley and Wendy Wasserstein all received the Pulitzer Prize for their plays in the 1980s – Beth Henley for *Crimes of the Heart* in 1981, Marsha Norman for *'night, Mother* in 1983, and Wendy Wasserstein for *The Heidi Chronicles* in 1988. Wasserstein was also the first woman to win a Tony for her play. Their dramas addressed the complicated relationships between men and women, mothers and daughters, and, in Wasserstein's work, the repercussions for upper middle-class women who aspire to professional achievement and yet continue to experience a double standard in the workplace and in family life. Furthermore, despite their aspirations for both work and family, they seem caught between a conflicting set of values.

In the 1990s, Wasserstein's *The Sisters Rosensweig* (1992) depicts the lives of three middle-aged sisters who celebrate the eldest's birthday in London, where she lives. All of the sisters experience frustration with their relationships and their life choices – subordinating themselves in marriage, effacing a Jewish identity for status, or forfeiting a career choice because it would not have met with their mother's approval. In 1996, Wasserstein's *An American Daughter* takes on the double standard confronted by ambitious and talented women in politics. Her protagonist, a woman physician about to be appointed Surgeon General, is undermined by an error in her domestic life that mirrors the Zoe Baird case when Baird, nominated for Attorney General by President Clinton in 1994, had to withdraw because she and her husband had hired illegal immigrants for domestic work in their home.[126] Although some feminist critics maligned Wasserstein's plays for focusing on privileged characters that 'react' rather than 'act', or pursue individualist goals, her work continues to be produced, after her untimely death at fifty-six in 2006.

Plays by Tina Howe and Emily Mann, though not explicitly feminist, placed women in the subject position. Although Howe and Mann are stylistically worlds apart and have focused their work on myriad issues, in the 1990s they both created aged women characters who reflect on their life choices. Howe depicts women on the brink of death in her plays *Approaching Zanzibar* (1989) and *Pride's Crossing* (1997). In the former play, she dramatizes a family on a journey to visit a dying woman, Olivia, an artist (many of her women characters are artists). Bigsby notes that the drama 'places special emphasis on the anxieties, pain, and sublimities of women's experience but that is integrated with larger concerns'.[127] In *Pride's Crossing*, ninety-year-old Mabel Bigelow recalls the various stages of her life, the circumstances and conventions that shaped her identity. The play concludes with Mabel, who at twenty-one was the first woman to swim the English Channel, envisioning her final swim. *Pride's Crossing* won the Drama Critics' Circle Award and was a finalist for the Pulitzer Prize.

Emily Mann, associated with some of the strategies of documentary theatre, weaves interviews, transcripts and journalistic accounts into her creative process to render significant historical events. Her 1996 *Having Our Say: The Delany Sisters' First Hundred Years* presents two African American sisters at 100 plus years, one a retired schoolteacher and the other a dentist, whose father had been a slave. They recall the stories of their lives as they bear witness to major events of the twentieth century that have not only shaped their lives but also give viewers a much needed perspective on the American century from their particular vantage point: Jim Crow laws, lynchings, the civil rights movement, the assassination of Martin Luther King and the congressional hearings involving Clarence Thomas and Anita Hill.

Feminist plays of the 1990s often shared concerns about women's attitudes toward their bodies, women's sexuality, the objectification of the female body, abuse, rape and sexual harassment. Perhaps the most well known work that addresses several of these issues is Eve Ensler's 1996 *The Vagina Monologues*, a series of monologues in which women speak about their vaginas in a range of contexts and from various perspectives and voices, distinguished by race or ethnicity, region, class status, sexual orientation and age. Over the last twenty years the play has become a global phenomenon, 'a mass culture event', performed hundreds of times each year, often on college campuses, giving rise to V-day, an organization to end violence against women and girls. Its success has raised a great deal of money for grassroots advocacy organizations.[128] Examining the relationships between the mission of *The Vagina Monologues* and its aesthetic form from the vantage point of twenty-first-century feminist theories, Christine M. Cooper problematizes the link that the monologues create between the vagina and female identity. For Cooper, although the monologues enable and encourage women to speak about their bodies without shame in myriad situations, at the same time they also convey the idea that 'sexuality is the very core of women's identities'. In other words, the vagina becomes a 'metonym for female consciousness' and 'empowerment through flesh', and the play moves away from 'social transformation, economic and racial as well as antipatriarchal'.[129]

In the 1990s, Rebecca Gilman won critical acclaim for plays that involved sexual assault and destructive relationships. In *The Glory of Living* (1996), the daughter of a prostitute enters into a relationship with a man who depends upon her for luring young girls to a motel where he rapes and abuses them. She is then left to dispose of the bodies and deal with the repercussions of this disastrous cycle. The play was a finalist for the 2002 Pulitzer Prize. In 2000, Gilman's *Boy Gets Girl* depicts a young woman whose blind date becomes her stalker, eventually turning violent to the point that she must leave her job and her home and establish a new identity. The play received nominations for the Outer Critics'

Circle Award in 2001 and the Olivier Award for Best New Play in 2002.

Among the many playwrights that addressed sexual abuse and violence, Paula Vogel has created the most provocative and complex renderings of trauma – 'the disturbing capacity of the past to reach into and disrupt the present' – as well as the ubiquity of some forms of violence, such as homophobia, racism and sexism, and of course the brutality of domestic violence.[130] Vogel's plays address AIDS, domestic violence, prostitution and paedophilia, among other issues. However, her aim is not to simplify her characters as aggressors or victims but to probe the ways in which we all participate in the dynamics of hurt and oppression and the ability to comprehend our past and seek agency in the present, even in pain.

In 1998, Vogel won the Pulitzer Prize for her most complex play, *How I Learned to Drive*, about a young woman who reconstructs scenes from her incestuous relationship with her uncle that began when she was eleven years old. The young woman has experienced trauma and, as she says, 'ceased to live in her body', but in grappling with and recounting/reordering these memories, she achieves a kind of understanding of herself and her uncle and gains agency as well. The play stirred a great deal of discussion about whether Vogel had gone 'easy' on the paedophile Uncle Peck, whom the playwright clearly portrays as harming his niece. In a candid interview, Vogel replied, 'I would say that we can receive great love from the people who harm us' and 'gifts from the people who hurt us'.[131] (See Chapter 4 for a full discussion of Paula Vogel's plays in the 1990s, and the 'Documents' section for an excerpt of this interview.)

In the early 1990s, the first Gulf War generated the beginnings of a theatre of war that has proliferated in the 2000s in the context of protracted wars in Iraq and Afghanistan. Naomi Wallace was among the first dramatists to render gendered violence in war zones, as well as racism and homophobia in the military. Her complex, multilayered surrealistic play *In the Heart of America* juxtaposes scenes from the Vietnam War with contemporary scenes of an American Palestinian woman searching for her missing brother in Iraq, attacked for homosexuality. As Jean Colleran argues, Wallace 'shows how the visible violence of war and the less-visible violence of social domination activate and sustain each other'.[132]

Lesbian/gay/queer theatre

Queer theatre has become the umbrella term for various forms of performance – drama, collective and solo performances, alter-ego performances – that render same-sex desire and/or the multiplicity of identities and practices that upend social norms related to sexual expression, for example, bisexual, transgendered and/or queer individuals and communities. The adjective 'queer' appropriates the stigmatized term for homosexual to subvert any form of stable or fixed biological relationship between sexuality and identity, and connotes 'multiplicity, openness, contradiction, contention, the slipperiness of sexual practice seeping into discourse, into fashion, into style and politics and theater'.[133] Clearly the performativity of theatre enables artists to adopt various gender and sexually-oriented guises so that audiences can see the constructed nature of sexual identifications. At the same time, theatre artists communicate to audiences the issues that have concerned those who have been open about their sexual preferences and conduct in daily life.

As with race, ethnicity and gender, the constructed categories around sexuality have informed theatrical work that represents marginalization, prejudice, exclusion, violence and hate crimes, resistance to stereotypes, the importance of relationships and community and the open expression of desire in its many forms. Queer theatre has a long history, and it is impossible to comprehend its forms and themes in the 1990s without understanding its roots in gay and lesbian theatre, feminist theatre collectives and experimental theatre of the late 1960s through to the 1980s. These performances developed in the context of a social movement ignited by the Stonewall uprising of 1969 when patrons of a gay bar in Greenwich Village resisted police arrest and harassment. The riots lasted for several days and the activist organizations created in its wake led to the repeal of discriminatory laws against homosexuality. Furthermore, lesbian and gay studies had gradually developed during the same period. It was not until the 1990s, however, that gay and lesbian theory emerged as a distinct field of study that sponsored conferences, journals and edited collections, such as the landmark *Lesbian and Gay Studies Reader* (1993), which incorporated queer theory, and the Queer Theater Conference (1996), sponsored by the Center for Lesbian and Gay Studies (CLAGS) at City University of New York. In tracing the history of queer theory and American literary studies, Scott Herring argues that 'during and after the 1990s ... the field intersected with issues of race, ethnicity, class, region, religion, disability, and nation state'.[134]

Early gay and lesbian theatre often took the form of raucous, campy, witty performances about gay or bisexual characters, primarily staged in the Greenwich Village enclave of New York City. Venues such as Caffe Cino, Judson Poets Theatre, Café La Mama and Theatre Genesis eventually developed into Off-Off-Broadway. Jill Dolan observes that early lesbian drama was experimental in style and tone, and that plays about lesbian relationships or intimate relationships among women were generally produced in radical feminist and lesbian theatre companies beginning in the 1970s.[135] However, a small canon of drama about gays attracted attention from a wider range of theatre-goers. Given the prejudice endured by gays as well as the preponderance for closeted behaviour, plays, such as Mart Crowley's *Boys in the Band* (1968), often focused on homophobia as well as the shame that thwarted relationships even when these characters are depicted in gay communities. Jane Chambers's *Last Summer at Bluefish Cove* (1980) presents a lesbian community on vacation in a secluded enclave, closeted in their public lives. Other lesbian-themed plays of the period sometimes mirror the angst of early drama about gay men. Dolan describes plot devices such as death, exile, or characters who remain 'odd and alone' or symbolically punished.[136] Marking a gradual shift to more 'accepting' attitudes among general audiences, Harvey Fierstein's comedy *Torch Song Trilogy* (1982), which eventually transferred to Broadway, focused on coming out, gender identity, relationships with family and friends, and gay parenting.

From the mid-1980s through the 1990s, gay playwrights turned to the subject of AIDS that had finally been named and recognized as a national epidemic. There exists a voluminous literature on the history of AIDS activism and theatre that examines the changes in the representations and discourses surrounding AIDS, its decimation of the gay community among other populations, and its associations with homosexuality in the public imagination. For example, a prevalent homophobic view conceived of the disease as a moral punishment for its victims. In *Acts of Intervention*, David Roman analyses the range of theatre and performance forms that gay men used 'to intervene' in the AIDS crisis, and interprets how that 'performance has participated in shaping our understanding and experience of AIDS'.[137]

Most famously, two plays produced by established Off-Broadway theatres in 1985 mainstreamed AIDS to larger audiences: William Hoffman's *As Is*, produced at the Circle Repertory Company, and Larry Kramer's *The Normal Heart* at the Public Theater. These plays 'humanized AIDS', rendering sympathetic characters that attempt to live their lives and sustain relationships surrounded by illness and death. They also debunked myths about AIDS, portrayed a community of support groups and 'hotline interactions', and in Larry Kramer's angry 'agit-prop' drama, castigated the media, the government and health organizations for inaction or mismanagement of a crisis.[138] These works provide an important context for the theatre that emerged in the 1990s when AIDS had become part of the national register of tragedies that had befallen the nation.

In the 1990s, playwrights such as Terrence McNally, Tony Kushner and Paula Vogel garnered wide recognition for works that presented gay characters in complex relationships and in a range of contexts. It is telling that these playwrights are represented in this book as among the most groundbreaking, stylistically diverse and enduring dramatists of the decade. At the height of the AIDS epidemic their plays took on greater urgency for the theatre-going public (see Chapters 3, 4 and 5 of this volume).

Theatre scholar David Savran observes that US theatre in the 'gay nineties' was '*out*' in the unprecedented numbers of theatre artists who were 'joyously, proudly, and matter-of-factly – queer', citing the proliferation of productions of uptown successes such as Kushner, Vogel, McNally and also Jon Robin Baitz, Paul Rudnick, Lanford Wilson and Craig Lucas. However, Savran also emphasizes the 'downtown' and 'West Coast' avant-garde performers whose work had become prevalent in alternative venues: 'Whether on Broadway or off, the new theater of the 1990s that both deconstructs and universalizes the queer subject, represents a utopian project dedicated to spectatorial pleasure, to the crossing of identifications and desires, to a queer colonization of the public sphere, and to community formation.'[139]

Performance art

Beginning in the 1970s and continuing into the twenty-first century, a great deal of 'subversive energy' came from performance art, defined by solo performer and theatre scholar Lenora Champagne as ranging from 'highly personal solo monologues to comedy routines, to large multimedia collaborations between artists from different disciplines'.[140] Champagne argues that many artists used performance to explore 'self-definition' as well as aesthetic forms that contributed to Postmodern experimental theatre. Performance artists projecting various identifications or speaking from specific and often intersecting communities – ethnic, feminist, lesbian/gay/queer – developed a 'persona' or several to undermine stereotypical constructions of identities and 'to make shocking and explicit personal revelations', confront taboos and address political issues in highly personalized terms.[141]

Performance artists often used their bodies as a site for disrupting or challenging objectified representations of gender and sexuality and calling attention to the experience of degradation. For example, Karen Finley's *Shock Treatment* (published in 1990) includes *We Keep our Victims Ready* in which she smears chocolate and yams on her body as visual language for abuse. In Tim Miller's *Naked Breath* (1994), he seated himself, naked, among audience members to not only celebrate gay male sexuality, but also to counter the alienated and horrified view of those with AIDS. It is worth remembering that Finley, Miller, Holly Hughes and John Fleck constituted the NEA Four accused of obscenity when their grants from the US government's National Endowment for the Arts were vetoed (see pages 41–2).

In the mid-1980s, WOW Café, a women's experimental theatre/performance club that continues to this day, became central to the edgy and often farcical performance art scene on the Lower East Side of New York City (downtown theatre). Adapting aspects of vaudeville and drag, they parodied cultural icons, familiar plays and films, and conventional family situations. Among those who made WOW legendary are Holly Hughes; the Split Britches collective of Peggy Shaw, Lois Weaver and Deb Margolin; Sharon Jane Smith; Dancenoise; Carmelita Tropicana (alter ego for Alina Troyano); and the collective the Five Lesbian Brothers (Lisa Kron, Peg Healey, Moe Angelos, Babs Davy and Dominique Dibbell), whose name signifies the fluidity of gender. Holly Hughes's 1990s solo works include *Clit Notes* (1990) and *Preaching to the Perverted* (2000), the latter about her experience as one of the NEA Four. In 1991, Shaw and Weaver collaborated with a gay British group, Bloolips, to alter and reverse the gender roles in Tennessee Williams's *A Streetcar Named Desire* to underscore the performance of gender in the play that exacerbates the characters' struggle for power. In the 1990s, the Five Lesbian Brothers parodied genre films that stereotyped lesbians, and horror films that projected lesbians as dangerous and homicidal.[142]

Performance art has been innovated by many theatre artists who drew on their intersecting concerns about race, ethnicity, gender and sexuality. For example, Robbie McCauley's Obie Award-winning *Sally's Rape* (1990), the third instalment of her serial performance *Confessions of a Black Working Class Woman*, used her body, stripped naked as if on a slave auction block, to render the experience she envisions sharing with her great-great-grandmother Sally and the other African American women under slavery. In the 1990s, Dael Orlandersmith created a trilogy of one-woman shows recounting the tales of young women in Harlem; Alina Troyano as her alter-ego persona, Carmelita Tropicana, performed *Milk of Amnesia* (1994) in which she conveyed a fragmented self, disoriented and oscillating between the Cuba of her childhood, where she is now viewed as an American, and her position in America, in which she feels 'othered'; Dan Kwong, born to a Chinese American father and a Japanese American mother, used a multimedia approach to tell autobiographical stories with varying themes, such as family dysfunction, Asian American men and HIV/AIDS, and homophobia in Asian American communities. And fourth generation Japanese American born Denise Uyehara, in such works as *Hello (Sex) Kitty* (1994), addressed sexuality, domestic violence and the AIDS epidemic by portraying a range of caricatures of Asian women and men (e.g. 'Asian Chic', 'Dyke Asia', 'Vegetable Girl'). Like many performance artists of her generation in the 1990s, she revelled in 'hybridity and multiplicity, especially in terms of sexual identity'. In 1993, Uyehara co-founded a performance collective of women with diverse cultural backgrounds, sexual orientations and ideological perspectives.[143]

Among numerous Latina/o theatre artists, several have become noted performance artists, playwrights and directors. Luis Alfaro's versatility as a theatre artist deserves special attention. Co-founder (with Diane Rodriguez) of the Latino Theatre Initiative and Director of New Play Development at the Mark Taper Forum, he was the recipient of the John D. and Catherine T. MacArthur Foundation

Fellowship (1997–2000) for his contributions to American theatre. Alfaro's works, such as *Downtown* (1993), *Bitter Homes and Gardens* (1994) and *Straight as a Line* (1997), focus on social and familial issues of his East Los Angeles neighbourhood, particularly the Pico Union district, as well as Chicano gay rights. The widely recognized comedian and solo performer John Leguizamo has won numerous awards, including an Obie and an Outer Critics' Circle Award for *Mambo Mouth* (1991). This first play as well as later works *Spic-O-Rama* (1993) and *Freak* (1998), the latter nominated for a Tony Award, parodied Latina/o family life and father–son relationships in relation to cultural identity.[144]

In addition to a proliferation of Latina/o solo performance artists, directors, writers and performance troupes, collaborations between artists were also prevalent, beginning in the 1980s and continuing into the present. The Chicano Secret Service and Culture Clash are among the best known groups, creating comic characters and satirical and often irreverent sketches, some using multimedia and improvisation to address a range of political and cultural issues confronted by Latina/os.[145] Performance artists Coco Fusco and Guillermo Gómez-Peña collaborated on performance art works from 1989 to 1998, in which they situated themselves in the histories and legacies of 'conquest and colonization of the Americas'. In perhaps their most provocative work *Two Undiscovered Amerindians Visit New York* (1993) they exhibited themselves in a cage, satirizing their objectification as two 'undiscovered' natives from a fictitious island in the Gulf of Mexico.[146] S. E. Wilmer observes that Gómez-Peña's performances of border culture envision 'the possibility of a borderless zone,' in which Chicanos/as and Mexicanos/as are full citizens, not 'exotic minorities'.[147]

In addition to mixing genres, theatre artists brought together different art forms and new media to create performance texts, such as the dance/music/theatre pieces of Meredith Monk and Ping Chong, or installations, such as the work of Gómez-Peña and Coco Fusco described above. The 1990s saw the further development of visionary auteur directors, creating productions that span the last three decades of the twentieth century and into the twenty-first century, such as Richard Foreman and his Ontological Theatre, Robert Wilson, Lee Breuer and Mabou Mines, and Elizabeth LeCompte's Wooster Group, creating collaged texts that draw on various sources, both canonical and pop culture. Alternative theatre demonstrated the power of spectacle using multicultural forms and multimedia productions that included innovative uses of technology, such as film, slide and 3-D projections, TV monitors, tape players, the internet and expressive lighting.[148]

Theodore Shank sees two 'driving forces of earlier alternative theatres that continue to motivate these artists and groups': those who 'direct their energies outwardly to social issues' with the intention of both informing and entertaining their audiences, and others who are 'inwardly focused on their own psyches and intuitive thought processes and attempt to express them directly in theatrical forms'.[149] All of these works represent the expanding parameters of American theatre in the 1990s.

Conclusion: A theatre of diversity in form and intention

By the 1990s, experimental theatre had become a major force in expanding and redefining the theatrical enterprise. Although realism was alive and well on the American stage, many artists eschewed traditional genres of dramatic writing, especially its emphasis on the 'aesthetic of psychological realism', linearly structured plot, familiar dialogue and domestic or work settings, as Ehren Fordyce has written, to give primacy to the performance text, the *mise-en-scène* – the conception and staging of a work.[150] Characters were not always consistent or integrated into a coherent identity. Realism as a form had become even more flexible, and playwrights often mixed genres within one work. Fordyce provides a compelling illustration in the work of the aforementioned Adrienne Kennedy, specifically *Motherhood 2000* (1994), a fictionalized autobiographical play about a mother's response to her son's experience of police brutality, in which she juxtaposes different forms and tones – monologue, passion play and a 'hyperbolically apocalyptic, almost sci-fi description' of New York City's Upper West Side.[151]

The theatre of the late twentieth century, however, also innovated familiar forms, such as adaptations of classic texts and docudrama, to encourage audiences to revisit texts and events that they think they know, to see again or, in Brechtian terms, to make the familiar strange in order to rethink our assumptions.

Adaptations of canonical texts gradually took the form of radical revisions, often in a subversive mode, including reinterpretations of myth, classical and modern drama, the novel and even the personal and philosophical essay.[152] I have argued elsewhere that 'productions with an explicitly political perspective altered or parodied a text, interjected anachronistic language and, re-arranged its parts to denaturalize the values we have come to associate with its iconic figures moving through seemingly inevitable destinies'. These distancing devices draw our attention to ideology encoded in the plot, language and structures of the drama.[153] Many of these revisions were informed by the politics and ideologies of gender, race, class and sexuality, and also troubled the trope of heroism in war. For example, following the Gulf War, Charles Mee presented revisions of the Greek classics about the Trojan War, such as *Orestes* (1992), *Agamemnon* (1994) and *The Trojan Women: A Love Story* (1996), and Ellen McLaughlin's *Iphigenia and Other Daughters* (1995) focused on Sophocles' and Euripides' depiction of female figures sacrificed to war. In the 1990s, adaptations of Shakespeare's tragedies, such as Paula Vogel's *Desdemona* (1994), underscored the high cost of patriarchy as interpreted by feminist playwrights, directors and scholars. Lee Breuer's and Ruth Maleczech's Mabou Mines female *Lear* demonstrated the effectiveness of cross-gendered casting to call attention to the gendered dynamics of power.

It would seem that the genre of docudrama was among the most politically motivated forms amid the strife of war and identity politics. Carol Martin uses the term 'theatre of the real' that includes 'verbatim theatre, reality-based theatre, theatre-of-fact, theatre of witness, tribunal theatre, nonfiction theatre ... war and battle reenactments and autobiographical theatre', all claiming a relationship to reality and 'reframing what has happened'.[154] The 1990s saw works that drew on the use of transcripts, films, photographs, trials, interviews and oral histories by such theatre artists as Anna Deavere Smith, Emily Mann, Moises Kaufman and the Tectonic Theater Project, already mentioned in this chapter, to create narratives about race, urban conflict, homophobia and violence. Ryan M. Claycomb observes that 'some of the hottest tickets to a theatrical event in the 1990s provided entrance not to the bombastic Disnified musicals that have come to define Broadway, nor to the intense, intimate family psychodramas' of Williams, Miller or Shepard, but to docudrama and oral history performance that constitutes a '(ch)oral history', refiguring 'conventional notions of community [and] subjectivity'. This approach to theatre integrates the audience as well into the 'sense of community' created by the theatrical event itself.[155] Martin notes the political stakes in contemporary documentary theatre that represent a 'struggle to shape and remember the most transitory history'. Often written contemporaneously with events as they are happening, this form of theatre 'directly intervenes in the creation of history by unsettling the present'.[156]

Although documentary theatre might seem like the genre most conducive to audiences ready and willing to 'perform democracy', to quote Jill Dolan's inspiring words, certainly the range of genres and dramas surveyed in this chapter gives us the means to rethink the beliefs and practices that we live by as we engage conflicts, subjectivities and diverse perceptions of American life rendered onstage. From the vantage point of the twenty-first century, many American theatre artists in the 1990s seem not only purposeful in galvanizing theatre's potential for contributing to social change, but also clear-eyed in recognizing theatre as constitutive of the social and cultural fabric of our lives.

3

Terrence McNally

John M. Clum

Introduction

Although Terrence McNally's career spanned over half a century, the 1990s were a boom time for the Texas-reared playwright who had come to New York City to study at Columbia University in 1956 and never left.[1] During the 1990s, the prolific McNally had five full-length plays produced in New York, one of which (*Master Class*, 1995) was a commercial success and another (*Love! Valour! Compassion!*, 1994) moved from Off-Broadway to Broadway before being turned into a film. In addition, during the decade he wrote the books for three Broadway musicals (*Kiss of the Spider Woman*, 1992; *Ragtime*, 1996; *The Full Monty*, 2000), all adaptations of novels or movies; and three plays for television (*Andre's Mother*, 1990; *The Last Mile*, 1992; and 'Mr. Roberts', a segment of the Showtime trilogy *Common Ground*, 2000). *Frankie and Johnny*, the film version of his 1987 Off-Broadway hit *Frankie and Johnny in the Clair de Lune*, was released in 1991. Three of the prolific playwright's richest and most stylistically adventurous works – *Lips Together, Teeth Apart* (1991), *A Perfect Ganesh* (1993) and *Love! Valour! Compassion!* – were produced in the 1990s. All three works are responses to the AIDS crisis that was decimating the gay community at the time.

During McNally's half-century career as a playwright, serious American drama moved from Broadway to Off-Broadway and non-profit theatre. All of McNally's plays from 1974 to the present began Off-Broadway or in regional theatres. For years, McNally was the unofficial house playwright of the Manhattan Theatre Club, which produced eight of his plays. A number of his plays transferred to Broadway, but, for the most part, McNally's commercial success has come from his work in musical theatre.

McNally's primary subjects are the interests and concerns of gay men and the evolving place of gay men in American society over the past half-century. His dramaturgical trajectory ranges from the fatal shame of the young man in *And Things That Go Bump in the Night* (1965) to sexually liberated gay men in *The Ritz* (1975); from responses to the AIDS crisis in a number of plays from the late 1980s through to the mid-1990s and vicious gay-bashing in 'Mr. Roberts', *A Perfect Ganesh* and *Corpus Christi* (1998) to gay marriage and families in his more recent plays, *Some Men* (2006) and *Mothers and Sons* (2014). Homophobia is always on the minds of gay men and heterosexuals. Chris, the epitome of the liberated gay man in *The Ritz*, declares, 'I'll tell you something about straight people, and sometimes I think it's the only thing worth knowing about them. They don't like gays. They never have. They never will. Anything else they say is just talk.'[2] This conviction is echoed by Perry in *Love! Valour! Compassion!*: 'They hate us. They fucking hate us. They've always hated us. It never ends, the fucking hatred.'[3]

No American playwright has explored middle-class homophobia as deeply or compassionately as McNally does in *Lips Together, Teeth Apart* and *A Perfect Ganesh*. The focus of many of the works McNally wrote in the 1990s is the conditional love of family members toward gay men. As Cal reveals to the title character in the teleplay *Andre's Mother*, 'God, how many of us live in this city because we don't want to hurt our mothers and live in mortal terror of their disapproval ... A city of fugitives from our parent's scorn or heartbreak.'[4] Characters who have been cruel to gay sons or siblings are riddled with guilt.

There is great stylistic variety in McNally's work: from conventional realism in *Frankie and Johnny in the Clair de Lune* and *Mothers and Sons*, to plays that break the fourth wall and linear time such as *Love! Valour! Compassion!*, *A Perfect Ganesh* and

Corpus Christi, to *Some Men*, which is a series of sketches, often involving the same characters. All of the works he wrote during the 1990s break through the fourth wall of realistic drama, all in different ways. McNally is at his weakest stylistically in conventionally realistic plays like *Mothers and Sons* and strongest when his plays call attention to their theatricality.

McNally has said of his work: 'I suppose I have to grit my teeth and refer to my plays as "comedies," which I get a little tired of, but people do like handles, I suppose, and I think there's laughter in my plays, and I think I have a comic sensibility, but I don't think I write comedies.'[5] Nevertheless, McNally's greatest gift was for comedy. His most successful works from the 1970s, *Bad Habits* (1973) and *The Ritz*, both of which transferred to Broadway (*The Ritz* was also made into a film in 1976), verge on farce, with stylized characters in absurd situations. *Bad Habits* was the collective title for two one-act comedies about opposing therapeutic communities: one totally permissive, the other geared toward self-improvement through eliminating all bad habits. Characters in *Bad Habits* had names taken from commercial products (Dr Pepper, nurses Benson and Hedges). *It's Only a Play* (1985; revised for Broadway, 2014) harks back to the great Broadway comedies of the 1930s. All McNally's work is leavened by comedy and has brought out the best in comic actors, particularly Nathan Lane, who has created leading roles in four of McNally's most successful works.

McNally was a satirist and, like most satirists, a moralist. He wasn't interested in psychological realism – the whys of the choices his characters make – but rather the moral implications of those choices. His world is one of good and evil, within which there are characters who can't avoid negative, cruel behaviour. His characters, gay and straight, often hate themselves, which makes it difficult for them to give or receive love. Some are able to break through the wall of solipsism through the love of a spouse, lover or friend. The ability to love and the ability to accept love are the saving traits in McNally's work.

McNally said of his work, 'I'm not a naturalistic writer – I think sometimes I'm operatic.'[6] Opera plays a role in most of his works and informs McNally's style. It was a crucial part of McNally's life. He was a dedicated opera fan who appeared regularly on the 'Opera Quiz' intermission features of the Metropolitan Opera Saturday broadcasts and wrote the libretti to operas including Jake Heggie's *Dead Man Walking* (2000). Opera is a heightened, perhaps the most heightened, form of theatrical performance, and McNally's characters tend to be performers, to be playing roles, sometimes actually onstage and, at other times, seeing the world as their stage. His characters, often deeply self-conscious, see themselves as performers in their own lives. Moreover, McNally's variety of theatrical styles often calls attention to this notion of performance.

Furthermore, opera, like musical comedy, was a crucial element of pre-Stonewall gay culture, and McNally was fascinated with the role opera played in the lives of older gay men, particularly the adulation of the diva Maria Callas. McNally satirized gay men who lived for opera, and in particular for Callas, in *The Lisbon Traviata* (1989), then went on to create a version of Maria Callas in his hit play *Master Class*. Later he wrote *Golden Age* (2009), about the great bel canto composer Vincenzo Bellini, set on the opening night of his final masterpiece, *I Puritani*.

By the time *Lips Together, Teeth Apart*, arguably Terrence McNally's best play, was produced in 1991, he had been writing for the stage for over a quarter of a century. The works immediately preceding *Lips Together, Teeth Apart*, particularly *The Lisbon Traviata* and the short television play *Andre's Mother*, were responses to the AIDS epidemic that had been ravaging the gay community since 1981. Stephen, the protagonist of *The Lisbon Traviata*, refers to AIDS as 'our very own bubonic plague' (164). The spectre of AIDS certainly darkens the spirits of the heterosexual characters in *Lips Together, Teeth Apart*, a theatrical meditation on mortality. Indeed, the AIDS crisis put the focus onto mortality: disease, death, loss, grief, rage and fear seem omnipresent in McNally's work during the 1990s.[7]

McNally's characters, particularly his female characters, are often frozen in time, particularly at a moment of loss. They can't overcome the grief that envelops them from the loss of a child or a beloved sibling. The grief is often connected to guilt at having been incapable of unconditional love toward a gay man. Connected to this grief and guilt is fear – of disease, of death and of a chaotic existence one can't understand or order. Two statements of Sally, a character in *Lips Together, Teeth Apart* who is grieving over the loss of a brother to AIDS, are paradigmatic of the attitudes of all these characters. 'I think these are difficult times to be anything in'

(230) she says – as difficult to be a straight woman or man as a gay man. The fear is universal. So is the sense of formlessness, of chaos. 'The truth is just too formless to grasp' (193) Sally says, and it is the formlessness of experience, even of one's own personality, that McNally's characters find frightening. The gay men feel it through the fear of violence and the fear of AIDS. The heterosexuals have the same fear of mortality, but also a profound sense of loss.

Lips Together, Teeth Apart (1991)

I don't know about pools and AIDS and homosexuals. I don't want to. It frightens me, all right? All of this. (250)

The central event in Blanche Dubois's backstory in Tennessee Williams's classic *A Streetcar Named Desire* (1947) is a moment of homophobic rage. Blanche discovered Allan Gray, her sensitive young husband, in bed with an older man. Later, on a crowded dance floor at a lake resort, she exposes and rejects him – 'I saw! I know! You disgust me!'[8] Blanche's public rejection leads to her husband's suicide. It also haunts her for the rest of her life. Blanche becomes the victim of even greater psychological and physical violence at the hands of the very heterosexual Stanley Kowalski, a kind of horrible karma for her cruelty toward Allan. McNally's *Lips Together, Teeth Apart* focuses on characters who, like Blanche, are haunted by their cruelty toward gay loved ones – who cannot recover from the guilt they feel.

Lips Together, Teeth Apart takes place at the Fire Island summer house, previously owned by David, who has died of AIDS. David has left the house to his sister, Sally Truman, an artist who is consumed by guilt and thoughts of death. Sally could never accept her brother's homosexuality – 'I hated him being gay' (253). Having helped her brother to die, Sally sees herself as a harbinger of death. She becomes obsessed by the vision of a young gay man swimming out to sea to commit suicide, a projection of her own death wish and what her brother must have felt from his family's rejection: 'I saw what happens when we're not loved and protected and feel so alone' (243). As Sally helped her brother to die, so she feels that she encouraged the suicidal young man to drown. When their eyes met briefly, 'My eyes didn't say "Stay, life is worth living." They said, "Go. God speed, God bless"' (244). Later Sally splashes water from the pool everyone is afraid of: 'One drop of water in your mouth or on an open sore and we'll be infected with my brother and his black lover and God knows who else was in here. Pissing and ejaculating' (249). She goes so far as to make her husband kiss her when she has a mouthful of water from the pool: 'Then let's all get AIDS and die' (250).

Mortality is everywhere in this play. John Haddock, Sally's brother-in-law and erstwhile lover, has been diagnosed with cancer of the oesophagus and is painfully aware that AIDS is not the only malevolent force 'at work on God's miraculous planet' (251). Sam, Sally's husband, aware of his wife's infidelity, kills a phallic snake, an objective correlative for the sexual and emotional insecurities of the men. At the end, the two couples, Sally and Sam and John and Chloe, his wife, are watching a shooting star as the zapping sounds of a bug-killing machine can be heard, visual and aural images of mortality.

Spiritual death, self-loathing and despair also permeate the play. Chloe says in response to her sensitivity to her sister-in-law's feelings toward her, 'Just about everyone is superior to me' (221). Her husband John is aware that 'To know me is not necessarily to like me' (251), and Sam doesn't want to be a father because, 'I'm empty. I'm just coasting. You don't love empty' (265). John is the most painfully aware of his negativity. When his cancer diagnosis is revealed, he tells the others, 'Riddled with the stuff, I'm still going to be the same rotten son of a bitch. I wish I could change. I really, really do. Profoundly. I can't' (262–3). John's self-diagnosis will be echoed by another John, John Jeckyll, in *Love! Valour! Compassion!*, who tells his twin brother, 'You got the good soul. I got the bad one' (454). The only antidote to the emptiness of John and his companions is passionate sexual and spiritual love, yet the characters expend a great deal of energy closing themselves off, not connecting. Sam watches a gay couple have sex in the bushes, an act that begins with physical passion and ends with 'I love you', followed by a literal burst of fireworks. Yet as Sam watches this physical and spiritual moment of connection, he and the other characters in the play are voicing their separate thoughts, which they are unwilling or incapable of expressing to each other. As Sally puts it, 'Even from a great distance we know so much about each other but pretend we don't' (244).

The isolation of the characters in *Lips Together, Teeth Apart* is reinforced by the play's style. Dialogue alternates with characters voicing their unspoken thoughts, which are far more revealing than what they say to each other. One can see dramatic precedent for McNally's technique here in Eugene O'Neill's *Strange Interlude* (1928), but the more powerful influence here is opera. McNally has said that this is 'my most operatic play – Mozart even opened the play. And now when I see it or read it I say, My God, there are quartets, or trios, or duets.'[9] The play opens with the sublimely beautiful trio from Mozart's *Cosi fan Tutte*, 'Soave sia il vento'.[10] Against this achingly beautiful music, with an undulating orchestral accompaniment suggesting the ocean current, we see the more turbulent emotions of the occupants of David's former home. The play is full of music, most of it emanating from the adjoining houses filled with gay men celebrating the Fourth of July. There's opera, show tunes, dance music – all music associated with urban gay culture. The gay men who occupy the houses on either side of the Truman house celebrate life even in the face of disease and death. The only music that emanates from Sam and Sally's house is the taped piano accompaniment to which Chloe briefly practices her dance number for an upcoming community theatre production.

The music from the unseen occupants of the surrounding houses underscores the irony of the position of the play's four characters. On Fire Island these heterosexuals are in the minority and are intensely conscious of being watched and, they believe, judged negatively as they are judging their gay neighbours. Over and over characters think the gay men are looking at them. Chloe says at one point after John and Sam have fought, 'Are they still looking over here? I'm too embarrassed to look' (225). Sam wants to raise their deck to the level of the surrounding balconies because, 'I don't want people looking down on me' (192), literally or figuratively. Sam doesn't like the idea of the neighbours thinking they are 'queer'; 'I'm gonna sit with my legs apart and smoke a cigar all weekend' (191). This, of course, would be a stereotypical performance of masculinity, ironic for men who feel inadequate as husbands or lovers. Chloe can't help but admire the attractive, scantily clad gay men around her – 'You are so fucking hot, honey!' (207). Neither can she help performing for them – 'I hope you boys don't mind a little show' (233) she says as she rehearses the steps for her next appearance in a community theatre musical. Even though the gay men are in the majority in this community, to the foursome they remain the nameless 'them' – the other. To Sam, they are 'the boys from Ipanema' (183); to John, they are simply 'Goddamn fairies' (204). Sally hates the homophobic language, but still admits that 'seeing them sort of sickens me' (256). The men in the neighbouring houses invite the foursome to join them in their festivities. They even throw down American flags for them to wave. However, the four refuse to join the celebration.

At the end, the two couples, Sally and Sam, Chloe and John, are still both together and apart. Sally has not yet told her husband that she is pregnant because she doesn't believe that she could possibly be a good mother. Sam feels too inadequate to offer a child anything. John can think about his gratitude for his wife's love but cannot express it. The play's title comes from a doctor's advice to Sam on how he can avoid grinding his teeth at night: 'Lips together, teeth apart.' Closed lips may stop the grinding of teeth, but it also makes communication impossible.

For all its darkness, *Lips Together, Teeth Apart* has very funny moments, mostly provided by Chloe's perpetual activity and over-the-top performances and Sam's humorous lines. Certainly the casting of three fine comic actors, Nathan Lane and Christine Baranski as Sam and his sister Chloe, and Swoosie Kurtz as the melancholy Sally (Anthony Heald played angry, mordant John), insured that the play would never become lugubrious. What the gay characters surrounding Sally, Sam, Chloe and John have realized is that one must celebrate life in the face of death. Slowly, in their own limited way, the four heterosexuals come to do that at the end of the play. The trio from *Cosi fan Tutte* suggests that McNally is aiming for the bittersweet character of that great Mozart–da Ponte collaboration in which things are never quite what they seem and the marriages that end the opera do not seem very happy.

In one of Sally's few specific memories of her brother David, she recalls his response to her family's homophobia. When their mother told him at his father's funeral that he couldn't possibly feel the loss she felt because the love of a man and woman was different from anything he would feel, 'I just looked away. Instead of feeling comforted, he told me, he felt rejected and *diminished* by us both. What a terrible word. *Diminished*' (198 – italics mine). Toward the end of McNally's next full-length play – his most daring stylistically – *A Perfect Ganesh*, Katharine Brynne, a middle-aged woman visiting India, is talking to a little Indian boy, actually the god Ganesha in disguise. Haunted and guilt-ridden by the death of her son Walter, who was gay-bashed on a New York street, Katharine tells the boy, 'When you grow up, I won't like you. I will hate and fear you because of the colour of your skin – just as I hated and feared my son because he loved men. I won't tell you this to your face but you will know it, just as he did and it will sicken and *diminish* us both' (347). Homophobia, particularly from a loved one, diminishes both the homophobe and her victim. In *Lips Together, Teeth Apart*, it is a sister who feels guilt at not being able to accept her brother's sexuality; in *A Perfect Ganesh* it is a mother whose guilt cannot be fully healed.

A Perfect Ganesh (1993)

I came here to heal but I can't forgive myself. (348)

While *Lips Together, Teeth Apart* was a relatively realistic, linear play in terms of setting and time scheme, the style of *A Perfect Ganesh* is much freer. The play's narrator is an elephant-headed god, Ganesha, who plays multiple male and female roles, as does another male actor. The action transpires on a bright white bare stage. The narrative jumps from the central characters Katharine Brynne and Margaret Civil, sitting on a plane, to Katharine's dead son Walter and Ganesha having a conversation on the plane's wing. Is Katharine imagining that conversation or are we in the realm of magic realism? Much to Margaret's irritation, Katharine keeps invoking the prologue to Shakespeare's *Henry V*, which asks the audience to believe that the bare stage, the 'unworthy scaffold' of Shakespeare's theatre, holds 'the vasty fields of France' (quoted in *A Perfect Ganesh*, 306). McNally wants us to accept that his bare stage can hold India. It is the bare stage that allows the play to move freely in space and time as it allows the real and the fantastic to merge.

Katharine is touring India with her friend, the prickly, not always civil Margaret Civil. Margaret has had her own loss – Gabriel, her four-year-old son, was run over on a New York street. Unlike Katharine, who speaks of little else but the loss of her son,

Margaret has kept her loss to herself and moved on. Both sons were killed by African Americans. Katharine can never forgive the young Black men who brutally murdered her son: 'They get off (Walter was a faggot, after all) and I don't even get to say "nigger"!' (338). Margaret, on the other hand, remembers the Black woman who accidentally killed her child interrupting his funeral by singing a spiritual magnificently: 'Such a vibrant, comforting sound it was!' (314). There's forgiveness in those words.

In the magical world of *A Perfect Ganesh*, the sons appear to their mothers, as if men at the country club dance where Katharine met her husband, and dance with them. Walter concedes his failure as a son, 'God, I was a judgmental little shit where you and Dad were concerned' (325), but the scene becomes too Oedipal for Katharine:

> **Katharine** You still don't know how to hold a woman.
> **Man [Walter]** You mean, like this?
> (*He pulls her to him hard and close*)
> Is this how you mean?
> (*She slaps him*)
> **Katharine** I'm sorry. I'm sorry.
> **Man [Walter]** No, you're not. (325–6)

The Man then becomes a grown-up version of Margaret's dead son:

> **Man [Gabriel]** You should be happy.
> **Margaret** I can't be.
> **Man [Gabriel]** I never knew what hit me. (327)

Like the characters in *Lips Together, Teeth Apart*, Katharine and Margaret have very little self-esteem. Katharine can't get over her guilt, and Margaret knows she is not easy to like. The friendship of these two women has its limits. Margaret observes, 'We know each other. We love each other. We just don't especially like each other' (337). Yet these women can comfort each other. It is typical of McNally's work that his protagonist's main problem is not psychological, social or merely emotional. In the guise of a Japanese tourist, Ganesha tells Katharine, 'You think it is only your heart that is broken. May I be so bold as to suggest that it is your soul that is crying out in this Indian dawn? Hearts can be mended. Time can heal them. But souls ...? Tricky, tricky' (310). McNally believes in sickness of the spirit that can poison one's life. We see it in Stephen in *The Lisbon Traviata* and John Jeckyll in *Love! Valour! Compassion!* It is evident in all four characters in *Lips Together, Teeth Apart* and in McNally's mothers, from the lethal Ruby in *And Things That Go Bump in the Night* right through to Katharine Gerard in *Mothers and Sons*. This is why a god presides over *A Perfect Ganesh*. The elephant-headed Ganesha is the Lord of Obstacles, the deity who can remove obstacles or place them in one's path. In McNally's play, he is a guide for Katharine and Margaret's journey toward enlightenment and spiritual renewal.

There is no easy, complete healing for Katharine and Margaret. In their last scene in India, the women confront a poor leper who begs not only for money, but for love. Neither woman can offer the leper what he needs from them. Katharine gives him 50 rupees and one of the many statues of Ganesha she has purchased in her search for a perfect one (there is no perfect Ganesh – nothing is perfect). Ganesha tells us, 'She did not sleep well that night. She worried about her soul. The man, however, had the finest meal of his entire, miserable life' (353). In an imperfect world – and Ganesha understands that the world is not perfect – Katharine has done some good. Yet her failure to love the leper – as she could not love her own son until it was too late – leads her to see the whole trip as a failure. In one sense it has been. Katharine has not been fully healed by India, yet she and Margaret have heard Ganesha's message as they float among the dead bodies on the Ganges:

Katharine We all have a place here. Nothing is right, nothing is wrong. Allow. Accept. Be.
Margaret Yes. (352)

The leper is one manifestation of the disease and death that permeates this play, written while AIDS was still a deadly disease in the gay community. While Katharine is in India, her husband dies in an automobile accident. Margaret discovers a lump in her breast. Katharine befriends an American gay couple who both have AIDS. India is as full of poverty, death and disease as it is of beauty. Ganesha tells Katharine, 'I prove that the world is full of opposites which exist peacefully side by side' (327). At the end, the women are back in their beds in their separate homes in Connecticut. Katharine's husband is dead, and Margaret's philandering husband is absent, as usual. They have received a message from India – a postcard from the gay couple with AIDS they befriended. The picture is of Ganesha, the message one of acceptance: 'We're both hanging in there. What else are you gonna do?' (357). The songs the women sing as they fall asleep in their Connecticut homes after their journey suggest that they still mourn their lost sons. Katharine sings Walter's favorite song, 'Blow the Wind Southerly', while Margaret sings 'Swing Low, Sweet Chariot', the song sung so powerfully at her son's funeral by the woman who accidentally killed him.

It is interesting that again and again in McNally's work, it is the mother, not the father, who diminishes her son, by withholding her unconditional love.[11] The fathers barely exist. In the 1990 teleplay *Andre's Mother*, the title character, who never accepted her son's sexual orientation, remains silent and apart during his Central Park memorial service. Andre's mother reappears in the 2014 play *Mothers and Sons*, still overcome with rage, grief and guilt twenty years later: 'I don't want peace or closure – another word I detest. I want revenge' (643). Yet for all her devotion to her son's memory, Katharine, Andre's mother, could not accept her son's sexuality: 'I know why you're crying. You're not crying for your father. You're crying because of what you are ... Can you imagine a mother saying that to her son?' (656). In *A Perfect Ganesh*, written twenty years before *Mothers and Sons*, Katharine Brynne is, at least, overwhelmed by guilt over her treatment of her son: 'I came here to heal but I can't forgive myself' (348). Walter sees his mother as the source of the violence that killed him: 'All of them you!' (294). It is only by shouting the language of hate, the words her son's attackers used as they killed him, that Katharine can purge herself of guilt.

Love! Valour! Compassion! (1994–5)

Buzz Who's going to be there for me when it's my turn?
Perry We all will. Every one of us. (459)

If *Lips Together, Teeth Apart* gave us married heterosexuals who feel isolated and frightened in the age of AIDS, *Love! Valour!*

Compassion! gives us a group of gay men who have created a sense of family during the same period:

Perry We could be the last eight people on earth.
Buzz That's a frightening thought.
Perry Not if you're with the right eight people. (428)

There's a black sheep, the aptly named John Jeckyll, and a gorgeous sexy outsider who causes a great deal of sexual tension, but even these people are part of this intentional family.

Love! Valour! Compassion! (the title enumerates the cardinal virtues in McNally's worldview) takes place on a bare stage on which the actors have to create a number of interior and exterior spaces. The fourth wall is regularly broken by characters narrating moments or speaking directly to the audience. While the play seems to have a clear time frame – three summer holiday weekends – that time frame is regularly broken. The play opens with Gregory Mitchell, a celebrated choreographer, and his friends describing the setting, Gregory's upstate New York country home. This introductory moment is out of time, as if the characters appear before they take their place in the narrative. Characters often step outside of time to comment on the events or to describe characters. The bare stage allows this kind of freedom. So does the sense of ensemble created from the very beginning of the play. The actors' singing of Stephen Foster's 'Beautiful Dreamer' offers a prelude to the play. From the beginning, the disparate characters form an ensemble. Toward the end, six of the characters don ballet costumes and rehearse dancing the 'Dance of the Little Swans' from *Swan Lake*, a tricky ensemble that requires unity and precision. It's a funny moment, but one that celebrates cohesion.

Every member of the group depicted in this play has some kind of physical or spiritual flaw. Gregory's is his stammer. His means of expression is dance, not speech. Gregory's lover Bobby, twenty years his junior, is blind, though Bobby is the most spiritual of the group. When he arrives at the house, he literally blesses the house and its surroundings, though he cannot see them: 'I was thanking God for all this,' he tells another guest, 'The trees, the lake, the sweet, sweet air. For all of us together in Gregory's house' (394). Bobby loves Gregory, but cannot resist the advances of the wild card in the group, the young, beautiful, very cocky in all senses of the word, Puerto Rican dancer, Ramon Fornos.

As with many gay groups, all the guests invited to the weekends in the country are related through sex or through work. Perry is a lawyer who does pro bono work for Gregory's company. He was also at one time the lover of John Jeckyll, who is the company's rehearsal pianist. Perry is at Gregory's house with his long-time partner, Arthur. Buzz, an ardent show queen, is the company's costume designer and was also at one time involved with John. Perry and Buzz were roommates when they first arrived in New York. The newcomers over the summer during which, Gregory tells us, 'everything changed, for good and bad but forever' (370) are Ramon, who comes as John Jeckyll's date but becomes smitten with Bobby, and John's twin brother James, who works in the wardrobe department of the National Theatre of Great Britain (the Jeckyll twins are played by the same actor). Both James and Buzz have AIDS, and over the course of the summer they become a devoted couple. Within this group, there are generational differences as well as differences in temperament: from Buzz, the flamboyant show queen, to Arthur, who worries that he isn't conventionally gay; from sweet Bobby to bitter John Jeckyll.

The action of the play begins with the first sexual encounter between Gregory's young, blind lover, Bobby, and Ramon. This isn't the first moment in the chronological order of events, but a kind of prologue that establishes a number of the themes of the play. Ramon seems fascinated and smitten with Bobby from first sight. One could ask why Ramon, the character who revels in being looked at and is indeed the object of the appreciative gaze of most of the characters – he spends much of the play nude – is so drawn to the one person who cannot see him. John Jeckyll points out that Bobby's older lover Gregory, a dancer and choreographer, has chosen a lover who cannot see his work. Bobby also cannot see that Gregory has the bruised, injured body of an aging dancer. Does Bobby sense that Ramon, who embraces him in the dark kitchen, is young and attractive? He has to ask Arthur what Ramon looks like. Throughout the play, Ramon and Bobby represent two sides of youth and beauty. Ramon, who lives for his body, offers a litany of all the ways he loves himself; while Bobby, the most spiritual character in the play, is (though blind) more connected to things outside himself – the people he loves, nature and God:

'Only God is unconditional love, and we don't even have to love him back. He's very big about it. I have a lot of reservations about God. What intelligent, caring person doesn't lately? But the way I see it, He doesn't have any reservations about me' (427).

Two events follow the late-night encounter of Bobby and Ramon, which is orgasmic, at least for Bobby, who has the telltale stain on his pyjama bottoms. During the embrace, Bobby drops the bottle of milk he is holding (yes, the spilled milk will later be cried over), and cuts his foot while cleaning up the glass, the first outcome of his infidelity. Arthur hears the glass breaking and goes to the kitchen where he bandages Bobby's foot. The stage directions tell us that Arthur's *'hand goes and would touch Bobby's bare chest or arms or legs, but doesn't'* (374). Monogamy doesn't come easily to Arthur, particularly in the presence of beautiful young men. Arthur admits to Bobby that his relationship with Perry was affected by his single experience of cheating: 'I told him and it's never been the same' (376). Controlling his desire for Bobby was difficult: 'He's so young, Perry ... I wanted to hold him ... Desire is a terrible thing. I'm sorry we're not young anymore' (377). Later in the play, Arthur will flirt – unsuccessfully – with Ramon.

This opening sequence establishes the pain of desire that is mitigated by age and physical limitations. Everyone is measured against Ramon's youth and physical perfection. John, who brings Ramon to Gregory's home, uses Ramon to recall his first sexual experience in his father's garage. In John's mind, the object of his first infatuation 'will always be seventeen and I will always be nineteen. No one grows old in this story' (433). This youthful sexual encounter involved bondage but no touching. Proximity was enough.

If John and Arthur have to cope with their painful awareness of advancing age in the presence of beautiful youth, Buzz and John's brother James have to cope with the knowledge that the disease they carry will kill them. James seems resigned to his fate, but Buzz copes by withdrawing into the fantasy world of musicals or through rage. At times, the two impulses combine, as in his rant to Perry, his best friend: 'Once, just once, I want to see a *West Side Story* where Tony really gets it, where they all die, the Sharks and the Jets, and Maria, while we're at it, and Officer Krupke, what's he doing sneaking out of the theatre? – get back here and die with everyone else, you son of a bitch!' (458). The healthy ones, like

Arthur and Perry, deal with survivor guilt: 'I will always feel like a survivor at the genocide of who we are' (452).

With disease and age comes an overwhelming sense of mortality. As with all of McNally's plays, particularly those written when AIDS was decimating the gay community in New York, mortality is a central theme. Bobby discovers that his sister has been killed in a freak accident at a carnival in India. In what might be considered the climax of the play, as the men dance to Petipa's choreography for *Swan Lake*, they step forward and tell the audience how they will die. AIDS isn't the only death sentence here. Everyone will die.

Yet the title of the play suggests the saving virtue that most of these men possess to varying degrees – love, valour and compassion. The play is about love in the face of age, disease and mortality. At the end of the play, this intentional family sings together, then the men strip and go skinny-dipping in the pond. One has only to Google *Love! Valour! Compassion!* to see how often the male nudity in the play is mentioned and how it has been on occasion the object of attack from the religious Right as it was in Grand Rapids, Michigan, in 2013. However, *Love! Valour! Compassion!* is about all aspects of these men, and bodies are crucial – aging, diseased, dying bodies as well as youthful, beautiful ones. The physical and spiritual merge in this play. There are also the positive traits we see in the men's behaviour: creativity, love, even spirituality. Bobby celebrates God's unconditional love. McNally celebrates flawed human love as gay men of the time experienced it.

There isn't a strong narrative arc to *Love! Valour! Compassion!* Gregory and Bobby separate temporarily after Bobby confesses his infidelity. Gregory goes from jealous fury at Ramon to hiring him to dance the lead in his new work. James and Buzz become a couple. There are heated dinner table arguments and moments of tenderness. In other words, these men behave like a family.

Master Class (1995)

A performance is a struggle. You have to win. The audience is the enemy. (502)

Maria Callas, like singer and film star Judy Garland, was a gay icon. There is no doubt that she was a great artist, but her diva persona and unhappy personal life also attracted gay men, particularly of the pre-Stonewall generation. In his brilliant book, *How to Be Gay*, David M. Halperin discusses the traits of singers and movie stars who have had a particular appeal to gay men: 'strength and suffering, glamour and abjection, power and vulnerability'.[12] In *The Lisbon Traviata*, named after an obscure 'pirate recording' of a Callas performance,[13] Mendy and his friend Stephen are more in tune with opera than with life outside their apartments. Mendy and Stephen may admire these qualities in Callas, but in their own interactions we see only suffering, abjection and vulnerability.

The long run of McNally's Tony Award-winning play *Master Class* suggests that Maria Callas's life, if not her singing, had an appeal far beyond the gay community (there are plans for an HBO production of the play). *Master Class*, a highly fictionalized version of Callas's master classes at the Juilliard School in 1971–2, would seem an unlikely play to be a commercial success. A version of the diva comments on a succession of young opera singers who sing arias to piano accompaniment. Unlike the real Callas, who, according to John Ardoin, 'wished to bring out the best in the talents of those who sang for her rather than to impose herself on them',[14] McNally's Maria is a study in self-absorption. She is rude to her pupils and uses their performances to talk about herself. During their singing, she soliloquizes about her life: her sense of her homeliness, her loveless marriage to an older man who promoted her career, her love of Aristotle Onassis, her abortion of Onassis's child, and his leaving her for an even more famous woman.

We see in McNally's Callas all the traits of the diva that David Halperin enumerated – the traits that attracted gay men. Like Floria Tosca, one of her most celebrated roles, Callas is the ruthless diva – 'I was never young. I couldn't afford to be. Not to get where I was going' (514) – as well as a woman capable of great love, expressed in her long romance with shipping tycoon Aristotle Onassis, and grand self-pity: 'You will. In time. Know how much suffering there can be for a woman' (514). McNally's Callas recalls how she felt as her career took off: 'When I sing, I'm not fat. I'm not ugly. I'm not an old man's wife' (517). Her art allowed her to forget her negative self-image. This is one aspect of the diva that pre-Stonewall gay men, educated to hate themselves, identified with. The fat, nearsighted ugly duckling could become a swan, and a very grand swan at that, but never totally lose the ugly duckling inside.

McNally had created an earlier portrait of a much healthier diva in his teleplay *The Last Mile* (1992). This diva, an American soprano (portrayed by Bernadette Peters), is about to make her Metropolitan Opera debut as Floria Tosca, one of Callas's most famous roles. In her dressing room, she remembers the people she loves most: her parents, her most important teacher and her brother Scott, who has died of AIDS-related infections. Her performance is for the people she loves as well as for herself. As the stage manager (Nathan Lane) leads her to her place backstage, she sees his AIDS ribbon – he is HIV-positive. She shows him that she has an AIDS ribbon hidden in her costume in memory of her brother. Unlike *Master Class*, in which Maria Callas is totally self-absorbed, *The Last Mile* depicts a diva who is connected, particularly to what gay men are suffering. Her brother appears to her in her dressing room and tells her, 'You would have died for me if you could have.'[15]

Corpus Christi (1998)

We're each special. We're each ordinary. We're each divine.[16]

By the mid-1990s, thanks to new drugs, HIV went from a death sentence to a relatively controllable infection. McNally's focus transferred from living in the plague years to living in a society that was still homophobic, particularly to what it is like to grow up gay in such a society. In McNally's controversial retelling of Christ's life, *Corpus Christi*, positive self-love becomes a religion. Before Judas betrays his friend and onetime lover Joshua, the Christ figure in this contemporary passion play, he has a discussion with the High Priest:

> **Judas** What is his crime?
> **High Priest** Blasphemy.
> **Judas** Because he says he's the son of God?
> **High Priest** No, because he says you're the son of God as well.

Judas We're all the sons of God.
High Priest Unless you're looking for trouble, I would keep that to myself. The son of God is a cocksucker? I don't think so. (65)

Joshua's message is one of human divinity: 'We're each special. We're each ordinary. We're each divine' (50). McNally is not offering pure secular humanism. Jesus is passing on God's message, the heart of which is the same as Bobby's in *Love! Valour! Compassion!* When Bobby first arrives at his lover's lakeside home, he blesses and gives thanks for things he cannot see. Joshua admonishes Lazarus, 'Be awake every moment and give thanks to God the Father for it' (58). The only unforgiveable sin is bigotry: 'All who do not love all men are against me!' (63).

Unfortunately, Joshua's theological language is not inclusive. A male God offers his son as teacher and sacrifice to an all-male world. Even the few female characters in *Corpus Christi* are played by men. McNally admits that one of the inspirations for *Corpus Christi* was a GAP ad: 'A lot of cute young guys in their white shirts and khakis barefoot. I said "That's what they should look like. T-shirts and khakis are what I had to wear to Catholic school."'[17] One is reminded of Wagner's *Parsifal*, where an all-male society guards the symbolic relics of Christ's passion: the cup of the Last Supper and the spear that lanced Jesus's side on the cross. The sole woman is the temptress. The men are the true believers, wounded only by their carnality.[18] In McNally's passion play, carnality is a virtue. Unfortunately the cute young all-male cast and the patriarchal language restrict McNally's message. The film *Corpus Christi: Playing with Redemption* documents the five-year history of a production of *Corpus Christi* that began in a Los Angeles area church and eventually toured parts of the United States, England and Ireland. This production, directed by Nic Arnzen, featured a multiracial cast of men and women of all ages, thus making the play available to all.

The prime example of lack of love for all men – bigotry – is homophobia. Joshua is gay, as are Judas and Peter. The vicious homophobes who taunt Joshua/Christ on the cross are the same voices who taunted and bullied Joshua in high school. Joshua dies for his Whitmanesque message of universal love, including self-love, and for his sexuality.

There is no resurrection in *Corpus Christi*. The Christ figure lives on through the ritualized re-enactment of his story. What the audience witnesses is such a re-enactment. The stage is bare except for a flame and a small pool of water. An actor steps forward to greet the audience and to inform them that 'We're going to tell an old and familiar story' (1). Then the actor playing John baptizes each actor, who introduces his character. The audience is made aware that they are seeing a performance in which the parts are being acted by thirteen actors who are introduced by name as they take on the roles of the disciples and Jesus. This underscoring of the artifice of performance, of the split between actor and role, is common to many of McNally's plays. At the opening of *Lips Together, Teeth Apart*, the actor/characters are frozen in a bright light as the trio from *Cosi fan Tutte* begins. Gradually they begin to move realistically. At the beginning of *Love! Valour! Compassion!*, the actors sing 'Beautiful Dreamer' as an ensemble before they take on their roles. In *Corpus Christi*, the actors are blessed and baptized as they become their characters.

The disciples have a variety of professions, from upper middle-class professions like doctor, lawyer, architect, to artists (actor, singer), to fisherman, hairdresser, masseur and male prostitute. The only one who isn't initially identified by a profession is Judas. The other actors begin their character descriptions in the third person, but Judas is all 'I': 'I'm smart. I like to read. I like music. Good music. I like the theatre. Good theatre. I like some sports. I like violence. I take good care of myself. Weak bodies disgust me. I've got a big dick' (8). We also know from the very beginning the primary cause of his betrayal of Joshua:

Joshua I did love you, you know.
Judas Not the way I wanted. (8)

In the ritualized re-enactment of Joshua's life, we have flashbacks of him as a gay teenager. He and Judas were high school lovers, but from their first encounter Joshua makes clear that Judas's nature imposes limits on their relationship: 'You can come no closer to Me than My body. Everything else you will never touch. Everything important is hidden from you' (37). He repeats those lines before Judas's betrayal.

The Christ figure's sexual orientation is not the only unique, transgressive, aspect of *Corpus Christi*. McNally also inserted aspects of his own experience into Christ's story. Corpus Christi, the setting of much of the play, is McNally's home town, and many of the cultural references place the action of the scenes of Joshua's adolescence at the time McNally was in high school. The name of Joshua's high school English teacher is Mrs McElroy, the name of McNally's favourite teacher.[19] The song 'Unchained Melody', which is sung at the high school prom, was a number one hit in 1955 when McNally was in high school (he graduated in 1956). James Dean, whose three films were released when McNally was a teenager, appears to Joshua during his wanderings in the desert. Why make the Christ figure's backstory similar to the playwright's? When I first wrote on *Corpus Christi*, I saw this identification as an act of hubris.[20] I now see it as part of the way McNally thought an individual must connect with Christ and his story. McNally wrote in the preface to the published edition of the play, 'If He is not created in our image as much as we are created in His, then He is less a true divinity for all men to believe in than He is a particular religion's secular definition of what a divinity should be for the needs of its followers' (v). What follows in the play is a working out of this idea. By having the actors tell us aspects of themselves as they describe their characters, McNally is saying that we all must bring ourselves to this story in order to identify with it and learn from it. The message is the same although the details have been changed. To some extent, the creators of medieval biblical plays did the same thing: for example, the shepherds in the *Second Shepherds' Play* speak in the dialect of the time they were created, and their gifts to the Christ child are gifts a thirteenth-century shepherd might offer. *Corpus Christi* here is also Corpus Christi in 1956.

Joshua's time in the wilderness is a time of self-acceptance. His negative statements about himself are the sorts of things a young gay person feels, the products of his education in a homophobic society: 'How can He be pleased with Me when I am so displeased with Myself?' (42) he asks. Later he tells James Dean, 'I don't want to be different, Jimmy. I want to be like everyone else. I want to be happy' (44). Finding his way to God is also finding his way to accepting and loving himself. That becomes his message.

McNally wrote this play before most religions had begun accepting lesbians and gay men and their relationships. The thought of gay marriage seemed very far away in 1998. Sodomy laws were not struck down by the Supreme Court until 2003, and the first state to legalize same-sex marriage, Massachusetts, did not do so until 2004. So Joshua's presiding over the marriage of James and Bartholomew was a defiant act. The High Priest echoes the attitudes of many religious figures: 'It is one thing to preach your perversions to ignorant and sentimental men such as yourselves, but such travesties of God's natural order will never be blessed in the House of the Lord by one of His ordained priests' (62). *Corpus Christi* offered an alternative to conventional Christianity for gay people when many denominations still turned them away. That was the play's challenge. That is why the New York production was almost cancelled, and why there were religious protestors across the street from the theatre before all performances of the play.[21]

Conclusion

It is important to note that in McNally's work, hatred and bigotry are not the special province of heterosexuals. Stephen, the central character in *The Lisbon Traviata*, voices a shockingly hateful opinion of gay men with AIDS: 'Wouldn't we all rather be at a nice restaurant than sitting here moping over someone who probably, if the truth could be faced up to, even just a little bit, got what was coming to him' (161). Stephen is rightfully terrified of losing his lover and being left on his own in the age of AIDS, but his hateful comment only reinforces his lover's desire to leave him. After voicing equally heartless comments, Perry in *Love! Valour! Compassion!* tells his lover, 'I just get so frightened sometimes, so angry' (409). The fear and anger are a result of a lifetime of experiencing homophobia and seeing the horrible devastation wrought by AIDS. Yet in *Lips Together, Teeth Apart* and *A Perfect Ganesh*, McNally offers a compassionate presentation of the pain homophobia causes to the person who expresses it.

There's a spiritual quality to McNally's work that transcends the loss, pain and grief his characters experience. It can be summed up in the title of one of his most ambitious plays, *Love! Valour! Compassion!* McNally celebrated the bravery of gay men in the face of disease and prejudice, which is caused by a lack of compassion. Above all, McNally was interested in people who are blocked from feeling love for themselves and for others. 'Why do we get involved with people it turns out hate us?' Frankie asks in *Frankie and Johnny in the Clair de Lune*. 'Because we hate ourselves' (63). We see that self-hate cripples characters in a number of McNally plays. We also see the healing power of love. In *Corpus Christi*, God tells his son Joshua, 'Men are cruel. They are not happy. They sicken and die and turn away from love. I want You to show them another way. The way of love and generosity and self-peace' (19). This conflict between self-hatred and love, for self and for others, runs through all of McNally's work.

Same-sex marriage and families are at the heart of Terrence McNally's work in the twenty-first century, reflecting the current chapter in the history of lesbians and gay men. In *Mothers and Sons* (2014), Will, a thirty-something gay novelist who never had to live through the more painful eras of the history of gay men, says, '"What Happened to Gay Men in the Final Decades of the Twentieth Century." First it will be a chapter in a history book, then a paragraph, then a footnote. People will shake their heads and say, "What a terrible thing, how sad." It's already started to happen. I can feel it happening. All the rough edges of pain dulled, deadened, drained away' (649). 'What Happened to Gay Men in the Final Decades of the Twentieth Century – and the First Decades of the Twenty-First' could be the title of McNally's collected work. If *Mothers and Sons* shows us how far upper middle-class urban gay men have come in half a century, McNally's earlier plays show us the obstacles to social and self-acceptance we faced along the way.

4

Paula Vogel

Joanna Mansbridge

Introduction

Although Paula Vogel's early formation as a playwright took place in the 1970s and 1980s – as a graduate student at Cornell University, a young feminist steeped in the emergent discourse of feminist theory and activism, and a lesbian coming out before it was trendy to do so – it was in the 1990s that her plays found their audiences. Vogel honed her craft by reading the Russian formalists, Kenneth Burke, Brecht, Artaud and Strindberg, supplemented by feminist theory, Broadway musicals and John Waters' films. Her plays are both politically and aesthetically challenging, talking back to the canon – William Shakespeare (*Desdemona*), Thornton Wilder (*The Long Christmas Ride Home*), Edward Albee (*And Baby Makes Seven*), Sam Shepard (*Hot 'n' Throbbing*) and David Mamet (*The Oldest Profession*) – while also initiating a conversation with the culture in which she lives and writes. Foregrounding vexed issues like domestic violence, pornography and AIDS, Vogel examines how these topics have come to be framed as sensationalized 'issues' and focuses on the histories and discourses that have gone into defining them, as well as on the bodies that bear their meanings.

Paula Vogel was born on 16 November 1951 in Washington, DC, to Donald Stephen Vogel and Phyllis Rita Bremerman, the youngest of three children. At five years of age, Vogel saw Mary Martin's performance of Peter Pan and immediately fell in love with theatre. She attended prestigious Bryn Mawr for two years before transferring to Catholic University, where she completed a BA in drama in 1974. She was rejected by the Yale School of Drama for graduate studies, and instead entered the Theatre Arts programme at Cornell University. Her dissertation topic – closet scenes in Restoration comedy – predated queer studies by over a decade, but when her committee all left for positions elsewhere, Vogel could not find anyone to replace them. She thus left Cornell ABD (all but dissertation). In 1985, Vogel began a twenty-three-year teaching career at Brown University, where she mentored Nilo Cruz, Lynn Nottage and Sarah Ruhl, among others. On 26 September 2004, Vogel married long-time partner Anne Fausto-Sterling. In July 2008, Vogel became the Eugene O'Neill Chair of the Playwriting Department at the Yale School of Drama, but, in 2012, she stepped down as chair to focus on writing projects. Vogel continues to teach at Yale as a lecturer in playwriting.

When writing the first drafts of *Desdemona*, *Hot 'n' Throbbing*, *The Oldest Profession* and *And Baby Makes Seven* in the 1970s and 1980s, Vogel found herself excluded by feminist theatre. Uninterested in creating a definable feminist or lesbian aesthetic or valorizing women on stage, Vogel was, instead, keen to borrow the tools and tricks from the canon she inherited in order to construct complex female characters who were neither idealized heroines nor victims of patriarchy, but rather active participants in culture and history. These flawed heroines and challenging subjects meant Vogel struggled to find theatres that would produce her work. C. W. E. Bigsby succinctly summarizes the complicated reception of Vogel's plays in the early stages of her career: 'Her plays were not offered as an antidote, still less as a palliative, but they were offered as an irritant. She aimed to disturb and for much of the 1980s she found herself operating in a theatre where that was not a priority.'[1] She herself admits, 'I guess I've sort of fallen between the different models of what feminist theatre is ... or queer theatre.'[2] Rather than developing an aesthetic based on her sexual orientation or gender, Vogel tried to show how all social identities take shape over time and through multiple levels of cultural learning.

Beginning with her breakthrough play *The Baltimore Waltz* (1992) and culminating with *How I Learned to Drive* (1997),

Vogel hit her stride in the 1990s, a decade defined, intellectually, by poststructuralist theories of language and identity; culturally, by renewed 'culture wars' surrounding race, multiculturalism, homosexuality and family values; politically, by the collapse of the Soviet Union and end of the Cold War, the Clinton administration and identity politics; and economically, by a prosperity that had not been seen since the immediate post-war period. Although bookended, on one side, by the George H. W. Bush administration's short-lived invasion of Iraq and, on the other, by George W. Bush's more enduring 'war on terror', the 1990s was a period of relative peace, at least internationally. National events, however, included the Rodney King riots, the O. J. Simpson trial and the Columbine High School shootings. Violence was as ubiquitous in the 1990s as ever, and while the Clarence Thomas–Anita Hill hearings and the Monica Lewinsky–Bill Clinton scandal produced sensationalized public debates around issues of race, gender and sex in popular culture, Quentin Tarantino's *Pulp Fiction* (1994) hit cinema screens with Postmodern nostalgia and sexy, stylized violence.

Vogel's contention is that 'defamiliarization is the purpose of drama'.[3] She defamiliarizes subjects through her formal experiments, which undermine habituated responses and insist instead on a mode of spectatorship that tolerates, and even takes pleasure in, contradictions. The aesthetic architecture of Vogel's plays is characterized by sharp juxtapositions, formal innovation and campy humour. She often deploys camp as a tool of defamiliarization. Her plays are camp in their incongruity, their blending of high and low culture, their oscillation between humour and pathos, their exaggerated display of the conventions governing gender and sexuality, their juxtaposition of past and present, and their deliberate confusion between heterosexual and homosexual, fantasy and reality. Camp is both method and tone, a strategy aimed at defamiliarizing the normative, the everyday, the profane and the discarded, and a kind of humour that is, at once, biting and bawdy, erudite and audacious.

Gender and sexuality are not fixed identities in Vogel's playworlds, but shifting positions and learned dispositions. In this way, her plays anticipated the theories of gender performativity developed by Judith Butler in the early 1990s, which stress the social, historical constitution of gender. The 'reality' of gender, Butler theorized, is 'an effect' of repeated acts 'which congeal over time to produce the appearance of substance'.[4] Normative genders are legitimized through the repetition or 'citation' of previously authorized acts. Gestures may, however, 'misquote' authority if, for example, a man performs gestures coded as feminine or a woman behaves in a conventionally masculine way – or if a feminist playwright rewrites a male-authored dramatic canon. In her revisions of canonical texts, Vogel deliberately misquotes, saying what has not yet been said and rephrasing what has been said over and over. Her characters often challenge the social, historical and theatrical conventions through which normative gender and sexuality establish their authority, even as they are also inevitably bound by them. Vogel's plays found their place in the 1990s, when performativity had become axiomatic and identity politics and confessional culture made talking about gender, sex and sexuality not only acceptable, but de rigueur.

The Baltimore Waltz (1992)

The Baltimore Waltz is a commemoration of Vogel's brother, Carl, who died of AIDS-related complications on 9 January 1988. It is her breakthrough play and, in her words, 'the greatest play I ever wrote'.[5] First staged in Perseverance, Alaska, in 1990 and directed by Molly Smith, *Waltz* moved to New York City's Circle Repertory Company in February 1992 in a production directed by Anne Bogart. After Vogel's success with *Waltz*, her earlier works, such as *Desdemona* and *And Baby Makes Seven*, were produced in the early 1990s at Off-Broadway theatres like Circle Repertory and Lucille Lortel. And after the resounding success of *How I Learned to Drive* at the end of the decade, Vogel's place in the American dramatic canon was secured. New York City's Signature Theatre devoted its 2004–5 season to Vogel, staging *Waltz*, as well as revised versions of *Hot 'n' Throbbing* and *The Oldest Profession*.

Vogel asks that all productions of *Waltz* include in their programme Carl's letter to her, which he wrote after his first bout of pneumonia at Johns Hopkins Hospital in Baltimore, Maryland, a request that imprints each production with the warmth and humour of his voice. The play's dedication reads, 'To Carl – because I cannot sew',[6] which implies that *Waltz* is Vogel's version of an AIDS quilt. In 1990, Ronald Reagan offered an official apology for his administration's dismissal of the crisis during the 1980s, and that same year, the symbolic red AIDS ribbon was introduced to America at the Tony Awards. AIDS was woven into practically every part of American theatre and culture, and plays like Cheryl L. West's *Before it Hits Home* (1990), Terrence McNally's *Lips Together, Teeth Apart* (1991), Steven Dietz's *Lonely Planet* (1994) and Tony Kushner's *Angels in America* (1993) engaged with the disease not as a marginal social issue, but as a central concern.[7]

Waltz begins with a moment of personal loss, suspending and expanding it into a public commemoration. The entire action of *Waltz* occurs in the moment that Anna hears her brother Carl has died. Crucially, however, the audience does not realize this until the play has ended, and so we watch the action unfold believing that Anna has just been diagnosed with Acquired Toilet Disease (ATD), while Carl is the healthy brother who accompanies his sister on a European adventure. The premise of a European trip in *Waltz* stems from a trip Carl asked Vogel to take with him in 1986, an invitation that she declined, not having the money and not realizing that Carl was HIV-positive. He died just over a year later, and Vogel wrote her play as a way to take that trip with him. Suspending time and endlessly deferring the conclusiveness of death, *Waltz* is a celebration of Carl's life, a theatrical translation of loss into remembrance, and a dramatic condensation and displacement of the emotion that emerges in a moment of grief, when there is an urge to flee from the finality of death, if only through fantasy. Reconfiguring time through the round-trip journey and the act of remembering, *Waltz* stages a complex temporality that involves stopping time, folding the past into the theatrical present and bringing the past/passed back to life.

Reality and fantasy in *Waltz* are interconnected registers distinguished visually through lighting. It is a play built on juxtapositions, with the sterile realism of the hospital scenes standing out against the fecund chaos of the fantasy scenes they frame. Most of the action in *Waltz* takes place in lighting that is 'stylized, lush, dark and imaginative', which sharply contrasts with 'the hospital white silence of the last scene'. As in all of Vogel's plays, music evokes social context and subtext, which here recycles 'every cliché of the European experience as imagined by Hollywood' (6). Lighting, music and an episodic structure work together to create the dream-like *mise-en-scène*.

Language lessons, travelogues, parodies of psychiatric models of grief, frisky sex scenes and political satire further contribute to the play's exhilarating capriciousness. References to *The Third Man* (1949) permeate the playworld with the anxious atmosphere of noir films, which parallels the secrecy, paranoia and moral panic surrounding AIDS and homosexuality in post-Cold War America. In *Waltz*, the devoted Anna Schmidt is recast as the licentious Anna and AIDS is renamed ATD, an incurable illness contracted primarily by single female schoolteachers and transmitted through contact with the toilets used by children. Since ATD is not sexually transmitted, Anna, who is infected with the virus, intends to 'fight the sickness of the body with the health of the body', by sleeping with every 'Thomas, Deiter, and Heinrich' (42) she encounters in Europe, all of whom are played by the play's third character, the Third Man. The play eschews sexual moralism and the privatization of sex in favour of an exuberant promiscuity and pointed political statements.

Lost and disoriented, Anna opens the play with a direct address to the audience, which is at once a language lesson, a plea for help and an invitation into the playworld:

> Help me please. (*Recites from memory*) Dutch: 'Kunt U mij helpen, alstublieft?' 'There's nothing I can do.' French: (*Searches in vain*) I have no memory. (*Reads from the Berlitz*) 'Il n'y a rien à faire.' ... I've never been abroad. It's not that I don't want to – but the language terrifies me. (7)

These lines are Anna's response to the words of the doctor at Johns Hopkins Hospital: 'I'm sorry ... There's nothing we can do' (9). This line echoes throughout the play, in various tenses, and it provides the point of return at the play's end. All of Anna's language lessons in the play relate back to this moment, and it is this moment that *Waltz* stops and expands into fantasy. Asking the audience to help her understand her brother's passing and help her remember, Anna takes a fantasy journey that translates loss into acceptance. Reinforcing this work of translation, Anna's final lesson introduces the three moods of the verb 'verlassen: to leave, to abandon, to forsake' (40).

In the play's penultimate scene, Anna sits alone, remembering a game she used to play 'in the days before I could read'. In this pre-linguistic game, before language fully defined her world, Anna would 'make up stories about my hands – Mr. Left and Mr. Right'. She explains to the audience:

> Mr. Left would provoke Mr. Right. Mr. Right would ignore it. The trouble would escalate, until my hands were battling each other to the death. (*Beat*) Then one of them would weep. Finally they became friends again, and they'd dance. (52)

The war and reconciliation between her two hands acts as a condensed metaphor for the play, as Anna tries to translate her brother's death from something that 'terrifies' into memory that consoles. Moreover, the game re-enacts, in miniature, the play's final image: a waltz.

After a frightening encounter with the Strangeloveian Dr Todesrocheln (translation: 'death rattle'), who enacts a darkly comic performance of Anna's childhood game, Anna, still hovering between fantasy and reality, sees her brother lying on the hospital bed. The 'Emperor Waltz' blares, and Carl 'becomes animated, but with a strange, automatic life of its own' (56). He and Anna dance an awkward waltz. But Carl's body gradually 'winds down' and a shrill alarm clock sounds, abruptly ending Anna's fantasy and returning her to the initial scene of loss. Now, back in the present tense, the Johns Hopkins doctor reappears, the harsh white light extinguishes the warm glow of the fantasy journey, and Carl's death is understood by Anna in/as the past tense: 'I'm sorry. There was nothing we could do' (56). And yet she refuses the finality of the past tense. A Strauss waltz softly begins to play, and 'Carl, perfectly well, waits for Anna. He is dressed in Austrian military regalia. They waltz off as the lights dim' (57). The play yields to fantasy and to the suspended 'now' of the theatrical present tense. Carl is immortalized in *Waltz*, his voice and body brought back to life every time the play is staged and in that suspended moment from which the action unfolds, where it remains always.

Baltimore Waltz received almost unanimous praise from critics, winning an Obie Award and gaining Vogel national recognition. In his review of Bogart's production, David Roman writes that *Waltz* is not only 'one of the funniest plays of the past few years', but also 'a beautiful play that celebrates with such honesty, warmth, and conviction the relationships we continue to lose twelve years and counting into this epidemic'.[8] Amid the praise, however, the *New York Times*'s Frank Rich registered an impatience with the tone and structure of Vogel's play, describing it as 'a crazy-quilt patchwork of hyperventilating language, erotic jokes, movie kitsch and medical nightmare – that spins before the audience in Viennese waltz time, replete with a dying fall'. Curiously, Rich critiques the play for enacting a kind of hubris in its attempt 'to rise above and even remake the world in which the disease exists'.[9] *Waltz* defamiliarizes the affective, moral and social meanings surrounding AIDS; even more, it demonstrates the way theatre can operate as a civic space, in which fantasy and memory can, if only provisionally, remake the world.

Hot 'n' Throbbing (1995)

Vogel began the first draft of *Hot 'n' Throbbing* (1995/2000) in 1985, after witnessing a violent domestic dispute in her hometown of Providence, Rhode Island. She began collecting newspaper reports on other such incidents from the *Providence Journal*, and within a year, her file was overflowing. In the 1980s and 1990s, not only was the topic of domestic violence entering public discourse, but the pornography debate was also in full swing. Anti-pornography feminists denounced all pornography as intrinsically harmful to women, a position shared by the Meese Commission on Pornography, a 1986 report released by US Attorney General Edwin Meese that sought broader definitions of pornography and stricter anti-obscenity laws making more types illegal. Vogel's concern is with 'what we censor in this country',[10] and her position is voiced by Charlene Dwyer, a single mother in *Hot 'n' Throbbing* who writes erotic screenplays for a living: 'It's only pornography when women and gays and minorities try to take control of their own imaginations. No one blinks an eye when men do it.'[11]

When Vogel applied for and received a grant from the National Endowment for the Arts (NEA) to write *Hot* in 1994, she knew she would juxtapose domestic violence and pornography as a way of both bringing to light the ubiquity of domestic violence and challenging the censorship of art in the United States. In 1990, NEA chair John Frohnmayer vetoed the grants to four performance artists – John Fleck, Holly Hughes, Karen Finley and Tim Miller, aka the 'NEA Four' – on the basis that the explicit homosexual and feminist content in their performance pieces did not benefit the public and so was deemed obscene. In her 'Author's Note' to the 1997 playtext, Vogel wrote, 'I was interested to learn that "obscene" came from the Greek, for "offstage." Violence in the Greek theatre was kept offstage.'[12] That 'obscene' has become a word signifying a sexual image or act put inappropriately into public view suggests that modern divisions between private and public have shifted in relation to the divisions between heterosexuality and homosexuality that they structure. The play's epigraph exposes the zone of heterosexual privacy that censorship protects: '*Hot 'n' Throbbing* was written on a National Endowment for the Arts Fellowship – because obscenity begins at home.' In the play's 1994 American Repertory Theater production, directed by Anne Bogart, this epigraph was the play's subtitle, making it clear that 'obscenity' would be placed centre stage.

Hot reveals the public nature of the private sphere and the collective nature of individual fantasies. The play takes place in a single evening, in the Dwyers' working-class townhome, where Charlene lives with her daughter, Leslie Ann (or Layla, as she prefers to be called), and son, Calvin. Charlene is recently separated from her abusive husband, Clyde, and writes for Gyno Productions, a film company that produces feminist erotica. The action of *Hot* alternates between two competing and overlapping playworlds, 'the stage lights and the red lights – reality, constructed as we know it, and a world that sometimes resembles the real – as we fantasize about it'. The stylized theatricality of the red-light area contrasts sharply with the mundane realism of the Dwyers' 'living room in a townhouse that cost $79,900 ten years ago. On a 9 per cent mortgage, no deposit down.'[13] These two realms – fantasy and reality – are far from separate, however. Fantasy intersects with and influences the 'real world', shaping the desires and thoughts of the characters in it. Moreover, invoking the canon of literature – from Herman Melville to Vladimir Nabokov to Henry Miller – and of popular culture – horror film, detective stories, pornography – Vogel stages the history of male-authored fantasies of female pleasure, showing the way these canonical narratives shape our imaginations and teach women how to cast themselves as objects of desire – and to find pleasure there.

The remaining two characters in *Hot* are the Voice and the Voice Over (VO). The Voice is both an embodied, male character and an omniscient voice who narrates the canonical texts that pervade and interrupt Charlene's own narrative voice. The VO is a female character who enacts – more particularly, overacts – and directs the erotic screenplay that Charlene is writing. As a 'sex-worker' and Charlene's 'inner voice', the VO represents women's most commodified role on the popular American stage – the stripper – but she is also the narrator and director of Charlene's screenplay, initiating scene changes by commanding, 'CUT TO'. The VO enacts the hypersexualized female body in popular culture, while the Voice embodies literary history and dominant culture. Charlene is negotiating her place between these two traditions, trying to become an author of female pleasure and desire within a history that persistently positions women as object and spectacle.

Hot is built around juxtapositions – between sexuality and violence, body and voice, fantasy and reality, high culture and low culture, masculinity and femininity, public and private. The stage design makes visible what is typically kept private – the domestic sphere and erotic fantasies – and makes it available for public viewing. Implicating the audience as voyeurs, the two spaces are both described as 'stages for performance, for viewing' (6). Leslie Ann and Calvin too are described in the character list as 'voyeurs, as teenagers are, hooked on watching – TV, Nintendo, music videos, parents' (5). The two stage spaces and the characters in them are in constant tension – the stripper and the single mother writing erotic fiction to make ends meet, the girl dancing erotically and the daughter being praised by her dad for her sexual appeal, the horror film that two young girls watch and the play's final, fatal scene. Vogel represents pornography and domestic violence not as obscene (offstage), but as a spectacle for public witness.

The play opens with the juxtaposition of sexualized body and narrative voice. Under 'a growing red light' the audience sees '*Leslie Ann dressed in very tight pants and a halter top, making suggestive stripper ... movements*', as Charlene sits at her typewriter. The VO narrates the play's first lines, which are the words that Charlene types: 'She was hot. She was throbbing. But she was in control. Control of her body. Control of her thoughts. Control of ... him ... He was hot. He was throbbing. And out of control. He needed to be restrained. Tied down. And taught a Lesson. But not hurt too much. Not too much. Just ... enough' (9). As Charlene shifts the power dynamics of heteronormative relations, positioning the man as dominated erotic object, she also questions her authority to revise this script. Cultural discourses – both written and performed – conflict and converge with Charlene's erotic voice, suggesting the way our imaginations, far from being within our control, are structured by a history of images and narratives. *Hot* is deeply concerned with the complexity of women's claim to authority – control – especially over representations of sexuality. As Charlene's authority as a pornographer is placed in dissonant tension with her authority as a mother, the play destabilizes conventions of both motherhood and female sexuality in far-reaching ways.

As the play's leitmotif, control over language is presented as a complex historical struggle. The writer does not possess the words she uses; they possess her. And narrative authority is, in the play, inextricable from control over one's body, its pleasures, desires, impulses. Charlene explains her writing strategy to Clyde by emphasizing the centrality of language, rather than physical acts, in women's erotica: 'For one thing, desire in female spectators is aroused by the cinema in a much different way. Narrativity – that is, plot – is emphasized.' In a passage that suggests something of Vogel's own playwriting strategy, Charlene adds, 'Most importantly, we try to create women as protagonists in their own dramas, rather than objects. And we try to appreciate the male body as an object of pleasure' (39–40). The challenge is finding a language that does not return to the same script.

Clyde is conflicted by Charlene's new writing career, both turned on and threatened by her newly claimed authority. In a vulnerable moment, he tells Charlene, 'you taught me about desire' (41). But he also mocks her work. As a working-class White man who does not meet the ideal of the economically successful and socially powerful American male, Clyde maintains his claim to masculine power through physical force and verbal humiliation. Clyde's hyperbolic performance of a failed masculinity induces a kind of empathy; he seems powerless over his words and actions. In his increasingly erratic performance, we can see him flailing for some other way to 'do' his gender. Clyde seems to be, like Charlene, in search of a new script. When the audience finds out that Charlene has a restraining order against Clyde and that he has cut the phone lines before barging into the house, the history of the relationship comes into focus.

Fantasy and reality converge when a spontaneous erotic encounter between Charlene and Clyde turns violent, and both are suddenly caught in scripts that neither is able to control. In an eerie echo of Charlene's explanation to Clyde of the power she feels when writing, the VO states, 'And the words become flesh' (67). As violent snuff film replaces feminist erotica, Calvin and Leslie Ann watch the unfolding scene from outside the sliding glass doors. Clyde beats Charlene in stylized slow motion, lip-syncing a script spoken by the Voice: 'You. Goddamn. Whore ... You're the one making me do this, Charlene' (71, 73). The ventriloquism and 'elaborate pantomime' (71) disconnect body from voice, the speaker from the history of the words spoken. This stylized theatricality distances the audience from the brutality, taking the action beyond its private setting of a working-class living room and into the realm of public fantasy. We are all familiar with Clyde's words; they are not his alone. Juxtaposing violent image and erotic language, contemporary culture and canonical history, Clyde strangles Charlene as the Voice reads Molly's soliloquy from James Joyce's *Ulysses*. Joyce's authorization of Molly's pleasure resonates in dissonant relation to Charlene's flailing body and the helpless warnings of the VO. As Clyde tightens his grip on Charlene's neck, the Voice whispers Othello's deadly poetry: 'Put out the Light and then Put out the light' (73). And Charlene's silent and lifeless body becomes the sign of this authority.

Three different endings, which directly follow this moment, have been staged in productions of *Hot*. In Anne Bogart's 1994 American Repertory Theater production, the play's conclusion suggests an endless cycle of violence. Leslie Ann enters, sees her dead mother and then walks under a spotlight, where she strips to the music of the 'stripper theme' in a spectacle devoid of eroticism. Leslie Ann takes off her clothes, dons her mother's and takes Charlene's place at the computer, typing the words that begin the play: 'She was hot. She was throbbing. But she was in control. Control of her body. Control of her thoughts.'[14] The second ending emerged from a conflict of opinion between Vogel and Molly Smith, a frequent Vogel collaborator and artistic director of Arena Stage. The ending Smith envisioned had Leslie Ann enter to find her mother's dead body, freezing in a tense pose of fear and anger. Then the VO responds to her fear in a soothing, maternal voice: 'It's okay. It's all right,' and Leslie Ann's body relaxes.[15] Vogel was unhappy with the decision to stage it that way; its very ambiguity seemed irresponsible toward audience members who may have experienced abuse.

The third version – Vogel's preferred ending – was staged in Les Waters' 2005 Signature Theatre production. This conclusion flashes forward ten years to show Leslie Ann as a literature professor teaching her students to question the canon they inherit. As she instructs her students on their *Moby-Dick* essays, 'I expect you to be in control of your arguments, in control of your words, and in control', then Leslie Ann and her mother's voice say in unison, 'of your thoughts'. The stage directions read, '*Leslie Ann Dwyer freezes at the sound of her mother's voice*' (75). This maternal echo perhaps signals a new legacy, an inheritance that displaces the voice of the master with other voices, other desires. In any case, the multiple endings suggest that it is always possible to 'change the storyline'.

Reviews of *Hot* were decidedly mixed. The *Washington Post*'s Lloyd Rose, reviewing the Arena Stage production, positioned *Hot* as a male-bashing counter-statement to David Mamet's *Oleanna*:

> In the center of this play there's some genuine, risky ugliness – the female suspicion that masculine strength will always ensure masculine control; that a woman's tender emotions – her socially approved love and compassion – are her worst enemies; that there's something fundamentally, unalterably wrong with men. Vogel slaps these nasty fears smack in the audience's faces. 'Hot 'n' Throbbing' ought to be on a double bill with David Mamet's fear-of-feminism 'Oleanna.'[16]

The 'ugliness' of *Hot* is found in the cultural scripts of sexualized violence that it recites. As *Pulp Fiction* was released that same year to great acclaim and as the O. J. Simpson trial became a media frenzy just two months after the play's premiere, theatre critics still did not have a vocabulary for discussing stage violence that was not sensationalized nor romanticized, but rather problematized and historicized. In her *Village Voice* review of Les Waters' 2005 production, Alisa Solomon explained that the play was responding in part to the NEA obscenity trials. Solomon underlined the play's tension between farce, fantasy and an 'edgy sense of real', referring to Vogel as 'one of America's most daring and complicated dramatists'.[17] In *Hot*, Vogel juxtaposes sexuality and violence, private and public, fantasy and reality, staging the texts and images that structure our imaginations and provide the setting for our desires.

The Mineola Twins (1997)

As Vogel puts it, '*Mineola Twins* was created by me thinking, "Okay, I wrote *Hot 'n' Throbbing*, it's time for me to laugh".'[18] She also wondered, however, 'Would it be funny if women told the jokes?'[19] In all of her plays, Vogel uses comedy as a technique that both brings audiences closer and disorients their perspectives. Sometimes campy, often clever and always disarming, the humour in Vogel's plays is also edged with something darker, as in *How I Learned to Drive*. She explains, 'Whether I'm writing a comedy or a tragedy, they come from the same source. This is what I'm worried about. This is what I'm fearful about.'[20] Comedy in Vogel's plays comes from a place of incongruity and irreverence, of questioning; it is not meant to reinforce the audience's assumptions, but overturn them.

The Mineola Twins was workshopped in 1995 at the New York Theatre Workshop and had its world premiere at the Perseverance Theatre in Douglas, Alaska. It had its New York premiere in 1998 at Laura Pels Theatre, after Vogel had earned recognition from *How I Learned to Drive*. *Twins* is a political satire of post-war American culture. Director Joe Mantello (who played the Third Man in Bogart's production of *Baltimore Waltz*) exploited the theatricality of *Twins*, achieving a cartoon aesthetic that, in many ways, captures the way we remember the 1950s and 1960s – as one-dimensional Technicolor images and stereotypes. The play uses the theatrical device of the split protagonist – in this case twin sisters – to allegorize a nation divided between political Right and Left. Vogel frames the play as an epic battle of warring twins:

I have been extremely upset at the Republican right taking over our Government. So I thought, okay, let's go back to the 50s, with its quintessential combination of comedy and terror. As a culture then, we went into science fiction, invaders from Mars, instead of looking at those who were invading us from within ... We used our fear of aliens to mask our terror at what was the heart of America. I used the image of twins that war: Jacob and Easu, a blood hatred between them. It's where we are emotionally as a country.[21]

Replacing warring brothers with battling sisters, *Twins* conjures the affective energy of an increasingly polarized and conflicted post-war America, from the Cold War panic of the 1950s and 1960s to the revolutionary activism of the 1970s, to the culture wars of the 1980s. The femininities embodied by Myrna – the 'good girl' who dreams of becoming a wife and mother – and Myra – the 'bad girl' who rebels against sexual mores and social institutions – work in the play as extensions of America's political polarization. The twins, both played by Swoosie Kurtz in Mantello's production, are identical 'except in the chestal area'. Myrna, the virginal 'good twin', is 'stacked', while Myra, the promiscuous '"evil" twin', is 'flat as a pancake'.[22] Satirizing the post-war fixation on apocalyptic endings, sex and female bodies, *Twins* takes the audience on a 30-year romp from the 1950s to 1989, presenting women as both products and producers of history, popular culture and politics. Coming of age in post-war American popular culture, Myra and Myrna present a vivid image of a divided post-war femininity, perhaps best captured in Revlon's massively successful 1950s 'Fire and Ice' campaign: 'In every good woman there is a little bad.'

The signs of popular culture abound in *Twins*. Ford cars and Maidenform bras further reveal the social forces at work in the construction of post-war middle-class heterosexuality, while songs from each decade permeate the playworld with powerful social messages. As Vogel argues, music is 'important as a way of saying "This was gender in 1960."'[23] In the 1950s and 1960s, young girls were sent contradictory messages; they could sing along with 'My Guy', 'I Will Follow Him' and 'Baby It's You', or loudly proclaim 'Don't Make Me Over' and 'You Don't Own Me'. Myrna and Myra Richards embody these contradictory messages, performing the divided politics and paranoia of post-war America. Amplifying gender as a masquerade, Vogel suggests two ways to do the play: '1. With good wigs. 2. With bad wigs.' 'Personally,' she writes, 'I prefer the second way' (97). The remaining characters are Jim and Sarah (played by the same actor), the romantic partners of Myrna and Myra, respectively; Ben and Kenny (also played by the same actor), Myra and Myrna's respective sons; and two mute male characters, who move furniture, play psychiatric aides and act as wardrobe assistants. The final casting element includes 'The Voice', the shared consciousness of the twins: 'Either brainwashing or subliminal seduction, it's the way the sisters talk to each other. In dreams' (97).

In its episodic structure, its double-role casting and its use of history as a theatrical device, *Twins* is Vogel's most Brechtian play, with nods to both *Seven Deadly Sins* and *The Good Person of Setzuan*.[24] The subtitle, *A Comedy in Six Scenes, Four Dreams, and Six Wigs*, reveals the play's campy tone, formal symmetry and imaginative theatricality. Set in the middle-class Long Island suburb, Mineola, the play blasts through three eras, each signalled by skirt lengths, hairstyles and hot-button issues. The first set of scenes takes place during the 1950s Eisenhower era; the second period takes place during Nixon's epoch in the late 1960s; and the last scenes take place in 1989, just as Bush Senior takes over from the Reagan administration. In the 1950s, the twins are polarized according to their sexuality; in the 1960s, they are divided by their political beliefs; and in the late 1980s, they are separated by their cultural values and lifestyles. The twins' extreme political and sexual roles – far Left/far Right and good virgin/evil whore – contrast with the more fluid political and gendered dispositions of the supporting characters, while the manic tone of the playworld swings between frenzied desire and panicked paranoia.

In the 1960s, the twins and the country are dealing with Nixon, Vietnam, Women's Lib and the Cold War. Myra is a radical anti-war activist, while Myrna is a Long Island housewife with a philandering husband and a nervous condition stemming from her time spent in the psychiatric ward. Myrna retaliates for being committed by her sister by giving the police information on Myra's whereabouts. Consequently, Myra does time in jail, where she 'discovers' lesbianism. By 1989, the twins' domestic lives have become the reverse of their political values. Myra has settled into a comfortable domestic life with her lesbian partner,

Sarah, and son, Ben. And while Myra was the radical in the 1960s and 1970s, the conservative Myrna, now divorced, has joined the Reagan-era feminist backlash and become a right-wing radio shock jock à la Rush Limbaugh, decrying the influences of multi-culturalism and 'tofu-eating-feminazi-fetus-flushing' and calling for the reinstatement of true American 'cultural values' (167). Her son, Kenny, predictably, has turned rebelliously to the Left, looking to his freewheeling Aunt Myra for guidance, while Myra's son, Ben, looks to Myrna as his right-wing role model, adopting her book on family values, *Profiles in Chastity*, as his life manual. The polarization in this period is almost complete.

The play ends with a dream sequence, in which the sisters, having driven themselves to the point of exhaustion, long for some kind of reconciliation. Interrupted by a 'crash and flash of light' (184), Sarah awakens Myra, reassuring her jokingly, 'We almost blew up, just like any other happy nuclear family' (185). Although the play ends on an unsettling tone that highlights the (still) deeply conflicted nature of American politics, it also depicts a new family scene: the image of Sarah and Myra lying together in their bed. As Doris Day belts out, 'I'll See You in My Dreams', we can see the play as a parody of the post-war American culture, packaged as part sci-fi film, part domestic drama and part campy comedy.

To critics already familiar with Vogel through *Baltimore Waltz* and *How I Learned to Drive*, *Twins* was seen as an unsophisticated attempt at political farce. Vogel had wished to have the 'ha-ha funny' tone of *Twins* produced before she dug in with *Drive*, which implicitly says, 'This is how it feels on the inside.'[25] However, the reverse happened, with *Drive* premiering in New York first – to wide acclaim – and *Twins* following its trail of praise, only to be received as a frivolous follow-up to its more sensitive predecessor. Ben Brantley criticized Vogel for 'manipulating cultural clichés' and contended that 'much of [Vogel's] gender-twisting satire would undoubtedly seem stale to a downtown audience' familiar with 'performers like Lypsinka and Five Lesbian Brothers'. Comparing Vogel's farce to the edgier lesbian theatre downtown, Brantley fails to take *Twins* on its own terms, as a legitimate political farce that is closer to Christopher Durang than Split Britches. Brantley dismisses the sisters as caricatures who are 'never much more than the sums of their slogans and fashion accessories'.[26] Vincent Canby thought that 'the politics of the play are fairly rudimentary'. The title of his review alone – 'The Mad History of Women as Told by Twin Barbies' – suggests a dismissal of *Twins* as a kitschy take on pop culture, and his description of the play as an 'insane' 'history of women' betrays a sexist snobbery.[27] Both Canby and Brantley seem resistant to watching women in drag, acting as representatives of political positions and national values, while at the same time hurling crude jokes at one another. Michael Feingold of the *Village Voice* pointed to the play's 'femaleness' as a feature that 'some male critics will no doubt resent'. For Feingold, the success of the play was in the 'triumphant performance' of Swoosie Kurtz (indeed, Kurtz won an Obie Award for her performance), but his most damning comment was the description of Vogel's play as a 'low rent' version of Wendy Wasserstein's *Heidi Chronicles*.[28] It was a startlingly off-the-mark comparison that suggests the limited vocabulary available to critics for talking about plays written by women, which, in the 1980s and 1990s, were often relegated to the ghetto genre of 'women's theatre'.

Despite the critiques, *Twins* has been produced regularly over the past two decades at regional and university theatres, becoming increasingly relevant as more women participate in the political sphere and in popular culture parodies. While Monica Lewinsky and Hillary Clinton were the duo many critics referred to after the play's 1998 New York production, in 2008 Hillary Clinton and Sarah Palin were the cultural touchstones. The twins are, like Tina Fey's and Amy Poehler's imitations of Palin and Clinton on *Saturday Night Live*, allegorical representations of a polarized national disposition, not realistic, moral examples of good/bad teenage girls, wives or mothers. *Twins* works when Myra and Myrna are taken seriously as social satirists and metaphors of a national 'split personality'. And in these first decades of the twenty-first century, with the convergence of politics and popular culture fairly complete, they are an increasingly pertinent pair.

Vogel contends, 'I actually take what I do as a playwright very seriously. I'm always asking, "What should we do? What should playwrights do?" Go back and look at what the Greeks did. One could not be a Greek playwright and write a tragedy without writing a satiric comedy on the same subject.'[29] If *Twins* presents a farcical vision of the split within American politics and American femininity, *How I Learned to Drive* gives us the darker side of that story. Published together as *The Mammary Plays*, *The Mineola*

Twins (1997) and *How I Learned to Drive* (1997) work dialectically as two sides of post-war American social history as seen through the lens of 'white, middle-class femaleness'. Vogel explains that she 'wanted the plays to travel the same time period, from the end of the 1950s to the end of the 1980s', with 'one play ... looking at the culture from the outside and one ... exploring how the culture feels on the inside'.[30] The exaggerated pop aesthetic of *Twins* works as the counterpart to the more minimalist style of *Drive*. In *Drive*, the frenetically divided Myra and Myrna re-emerge in L'il Bit, who tells a complex story of her internal division between objectified body and subjective voice, a split negotiated through recollected memories, reactivated affects and retraced roadways.

How I Learned to Drive (1997)

How I Learned to Drive is Vogel's most celebrated play and the work that earned her international recognition as an important voice in American theatre. In contrast to the broad caricatures in *Twins*, *Drive* is a precisely sketched story of a young girl's coming of age – and coming apart. While critics have defined *Drive* as a sensitive depiction of 'child abuse'[31] and even 'a love story',[32] Vogel says, 'I actually describe *Drive* as a comedy', adding, 'Of course it's not, but the first half very much functions as comedy. At some elemental level, it is who I am.'[33] Juxtaposing comic scenes with moving and at times disturbing ones, the play interrupts, at every turn, conventional patterns of identification and spectatorship. Vogel wrote *Drive*, in part, as a response to the uneven representation of sexual harassment in David Mamet's 1992 polemical play *Oleanna*.[34] In contrast to the linear naturalism of *Oleanna*, which makes its conclusion logically inevitable, *Drive* has a recursive structure that defies resolution. *Drive* is not a psychological portrait of sexual abuse, nor is it concerned with getting at the truth of the present by uncovering the trauma of the past. Rather, the play shows the way our desires, sexualities and our subjectivities are not 'ours', but rather the products of culture, history and memory.

Drive is a memory play. It looks closely at the process of using pieces of the past to reconstruct a present self. L'il Bit remembers her past with the distance of a director observing a rehearsal.

Moving between exposure and concealment, she gives shape to her memories and forms them into a newly made self, born of recognition and forgiveness. *Drive* employs a non-chronological structure, using detours and reverse movements to mimic the workings of memory, to reorient structures of empathy and to map out a temporal terrain both individual and collective. These devices displace psychological realism and linear action with varying speeds and movements, all of which reorient the audience's sense of time and character. Dramatizing history as memory, the play stages the last four decades of the twentieth century from the perspective of a now forty-something woman, L'il Bit, who looks back on her adolescence and, specifically, her relationship with her Uncle Peck.

Drive draws, in part, from Vogel's fascination with Vladimir Nabokov's *Lolita*. Like *Lolita*, *Drive* is a story of seduction, a picaresque tale and a satiric examination of American culture. Unlike *Lolita*, *Drive* puts the young woman in the driver's seat, giving her the narrative voice through which to direct the story. Vogel brings the Lolita myth – the myth of a female sexuality that is both innocent and cunning – in direct tension with the stigmatized paedophile. Writing in the 1990s, when 'politically correct' became the easy answer to difficult differences, Vogel insisted, 'In my sense of the political, you can never be politically correct. To be political means to open up a dialogue, not to be "correct."' Vogel's plays encourage the kind of complex, contradictory perspective that political correctness seeks to smooth over. With *Drive*, she wanted 'to see if the audience would allow themselves to find this erotic; otherwise, they only see victimization without empowerment'.[35] If the spectator finds the relationship erotic, they are immediately implicated in Peck's seduction of L'il Bit and perhaps then compelled to reflect and empathize rather than demonize.

By encouraging the audience to identify with Peck, the play transforms what is shameful or threatening into an experience of uncomfortable recognition. Andrew Kimbrough argues that *Drive* 'testifies to the radical and self-implicating belief that community begins when we recognize that what we find most abhorrent and intolerable in others is really that which we find most fearful and shameful about ourselves'.[36] Demonizing Peck for his 'deviant' desire works of course to define what is 'normal' desire. These categories, however, evade the way, as a culture, we fetishize youth and sexualize girls and boys at an increasingly young age.

As sexual images fill the cultural landscape, we become ever more vigilant about identifying and policing non-normative sexualities. Kimbrough reminds us that, in the 1980s and 1990s, there was 'a sharp rise in the awareness of perceived sex crimes against children and the propagation of the unquestioned belief that these crimes are on the rise'.[37] Indeed, the creation of the 'paedophile' fuels the paranoia surrounding his or her detection. The escape valve for this paranoia is the voyeuristic consumption of hypersexualized images of young people, which offers some of the same titillations sought by the paedophile, but from a morally sanctioned position.

Vogel's dramaturgy works as a kind of pedagogy in the way it uses form to encourage audiences to expand their critical thinking and feeling capacities beyond habituated assumptions or predetermined moral categories. That Peck first made sexual contact with L'il Bit when she was eleven years old is revealed late in the play, after the audience has seen their relationship develop as one of mutual respect and affection and as one formed out of larger cultural attitudes and affective structures. L'il Bit begins the play by saying to the audience, 'Sometimes to tell a secret, you first have to teach a lesson.'[38] L'il Bit claims authority over what she will and will not disclose to the audience, keeping aspects of her sexuality private, even as she performs them publicly, and often using metaphor to translate her story of sexual coming of age. Seducing the audience with the promise of an exposed private secret, 'the dirt' buried in her past, L'il Bit offers instead a public lesson about the complexity of sexual desire.

This perverse pedagogy is given a classical imprimatur through the incorporation of a Greek Chorus, or in this case, three choruses – the Male, Female and Teenage Choruses perform the function of both comic and cultural commentator. The communal choric voice is revised here as a collection of disparate, conflicting and often very funny voices. The multiple choruses theatricalize the relationship between individual and collective, private and public, while suggesting that an individual's voice is, like memory, not actually individual, but a learned, internalized script made up of multiple cultural messages passed on over generations. The three actors who play the choruses enact various parts. They also give advice; criticize; insult; sing doo-wop songs in three-part harmony; witness the relationship between Peck and L'il Bit; and give L'il Bit a voice when she is unable to speak. They provide both formal complexity and aesthetic distance. Above all, the choruses are the contradictory voices that teach L'il Bit how to live in the world.

In the opening scene, a seventeen-year-old L'il Bit sits in a car with her Uncle Peck, who fumbles to unlatch his niece's bra during one of their weekly driving lessons. The Vineyard production provided emotional distance from this and other moments like it through non-naturalistic acting and an abstracted set design. Facing the audience and sitting in two chairs that signal a Buick Rivera, Peck fondles L'il Bit's breasts, while their bodies remain 'impassive' and 'only their facial expressions emote' (8). Refusing the comfort (or voyeurism) of the fourth wall, and other conventions of realism, the play works as a kind of public staging, an encounter between audience and performers. Further defamiliarizing the action is the voice of the driving instructor, whose disembodied authority guides us through the lessons, telling us what gear is being used, the direction in which we are moving and the precautions we should take. The driving instructor also signals the temporal shifts of L'il Bit's memories, as they move back and forth between 1962 and the play's present.

Driving lessons are the play's primary conceit, working analogously as lessons in gender formation. Through Peck's driving lessons, L'il Bit learns to assume a position of control, both in and outside the car. In a scene entitled 'You and the Reverse Gear', Peck instructs a fifteen-year-old L'il Bit:

> When you are driving, your life is in your own two hands. Understand? ... There's something about driving – when you're in control of the car, just you and the machine and the road ... A power. I feel more myself in my car than anywhere else. And that's what I want to give to you. There's a lot of assholes out there ... And you have to be ready for them. I want to teach you to drive like a man ... Men are taught to drive with confidence – with aggression ... Women tend to be polite – to hesitate. And that can be fatal. (50)

This passage is rife with all the contradictions that animate the relationship between Peck and L'il Bit: he wants to protect her, and yet he also violates her; he wants to invest her with a sense of power and authority, and yet he also leaves her powerless to his advances; he wants her to experience the freedom and autonomy of driving, and yet he damages the possibilities she may have had to experience her body in that same way. Peck teaches L'il Bit 'to drive like a man' and survive in a world that constructs her as an object, even as he sexualizes her female body. The metaphor of the driving lesson reinforces that gender is not something that originates in the body, but something that is taught and internalized as 'natural'.

Sexuality that is kept 'secret', the play suggests, is damaged. The central scene is titled '1965. The Photo Shoot'. A thirteen-year-old L'il Bit moves swiftly through the performative gestures of feminine embodiment: self-consciousness, shame and defiance. Looking back to this moment without any visible traces of emotion, L'il Bit sets the scene, which takes place in Peck's basement, a place where, she says knowingly, 'he keeps his secrets' (59). In this space of secrets and domestic privacy, L'il Bit learns to transform shame into seduction and to see herself as a sexual object. As Peck prepares her for the photo session, we see his desire for L'il Bit as, in part, a desire for command over her body. He prompts her to move seductively with affirmations of her beauty and unbuttons her blouse with the calculated detachment of someone seeking, above all, to be in control. Moving her body in response to his affirming voice and desiring gaze, L'il Bit becomes sexualized for and because of Peck's gaze. L'il Bit feels betrayed, however, when she realizes that Peck is planning to send the photos of her to *Playboy*. Her body made into a public commodity, L'il Bit feels violated and vulnerable, as if Peck can 'see right through' her. Mark Brokaw's 1997 production at the Vineyard Theatre complicated interpretations of this scene by projecting the photos of L'il Bit that Peck was taking on a screen above her, interspersing them with images of *Playboy* bunnies, popular celebrities and even Alice Liddell, Lewis Carroll's child muse. In this way, the 'private secret' unfolding in Peck's basement was contextualized within a long tradition of sexualized images in visual art and media. The audience was invited into the historical complexity of this scene and divested of the comfort of clear moral responses.

L'il Bit is an astute student, transforming Peck's lessons into a form of sexual authority. On a bus trip to upstate New York in 1979, L'il Bit, now a 27-year-old teacher, seduces a seventeen-year-old boy. She tells the audience, 'I was only into the second moment of conversation and I could see the whole evening before me':

And dramaturgically speaking, after the faltering and slightly comical 'first act', there was the briefest of intermissions, and an extremely forceful and sustained second act. And after the second act climax and a gentle denouement – before the post-play discussion – I lay on my back and thought about you, Uncle Peck. Oh. Oh, this is the allure. Being older. Being the first. Being the translator, the teacher, the epicure, the already jaded. This is how the giver gets taken. (41)

This metatheatrical scene describes gender and desire as prescripted roles that play out in a drama of seduction. In this scene, L'il Bit is both director and leading role, acknowledging the man from whom she learned her timing and techniques.

In the devastating penultimate scene, we witness the moment at which the power dynamics shift between uncle and niece. On the eve of L'il Bit's eighteenth birthday, a desperate Peck, bearing the gift of a new Cadillac, begs L'il Bit to marry him, but she cuts all ties with him. After this encounter, she tells the audience, 'I never saw him again ... It took my uncle seven years to drink himself to death. First he lost his job, then his wife, and finally his driver's license' (85). Spoken matter-of-factly, this elegiac moment is haunted by Peck's physical presence, as he remains still seated beside L'il Bit on stage. With a present filled with the past, L'il Bit sits, calmly and assuredly, beside Peck, ready to remember and re-enact their first encounter.

The Teenage Chorus speaks all of L'il Bit's lines in this scene, performing the dislocation of body and voice incited by this experience and creating a sense of distance between the encounter and its remembrance. L'il Bit sits silently in the passenger seat beside Peck and 'looks at him closely, remembering' (88). In the first direct look she and Peck exchange during a sexual encounter, L'il Bit confronts her past, her gaze compensating for her disembodied voice. Initiating their first driving lesson in 1962, Peck asks L'il Bit, 'Do you want to drive?' (88). While teaching her how to operate the steering wheel, Peck places 'his hands on her breasts', an image of violation that contradicts his instructions always to stay in control of the wheel. L'il Bit sees in retrospect Peck's conflicted desires: he wants both to protect and prepare her, and also to satisfy his sexual desire and exercise his own control. As Peck 'tenses against L'il Bit', she sits on his lap, facing the audience, 'trying not to cry', and comforting herself by insisting, 'This isn't happening.' The audience watches her words disproved in a disturbing moment filled with a mixture of uncomfortable eroticism, sadness and panic. There is an urge to plead with Peck, along with L'il Bit, who begs him, 'please don't do this' (90). And yet there is also a moment of shameful recognition, a painful awareness of the inevitability of such an encounter in a culture saturated with images far less sensitively drawn.

L'il Bit concludes the play with a direct address to the audience, a narrative strategy that brings the audience back to the beginning of the play and suggests that the lesson was, itself, the secret, the lure to look at sexual desire in a different, more difficult way. 'That was the last day I lived inside my body,' L'il Bit tells the audience. And yet, in a reflection that suggests driving has become a kind of compensation, she adds, 'The nearest sensation I feel – of flight in the body – I guess I feel when I'm driving' (91). This final scene stages the importance of L'il Bit's narrative voice as the agency with which she gives shape and meaning to her memories, her story. As L'il Bit (and the audience) remembers Peck, she (and we) gets remade through the process. In the play's final image, she gets into her car, where 'a faint light strikes the spirit of Uncle Peck, who is sitting in the back seat of the car. She sees him in the mirror. She smiles at him. He nods at her. They are happy to be going on a trip together' (92). In a look of recognition and forgiveness, L'il Bit sees her own image reflecting back at Peck's, acknowledging him as part of her remade self. She redirects the narrative conventions of closure and resolution, along with the safety they promise, opting instead for an uncharted path. With the car in first gear, L'il Bit, together with the ghost of Peck, drives off into an unknown future: 'And then – I floor it' (92).

Drive premiered in February 1997 at the Vineyard Theatre in a production directed by Mark Brokaw and featuring Mary-Louise Parker and David Morse in the lead roles. It moved across the street to the Century Theatre in April 1997 for a commercial run, where Jayne Atkinson (and later Molly Ringwald) and Bruce Davison took over the lead roles. After 450 performances over a fifteen-month run, *Drive* went on to be produced across the country and around the world. Winning the 1998 Pulitzer Prize for drama, *Drive* confirmed Vogel's reputation as an important American playwright. Ben Brantley praised the play's skilful balance of delicate subject matter:

'It is hard to say who is the more accomplished seducer ... Uncle Peck, surely the most engaging pedophile ever to walk across an American stage, or the woman who created him.'[39] Michael Feingold lauded Vogel's courage, writing, 'She doesn't flinch from any of the awfulness involved', and the 'gentleness and precision in her touch' makes *Drive* 'the sweetest and most forgiving play ever written about child abuse'.[40] Jill Dolan's pithy review in *Theatre Journal* points out, however, that '*Drive* is only "about" incest after the scene of L'il Bit's first molestation', which occurs very near the end of the play. Until then, it is a play about 'forgiveness and family, about the instability of sexuality, and the unpredictable ways in which we learn who we are, how we desire, and how our growth is built on loss'.[41]

Drive's immediate success emerged in part because it arrived amid a period where sexual abuse stories were gaining in public visibility, on and off stage.[42] However, as noted, *Drive* is unique in the way it resists placing L'il Bit in the role of either confessor or victim. In his review of the 1997 Vineyard Theater production, *New York* magazine's John Smith found fault with this ambiguity,[43] while the *New York Observer*'s John Heilpern took issue with Vogel's admission that she wanted to see whether the audience would 'allow themselves to find this erotic', contending that 'Ms. Vogel would like us to be turned on by child molesters like Uncle Peck.' Heilpern concluded, somewhat paradoxically, that Vogel 'has neutralized the issues making them more or less harmless'.[44] Similarly, in his review of a 2004 production of *Drive*, Michael Toscano of the *Washington Post* was concerned with 'Vogel's seeming inability to clearly state who or what is right or wrong' and expressed disappointment that a 'courageous feminist, lesbian playwright' like Vogel did not 'take a strong position' by portraying 'the predator' as 'clearly ... evil' and making it clear 'who is preying on whom'.[45] *Drive* cultivates not moral certainty, however, but moral complexity, and the ambiguity and unresolved affective aftermath are the play's greatest power. Regardless, *Drive* was ultimately canonized using highly traditional terms. As Robert Brustein writes, 'Vogel moves her characters out of the provisional world of morality into the timeless world of art.'[46] To praise the play using such sanitizing aestheticism seems ironic. Nonetheless, *Drive* stands as Vogel's most produced play to date, and it continues to tell us – to teach us – about what it means and how it feels to live in a body not entirely your own.

Conclusion

Vogel continues to write plays that provoke questions, provide pleasure and produce a feeling of (sometimes uneasy) complicity that culminates not in a resolution, but in an unravelling of the material history that constitutes gender, sexuality, class and, more recently, race and ethnicity. Her latest plays continue to rework material from the dramatic canon and cultural history in ways that pose pressing questions to the present. *Don Juan Comes Home From Iraq* (2014), for example, revises Ödön von Horváth's *Don Juan Comes Home From the War* (1936) and, with expressionistic brushstrokes, registers the experiences of Iraq and Afghanistan war veterans returning home not to a hero's welcome, but to a life of invisibility and psychological trauma. Her latest work, *Indecent*, co-created with Rebecca Taichman, premiered at Yale Repertory on 2 October 2015. This play with music traces the vexed production history of Polish-Jewish writer Sholem Asch's *God of Vengeance* (1907) and its controversial 1923 Broadway debut. Asch's play tells the story of a brothel-owning Jew whose teenage daughter falls in love with a prostitute working for him; Vogel and Taichman's retelling provokes questions that echo throughout Vogel's oeuvre: whose authority counts as legitimate? What kinds of desires get deemed obscene? How do the particulars of time and place shape perception? What gets recorded as history? What role does theatre play in the preservation of cultural memory? *Indecent* moved to Broadway's Cort Theatre in April 2017, after a sold-out run at the Vineyard Theatre in spring 2016. The play also served as Vogel's revised PhD thesis in Cornell's Theatre Arts programme. A fitting final requirement for her doctorate degree, this play marks the completion of an academic journey of more than forty years and a high point of a playwriting career still in full force.[47]

5

Tony Kushner

James Fisher

Introduction

Many critics would concur that Tony Kushner's playwriting career reached its high point in the early 1990s, with the extraordinary success of his two-part masterwork *Angels in America*. Kushner's work in the 1990s marked the culmination of his formative period as a playwright during the turbulent 1980s when, as a liberal-minded political activist and aspiring theatre director, he contemplated Ronald Reagan's new conservative era, the spectre of HIV/AIDS and his own sexual orientation. In a sense, Kushner's timing was perfect. Reagan's expressed values collided with those of the activist homosexual community, and this tension proved fertile for Kushner's drama. The early failures of the government, the media and the medical community to face AIDS, which seemed to be killing gay men at an alarming pace, energized the gay community and Kushner himself. A student of history, he found the 1980s a vantage point from which to probe America's political landscape, its history, its religious underpinnings and its art, finding in the cultural complexities of the second half of the twentieth century a thick underbrush of betrayed ideals, outmoded values and misguided beliefs fuelled by bigotries and political division. Seeking a creed for the future, Kushner looked to the struggles of gay Americans as a means by which to rediscover those principles of value that might provide a strategy for survival into an unknowable future. As a gay man slowly embracing his sexual orientation, Kushner felt the anger that inspired some to activism and others to despair as the deaths from AIDS spiralled into a worldwide pandemic.

Two generations of AIDS-era dramatists – Larry Kramer, William Hoffman, Harvey Fierstein, Terrence McNally, Paula Vogel and Kushner, among others – present a range of views on the intersections of love and sex among homosexuals, but all were compelled to grapple with the death toll of AIDS and its impact on sexual politics. In Kushner's hands, rage at the inaction of American society to face the AIDS crisis is transmuted into compassion for the experience of ordinary individuals who, in his observation, are buffeted by the powerful cross-currents of history, politics and religion. In the face of horrific levels of human suffering Americans are unaccustomed to (and protected from, compared to those in many other countries), Kushner created works investigating late twentieth-century American values and beliefs, and strategies to move forward for those who found those values and beliefs wanting. As he writes, 'people do go to art in general as a way of addressing very deep, very intimate, very mercurial and elusive, ineffable things in a communal setting. It ends a certain kind of inner loneliness. Or it joins one's own loneliness with the inner loneliness of many other people. And I think it can be healing.'[1]

Since childhood, Kushner has found healing through art. Born Anthony Robert Kushner in Manhattan on 16 July 1956, the son of classically trained musicians who encouraged his interest in art and literature, Kushner spent much of his youth in Lake Charles, Louisiana. His mother performed in amateur theatre, entrancing Kushner with the emotional and intellectual impact of drama. As he later recalled, 'I have very strong memories of her power and the effect she had on people ... I grew up very, very closeted, and I'm sure that the disguise of theatre, the doubleness, and all that slightly tawdry stuff interested me.'[2] His escape from the closet came when he moved to New York in 1974 to pursue a BA degree in English Literature at Columbia University.

During this time, he also immersed himself in the New York theatre scene, subsequently completing a Master of Fine Arts degree at New York University's Tisch School of the Arts, where he trained as a director under the guidance of Bertolt Brecht specialist Carl Weber. In this period, Kushner directed his own original plays with fellow students, including an opera, *La Fin de la Baleine: An Opera for the Apocalypse* (1982), an adaptation of Goethe's *Stella: A Play for Lovers* (1987), theatre for youth plays *Yes, Yes, No, No* (1985) and *The Protozoa Review* (1985), and one-act and full-length plays including *The Heavenly Theatre* (1986) and *In Great Eliza's Golden Time* (1986). In these earliest works, Kushner examines themes and explores techniques evident in his full-length plays from this period, *A Bright Room Called Day* (1984) and *Hydriotaphia, or The Death of Dr. Browne* (1987), and in the earliest of his many adaptations, *The Illusion* (1988). The latter play is freely adapted from Pierre Corneille's obscure 1636 comedy, *L'illusion comique*.

Kushner's artistic and political concerns came to full fruition in his major works beginning with his two-play epic *Angels in America: A Gay Fantasia on National Themes* (1991–2), followed by a serio-comic vaudeville, *Slavs! Thinking About the Longstanding Problems of Virtue and Happiness* (1994), as well as his adaptations of Brecht's *The Good Person of Setzuan* (1994) and S. Ansky's Yiddish theatre classic *A Dybbuk; or, Between Two Worlds* (1995, 1997). In the late 1990s, Kushner also laboured over two works that would be produced in the early 2000s. The one-act monologue *Homebody*, first produced at London's Chelsea Centre in 1999, evolved into the darkly tragic *Homebody/Kabul* (2001). And, as the decade of the 1990s ended, Kushner was at work on the sung-through musical drama *Caroline, or Change* (with music by Jeanine Tesori), which premiered at New York's Public Theater in 2003 followed by a Broadway run in 2004. His prodigious output of the 1990s also included several as-yet unproduced works: an original opera, *St. Cecilia; or, The Power of Music*; a teleplay, *East Coast Ode to Howard Jarvis* (1995); a screenplay *Grim(m)* (1995); and one-acts and other smaller projects.

Kushner told the *New York Times* that he is 'drawn to writing historical characters. The best stories are the ones you find in history,'[3] and much of his full-scale work is similarly sweeping in scale, theme, characterization and language. Kushner contends that 'all theatre is political', that drama, like democracy, springs from the 'frazzle, the rubbed raw, the unresolved, the fragile and the fiery and the dangerous'[4] in human circumstances and political discourse. His own politics formed in college after he read Ernst Fischer's *The Necessity of Art: A Marxist Approach*, as well as plays by Brecht, Clifford Odets and Arthur Miller. Kushner's commitment to the social responsibility of the stage came at a time when few mainstream American dramatists featured overt political themes and, when they did, presented them with utmost realism. For his approach, Kushner instead turned to Brecht's epic theatre and lyric realism as found in plays by Tennessee Williams and John Guare, though his recent work *The Intelligent Homosexual's Guide to Capitalism and Socialism with a Key to the Scriptures* (2009) evokes the realistic tradition in the manner of Miller's *A View From the Bridge* (1955–6).

Kushner's work is rife with the problems of balancing human desires with lofty ideals. The attitudes of his characters are complex and often contradictory, reflecting the political divisions exemplified in the so-called 'culture wars' of the 1990s, but in Kushner's hands instead of a liberal versus conservative divide, he offers a more complicated mix of diverse values and matters of individual conscience. The impact of economics, and especially the resulting moral dilemmas faced by those for whom material success became synonymous with conceptions of the 'American Dream', becomes a theme in Kushner's plays that resonates with the works of Miller and, to a lesser extent, Odets. But beyond these theatrical influences, it is of major significance that Kushner self-identifies as a gay man while his works include but extend far beyond the LGBTQ community. In his most representative works, Kushner explores characters of all stripes caught up in periods of wrenching cultural transitions and vast socio-political upheaval, although in both his historically-based and contemporary plays issues of change are inextricably woven together with the smaller lives of ordinary individuals facing parallel personal upheavals and challenges to their moral certitudes.

Like George Bernard Shaw and Brecht, with the latter supplying a dramatic structure Kushner employed in his earliest plays, he uses the stage as a platform for social, political and religious argument, but in ways that neither Shaw nor Brecht, nor, for that matter, any other American dramatist has previously done. The ideological debate in his plays emerges from a composite of rhetorical rationality, literary and cultural imagery drawn from the dogmas of the past, and wildly imaginative fantasy to unfold the complex cross-currents of history and culture. Along with socialist proclivities inspired by Karl Marx and Leon Trotsky and, in literary and dramatic terms, by Brecht and Walter Benjamin, Kushner melds together an aesthetic drawn from aspects of post-naturalistic European theatre, including elements of realism. Influences from literature, art and thought of the ancient world through to the Renaissance also blend together in Kushner's plays.

Kushner's study of the great religions, from Christianity and Judaism (his own faith) through a variety of Eastern religions, mingles with his love of Modern and Postmodern literary influences too wide-ranging to adequately index. These include writers from the classical realm to nineteenth-century German classicism, poets ranging from Rilke to Stanley Kunitz, French Renaissance to Yiddish theatre, and modern dramatists from Brecht, O'Neill and Williams to contemporaries such as Guare, Richard Foreman, Maria Irene Fornés and Sarah Ruhl, and such British counterparts as Edward Bond, Caryl Churchill and David Hare. From Williams to Hare, modern playwrights often sought expressive means to bring the fantasies and images of the historical past together with the real or imagined lives of their characters. Kushner has similarly sought to do so, but much more overtly and with a particular emphasis on fantastical elements, whether bringing on stage angels, devils and deceased historical figures, or making use of anthropomorphic characters along with heightened, lyrical language evident only in the most experimental of Williams's plays.

Kushner is often described as a 'gay dramatist', but is, in fact, better understood as a 'political dramatist'. His brand of socialism might better be labelled progressivism, a politics he calls 'socialism of the skin', which honours the values of the past without slavish adherence to belief systems whose traditions exclude or oppress diversity in culture, sexual orientation, gender and politics. Kushner insists that unshakable dogmas of any variety are at times comforting, but fraught with problems in a rapidly changing world, and that attempting to understand the world solely in rational terms is potentially catastrophic; for him, the unspoken, the unseen and faith in hard-won progress built on compassion and humanism may permit society to proceed most constructively into the fearful future. The failure of humanity to achieve connection and compassion and the denial of society's accountability for the well-being of all its citizens is found in *Angels in America*, as well as such later Kushner works as *Slavs! Thinking About the Longstanding Problems of Virtue and Happiness*, the one-act teleplay *East Coast Ode to Howard Jarvis* and the screenplay *Grim(m)*.

Angels in America (1991–2)

Kushner won unprecedented critical acclaim for his Pulitzer Prize-winning *Angels in America: A Gay Fantasia on National Themes*. This two-play epic dealt with some of his recurring themes while turning his gaze toward the impact of HIV/AIDS on American society, particularly as seen in the lives of a gay couple (Prior Walter and Louis Ironson), a seemingly straight couple (Joe and Harper Pitt) and an infamous historical figure, Roy Cohn, as all are facing shattering crises in their lives. The two *Angels* plays, *Millennium Approaches* and *Perestroika*, are of a piece; separately and together they explore in linear fashion the lives of the aforementioned individuals, while making fantastical digressions into the drug-induced delirium of three of its characters (Prior, Harper and Roy Cohn) with imaginative journeys to Antarctica, Heaven and Hell.

In *Millennium Approaches*, internal conflicts surface in intertwining relationships with others in this burgeoning cast of characters. Law clerk Joe Pitt struggles to be true to his Mormon upbringing while coming to the realization that he is a closeted gay man; meanwhile his wife Harper, agonizing over her suspicions about Joe's true sexuality, treats her deep depression with Valium and an escape into fantasy. Roy Cohn, who, by 1985, is a disreputable divorce lawyer on the verge of disbarment, intends to secure a position for Joe in the Reagan administration's Justice Department in Washington, DC, where Cohn, who learns he is suffering from AIDS, hopes that Joe will serve as his informant. Louis, a liberal court reporter working in the same building with Joe, abandons his HIV-positive partner Prior and spirals downward into despair and self-recrimination. Belize, an African American nurse and sometime drag queen, cares for Prior and offers a humanistic response to the play's divided politics. Joe finally embraces his true sexual identity, 'comes out' to his repressed mother, Hannah, and leaves Harper to pursue Louis. The physical conditions of Prior and Cohn deteriorate as *Millennium Approaches* moves forward. Delirious from his illness, Prior encounters an overdosed Harper in a mutual fever dream, while Cohn is haunted by the spectre of another historical figure, Ethel Rosenberg, who, along with her husband Julius, was executed in the early 1950s as a Soviet spy. Cohn reveals to Joe that he had illegally pressured the judge in the Rosenberg case to apply the controversial death sentence. Cohn also refuses to acknowledge his homosexuality – gay men, in his opinion, are powerless and faceless people. As the play moves to its conclusion, Harper sinks more deeply into depression and drugs, and Prior is haunted by the ghosts of two ancestors – 'prior Priors' – both of whom have died of plagues in previous eras and recognize the AIDS pandemic as similar to their horrific deaths. Prior also intermittently hears the voice of an Angel calling him 'prophet'. In the play's final scene, the Angel crashes through the ceiling of Prior's bedroom announcing that 'The Great Work Begins'.

In and around the personal crises of the characters, *Millennium Approaches* continues to explore late twentieth-century attitudes about American history, sexuality, race, religion and the traditional poles of conservative and liberal politics. *Perestroika*, the second of the *Angels* plays, picks up where *Millennium Approaches* leaves off, continuing to follow the same set of characters as the Angel, Hannah and Belize evolve from secondary characters to figures as significant as Joe, Harper, Prior, Louis and Cohn. The Angel that has named Prior a prophet takes Prior to encounter a heavenly council of angels attempting to find their way in the absence of God, who has not been seen or heard from since the San Francisco earthquake of 1906. The Angels encourage Prior to stay in Heaven, but he pleads for more life despite his suffering, suggesting that life continues even beyond the loss of hope.

As the characters confront their choices, their relationships shift. Returning to life, Prior faces a repentant Louis, who has discovered that despite his physical attraction to Joe, he wants to return to Prior. Prior refuses even as they discover that Joe has written anti-gay legal opinions. Appalled, Louis breaks off their relationship. Joe's mother Hannah, who has arrived in New York from her Salt Lake City home in order to face Joe, instead ends up caring for a deeply disturbed Harper. Working with Hannah at the Mormon Welcome Center, Harper becomes fixated on a diorama of a Mormon pioneer family. Miraculously, the Mormon Mother comes to life and shares her life's hardships with Harper, making it clear that Harper must face her pain and journey forward. Cohn, semi-delirious and dying in the hospital, is nursed by Belize, despite Cohn's hateful racial taunts. The ghost of Ethel Rosenberg reappears, this time to punish Cohn with the news that the Bar Association committee has formally disbarred him. With Belize's advice, Cohn has secured a cache of AZT, a new and apparently effective drug for AIDS suffers. When Cohn, for whom the drugs are too late, succumbs, Belize enlists Louis to steal the medicine to help Prior and other AIDS sufferers. In return for this 'gift' from Cohn, Belize encourages Louis to perform the Kaddish over Cohn, during which he is joined by the spectral Ethel Rosenberg, in a moving act of forgiveness for their political nemesis. Harper has pulled herself together and leaves Joe, presumably to start her life over without him. Hannah becomes friends with Prior and, through this relationship, comes to some understanding of her son's sexual orientation. Hannah also encounters Prior's Angel, who provides an orgasmic experience that liberates Hannah from her repressed existence and helps to create, by *Perestroika*'s final scene, set in 1990, a newly formed family of friends including Hannah, Prior, Belize and Louis. Prior, despite the ravages of AIDS, looks ahead to the future and offers his blessing to the audience as the play ends.

The acclaim for *Angels* was matched by controversy over its subject matter, language, images of homosexuality, and politics, but even naysayers were impressed by its scope and Kushner's lyrical language. *Angels* became one of the most talked-about plays since Edward Albee's 1962 drama *Who's Afraid of Virginia Woolf?* Critics rhapsodized about the plays. Frank Rich, writing in the *New York Times*, called *Millennium Approaches* 'a true American work ... a work that never loses its wicked sense of humor or its wrenching grasp on such timeless dramatic matters as life, death and faith even as it ranges through territory as far-flung as the complex, plague-ridden nation Mr. Kushner wishes both to survey and address',[5] while *Newsweek*'s Jack Kroll, echoing many other critics, described *Angels* (writing of both parts) simply as 'the most ambitious American play of our time'.[6]

In the manner of all Kushner's major plays, the two *Angels* plays are explorations of the eternal cultural struggle between reactionary and progressive forces. Kushner probes the ways in which the political poles of post-war conservatism and liberalism, changing sexual mores and long accepted belief systems have, for better or worse, shaped American life in the last decades of the twentieth century. *Angels*' subtitle, 'A Gay Fantasia on National Themes', was inspired by Shaw's subtitle, 'A Fantasia in the Russian Manner on English Themes', for his 1920 play *Heartbreak House*. *Angels*, like *Heartbreak House*, is set in a turbulent era of transition. In Shaw's case, it is those transitional moments before the start of the First World War in which he viewed the obliteration of Victorian–Edwardian values as welcome. Kushner, in *Angels*, also sees transitional changes inspired by the rise of Reagan conservatism, but questions what will happen to his characters in the unknowable future as they face these harrowing changes in both their personal lives and in the society in which they live. Their bewildered, pained existence, like that of Shaw's characters, is set against the hopes for progressive change espoused by both authors.

In *Angels*, Kushner argues for a re-evaluation of American society along the theoretical lines suggested by British socialist critic Raymond Williams, whose 1985 essay, 'Walking Backwards into the Future', posited, among other things, the value of socialist theory in forming an idea of a society that places a higher value on community than individualism. For Williams and, by extension, Kushner, this necessitated consideration of the question of whether life was about improving conditions for all or developing personal connections. Laced throughout *Angels* is an insistent plea for a re-examination of cultural certitudes, particularly those in the arenas of politics, economic justice, religion, morality and sex and gender. A reformed society, as Kushner sees it, must be built upon a progressive humanist doctrine founded in the hard lessons of history, a conception central to both Williams's theories and Kushner's *Angels* (as well as his other major plays).

For the characters in *Angels*, the anxieties of proceeding into an unknown future cause paralysis and considerable emotional suffering, but over the course of the two plays a few ultimately conclude that stasis is more painful than taking the fearful journey forward. Walking backwards into the future, as Williams articulates, is a means of facing the inevitability of change; by finding guideposts in past wisdom, the progressive traveller may avoid potential pitfalls. When Prior Walter, the pivotal emotional centre of *Angels*, invites the audience to imagine progress that, in his case, translates to 'more life', despite the ravages of AIDS and the emotional pain of abandonment he endures, he does so with his eyes firmly fixed on what lies behind him and the stagnation of stasis. He accepts, and even embraces, the agonies of his illness-ridden life and, as such, achieves redemption borne of a renewed hope, even if that hope is burnished with a knowledge that the joy of living is inextricably linked to loss and suffering. Prior acknowledges that humans live on past mere hope, discovering within themselves the personal and political will to fight for change, to create community and to believe, however improbably, in the possibility of a better world.

Kushner casts his major characters into a vortex of past, present and future values and questions; each character faces profound personal tragedy, ranging from abandonment and emotional despair to the collapse of the moral or religious certitudes that have guided their lives. The possibility of death looms over the characters, who encounter each other and the dead in the play's combination of realism and fantasy. Kushner acknowledges the wrenching pain of enduring tragic circumstances, but he insists that tragedy teaches. The lessons taught are brutalizing and the losses suffered staggering, but in Kushner's world finding the ability to accept the inevitability of loss and change, and to progress, is a strategy for survival, both for the individual and for American society.

As a social progressive, Kushner's personal politics are paramount in *Angels*; he allows both political poles – conservative and liberal – to be seen and heard at their best and worst. His most conservative character, the historical figure Roy Cohn, does and says reprehensible things, but so does the play's most liberal character, the fictional Louis Ironson, who abandons his long-time companion at his darkest hour of need. Cohn pays for his sins by suffering with AIDS, but the play's most sympathetic character, Prior Walter, also endures AIDS while the play's most innocent character, Harper Pitt, must bear abandonment and the loss of the person she loves. Regardless of their politics or actions, all of the characters face overwhelming ordeals testing their beliefs and their ability to survive loss. Strong characters become weak and those who consider themselves weak find unexpected strength within themselves. The survivors seen in the final scene of *Perestroika* have journeyed forth, carrying the lessons of their past – and the historical past – into a hopeful future.

The central male characters in *Angels* are either 'closeted' or 'out' homosexuals shown in varied circumstances but all connected by those circumstances while grappling with their individual struggles. The play's indictment of the failures of both conservative and liberal politics to address the social and political crises of the last decades preceding the new millennium is blunt. Its assault on the Reagan administration's particular failure to address the HIV/AIDS pandemic and what Kushner otherwise felt Reagan conservatism represented is also directly confronted. For Kushner, Reagan's presidency exacerbated the horrors of the mounting HIV/AIDS pandemic through its callous and politically calculated blindness to the crisis, as well as the multiple dilemmas facing gay citizens on both sides of the national political divide as gays left the closet behind to seek equality within American society.

Angels was recognized as a landmark in American culture, and Kushner's skills as a dramatist were lauded as the play entered the canon of foremost American dramas, including *Long Day's Journey Into Night* (1956), *A Streetcar Named Desire* (1947), *Who's Afraid of Virginia Woolf?* (1962), *A Raisin in the Sun* (1959) and *Our Town* (1938). Not overtly agit-prop like Larry Kramer's *The Normal Heart* (1985), not domestic drama like William M. Hoffman's *As Is* (1985), not historical tragedy like Martin Sherman's *Bent* (1979) and not an ensemble comedy/drama demonstrating the variety of gay life – and the normalizing of it – like Terrence McNally's *Love! Valour! Compassion!* (1994), *Angels* enfolds all of those elements in its dissection of deep political divisions in millennial America (and the roots of those divisions in the post-Second World War era). He gives ample attention to the intimate relationships of its characters, the varied ways gays live their lives in a deeply homophobic nation, and the search for guiding moral principles as old values fade and the future looms.

Along with the influence of Raymond Williams's Marxist criticism, Kushner also found a profound influence in Walter Benjamin's 'Theses on the Philosophy of History', which had inspired an important image for Kushner, and Paul Klee's painting *Angelus Novus*, depicting the Angel of History being blown into the future by the winds of progress while glancing back at the rubble of history. The influence of Klee's painting is inherently obvious, while the Benjamin essay meant enough to Kushner that he gave his protagonist, Prior, the last name Walter in tribute to

Benjamin. Using Klee's potent image as an overarching thematic motif, Kushner employs Brechtian epic theatre techniques, such as short truncated scenes, projected title cards and characters breaking the fourth wall to address audience members directly, encouraging them to think critically about the characters' respective crises and the possibilities of social change. Weaving together political drama with lyric realism, Kushner presents characters caught between two worlds – one dying and one being born – and his dual structural inspirations mirror the dualities facing his characters who are tormented by fear of an unknown future even more harrowing than their turbulent present, an uneasy sense of moral uncertainty and profound feelings of inexplicable loss. In one scene, a disturbed homeless woman offers the prediction that 'In the new century, I think we will all be insane.'[7] Near the end of *Millennium Approaches*, Kushner offers a *coup de theatre*, as the ghost of Ethel Rosenberg faces off with the frightened but unrepentant Roy Cohn, prompting him to boast, 'I have *forced* my way into history. I ain't never gonna die,' to which Ethel ominously replies, 'History is about to crack wide open. Millennium approaches' (118).

Ethel's prediction comes true in *Perestroika*, as great changes occur for all of the play's main characters while the oldest living Bolshevik berates his Soviet peers for abandoning socialism without a new theory to guide them into the future. Kushner's characters are similarly without guidance as they move forward. The more intellectually and thematically complex of the two *Angels* plays, *Perestroika* stresses the necessity for forgiveness and the acceptance of loss if the characters' lives, and their society, are to progress into a future that may (or may not) be better than the present in which they reside. Kushner depicts forgiveness and loss in many ways: for example, at one point Louis is appalled to find himself at the bedside of Cohn, who, despite persistent denials about his sexuality, is succumbing to AIDS. The ghostly Ethel joins Louis to chant the Kaddish over Cohn's corpse in an act of forgiveness from both his historical and present-day enemies. Transgression can and must be forgiven, Kushner implies, and is the means by which it becomes possible to journey forward, as hopes for a brighter future and society's progress result from facing up to hard truths.

In *Perestroika*'s final scene at Central Park's Bethesda fountain, with a statue of a healing angel at its centre, Kushner offers a newly created family from those who are forgiving and forward-looking.

In this essential scene, which brings to culmination the complex themes of the two plays, Kushner allows his characters to state his guarded optimism, asserting Kushner's mantra of the interconnectedness of all humanity, regardless of race, religion or sexual orientation, and the primacy of loyalty and commitment to others and to the community. Prior, Kushner's avowed prophet, speaks directly to the audience and points out the angel of the fountain, a figure commemorating death but suggesting 'a world without dying' (279). Giving voice to the human longing for transcendence and life-giving affirmation in the face of unspeakable suffering, Kushner has Prior, whose AIDS symptoms have stabilized, explain that though the healing waters of the fountain are not now flowing, he hopes they will flow again. Prior speaks for Kushner and those who have come before: 'This disease will be the end of many of us, but not nearly all, and the dead will be commemorated and will struggle on with the living, and we are not going away. We won't die secret deaths anymore. The world only spins forward. We will be citizens. The time has come' (280).

Angels, which won the Pulitzer Prize, Tony Awards for both plays and innumerable critics' awards, is most often identified as a gay play, and it is indeed a reflection of the reinvigorated homosexual activism of the early AIDS era. At the same time, Kushner moves beyond the political liberation of gays and the crisis of AIDS toward an exploration of the boundaries of gender (one of the play's conceits is that all of its characters are acted by a corps of eight actors, with men playing women and women playing men in some cases) and the complex intertwining of sex and love. In this, Kushner is indebted to Tennessee Williams, a dramatist similarly concerned with the brutalizing realities of sexuality on fragile souls seeking love. Anna Quindlen wrote at the time of *Angels*' Broadway premiere that it is 'a brilliant, brilliant play about love and the human condition at a time when our understanding of what it means to be human and loving has, thankfully, expanded'.[8]

Few plays in any era garnered as much critical and editorial attention as *Angels* onstage and in its six-hour television film version, a fact suggesting that despite culture wars controversies, audiences found *Angels* to be a compelling framing of the political, moral and sexual issues confronting Americans at the end of the twentieth century.

Codas to Angels: *Slavs!* (1994) and *G. David Schine in Hell* (1996)

Two subsequent Kushner works are loosely connected to *Angels*. *Slavs! Thinking About the Longstanding Problems of Virtue and Happiness* is a serio-comic vaudeville about the collapse of the Soviet Union and is partially made up of scenes and characters Kushner intended to include in *Perestroika*, though its length required the elimination of scenes set in the Soviet Union. Based around the relationship of a beleaguered woman doctor treating victims of the Chernobyl nuclear disaster and her lover, a young woman employed as a guard at a facility storing the brains of the dead 'great thinkers' of the Soviet experiment, *Slavs!* probes, albeit in a broadly cartoonish way, the irreparable social consequences of the failure of Soviet socialism. A speechless child, Vodya, damaged by the nuclear disaster, represents the tragic human toll of failed politics and international conflict, while elderly Bolsheviks sit in Heaven debating political theories, ending in puzzlement with Lenin's famous question, 'What is to be done?'

The other *Angels* coda, *A Backstage Pass to Hell*, sometimes titled *G. David Schine in Hell* (1996), is a satiric one-act in which Roy Cohn, now in permanent residence in Hell, encounters icons of twentieth-century conservatism also residing there, including J. Edgar Hoover and Richard Nixon. Cohn's alleged former lover, G. David Schine, whose relationship with Cohn precipitated the Army–McCarthy Hearings in 1954 that subsequently brought down McCarthy's career, also arrives. Kushner imagines the interactions of these particularly American legends with the purpose of examining the moral and political lessons recorded in history's log book. Its significant questions about the passing of old values in a time of moral, political, racial and sexual division, and the lack of moral and political direction, are issues at the heart of this slight work, as it is in *Angels* and *Slavs!*, and remain core issues in Kushner's subsequent plays.

Adaptations: *The Good Person of Setzuan* (1994)

In addition to the aforementioned free adaptations of plays by Goethe and Corneille, Kushner has produced numerous other creative adaptations of works by Heinrich von Kleist, S. Ansky, Ariel Dorfman and Brecht. The economic and social-political woes evident in much of Kushner's output from the mid-1980s through the 1990s are at the crux of his adaptations of Brecht's plays. *The Good Person of Setzuan*, Brecht's 1940 play adapted by Kushner and first performed at San Diego's La Jolla Playhouse in 1994 (followed by a Wings Theatre Company production Off-Broadway in 1999), examines the battle for the survival of the goodness of the human soul in a cruel, mercenary world. Existential questions surface centrally in Kushner's Brecht adaptations, but the harsh universe in which Brecht's characters find themselves stems, in part, from the economic and political construction of society, a concern Kushner significantly enhances in his otherwise faithful adaptation. The struggle of the individual against society is central in *Good Person*, a parable concerning attempts by a poverty-stricken Chinese woman to live a moral life within a corrupt society.

Through the simplicity of an episodic fable, themes unfold in layers, with increasingly complex (and contradictory) historical and cultural meanings arising. Liberated from the constraints of realistic illusion, the play's episodes exploit variations of a few overarching themes, an approach typically prized by Kushner, who adds his own cinematic sensibility to the traditions of Brechtian structure, overlapping episodes as in his own plays. Brecht's use of fable to recount (and re-evaluate) human history alienates his audience from distracting details of contemporary reality even as the story reflects upon them.

Kushner draws the Brechtian characters closer to his audience through his allegiance to American lyric realism, while also adopting Brecht's insistence that the theatre's mode of representation must come second to what is represented. The play's thematic concerns are bound up with political notions; in other words, *Good Person*'s emphasis rests on the relationship of the individual to the construction of society. Kushner largely eschews Brecht's distancing techniques regarding character – the characters in his adaptation (either invented or adapted from Brecht's originals) are more fully dimensional and distinctly individual than those in Brecht's play. Although they may step out of the 'reality' of their world, they are real people, not merely icons serving as thematic mouthpieces, as is typical of Brecht (although they may serve this function at times). This critical difference between Brecht and Kushner has an impact in Kushner's adaptations of Brecht (and, of course, his own original plays inspired, in part, by Brecht's *oeuvre*), although both playwrights share a sense of the changeable nature of situations, individuals and societies as deeply political and, at the same time, fundamentally dramatic.

The paradoxical nature of humans is taken to its extreme in *Good Person* as Brecht's protagonist, the good-hearted Chinese prostitute Shen Te, invents an alter-ego, Shui Ta, to guard (or supersede) her instinctively generous and compassionate spirit. Shui Ta's avaricious, ruthless nature protects Shen Te, providing a defence against the overwhelming tests of morality and compassion she faces. Brecht and Kushner are bound together in their belief that the exclusive province of the stage is to create such contradictions as a means of releasing both human nature and the inherent social questions shaping human experience. Kushner approaches *Good Person* as, he noted, 'agrarian folk poetry',[9] with a central character that is essentially a good person. Kushner's drama, like Brecht's, is inextricably bound to the problems of a capitalist society. *Good Person* employs Marxist concepts to depict the inequities inherent in capitalism that shape behaviour and to pose variant political views within a capitalist society. Locating counter-theories – or finding strategies for those disenfranchised by capitalism – is within Kushner's conception of Brecht's play. He is inexorably shaped by the triumph of capitalism in American society (and the world in the aftermath of the collapse of the Soviet Union). Stopping short of a call for class warfare, he questions the ways in which the disenfranchised suffer in any time and place, most particularly the present. Cultural clashes between rich and poor, and conceptions of the ways individuals experience good and evil at the opposite ends of the economic spectrum, are present in Brecht's *Good Person*, as well as Kushner's adaptation. Kushner enhances the effectiveness of the play by tightening its language, making it more accessible linguistically than most available translations of Brecht's work, and by subtly drawing parallels with the economic uncertainties resulting from the Reagan administration's trickle-down economics and an era of conflict in America over traditional moral certitudes involving sexuality and gender issues, class, and ethnic and racial identity.

Adaptations: *A Dybbuk; or, Between Two Worlds* (1997)

In many of his works, Kushner's politics become entangled with spiritual uncertainties, an area of significant interest for him beginning most obviously in *Angels*. Questions of God's will and the idea that He is not necessarily a benign (or even present) force are raised in many Kushner plays, most obviously in the errant, unseen God of *Angels* who disappears to parts unknown, leaving humanity to fend for itself during the disastrous twentieth century.

In Kushner's *A Dybbuk; or, Between Two Worlds*, freely adapted in 1994 from the Yiddish theatre chestnut by S. Ansky (written c. 1912–14), the prejudices directed at Jews in early modern Europe are set against the audience's awareness of international tragedies to come in two cataclysmic world wars and in the mass murder of Jews in the Holocaust, which would obliterate the society depicted in the play. Ansky, the pseudonym of Solomon Rappoport, an ethnographer who crafted the play from historical/mythical stories he had unearthed during the early twentieth century, recognized that the *shtetls* of Eastern Europe were vanishing, though Ansky could not have known that the encroachment of modernity as the agent of change would be overwhelmed by the horrific brutality of the Nazis in their attempt to exterminate all Jews and their societal values as enshrined in *shtetl* life.

Produced first by the Hartford Stage Company in 1995, followed by a subsequent New York Public Theater production in 1997, Kushner's adaptation is built on Joachim Neugroschel's literal translation of the original text. This free adaptation reveals Kushner's recurrent concerns with the joys and heartbreaks of love and his sense of the impact of sweeping socio-political and economic changes and realities on individual lives. Most centrally, the play renders a troubled religious scepticism coupled with a deep yearning for faith poised on a philosophical fissure between Modernist and Postmodernist thought.

As with his earlier adaptation of Corneille's *The Illusion*, Kushner finds in Ansky's play opportunities to enhance its inherent theatricality and passionate expression, while engaging in a Talmudic questioning of the natures of love, sex and faith and their intersections. He juxtaposes images of past Jewish life and a rigidly orthodox belief system depicted by Ansky with contemporary anxieties, as he also did with Brecht's plays. Kushner takes many more liberties with Ansky than he did with Brecht, and his adaptation, in essence, extends beyond Ansky's rendering of traditional stories to unlock Kushner's own ambivalence about religion in general and his own faith in particular.

That past life, the 'old world', is stage centre in the comparatively simple plot Kushner carries over from Ansky's play. Often referred to as the Yiddish *Romeo and Juliet*, the play recounts a tragic romance between Chonen, a young rabbinical student, and Leah, daughter of Reb Sender, a well-to-do merchant. Sender made a pact with Chonen's long-dead father that Chonen and Leah would one day marry, yet he breaks the pact and promises Leah to another young man whose family will bring financial opportunities. Chonen dies in despair over this betrayal, returning as a malevolent spirit – a *dybbuk* – possessing Leah's body. Sender sends for Rabbi Azriel, an exorcist, in hopes of freeing Leah from the *dybbuk*'s hold. After an epic struggle, Azriel succeeds at the cost of Leah's life, and the lovers, destined to be together, are united in another world. (Ansky, an ethnographer, learned of an actual incident in a small town where a monument was erected to a bride and groom killed on their wedding day in the eighteenth century.) Kushner maintains Ansky's basic plot and archetypal characters, introducing more dimensions into their personas, adding more complicated ideas of sexuality and stressing conflicts between Old World traditions and the dawning of modernity. These conflicts in Ansky's play, written as Modernist thought, widespread immigration and technological developments hastened the disappearance of traditional Eastern European Jewish life, are carried further by Kushner, who adds allusions to the coming Holocaust, the profound impact of technological progress and the resultant religious scepticism springing from both.

Kushner's most significant embellishment is in the introduction of scepticism in the character of Rabbi Azriel, whose own faith is shown to be deeply shaken by the multiple tragedies of the world and, in particular, the agonies of Chonen and Leah. Ansky's rabbi is a one-dimensional man of faith; in introducing ambivalence to the character, Kushner reveals his own mistrust of patriarchal tendencies in Judaism and, in fact, of most ancient religions. As a homosexual, Kushner condemns the long history of homophobia in religious tradition by imbuing *A Dybbuk* with homoeroticism, as when rabbinical students indulge in an orgiastic dance. Kushner critiques sexual repression in general with the conventional romantic passions of Chonen and Leah. For example, Kushner's Chonen delivers a passionate recitation of the 'Song of Songs' for Leah while stressing that Chonen, as the *dybbuk*, penetrates Leah's body in a sensual merger of spirituality and sexuality.

Kushner imagines Ansky's scepticism and the impact of European political upheavals emerging in that period as central to the play's continued viability. The intense intellectual debates on social and spiritual issues combine with fevered flights of fantasy in Kushner's adaptation as in his own plays. He grapples with social circumstances, the cultural and religious heritage of his characters and their contradictory emotions and desires, particularly regarding love and faith. *A Dybbuk*, like Kushner's other plays, evokes an anxious and troubled humanism. Kushner substantially restructures Ansky's text into a Brechtian episodic framework as in his early original plays from *A Bright Room Called Day* to *Slavs!*, a structure he moves away from, or significantly modifies, in the later, more cinematic *Homebody/Kabul* and *Caroline, or Change*. He brings to *A Dybbuk* the guarded optimism of his major plays, tempered by Postmodern doubt. Hope springs from the lessons learned from loss that Kushner stresses in his own plays, and in *A Dybbuk* he enhances those qualities of Ansky's text. Chonen is unable to bear the loss of Leah in this world, yet wins her in the next. Wrongs may ultimately be righted, Kushner implies, and the universe may be put in order, although not in expected ways.

As previously noted, Kushner foreshadows the coming horrors of the Holocaust which finally obliterated the Old World that Rabbi Azriel feels slowly slipping away, most obviously in the onstage arrival of Azriel in a railroad boxcar, a visual reminder of the forced transportation of Jews to Nazi death camps. More overtly, he offers a scene in which Azriel's Scribe records the exorcism and is stunned when an unseen hand fills a blank page with a description of the unimaginable horrors Jews will face only decades hence. Kushner's contemporary awareness negotiates an uneasy truce between fundamental religious faith (and mysticism) and the secular (and real) world. In his adaptation of Ansky's *A Dybbuk*, Kushner's focus on the historical ravages of the past, the fearfulness of a future without traditional faiths, individual human longing for atonement and spiritual redemption, and on honouring the dead and cherishing the living is intended to transform a dramatic curio into vital drama. Kushner's penchant for adapting plays by others, from his free adaptation of Corneille to his more faithful adaptations of Brecht's *The Good Person of Setzuan* and *Mother Courage and Her Children* (2006), provides evidence of his passion for international dramatic literature, especially those plays with the potential to speak to contemporary audiences, requiring only liberation from outmoded conventions and verbosity to deliver their messages. That the themes of these works extend those in Kushner's own original works simply confirms that his commitment to adaptation is a dimension of his search for the tools of language, style, structure and intellectual thought to enhance his own.

Homebody/Kabul (1999–2001)

Kushner's next full-length play did not appear in New York until 2001, though its genesis came in the 1990s at the request of an actress friend, Kika Markham, who asked Kushner to write a monologue for her to perform in the summer of 1999 at the Chelsea Theatre Centre. Kushner called it *Homebody*, a complex hour-long monodrama in which a middle-aged British woman is seen in her comfortable London home ruminating on her mild agoraphobia, unhappy marriage, troubled daughter and her flirtation with both the history and present circumstances of Afghanistan under Taliban rule. Over the subsequent two years, Kushner revised and expanded the work into a three-act, three-hours-plus epic, and in the late summer of 2001 the New York Theatre Workshop commenced plans and rehearsals for its premiere of the play. As they rehearsed, the terrorist attacks of 11 September 2001 occurred, bringing down New York's World Trade Center, damaging the Pentagon in Washington, DC, and killing plane loads of travellers as the terrorists used commercial airliners as bombs. As New York recovered from the disaster, *Homebody/ Kabul*, a disturbing drama about a British family drawn into the horrors of Taliban-ruled Afghanistan, opened to praise from critics who remarked on Kushner's prescience in his play's implication that the West could not afford to ignore threats from the East.

The play won the Obie Award for Best Off-Broadway Play and several critics' prizes, but Kushner went on to revise it for a 2003 production at Chicago's Steppenwolf Theatre under Frank Galati's direction, a production that moved to the Brooklyn Academy of Music that same year. Kushner stresses in *Homebody/Kabul*, as in earlier works, that social change becomes possible when the unstable dynamism of a chronically chaotic society or the acute turbulence of an important transition period shatters individual illusions of comfort and stability. Few lands have been as unstable as Afghanistan in the second half of the twentieth century, and Kushner considers the mayhem resulting from the historical legacy of colonization. The mother of the family, the titular 'Homebody', insists that those of the West living in comparable comfort and presumed safety are in grave danger of 'succumbing to luxury'.[10] She concludes that it might be better to live among the oppressed and suffering than to fade into a senescence built on ease and the arrogance resulting from the illusion of security. As in *Bright Room*, Kushner calls for engagement and activism, a willingness to aid those without luxury, though this particular path is fraught with multiple perils.

Kushner's characters are obliged to reap the consequences of choices that Western nations have made in response to the complexities of the Middle East. Fascinated by the vast history of Afghanistan, simultaneously a beautiful country, a wasteland of corruption and a hotbed of terrorism, the Homebody concludes a dizzyingly imaginative monologue about other worlds, particularly Afghanistan, as the play shifts from her cozy London living room to the wounded city of Kabul. Kushner explores the disturbing face of religious fanaticism as seen through the eyes of Priscilla, the Homebody's grown daughter, revealing his own aversion to the intolerance of religious zealots of any stripe. Kushner assails the Taliban for its misogyny and brutality, but humanizes other Afghani characters trapped by its tyranny.

Astonishingly, the Homebody departs from her comfortable London home, and her husband and daughter learn that she has gone to Kabul, where she has disappeared. Local Taliban officials claim that a badly dismembered body of a woman found on the streets are the remains of the Homebody, but Priscilla is unconvinced and, hidden under a burka, she leaves the relative safety of a motel room for the dangerous streets of the city in search of her mother or, at least, the full story. On her own in Kabul, Priscilla finds herself a guide, a poet who shows her the world her mother has either embraced or been destroyed by, a city, Kushner suggests, stamped by the myth that Cain's grave may be located within its environs. Ironically, its purported location is now a Taliban minefield, and Priscilla, wandering the figurative minefield that is Kabul, receives the startling news that her mother may be alive and living as the wife of a well-to-do Muslim. This character is never seen, but his Afghani wife, Mahala, is. Her rage at both the Taliban and the West is disquieting and in this Kushner's globalism takes on a darkly bitter edge.

Mahala, a former librarian who, like the Homebody, reveres language and books and is a woman of intellect and dignity, is obliged to beg Priscilla's help to escape Afghanistan. The constant terror and isolation, she reveals, are causing her to forget the alphabet, an insupportable loss. Mahala spews rage in various dialects demonstrating Kushner's facile manipulation of and appreciation for language. Priscilla grows in wisdom from this encounter, ruefully noting that Mahala 'isn't mad, she's fucking furious. It isn't at all the same' (80). If oppressions are severe enough, Kushner posits, they will lead inevitably to either the defeat of total resignation or an unending fury that true survivors require to soldier on.

Whether or not the Homebody is dead or alive is never confirmed, but this is not what interests Kushner. The violent collision of cultures, as the Homebody explains, is what intrigues him: 'Ours is a time of connection; the private, and we must accept this, and it's a hard thing to accept, the private is gone. All must be touched. All touch corrupts. All must be corrupted'(2). This corrupting touch may eventually bring greater understanding, but in the short term the shattered lives of both the citizenry of Kabul and the visiting Westerners are the result. Priscilla's yearning, desperate search for her missing mother expands into a deeper comprehension of difference and for the connection the Homebody insists is essential, both among nations and peoples.

The theoretical underpinnings of *Homebody/Kabul* emerge to some degree from Kushner's interest in Raymond Williams, most notably Williams's phrase 'thinking about the longstanding problems of virtue and happiness',[11] which Kushner interprets as a sceptical faith in progress, in the transformative power of compassion and in the perhaps unattainable dream of a true world community. He knows what progress costs – the process is painful, even destructive, and its benefits are hard won – but despite it all, progress is necessary and, in fact, inevitable. The purposeful dramatist, Kushner theorizes, is by nature overtly political and is likely to fit into one of two distinct categories: 'the ones who ask small questions but give great answers (the traditionalists) and the ones who ask huge questions and often, as a consequence of the ambitiousness of their questioning, fail to give good answers or even any answers at all (the experimentalists, the vessel breakers); both are necessary'.[12]

Speaking of *Homebody/Kabul*, Kushner explains that no theatre-goer attends a play about Afghanistan expecting an easy night, adding that he depends on 'an audience really wanting to ask a lot of questions and be asked to do a certain amount of thinking'.[13] His plays, from *Angels* to *Homebody/Kabul*, have engendered controversy, but Kushner believes that 'a God who gave us powers of creation, curiosity and love' would not then 'command us to avoid the ideas and art these powers produce'.[14] A society too fragile to value a questioning spirit is in danger of losing the best of itself, he posits; Kushner assumes his audience seeks interrogation, even as the inflamed post-9/11 patriotism that rose while *Homebody/Kabul* made its first run seemed to curtail dissent.

History and culture intersect in this epic play, an epic in both the classic and the Brechtian senses. Its theatrical fusing of the past, current events and Kushner's imaginings demonstrate theatre's transformative power and ability to clarify and frame difficult questions. *Homebody/Kabul*, James Reston, Jr writes, is for 'those who can see through the fog of patriotism to the finer distinctions, who are finally ready to ask how on earth do we get out of this godforsaken place, who can bear to contemplate the thought that we have participated to some extent in our own tragedy'.[15] Kushner asks his audience to contemplate it. As John Heilpern notes, *Homebody/Kabul* depicts a 'journey without maps to the ravaged, symbolic center of a fucked-up universe'. He has described the play as a 'towering drama' about lost civilizations and unsolvable paradoxes, furious differences and opposites, and disintegrating, rotting pidgin cultures. It's about desolation and love in land-mined places, child murderers and fanatics, tranquilized existence and opium highs, travel in the largest sense of the word – travel of the mind and soul. To where? An unknowable mystery, perhaps, where all confusion is banished.[16]

Homebody/Kabul's haunting timeliness contemplates love and connection, war, guilt, displacement, loss and the complex maze of history to ask complex questions about the present moment while illuminating hard lessons of the past.

Conclusion

Throughout the decade, Tony Kushner's success as a playwright paralleled a frustrating encounter with the movie business. As early as 1990, Universal Pictures optioned *The Illusion*, Kushner's Corneille adaptation, and in 1995 he was announced as writer of *The Mayor of Castro Street*, a film about the life of Harvey Milk starring Dustin Hoffman, though neither film came to fruition. During the 1990s, however, Kushner completed several screenplays, including *East Coast Ode to Howard Jarvis*, which commemorates the elderly Californian who led a grassroots tax revolt in 1978 aimed at curbing burgeoning property taxes. Jarvis became a populist icon and inspired similar tax revolts in other states. *East Coast Ode* was completed for Showtime television in 1996, but never produced. As with Kushner's plays, the collisions between politics and human nature are central to *East Coast Ode*, a work Kushner frequently read at colleges and universities during the late 1990s.

In 1995, Kushner completed *Grim(m)*, a teleplay inspired by the Brothers Grimm story *Two Journeymen*, focusing on Amanda, a young African American teacher, struggling to do right by her students in a poor Bronx school at the time of the 'Republican Revolution' and Newt Gingrich's 'Contract with America' in the mid-1990s.

Despite frustrating delays during the 1990s, Kushner ultimately found screen success, first with the HBO adaptation of *Angels in America* in 2003, directed by Mike Nichols and starring Meryl

Streep (in multiple roles), Al Pacino, Justin Kirk, Emma Thompson, Jeffrey Wright and Mary Louise Parker, among others.[17]

As the new millennium dawned, Kushner's rich oeuvre expanded with such works as the naturalistic domestic drama on economics, *The Intelligent Homosexual's Guide to Capitalism and Socialism with a Key to the Scriptures* (2009) and one-acts including an original opera (with music by Jeanine Tesori), *A Blizzard on Marblehead Neck* (2011), concerning the last days of Eugene O'Neill, and multiple essays on art, culture, gender and politics.

'The moments in history that interest me the most are of transition,'[18] Kushner said at the time of *Hydriotaphia, or The Death of Dr. Browne*'s 1998 productions. The play, originally presented in 1987, is an 'epic farce', a wild flight of intellectual and theatrical fantasy centred on an obscure historical figure, Sir Thomas Browne (1605–82), a seventeenth-century philosopher, writer and scientist. Browne's life is imagined as an embodiment of the emergence of the Industrial Revolution and the resulting capitalist greed, the human price of economic inequity, a subject often present in Kushner's work.

Kushner has often spoken of the guiding principle of his work, a '[p]essimism of the intellect, optimism of the will',[19] which merges a clear-eyed view of socio-political realities with guarded hopefulness about change and activism in achieving progressive change. Kushner's political activism is firmly tied to his art: good politics produce good aesthetics, he believes, and he remains alert to the raw edges of contemporary life and to those pressure points of our present international problems. Perhaps most importantly, he challenges his audience instead of providing satisfying answers to the unanswerable.

His work as a writer and his life as a politically engaged artist require, in Kushner's view, a belief in progressive change even in the face of personal or societal circumstances mediating against hope. For Kushner, finding hope through an exploration of the past, an engaged spirit in the present and openness to the unknowable future is not only an inspiration for his work, but also a strategy for survival.

Despite influences from classical to modern European theatre, Kushner's ambitious, boldly theatrical and overtly political style has been a revitalizing factor in contemporary American drama. His influence may ultimately equal that of O'Neill, Williams and

Miller (all of whom influenced him), for while his contemporaries Sam Shepard and David Mamet, among others, present increasingly minimalistic and fundamentally realistic dramas, Kushner provides a model for an American drama boldly mixing epic theatre, fantasy and lyric realism to explore history and politics. The ideals and moral issues of the American past and present facing the nation in the future has been the frequent terrain of the plays in Kushner's oeuvre. As gay activist playwright Larry Kramer has stated, Kushner is 'drunk on ideas, on language, on the possibility of changing the world',[20] and, at the same time, as John Lahr proclaims, Kushner guides his audience to 'that most beautiful, divided, and unexplored country – the human heart'.[21]

Kushner believes that the tragedies of the human heart – real and fictional – can inspire change, not only for society, but also for individuals, including the playwright himself. In bringing aspects of his own autobiography to the stage, like many of the greatest American dramatists, Kushner emphasizes that existence means learning to live with loss, political conflict and moral confusion. Belief in progress, however painful, and the transformative power of love, compassion and forgiveness, makes negotiating the rocky terrain of existence possible. As a gay man, a Jew, a political leftist and a Postmodern metatheatricalist, Kushner seems situated outside the traditional American mainstream, yet he continues to be guided by his mantra 'pessimism of the intellect, optimism of the will', focusing his gaze on the ways the past follows the present into the future – and what can be learned from this dynamic. The hard-won wisdom and strategies of survival found on this journey may lead to belief in the possibility of change and an improved world. The stage can be the conduit for such change, Kushner believes, because it is a realm for representing a movement into the light and out of the darkness of Postmodern isolation toward an unknowable, and perhaps frightening, future, which, in Kushner's view, is the sole path possible.

6

Suzan-Lori Parks

Kevin J. Wetmore, Jr

Introduction

The 1990s is the decade in which Suzan-Lori Parks became 'Suzan-Lori Parks', the American theatre phenomenon. The decade began with her winning an Obie for her 1989 play *Imperceptible Mutabilities in the Third Kingdom*, which premiered at Brooklyn Arts and Culture Association (BACA), directed by Liz Diamond. Five major plays followed in the decade: *The Death of the Last Black Man in the Whole Entire World* (BACA, 1990), *Devotees in the Garden of Love* (Actors Theatre of Louisville, 1992), *The America Play* (Yale Rep/New York Public Theater, 1994), which also had its text published in *American Theatre*, *Venus* (New York Public Theater, 1996) and *In the Blood* (New York Public Theater, 1999). She also wrote three radio plays: *Pickling* (1990), *Locomotive* (1993) and *The Third Kingdom* (1993), as well as four screenplays, two unproduced: *Gal* (1997) and *God's Country* (1997); and two produced: *Anemone Me* (Apparatus, 1992) and Spike Lee's *Girl 6* (40 Acres and a Mule, 1996). The decade ended with her writing the Pulitzer Prize-winning *Topdog/Underdog* in three days while premiering the Pulitzer finalist *In the Blood*. In that decade she demonstrated herself to be a protean dramatist, an Eshu figure whose every drama refigures the previous ones.

Susan Lori Parks was born to Donald and Francis Parks on 10 May 1963 in Fort Knox, Kentucky, the second of three children.[1] Due to her father's military career, she and her siblings frequently moved in their youth, spending a period of time in West Germany when Parks was in junior high school. As a child she was an avid reader, drawn to mythology and folklore. She attended Mount Holyoke College where she took a fiction class in 1982 with James Baldwin, who encouraged her to write plays. She graduated Phi Beta Kappa in 1985 with a double major in English and German. Her senior thesis, *The Sinner's Place*, was subsequently performed at a new play festival at Hampshire College. She then spent a year studying at London Drama Studio before returning to the United States and moving to New York City. Her time in London was primarily spent studying acting, not writing. Parks aimed to deepen her understanding of performance in order to be a better writer. In 1987 her first New York play, *Betting on the Dust Commander*, premiered at the Gas Station in Brooklyn, directed by Laurie Carlos.[2] The one-act concerns a married couple in Kentucky in the 1950s that recall meeting and marrying and then repeat the scene in a manner to suggest their lives together have been suffocating and unfulfilling. Although the scenes are fairly linear in presentation, the repetition of the scene already contains hints of the unique dramaturgy Parks would develop throughout the 1990s.

It is not an exaggeration to state that Parks has transformed the theatrical landscape in the past two and a half decades. Philip C. Kolin has maintained that 'her plays have recast and reconfigured the American theatre'.[3] Her career reads like a list of superlatives and firsts. She was the first African American woman to win the Pulitzer Prize for drama (after being shortlisted for *In the Blood* in 2000) and was a finalist again with *Father Comes Home from the Wars (Parts 1, 2, 3)* in 2015. Parks has changed the world of theatre, especially with *365 Days/365 Plays*, which in 2006 was the largest single, simultaneous world premiere and quite possibly the largest theatrical event in history. Parks decided in 2002 to write a play a day for a year, and then offered the resulting script to be presented in 14 regional 'hubs', as well as a university hub and an international hub, with each theatre company taking a week's worth of plays. So each hub had fifty-two companies performing the 365 plays over the course of a year, resulting in thousands of performances featuring thousands of artists. As Parks herself notes in the published script, 'it may also encourage us to radically change the way we produce/create/ critique/enjoy/think about/talk about theatre and the world ... As one colleague in Los Angeles said recently, "*365* isn't just a play, it's a movement!".'[4]

As I have argued elsewhere, writing about Parks's *oeuvre* for any period of time is particularly challenging 'because her most recent play does not fit into a preconceived notion or theory of what a "Suzan-Lori Parks play" is'.[5] Or, as Monte Williams wrote in the *New York Times* in 1996,

> Ms. Parks has been defying easy categorization in all her professional life. Critics have called her productions elliptical and, in places, purposefully unclear. One reviewer advised theatregoers looking for plays with neat little meanings, conventional narrative and character development to forgo Ms. Parks' nonlinear epics ...[6]

Parks herself insists there is no such thing as 'a Suzan-Lori Parks play' because she changes her writing with every play.

Her influences, both self-stated and argued by scholars, are many and varied: Greek tragedy, Shakespeare, William Faulkner, Gertrude Stein, the absurdist playwrights such as Samuel Beckett, Eugène Ionesco, Luigi Pirandello and Jean-Paul Sartre, not to mention Ntozake Shange, Adrienne Kennedy and James Baldwin. Her plays often form intertexts with their works, but Parks is a unique dramatist in her own right.

Her first major play, *Imperceptible Mutabilities in the Third Kingdom*, received a great deal of praise from the critics and heralded Parks's emergence on the Off-Broadway stage as a major new voice in both experimental theatre and African American theatre. *The Death of the Last Black Man in the Whole Entire World*, the second major work by Parks in New York, was recognized as further establishing Parks's dramaturgical structure, style and language.

In 1992, *Devotees in the Garden of Love* was commissioned by the Humana Festival, Actors Theatre of Louisville, as half of a double bill with David Henry Hwang's *Bondage* titled 'Rites of Mating'. The play takes the form of a drawing room comedy set in a war zone. Three Black women in white wedding dresses, including a mother and a daughter, are watching an offstage battle from atop a hill. The women's language of romance is set in contrast to the violent, never-ending battle playing out on the field below. Deborah Geis has described the play as 'a parody of the rhetoric ... in women's magazines ... that promise transcendence ... through the act of falling in love'.[7]

In 1993, Parks was named in the *New York Times* '30 artists under 30 and likely to change the culture for the next 30 years' list.[8] She also wrote *Locomotive* and *The Third Kingdom* (radio plays) produced by New American Radio. Much of the year was spent in workshop productions of *The America Play* at Arena Stage and Dallas Theater Center.

The following year, *The America Play* premiered at Yale Repertory Theatre and the New York Public Theater and was simultaneously published in the Theatre Communications Group's (TCG) *American Theatre* magazine. TCG would publish the script in Parks's collection of plays, *The America Play and other Plays*, the following year.[9] Five other plays are in the volume, including *Imperceptible Mutabilities in the Third Kingdom* and *Death of the Last Black Man in the Whole Entire World*.[10] In 1995, Parks also received the Lila Wallace-Reader's Digest Writers' Award.

Two major projects manifested in 1996. The first was the premiere of *Venus* at the New York Public Theater directed by avant-garde auteur Richard Foreman (a controversial choice of director, as discussed below). Parks also wrote the screenplay for Spike Lee's film *Girl 6*, a comedy about an aspiring actress named Judy (Theresa Randle) who takes a job as a phone sex operator in order to make ends meet after growing frustrated by the treatment of women in the entertainment industry. Although remarkably mainstream for Parks, the film still echoes many of her concerns and motifs (all of the women who work at the phone sex business are solely identified by number, for example, and the film examines the separation of voice from body as women are objectified on the phone). Parks was partly drawn to the project, she claims, because she worked as a phone sex operator when she first arrived in New York in the late 1980s.

On 6 January 1999, Suzan-Lori Parks began writing *Topdog/Underdog*, finishing the script in three days. It eventually played on Broadway and won Parks the Pulitzer Prize for drama in 2002. The year 1999 was also the one in which *In the Blood*, discussed below, premiered at the Public, followed rapidly in 2000 by its fraternal twin, *Fucking A*. In 1999, *Time* magazine also included Parks in the list of '100 Innovators for the Next New Wave'.

Parks has written extensively about her own stylistic inventions and thematic concerns, primarily through a series of linked essays on style in her published plays. When TCG published *The America Play and Other Works*, the volume also contained the first essay by Parks in a series entitled 'Elements of Style', featured in every TCG-published volume of Parks's except *Venus*. The 'Elements of Style' essay in *The America Play and Other Plays* is among the longest and introduces the central idea of her work: repetition and revision, or, as she calls it, 'Rep & Rev', defined by her as the core of jazz, which she states is arguably the most significant cultural influence on her work. She is writing jazz.[11] Let's unpack these two key concepts so integral to Parks: 'Rep and Rev' and dramaturgy as music, especially since Parks herself links them in 'Elements of Style'.

'Rep and Rev' is the concept most associated with Parks's dramaturgy. Repetition and revision: do it again, do it differently. It is a model she has followed since *Betting on the Dust Commander*. The practice allows Parks to 'unmoor' (to use Heidi J. Holder's term) history, people and events from their context, and signify in a new way on them.[12] Parks states that through 'Rep & Rev' she is 'working to create a dramatic text that departs from the traditional linear narrative style to look and sound more like a musical score'.[13] For example, in *The America Play*, and many others, she does not use the word 'pause' in the text. Instead, she writes 'rest'. She told Michele Pearce that 'rest' is a musical term, a break in the score before the playing continues.[14] Her rests are not a pause, a break in the action, but rather an active silence in between sounds. Director and frequent Parks collaborator Liz Diamond refers to approaching Parks's scripts as musical scores, looking 'for its rhythmic patterns', recognizing that Parks 'herself is a musician ... so the musicality in the plays is part of Parks's makeup'.[15]

The concept of 'Rep & Rev' is also integral to jazz, as Parks indicates: 'the composer or performer will write or play a musical phrase once and again and again; etc. – with each revisit the phrase is slightly revised'.[16] She calls it 'a drama of accumulation'. Rather than following a linear arc in a narrative, she finds meaning in the accumulated differences between repeated texts.[17]

Nicole Hodges Persley argues that Parks's canon, in particular the history plays such as *Venus* and *The America Play* that directly engage with problematic histories, can be examined through hip-hop theory, identifying sampling and remixing as two of Parks's dramaturgical strategies.[18] Parks 'samples' characters and themes to construct her narratives, especially visible in *The Death of the Last Black Man in the Whole Entire World*, which samples Richard Wright, the Bible, history and even James Joyce. Parks also remixes the past in the present, tragedy into comedy, and repeats the themes, lines and rhythms again. This, argues Persley, allows Parks to create 'a sonic remix of American history that challenges African Americans to define their own positions within and outside dominant discourses in order to shape new imaginings of blackness in the future'.[19]

To 'Rep' and 'Rev', I have suggested elsewhere that Parks might add 'ref' – reference, similar to Persley's theory of sampling. Parks's plays are never self-contained but always refer to other texts, including and often her own.[20] *The America Play* contains selections from *Our American Cousin*, the play President Lincoln was watching when he was assassinated. *In the Blood* and *Fucking A* are both riffs on Nathaniel Hawthorne's *The Scarlet Letter*. *Imperceptible Mutabilities in the Third Kingdom* contains an extended riff on the television programme *Mutual of Omaha's Wild Kingdom* and its host, Marlin Perkins. Lastly, *Topdog/Underdog* seems to be a remix of *The America Play*, featuring an African American man whose job is to impersonate Lincoln and allow people to pretend to assassinate him. Her plays are almost always in conversation with other works.

After 'Elements of Style', the volume also contains an essay entitled 'An Equation for Black People on Stage', one of Parks's most open statements concerning race in relation to her plays, and one which might serve as a model for how to 'shape new imaginings of blackness in the future'. For Parks, the problem is that too often the theatre (and African American theatre specifically) defines 'Black' through its 'non-whiteness', instead of its own thing.[21] Parks seeks to move beyond the simple binary of White oppressor–Black oppression, and the idea that there is always a white presence in a Black play. 'There is no such thing as THE Black Experience,' she insists.[22] There is no single African American experience; nor a single way to represent the experiences of African Americans. The first role of her drama is to refute any sense of a monolithic Black community.

Yet, she also seeks to define the elements that go into the creation of a Black identity and Black history. The one statement which might summarize her work of the decade, from *Imperceptible Mutabilities in the Third Kingdom* to *Topdog/Underdog*, is 'I'm continually encouraging myself to explore The-Drama-of-the-Black-Person-as-an-Integral-Facet-of-the-Universe.'[23] She states that she works to avoid 'insidious essentialism' and instead embrace 'infinite variety'.[24] The scholars and critics would seem to agree that she has succeeded in doing so. What Philip Kolin and Harvey Young affirm concerning *Imperceptible Mutabilities in the Third Kingdom* could summarize her canon of the 1990s: 'Parks's dramaturgy rewrites, reimagines, and restores a black historical presence.'[25]

History is, of course, another preoccupation of Parks's: 'I take issue with history because it doesn't serve me – it doesn't serve me because there isn't enough of it.'[26] This statement echoes a quotation from *The Death of the Last Black Man in the Whole Entire World* about writing history down so the future cannot claim that it never happened, discussed at greater length below. And yet, as Parks told Han Ong, 'I'm a poet – I'm not a journalist.'[27] She does not set out to dramatize history as it happened but rather to use the theatre to engage with history as an unstable narrative. She recognizes that the history of Black people in America is far from complete, filled with inaccuracies and riddled with vast holes. Parks seeks not only to redress the gaps; she seeks to make audiences think about how language makes those holes to begin with. For example, the name of the title character in *The Death of the Last Black Man in the Whole Entire World* is 'Black Man with Watermelon', which not only evokes a stereotype, but also evokes stereotyping, forcing the audience to think about why that stereotype exists in the first place. In asking that question, the entire historical construction of Black stereotypes is opened up for examination. Any discomfort the audience feels becomes a form of acknowledging one's complicity with that culture. Significantly, she does so through unrelenting humour (also linguistically based): 'I can get more out of history if I joke with it than if I shake my finger at it and stomp my feet.'[28] Parks's plays engage deep subject matter, but they are inherently funny.

Another major motif in Parks's work is the Black body – specifically, the studying/surveying and surveilling/examining of the Black body on display, especially the female Black body. *Venus*,

Imperceptible Mutabilities in the Third Kingdom, *Devotees in the Garden of Love* and *In the Blood* all feature female Black bodies on display to the audience and to the onstage audience for pleasure, for sex, to control. Parks highlights the objectification of Black female bodies as sites of sexual desire. The Black male body, on the other hand, is objectified as a site of violence. People pay to pretend to shoot the Foundling Father of *The America Play* in the head. The title character of *The Death of the Last Black Man in the Whole Entire World* is repeatedly killed or the damage to his body reported by choral figures onstage. In *In the Blood*, Hester La Negrita kills her own son Jabber for calling her a slut.

Heidi J. Holder identifies a 'preoccupation with death, endings and aftermaths' in Parks's work and her tendency to 'begin, rather than end with death'.[29] The irony, of course, is that by beginning with endings, her plays resist synthesis and closure, and often tend toward the circular, if not a non-linear openness. Several of her plays begin with the death of the protagonist. After The Foundling Father's opening monologue in *The America Play*, an individual dressed as John Wilkes Booth enters and shoots him in the head, the Foundling Father then 'slumps in his chair' and subsequently refers to those who shoot him as 'killers'.[30]

Venus opens with the proclamation that the title character is dead:

The Negro Resurrectionist I regret to inform you that thuh Venus Hottentot iz dead.
All Dead?[31]

The proclamation of her death ('I regret to inform you that thuh Venus Hottentot iz dead') is repeated three more times in the brief opening scene. She then enters. Similarly, *The Death of the Last Black Man in the Whole Entire World* begins with an announcement of the death of the title character, which will be frequently repeated throughout the play: 'This is the death of the last black man in the whole entire world' and then Black Woman with a Drumstick explains how he 'dieded' when he fell twenty-three storeys yesterday (101–2). The dead in Parks's plays are the returned dead – not just spirits but also the corporeal dead. The dead come to life. The Last Black Man in the Whole Entire World dies several times during the play named for him and continues to narrate his tale. The Venus Hottentot is dead but actively present in her play as well.

Parks's non-naturalistic approach partly explains how plays can begin with the death of the main character, who then continues to appear throughout the rest of the play. Also of significance is Parks's structure of time in her plays. The play is always 'now'. Shawn-Marie Garrett observes that Parks writes in 'a space of simultaneity'.[32] Everything that happens, happens in the present moment. There is no past, and a potential future never arrives. Every present moment becomes a past moment. Every past moment was once a present moment. In Parks's temporal geography, it is always now, which makes it possible to explore trauma, memory and constructed and performed identity since the moment of trauma is not in the past but still here. The memory is not only remembered, it is repeated and revised onstage.

As such, metadrama and metatheatre play a key role in all of Parks's plays.[33] *Venus* and *The America Play* contain plays within the plays. Her settings are often popular entertainments: sideshows, theme parks, theatres and television programmes. Even in *Devotees in the Garden of Love*, the offstage battle being waged is simply an entertainment for the women watching. The plays from the 1990s are full of performance and characters aware that they perform, which makes the plays self-reflexive; they constantly remind the audience of the performativity of the event. Parks frequently reminds the audience that they are watching (and just as often indicts them for simply watching). Her dramaturgy ensures that links are made between the choices of the onstage characters, especially choral characters that primarily watch the action onstage, and an audience she will not allow to remain passive. Young identifies a motif in Parks's work in which onstage choruses are linked with the audience; in doing so, Young argues, Parks 'makes a veiled critique of present-day, societal complicity in the objectification of others, and, in so doing, encourages her audiences to feel compassion for the black, female protagonist'.[34] He especially finds this motif in *Venus* and *In the Blood*, both analysed in greater detail below.

Lastly, Parks claims that an intense spirituality underlies all her work from this period and after. 'I write for God,' she has said, and argues for a process of creation which is divinely sparked and in which the words and ideas flow through her prophetically.[35] She has a tattoo on her wrist which states in Sanskrit 'Follow the Inner God', which she also describes as part of her creative process.

Imperceptible Mutabilities in the Third Kingdom (1989)

'Behind the imposing title "Imperceptible Mutabilities in the Third Kingdom" there is the voice of a thoughtful young playwright, Suzan-Lori Parks,' wrote Mel Gussow in his *New York Times* review of the production in late 1989, directed by Liz Diamond and marking the emergence of Parks onto the larger New York theatre scene.[36] Gussow went on to praise Parks's 'historical perspective and a theatrical versatility' and 'ingenuity and humanity', noting that her work reminded him of Adrienne Kennedy and Ntozake Shange.[37] The play won the Obie Award for Best Play in 1990.

Kolin and Young state, 'In *Mutabilities*, Parks explores the wide and stinging impact of slavery in America and its effects on black identity.'[38] In five scenes, 'Snails', 'Third Kingdom', 'Open House', 'Third Kingdom (Reprise)' and 'Greeks', Parks presents a series of scenes of African Americans encountering some aspect of their history or identity. In 'Snails', three African American women converse while spied upon by a naturalist who compares them with roaches and proposes extermination. One of the women then shares her first experience of things African while watching *Mutual of Omaha's Wild Kingdom*. In 'Open House', a former slave is dying and recalls the abuse she suffered at the hands of the children she helped raise. The scene links the Middle Passage with the Holocaust, with Miss Faith quoting statistics from *The Transatlanic Slave Trade* and Aretha eventually shouting 'Buchenwald! Buchenwald!' (a Nazi concentration camp) and stating that 'Nine million just disappeared' in the Middle Passage.[39] In 'Greeks', a Black marine sergeant is a good soldier whose family maintains a façade of happiness while he waits for his 'distinction'. Instead, he slowly goes blind. This scenario will be repeated in moments in *365 Days/365 Plays* and *Father Comes Home from the Wars*.

The eponymous 'Third Kingdom' has multiple meanings as demonstrated in the section called 'Third Kingdom'. In 'Part Two:

Third Kingdom', Kin-Seer, Us-Seer, Shark-Seer, Over-Seer and Soul-Seer tell 'where [we] comed from' – a ritualistic retelling of the Middle Passage that also mythically explains the history of humanity and reality (37). The world was split in two and the sea separated the two cliffs that made up the halves of the world. Over-Seer explains to the other Seers that the Third Kingdom is 'thuh space in between' which makes a 'Third Self' for those who travel across it (29). Or, as Jennifer Larson identifies it, 'The Third Kingdom evolves from the fragmentation of one world into two with a third space in between.'[40] This seemingly suggests both the Middle Passage (the space between Old World and New, in which Africans became African Americans) and the idea that the Third Kingdom is also the space between two people. Ritualized performances recreating the Middle Passage are not unique to Parks. They have been seen before and since onstage in ritualized contexts, most notably in Amiri Baraka's 1967 *Slave Ship* and August Wilson's 2003 *Gem of the Ocean*. In the former, subtitled 'A Historic Pageant', the horrors of the Middle Passage are dramatized through both image and sound to African drums and 'white voices' barking out orders on the ship; in the latter, the Middle Passage is reversed as Aunt Esther and Black Mary talk Citizen Barlow through a ritualized return to the City of Bones.[41] However, it is Parks's idea that the Middle Passage is a metaphor for the space between people and between worlds. A gap has been created and we must tell stories to fill that gap.

Larson also identifies the 'mutabilities' of the title as implying mutation, 'and this provides a valuable outline for understanding how language and identity co-exist'.[42] Language shifts and identity shifts may not be perceptible to us in the moment, but the title of the play seems to suggest an evolution of African American identity and language from the Middle Passage to the present.

The play is non-linear and the language is challenging. However, Parks links individual scenes about history and identity thematically in a non-literal, non-naturalistic manner that showcased her developing idiom. Gussow in the *New York Times* proclaimed, 'the title of the piece is entirely applicable. In this study of the Black experience from slavery to the present, the changes are almost invisible – like geological shifts in the earth.' The play already held the seeds for the plays to come: *The Death of the Last Black Man in the Whole Entire World* and *The America Play*. Yet crowds and critics were also struck by how much *The Death* was different from *Imperceptible Mutabilities*. It was the first indication that Parks does not do sequels and that each play would be its own unique thing.

The Death of the Last Black Man in the Whole Entire World (1989–92)

Parks's second major New York play, *The Death of the Last Black Man in the Whole Entire World*, further expanded her reputation and her dramatic milieu. While more fragmented in a sense than *Imperceptible Mutabilities*, it also represented a single narrative all the way through, thus setting up a key difference with the earlier play. In the *New York Times* review, Gussow, while proposing that her earlier work (specifically *Imperceptible Mutabilities*) was more precise, stated that *Death* 'has a rapturous feeling for the flow of ethnicity through language. Ms. Parks transforms patois into poetry.'[43] The play was not merely seen as an excellent play but was read as further proof of Parks's genius: 'Freewheeling and earthy, the play confirms Ms. Parks's indigenous theatrical talent.'[44]

The play presents stereotypical characters with names like 'Black Man with Watermelon', 'Black Woman with Fried Drumstick' and 'Old Man River Jordan', alongside evocative names designed to signify an African American history: 'Before Columbus', 'Queen-Then-Pharaoh Hatshepsut', 'Ham' and 'And Bigger And Bigger And Bigger', the last a reference to Bigger Thomas, the eponymous hero of Richard Wright's 1940 novel *Native Son*. The play begins with the characters identifying themselves and then informing the audience, 'This is the death of the last black man in the whole entire world.'[45] Gamble Major, the actual name of 'Black Man with a Watermelon', is then killed or has his death reported onstage multiple times: he bursts into flames, he is electrocuted, lynched, beaten and falls 23 floors to his death.

The play itself does not have a plot in the traditional sense. There is no narrative arc, no character striving for change and closure at the end. If anything, the play is a circular ritual with four important elements to note. First, that the play itself is concerned with violence toward Black bodies, and especially toward men of colour. Parks riffs on the history of Black men dying violent deaths in America from the Middle Passage to the present. Second, the play repeatedly expresses concern for how that history is reported. 'Yes and Greens Black Eyed Peas Cornbread' tells the audience, 'You should write that down and you should hide it under a rock', repeating the line several times (102). 'Yes and Greens Black Eyed Peas Cornbread' then warns:

> You should write it down because if you don't write it down then they will come along and tell the future we did not exist. You should write it down and you should hide it under a rock. You should write down the past and you should write down the present and in what in the future you should write it down ... You should hide it all under a rock so that in the future when they come along they will say the rock did not exist. (104)

The concern is that if the past and the present are not recorded, then others can erase them from history. The Black contributions to the United States as well as racist crimes are often erased from official histories. History must be recorded, protected and preserved while still recognizing that that history is itself questionable. Third, the play was profoundly shaped by Parks's own Roman Catholic upbringing, both in terms of ritual elements (ringing bells) and the overall structure of the play which reflects the Stations of the Cross.[46] Bells ring, words are intoned and the dramaturgy is meant to suggest the sacrifice of Christ.

Fourth and finally, this play is the one that truly established Parks's sense of perpetual simultaneity, as mentioned in the introduction, above. In *The Death of the Last Black Man* there is only now. This sense of nowness is most specifically articulated in the play when the Black Man with Watermelon proclaims:

> There is uh Now and there is uh Then. Ssall there is. I bein in uh Now: uh Now bein in a Then: I bein, in Now in Then, in I will be. I was be too but that's uh Then thats past. That me that was-be is uh me-has-been. Thuh Then that was-be is uh has-been-Then too. Thuh me-has-been sits in the be-me: we sit on this porch. Same porch. Same me. (126)

In *The Death of the Last Black Man in the Whole Entire World*, Parks links past, present and future, both on the personal level and on the historic level. The physical violence done to Black Man with Watermelon is the violence of the past, the present and, tragically, the future. But he also recognizes that humans are time-based creatures. We live in the now with a memory of the past and a plan of the future, all of which indicates the newness of every moment.

The America Play (1993)

By the premiere of *The America Play*, commissioned and developed by Theatre for a New Audience, New York City, and given workshop productions at Arena Stage and Dallas Theater Center (all in 1993), and at the Yale Repertory Theatre in January 1994, Parks's work had already received a great deal of support and attention. She had received a Whiting Foundation Writers Award, two National Endowment for the Arts playwriting fellowships, and grants from the Rockefeller Foundation, the Ford Foundation, the New York State Council on the Arts and the New York Foundation for the Arts. She had also been named an Associate Artist of the Yale School of Drama.

The play itself was written between 1990 and late 1993, with Parks claiming that on average it takes her five years to write a play from initial idea to first performance.[47] The premiere had been co-produced by Yale and the New York Shakespeare Festival, and after running from 13 January to 5 February in New Haven, the play was performed at the Public Theater in Manhattan from 22 February to 27 March. The Public's artistic director, George C. Wolfe, had wanted to commission a work from Parks, and this distinctive play was the result.

In the first act, the Foundling Father, a Black man with an uncanny resemblance to Abraham Lincoln and a gravedigger by trade, introduces himself and the world of the play. After completely making himself over as Lincoln, down to an entire collection of beards made from hair collected in a barbershop, the 'Lesser Known', as he also calls himself, attempted to have a career as a Lincoln impersonator. Although 'speechifying' as Lincoln did not earn him a living, letting people pretend to assassinate him with a gun full of blanks proved much more lucrative.

Parks's script lists the location as '*A great hole. In the middle of nowhere. The hole is an exact replica of The Great Hole of History.*'[48] Already Parks's penchant for wordplay is apparent. Instead of a founding father, the Black man is the 'foundling father'– the child abandoned by his parents with no sense of history or heritage. He attaches himself to Abraham Lincoln in order to have a sense of identity. 'The Great Hole of History' is also a homonym which is also an antonym. It is the 'hole' of history – a gap or maw into which everything falls. It is an absence. But it is also the 'whole' of history – it is everything. So the Great Hole of History contains everything and nothing simultaneously. But the Foundling Father must work at 'a replica' of it, not even the real Great Hole. There is nothing authentic in this experience in a theme park. Throughout the scene, individuals enter and shoot the Foundling Father in the head.

In the second half of the play, the audience is shown the actual hole and told the Lesser Known is dead. The Foundling Father's body is sought in the second half by Lucy, his wife, and Brazil, his son. Brazil refers to him as 'my foe father' (191), yet another of Parks's homonyms with multiple and contradictory meanings. 'Foe father' sounds and reads as African American vernacular English for 'forefather', the surface meaning of the text. However, it also sounds like 'foe father', as in the father who is one's enemy, not to mention 'faux father', a father who is not actually a father at all.

Lucy and Brazil dig for his bones and 'wonders' and discover the material detritus of America, including George Washington's teeth and a bust of Lincoln. Simultaneously, the Foundling Father appears on television and performs in scenes from *Our American Cousin*, the play Lincoln was watching when he was assassinated. As with *The Death of the Last Black Man*, there is no linear plot to follow and the structure and wordplay make the meaning of the piece complex, layered and subjective.

The *New York Times* review by Alvin Klein of the Yale Repertory production called the play 'a cerebral workout', 'neither fathomable nor cohesive' and 'jumpy', but also noted, '[Parks's] unanswerable questions are freeing, the verbal and temporal leaps, even the vastness of her intentions, are invigorating.'[49] In other words, the play is perplexing but possesses world-changing theatricality. During a preview for the Public Theater performances, Parks described the plot to a *New York Times* writer: 'A man is telling the story of his life and in the second act the family is coming to look for his remains; that's the story I want to tell.'[50] The family seeking to dig up and claim his remains is another literalization of a metaphor. They are digging through the (w)hole of history to find the Black man. Lucy and Brazil ironically dig holes in history in order to fill the holes in their history. The relics of the past are made present. This action ties the work to Parks's ongoing thematic concern with excavating history as both corrective and identity-creating.

Certainly the material world of the play is significant. The hole and the dirt that was displaced to make it, the assassin's gun, Washington's teeth and the other physical items of the play suggest a museum of sorts – our desire to link to the past combined with an inability to actually do so is somewhat ameliorated by being able to surround ourselves with the meaningful stuff of the past. Parks describes Lincoln as 'the sum of his outfit. You know, his beard ... and his hat, coat, vest and shoes.'[51] The 'Foundling Father' is not a true historic figure: he wears a costume to link him to the 'Greater Man', but it remains just that – a costume. His link to America's past and the Great Hole of History is one he himself has assumed as a costume, but there is no actual historic connection there. While the material world of the play is significant, Parks suggests that the stuff of history is just that – stuff, no different or more special than anything else, but which can be used to create an illusion of authenticity.

As the title suggests, this is a play about America, but also about how we understand 'America'. The programme and published script both have a quotation from John Locke: 'In the beginning, all the world was *America*,' which Parks states was to 'encourage people to think about the *idea* of America'.[52] For Locke, America represented the natural state that all human beings are born into, and that Europe's history and so-called civilized society moved one further away from this natural ideal. Parks, however, begins the play by deconstructing this idea. The Foundling Father represents both a critique of this Eurocentric, pejorative view of America and a reminder that part and parcel of the idea of America was the hypocritical irony that a nation founded on the principles of 'life, liberty and the pursuit of happiness' really only intended those principles to apply to property-owning White males, and that the exact opposite was the reality for all people of colour and White women. Parks wrote a play about myths, lies, history, time and memory – the myth of the nation, of 'America', but also the myth of Lincoln and the myth of the family. Even as the characters are aware of the myth and the artifice, they embrace it. To do otherwise is to leave yourself unmoored in the Great Hole of History, unattached to anything.

Venus (1996)

Venus earned Parks her second Obie Award but was also her most controversial play, based on the true story of Sartjie Bartmaan, a nineteenth-century Khoikhoi woman from what is now South Africa, brought to Europe and put on display as 'The Hottentot Venus', primarily due to her large buttocks.[53] In Parks's play, in 31 scenes, numbered backwards, the Venus arrives in England and is put on display by the Mother Showman who beats her, steals from her and invites men to rape her for money (Parks told Tom Sellar the Mother Showman is 'a sort of cross between P.T. Barnum and Mother Courage').[54] She is then brought to France by her lover (and exploiter), the Baron Docteur, and finally brought back to life by the Negro Resurrectionist. An ensemble plays all of the other characters in the play, including the 'Chorus of 8 Human Wonders', the other individuals in the side show. It is a play obsessed with bodies, both living and dead, and displays of bodies. It is also a play that reflects the objectification of the Black female body that was perpetuated in nineteenth-century Europe and America, along with the concurrent sexualization of that body. She is placed on display in a menagerie, implying bestiality as well as licentiousness.

Two controversies shaped the reception of the play at its premiere. The first was the Public Theater hiring of Richard Foreman to direct, which, according to Kolin and Young, 'compromised the expression of Parks's dramaturgical voice' with directorial overlays and conceptual designs seemingly unrelated to the play.[55] Numerous critics picked up on the tension between play and direction, and the play's reviews reflected these competing visions. 'That Richard Foreman, the revered playboy of the avant-garde, is the director for Ms. Parks's intense cause defeats it perversely,' wrote Alvin Klein in the *New York Times*, 'creating further distancing and reducing it to drivel and ostentation ... None of his recycled techniques ... serve Ms. Parks's material, intensifying its murkiness and killing all possibilities of emotional climax.'[56] Although Foreman received the brunt of Klein's scorn, the script was also criticized, with Klein concluding that *Venus* 'comes off as snob theatre, full of exclusivity, pretense and showy effects, signifying trendiness'.[57]

The second controversy had to do with the text itself and the complicity of the Venus in her own exploitation. Every time Venus has a decision to make she asks, 'Do I have a choice?' and is told, 'Just say yes', so she does. Critics took Parks to task for seemingly blaming the victim for her situation, but Parks resisted the easy categorization:

> I could have written a two-hour saga with Venus being the victim. But she's multifaceted. She's vain, beautiful, intelligent and, yes, complicit. I write about the world of my experience, and it's more complicated than 'that white man down the street is giving me a hard time.' That's just one aspect of our reality. As black people, we're encouraged to be narrow and simply address the race issue. We deserve so much more.[58]

For Parks, the Venus is not solely defined by her victimhood, her exploitation or her oppression, any more than she was defined by her buttocks. Parks also sees the Venus's willingness to go with the Baron Docteur as having a real-world equivalency of being 'like many poor people, willing to exchange her labor in order to get out of a poverty-stricken situation'.[59] The play does not set up a simple Black good/White bad dichotomy. 'Showing she has this much agency is not blaming the victim,' Parks asserts. 'Neither does it let the victimizer off the hook.'[60]

Although panned in its initial production, *Venus* has fared much better critically in subsequent productions in Canada and the United States. It is both Parks's most written-about play and the one most beloved by her fans. It is also unique in that it marked a move toward linear narrative, following a timeline and a character arc.

In the Blood (1999)

In the Blood was tremendously successful for a play that began as a joke. Parks tells the story that, 'I was in a canoe with a friend. We were paddling along a river or lake – this was years ago. I was in the back of the canoe and I said to her, "I'm going to write a play called 'Fucking A,' and it's going to be a riff on *The Scarlet Letter*. Ha, Ha, Ha." And I started laughing really hard.'[61] What began as a joke split into two plays that Parks refers to as 'almost-twins' and was subsequently published together as *The Red Letter Plays: Fucking A* and *In the Blood*.[62]

The play is a riff on Nathaniel Hawthorne's *The Scarlet Letter* (1850) and what Margo Jefferson calls 'American history and the larger pattern of sin, cruelty, punishment, and redemption'.[63] The novel begins with the public shaming of Hester Prynne, who has borne a child out of wedlock. She is led from the prison door to stand on a scaffold, holding Pearl, her illegitimate daughter, and wearing the 'A' so that every 'man, woman and child may have a fair sight of her brave apparel' and see that 'iniquity is dragged out into the sunshine!'.[64]

Already we are firmly ensconced in Suzan-Lori Parks's milieu: the female body on display for sexual pleasure. Shari Benstock sees the opening of the novel as parading 'the body of sin, or more accurately the woman's body as emblem of sin. The female body is both an agent of human reproduction and a field of representation,' symbolized on the scaffold by Hester's body, the infant child and the mandated 'A'.[65]

Similarly, *In the Blood* opens with a ritualistic shaming of Hester La Negrita, a single Black mother on welfare, as the entire company gathers on stage and shouts condemnations of her for giving birth to a fifth child:

All THERE SHE IS!
WHO DOES SHE THINK
SHE IS?
...

SHOULDN'T HAVE IT IF YOU CAN'T AFFORD IT
AND YOU KNOW SHE CAN'T

SHE MARRIED?
WHAT DO YOU THINK?
SHE OUTGHTA BE MARRIED
...

THIS IS HER FIFTH
FIFTH?
SHE GOT FIVE OF THEM
FIVE BRATS
AND NOT ONE OF THEM GOT A DADDY
...

SOMETHINGS GOTTA BE DONE TO STOP THIS SORT
    OF THING
CAUSE I'LL BE DAMNED IF SHE GONNA LIVE OFF ME[66]

In the Blood moves Hawthorne's narrative to a contemporary urban poor Black landscape, a new category in Parks's work, which tended toward the mythic and historic.

Parks's welfare mother engaged the discourse of the 'Welfare Queen', reported by Franklin Gilliam in 1999. Gilliam claimed that during the period from President Reagan through President Clinton, the media shaped a narrative of 'Welfare Queens' that portrayed the majority of people on public assistance as urban African American women who deserve public scorn:

> [P]oor women choose to be on welfare because they fail to adhere to a set of core American values. From this perspective, single motherhood, divorce, desertion and a failure to hold the family unit together become the causes of their impoverished condition. In short, welfare dependency is a function of the moral failings of poor women. Their unwillingness to adhere to the principles of hard work, family values and sexual control thus deem them as undeserving.[67]

This media-shaped attitude is a contemporary reflection of Hawthorne's own construction of sin and moral failing in the Puritan Boston colony during the early settlement of the nation. Furthermore, Gilliam states that although African American women represent only ten per cent of the individuals on welfare, the 'key image that emerges from the welfare queen script is that most women on welfare are African American'.[68] Whereas the dominant media representation of the average welfare recipient is an unmarried African American woman with multiple children by multiple fathers, Parks takes that image and deconstructs the social conditions which create both the image and the individual reality behind it. Just as Hawthorne indicates both the hypocrisy and the moral failings of the founding community, so too does Parks demonstrate the 'moral failing' of a society set upon exploiting and condemning the impoverished Black woman. The play critiques the image, but also holds up the experiences of Hester as her reality – it is one thing to say the media has created an image; Hester must actually live with the conditions that created the image and with the image as well.

In the Blood as a title carries great resonances, especially in the age of AIDS, the implication being that AIDS (which hit the African American community in far greater numbers than the Euro-American community) was the result of moral failings – homosexual sex, intravenous drug use or unprotected heterosexual sex – and therefore those who are HIV-positive somehow 'deserve it' or are directly responsible for their own plight. Such individuals then become carriers who could affect 'us', who are not in those categories, and thus must be protected from 'them'. The title also suggests the racial purity laws which mandated a Black identity if an individual possessed 'one drop of Black blood'. Illiterate and uneducated Hester, with her multi-ethnic children by different fathers, is thus the poster child for all of the social phobias of the late 1990s: welfare, miscegenation, AIDS, poverty and fear of African Americans. Her Black female body is commodified, exploited, used for pleasure (by all of the characters) but not pleasured itself, a recurring theme in Parks's work. When given the opportunity, she willingly agrees to her own exploitation in order to escape her situation. Hester is in many ways the great-granddaughter of the Hottentot Venus.

The remaining characters are played by five adult actors. Each actor plays one of her children – Jabber, Bully, Beauty, Trouble and Baby – as well as an adult who manipulates her. Each individual uses Hester for his or her own purpose and treats her as less than human. The Doctor (who goes under her skirt to give her an exam in the middle of the street) and Welfare Lady both want to sterilize her so she cannot have more children. Amiga Gringa ('White friend') steals from her, even as she looks down on Hester for sewing. Reverend D (based on Reverend Arthur Dimmesdale in Hawthorne), her lover and the father of her youngest child, refuses to publicly acknowledge her out of fear that it will damage his ministry, reputation and social status. Chili (the Roger Chillingworth character from *Scarlet Letter*), the father of Jabber, left her nine years ago and returns only to reject her again for being with other men in his absence.

Hester kills Jabber, her oldest child, for calling her 'slut'. He was the one who was teaching her how to read and write, so she writes a red 'A' in his blood next to his body. Larson reads this murder as a direct result of the social situation of the protagonist: 'Hester La Negrita, although she does bring sexual satisfaction to some of the play's characters and does attempt to feed and comfort her children, cannot respond to her oppression with compassion, and she turns to violence against her own child.'[69]

If *Venus* was and still is Parks's most controversial play, *In the Blood* was her most celebrated of the 1990s. The reviews were glowing, and Charlayne Woodard, who played Hester, received a number of accolades and award nominations. *New York Observer* theatre critic John Heilpern declared in his end-of-year summary that 'the award for best actress goes to Charlayne Woodard for her fantastic performance as Hester La Negrita in Suzan-Lori Parks's *In the Blood*. The tremendous love and waste and heartbreak within Ms. Woodard's utterly natural performance touched all hearts.'[70] Of the play itself Heilpern wrote, 'Ms. Parks's signal achievement here is to have put people we ignore, and never know, on stage.'[71] The *New York Times* review called the play 'extraordinary' and applauded Woodard as an actor who 'embodied with stunning coherence' the role of Hester, concluding, 'You will leave *In the Blood* feeling pity and terror. And because it is a work of art, you will leave thrilled, even comforted by its mastery.'[72]

Conclusion

In the decade and a half since *In the Blood*, Parks has remained inventive, prolific and mutable. The trajectories laid out in the 1990s have, for the most part, been followed, especially in the sense that every new play is a different kind of play, and that Parks continues to evoke many of the same themes, ideas and motifs that manifested in her work in the 1990s. In 2001, *Topdog/Underdog* premiered at the Public Theater and won the Pulitzer. In 2003, Parks published her first novel, *Getting Mother's Body*, which forms an intertext with Faulkner's *As I Lay Dying* (even her fiction is rev & rep & ref, sampling and mixing from other literature!).

As noted above, in 2002, Parks began writing a play a day for a year. In 2006, that project reached fruition in the year-long, nationwide *365 Festival*. In 2007, she wrote the book for the musical *Ray Charles Live!*, followed by co-adapting *Porgy and Bess* in 2011. In between those two projects, her straight play *The Book of Grace* was performed at the Public Theater in 2010. She won another Obie for *Father Comes Home from the Wars (Parts 1, 2 & 3)* in 2015, which was also nominated for Outstanding Play for the 2015 Lucille Lortel Awards and the 2015 Kennedy Award for Best Drama and was performed at the Public Theater.

Over the decade, Parks went from being an unknown playwright with a few New York credits to a major figure in world theatre whose work achieved the highest honours in American theatre. Her plays moved from a former gas station in Brooklyn to the Public Theater and Broadway. Her plays defined American theatre and America itself, while also offering a model for a new kind of dramaturgy and a new way of understanding African American identity.

Long-time collaborator Liz Diamond, an integral influence on the shape and reception of Parks's work in the 1990s, states that it is Parks's linguistic inventions and innovations, along with the cogent political content of her plays, that makes her such an important voice in American theatre:

> [I]t was the strangest, newest, most enticing playwriting I had ever read ... I had never heard language like that, theatrical poetry like that. I felt like I was in the presence of a completely new sound in the theatre ... I found her writing extraordinarily capacious in its themes, political concerns, psychological insight, and its passion.[73]

Diamond directed most of Parks's early New York plays and is credited by many, including Parks herself, with strengthening the stage performances of Parks's work. What seemed opaque on the page, Diamond was able to present vividly and with clarity onstage.

In the decade of the 1990s, Suzan-Lori Parks emerged as the singular most unique and significant voice in American theatre. In 1990, even in 1999, the Pulitzer, *365* and the Broadway shows were all still in the future. The major works from 1989 to 1999, however, demonstrate an arc – the development and evolution of a playwright determined to use a new dramaturgy to reflect upon African American identity and rethink how we tell stories and interrogate and deconstruct history. Before she was thuh Suzan-Lori Parks of this writing, she was thuh Suzan-Lori Parks of Then. Those Thens of the 1990s are what made her the playwright of Now.

Afterword

Cheryl Black and Sharon Friedman

Introduction

The four playwrights selected as representative of American drama in the 1990s have continued to make vital contributions to dramatic literature throughout the first two decades of the twenty-first century, particularly if one broadens the conception of 'dramatic literature' to include musical books and opera libretti, performance art and film, and the conception of 'contributing to dramatic literature' to include teaching and fostering the work of other playwrights.

Recent history has demonstrated that American citizens living in the 1990s had reason to fear the new millennium, but the devastation did not come from the expected sources of a technological catastrophe or a latter-day viral plague. The disaster struck on 11 September 2001, when two US airliners piloted by al-Qaeda hijackers flew into the twin towers of the World Trade Center. The nation watched, horrified, as the towers collapsed. A third plane crashed into the Pentagon in Washington, DC, and a fourth into a field in Pennsylvania. In all, the attacks claimed nearly 3,000 lives and caused $3 trillion in damage. It would be the defining moment of the next two decades, resulting in an ongoing 'War on Terror' that has been carried on in Iraq, Afghanistan and Syria. A 'new normal' has emerged of increased surveillance and security measures in all public spaces. A Department of Homeland Security was created in 2002, and a 'Patriot Act' increased law officers' ability to use surveillance and searches in cases of suspected terrorism. Related 'fallout' from the war(s) carried on in the Middle East includes increasing Islamophobia, isolationism and neo-nativist opposition to immigration.[1]

During the decade examined in this book, America struggled somewhat more successfully with the attack that had come in the form of a disease – AIDS – that not only affected individuals and their families but also decimated whole communities. Three of this volume's featured playwrights – Terrence McNally, Paula Vogel and Tony Kushner – identify as gay or lesbian, and issues specificallyurgent to the LGBTQ community were addressed in some of the decade's most notable works, including Kushner's *Angels in America*, Vogel's *Baltimore Waltz* and McNally's *Lips Together, Teeth Apart* and *Love! Valour! Compassion!* The shattering physical, psychological and emotional impact of AIDS, the dread disease that disproportionately impacted gay men, figured prominently in each of these works. Their combined, passionate and eloquent voices, along with many others, shed light on this crucial issue, and by the end of the 1990s, progress had been made.

In April 2000, President Bill Clinton declared HIV/AIDS a threat to national security; awareness, diagnosis and treatments improved steadily as new cases and death rates in the US decreased substantially. Concomitantly, substantial progress was made in combating homophobia and winning civil rights for sexual minorities. In 2004, Massachusetts became the first state to legalize same-sex marriage, and by 2015 it was legal nationwide. It seems reasonable to credit theatre artists/activists like McNally, Kushner, Vogel and others for the significant role they played in raising awareness of and changing attitudes toward diverse sexualities with their authentic, complex and empathetic dramatic portrayals of gay and lesbian identities and experiences. Interestingly, all four playwrights married in the twenty-first century, and all of their unions would have been illegal in most US states at the time they were born. Paula Vogel married Anne Fausto-Sterling in Truro, Massachusetts, in 2004. Tony Kushner married Mark Harris in 2008 in Provincetown, Massachusetts (they had celebrated a commitment ceremony in 2003 in New York City). Terrence McNally married Tom Kirdahy in 2010 in DC (they had celebrated a civil ceremony in Vermont in 2003). Suzan-Lori Parks, who was four years old when the 1967 Supreme Court decision in *Loving v. Virginia* overruled state laws prohibiting interracial marriage, married Paul Oscher, a White man, in 2001.[2]

The ideology of White supremacy, ineluctably tied to hierarchal ideas about race, ethnicity, religion, class and nationality, has plagued American society since the nation's inception, and was another common theme among these playwrights – explicit and profound in all of Parks's works and Kushner's *Homebody/Kabul*, inherent in McNally's *A Perfect Ganesh*, Kushner's *Angels* and Vogel's *Desdemona* (written earlier but first produced in the 1990s). As the twenty-first century unfolded, the sophisticated, and even prescient, critiques manifested in these works resonated even more powerfully, as the events of 9/11 fanned smouldering prejudices against ethnic and religious others into flames. In the twenty-first century, racial tensions between Black and White Americans were exacerbated by, among other things, the distinctly racial component in America's war on terrorism and increasing unease at immigration from south of the US border. Despite America's election of its first African American president in 2008 (re-elected in 2012), relations between Black and White America have grown increasingly strained, and political priorities increasingly polarized. Multiple cases of unarmed Black men shot and killed by police officers or volunteer 'watchers', a retaliatory slaying of police officers by a lone gunman in Dallas, Texas, and a mass shooting by a White supremacist in a Black church in Charleston, South Carolina, seized headlines throughout the first two decades of the twenty-first century.

Race and ethnic identity continued as major themes in the works of Suzan-Lori Parks in the twenty-first century, with *Ray Charles Live!* (2007), *The Gershwins' Porgy and Bess* (2011) and *Father Comes Home from the Wars* (2014). Race and ethnicity loomed large in Tony Kushner's *Caroline, or Change* (2002), his co-authored screenplay for *Munich* (2005) and adapted screenplay for *Lincoln* (2012). The musical *Ragtime*, with book by Terrence McNally, provides a penetrating exploration of turn-of-the-century attitudes toward immigration and race relations. Ethnic and cultural, as well as gender and sexual, identities are intersecting themes in Paula Vogel's latest play, *Indecent*, inspired by Sholem Asch's *The God of Vengeance*, premiering Off-Broadway in 2016, and running on Broadway from April-August 2017. The continued efforts by these playwrights to wrestle with issues of race and ethnicity reflect current concerns. In a 2016 Gallup poll, immigration and racism/race relations were listed as the second and third most serious non-economic problems facing America today (gay rights was no. 22 on the list).[3]

Vogel and Parks offered vivid critiques of sexism and the sexual subjugation/ 'colonization' of the female body in works like Vogel's *Mineola Twins* and *How I Learned to Drive* (the 'mammary' plays), Parks's *In the Blood* and *Fucking A* (the 'Red Letter' plays) and *Venus*. Parks's plays particularly illustrate how race and class intersect with gender in the sexual exploitation of her female protagonists. In the twenty-first century, statistics documenting cases of rape and sexual violence are staggering, yet the issue didn't make the list of 36 non-economic problems enumerated in the poll cited above.

As America struggled to adjust to the new normal of constant, low-level anxiety from terrorist attacks and mass shootings on the domestic and international fronts, escalating tensions between ethnic groups in the US and the devastating effects of Hurricane Katrina (2005) – the costliest natural disaster in US history, causing the deaths of nearly 2,000 people and $81 billion in property damage – it also faced the worst financial crisis since the Great Depression, the crash of 2007–8. Stock markets plunged worldwide, the real estate market plummeted and only a bailout by national governments kept many of the world's major financial institutions from collapsing. Eight years later, Americans (as well as citizens around the globe) are still recovering from the effects of the recession that followed. In the poll cited above listing national concerns, the economy was indisputably the top priority, with a category all its own. Polls, however, make no attempt to illuminate the intersections between 'economic' (jobs, income gaps, corruption) and 'non-economic' (attitudes concerning race, gender, sexuality) phenomena. For such nuanced illuminations, we turn to artists/activists like the playwrights profiled in this book.

Class identity also remained a concern with this volume's focus playwrights. Class is ineluctably integrated in all of Parks's works from the 1990s and into the twenty-first century, as the characters that inhabit her most notable works (including *In the Blood*, *Fucking A* and *Topdog/Underdog*) confront hardships wrought by multiple, intersecting forms of discrimination. The central characters in the Civil War-era *Father Comes Home From the Wars* are enslaved. Class (as well as its intersection with other cultural 'locations' like gender, religion and sexuality) frequently manifests in Kushner's twenty-first-century works, particularly *Caroline, or Change*, his new translation of *Mother Courage and Her Children* (2006) and *The Intelligent Homosexual's Guide to Capitalism and Socialism with a Key to the Scriptures* (2009). In 2016, Kushner embarked on a collaboration with actor/director/producer Denzel Washington to help bring August Wilson's Pulitzer-winning play *Fences* to the screen, receiving credit as co-producer of the film. Class and intersecting oppressions are also significant factors in musicals for which McNally contributed books, including *Ragtime* (1998–2000) and *The Full Monty* (2000).

At the turn of the twenty-first century, Broadway was producing more new works than revivals, but revivals and musicals were more profitable. Despite the ongoing economic malaise of the second decade of the twenty-first century, Broadway enjoyed steadily increasing ticket sales, reporting a record high income of $1,373,253,725 for the 2015–16 season, up from the $1,365,232,182 recorded for 2014–15. The bad news? Average ticket prices in 2015–16 were $103.11,[4] a circumstance that would seem to gall playwrights of social conscience, a trait shared by the four featured in this book. Much of Broadway's boom is due to the spectacular and perennially-running 'megamusicals', like *Les Misérables* and *Phantom of the Opera*; the hugely popular 'movicals' (stage works adapted from animated or live-action films) including Disney's *The Lion King* and *Aladdin*, Dreamworks' *Shrek: the Musical* and Monty Python's *Spamalot*; juke box musicals like *Jersey Boys* and *Mamma Mia*; and acclaimed revisionings of iconic works like Stephen Sondheim's *Company* and *Sweeney Todd*.

Musicals embodying serious social critiques, however, also proved profitable – the groundbreaking *Rent*, which depicted racial and sexual diversity, economic exploitation and AIDS, among other themes, closed a twelve-year run in 2008. Successful musicals that satirized capitalism, corporate greed, religion, homophobia, racism and legal and political systems include *Urinetown: The Musical* (2001–3), *Avenue Q* (2003–9) and *The Book of Mormon* (2011–). Metatheatrical musicals that critiqued racial representation include *The Scottsboro Boys* (2010), *The Gershwins' Porgy and Bess* (2012, with revised book by Suzan-Lori Parks) and *Shuffle Along: The Making of the Musical Sensation of 1921* (2016). Perhaps fated to be the most significant of all is the landmark *Hamilton*, a hip-hop biography of Alexander Hamilton featuring a young, ethnically diverse cast (mostly Black and Latina/o) as America's founding fathers and mothers (2015–infinity, if current box office sales are any indication). Winner of 11 Tony Awards in 2016, *Hamilton* also holds the record for the highest ticket price charged on Broadway ($998).[5]

Among the four playwrights featured in this volume, McNally has been most prominently represented on Broadway in the last two decades. He has had fourteen Broadway productions, including revivals, during that time. Parks and Kushner have each had two works performed on Broadway. Following Vogel's Broadway debut in 2017, a Broadway production of her Pulitzer-winning *How I Learned to Drive* was scheduled for spring 2020, but canceled due to COVID 19. A proposed revival of Kushner's *Caroline or Change* was also, apparently, a COVID casualty.[6]

Productions at professional regional theatres bring prestige, if not significant financial rewards, and frequently serve as developmental steps in creating a work that will transfer to Broadway. All four featured playwrights have enjoyed special relationships with Off-Broadway or prestigious, regional theatres (McNally with Philadelphia Theatre Company and Manhattan Theatre Club, Vogel with Perseverance Theatre, Kushner and Parks with the Public Theater), a circumstance which highlights the significant role these theatres play in the development of innovative work. All of these playwrights have enjoyed professional, regional theatre productions outside of New York since the 1990s. The Theatre Communications Group (TCG) lists the top ten most frequently produced works each season (reporting statistics from 524 member theatres). Works from two of our featured playwrights made this list within the past two decades – McNally's *Master Class* in the 1999–2000 season and Parks's *Topdog/Underdog* in the 2003–4 season.

These playwrights are being taught and produced in colleges and universities, although production records are scanty, and their works have been fairly frequently anthologized. A number of factors provide some information about the degree of scholarly attention accorded these playwrights, ultimately revealing that Parks and Kushner have received the lion's share. A keyword library catalogue search reveals forty works that treat Kushner's plays, with eight devoted exclusively to Kushner (1996–2014); thirty-seven works that treat Parks's plays, with four devoted exclusively to Parks (1995–2016); eighteen works treat McNally's plays, with three exclusively devoted to McNally (1972–2016); sixteen works treat Vogel's plays, with one devoted exclusively to Vogel (1999–2014).[7]

Perhaps because she is the youngest of the four writers (a generation separates McNally, born in 1938, from Suzan-Lori Parks, born in 1963; Vogel and Kushner were born in 1951 and 1956, respectively), Parks seems to be attracting the greatest number of young scholars at the moment.[8] Proquest Dissertation Abstracts database lists sixty-nine dissertations devoted exclusively or in part to Suzan-Lori Parks (completed between 1996 and 2015), sixty-one devoted exclusively or in part to Kushner (1995–2015), and eighteen each to McNally (1974–2013) and Vogel (1999–2015). These statistics may also suggest how frequently the playwrights are being studied in academic programmes. Four studies include comparative analyses of works by both McNally and Kushner (focusing on the performance of loss, queer identity and AIDS);[9] one study includes explorations of works by McNally and Vogel (AIDS as the common subject);[10] one includes studies of works by Kushner and Parks (addressing the politics of subjectivity);[11] and two include studies of works by Parks and Vogel: the fact that they are both women who have won Pulitzers as the common thread in one and the staging of identity in the other.[12]

Cross-over artistry is another feature of theatre in the twenty-first century, as works are adapted to and from various media (film/stage/TV/literature/animation/live action) and celebrated performers from TV, film and popular music (including Denzel Washington, Sean (Puff Daddy) Combs, Mos Def, Tom Hanks, Sean Hayes, Larry David, Jeff Daniels, Laura Linney, Hugh Jackman, Jude Law, Lucy Liu, Scarlet Johansson, Jessica Lange and Lupito Nyong'o) have appeared onstage in the past decade. Cross-over artistry has characterized the twenty-first-century careers of the four playwrights discussed in this book. All four have written for television. Both Vogel and McNally contributed episodes to the teleplay *Common Ground* in 2000. Kushner adapted *Angels* for HBO broadcast in 2004 (which racked up a record-breaking eleven Emmy Awards from twenty-one nominations, including an award for outstanding writing). Parks was one of three writers credited with adapting Zora Neale Hurston's *Their Eyes Were Watching God* for ABC-TV in 2005 (produced by Oprah Winfrey's Harpo Productions and nominated for a Black Reel Award).

Terrence McNally

Terrence McNally had already been inducted into the theatre hall of fame by 1996, but he showed no signs of slowing down in the new millennium, completing nine plays and contributing books to four musicals from 2004 to 2015. The experience of being gay in America, including the lasting impact of AIDS, was a recurring theme. However, even more prominent was a metatheatrical preoccupation with art and artists, manifest in at least five of these recent works, including another exploration of the inner life of an opera star in *Golden Age* (2009), which offers an imaginative backstage view of the opening night of Vincenzo Bellini's *I Puritani* in 1835, and *And Away We Go* (2013), a backstage tour through Athens's City Dionysia, Shakespeare's Globe, the royal theatre of Versailles, the Russian premiere of Chekhov's *The Seagull* and the US premiere of *Waiting for Godot*.

His achievements as a musical bookwriter continued with the very successful movical *The Full Monty* (2000), relocating the 1997 British film to Buffalo, New York, where six unemployed steel workers create a striptease act that not only earns them much-needed cash but a renewed sense of camaraderie, self-confidence and hope for the future; the metatheatrical movical *A Man of No Importance* (2002), based on the 1994 Albert Finney film, which dramatizes an amateur theatre's controversial staging of Oscar Wilde's sensuous play *Salome*; *Chita Rivera: The Dancer's Life* (2005); the movical *Catch Me If You Can* (2011), based on the 2002 film, which was itself adapted from Frank Abagnale, Jr's 1980 account of his extraordinary career as a con man; and a musical adaptation of Friedrich Dürrenmatt's *The Visit* (Broadway opening, 2015). Starring McNally's recent collaborator Chita Rivera, *The Visit* is a tale of a wealthy woman scorned who offers an economically stressed town a fortune if they will kill the man who abandoned her years earlier. McNally's most recent musical project, *Anastasia*, based on Disney's 1997 animated film and inspired by the legend of the Russian princess who escaped assassination during the Russian revolution, premiered in May 2016 at Hartford Stage. With a book by McNally, composed by *Ragtime*'s team of Stephen Flaherty (music) and Lynn Ahrens (lyrics), Anastasia opened on Broadway in April 2017 and ran until March 2019.

Perhaps unsurprisingly, McNally became an opera librettist in 1999, with *The Food of Love*, composed by Robert Beaser. *The Food of Love* was the final act of a trilogy of one-act operas sharing a Central Park location, with librettos by noted dramatists (the other two by Wendy Wasserstein and A. R. Gurney, composed by Deborah Drattell and Michael Torke, respectively). *The Food of Love* presents a haunting portrait of a homeless mother who tries to persuade passing strangers to take her baby and give him a future. McNally's foray into opera was followed by four collaborations with composer Jake Heggie (2000–15).

McNally remained a vital presence on Broadway, with twelve shows opening from 2000 to 2015 (six plays and six musicals), including revivals of *The Ritz* (2007) and *Master Class* (2011) and the Broadway premiere of his *Frankie and Johnny in the Clair de Lune* (2002), which had enjoyed a very successful Off-Broadway run from 1987 to 1989. A romantic comedy-drama featuring a short-order cook just released from prison and a waitress just released from an abusive marriage, the play was adapted by McNally for the screen as *Frankie and Johnny* in 1991, with Michelle Pfeiffer and Al Pacino in the leading roles.

One of McNally's most notable successes of the twenty-first century was the musical *Ragtime*, the book adapted from the acclaimed novel by E. L. Doctorow (published in 1975). A quintessentially American story, set during the first decade of the twentieth century, *Ragtime* featured the interwoven experiences of a Black couple from Harlem, a Jewish immigrant from Latvia and a privileged White family from New Rochelle, New York, with music and choreography that blended traditional musical genres with ragtime, gospel, marches and the cakewalk. After ending its original two-year run in 2000, *Ragtime* enjoyed a celebrated run in London's West End in 2003 and an award-winning revival on Broadway in 2009–10. In the twenty-first century, McNally's works garnered six Drama Desk Award nominations and three Tony nominations. In 2011 McNally received the Dramatists Lifetime Achievement Award, and in 2019 he received a Special Tony Award for Lifetime Achievement in the Theatre.

In 2010, the Kennedy Center honoured McNally with a special presentation of three of his works involving opera, titled *Nights at the Opera*. The pieces included the *Master Class*, *The Lisbon Traviata* and *Golden Age*. In 2012, the Philadelphia Theatre Company, which produced the world premieres of four McNally works, created the Terrence McNally New Play Award, given annually to

> recognize a new play or musical that celebrates the transformative power of art-pieces that call to mind the themes and resonance of McNally's *Master Class*, *Golden Age* (both PTC

premieres) as well as *The Lisbon Traviata*. We believe that the inherent humanity found in McNally's work, along with his belief in the indelible impact that art and beauty can make on our individual and universal soul should be recognized and celebrated.[13]

In 2015, the Eclipse Theatre in Chicago devoted a season to Terrence McNally, producing his three plays *Lips Together, Teeth Apart*, *A Perfect Ganesh* and *The Lisbon Traviata*. In the same year, McNally completed his innovative *Selected Works: A Memoir in Plays*, which includes eight works selected by McNally as the most significant of his five-decade career, along with personal essays by McNally that introduce each work. Four of the eight chosen are from the 1990s: *Lips Together, Teeth Apart*, *A Perfect Ganesh*, *Love! Valour! Compassion!* and *Master Class*.

Paula Vogel

Paula Vogel has continued to make major contributions to the American theatre in the twenty-first century with new plays, her commitment to developing regional theatre and university theatre programmes and her widely recognized teaching of many young playwrights at Brown University and Yale Drama School. During her legendary 'boot-camp' playwriting intensives, she has mentored some of the most exciting new playwrights in the country, including Nilo Cruz, Gina Gionfriddo, Lynn Nottage, Adam Bock and Sarah Ruhl.[14] In 2002, she collaborated with Oscar Eustis to create the Brown/Trinity Repertory Company Consortium, and she is currently an artistic associate at Long Wharf Theatre in Connecticut. Recognizing the value of her drama, New York's Signature Theatre devoted their well-known Playwright-in-Residence season (2004–5) to an in-depth exploration of three of her plays: *The Oldest Profession*, *Baltimore Waltz* and *Hot 'n' Throbbing*.

In addition to her ongoing experiments with aesthetic techniques, Vogel has expanded her engagement with canonical texts to which she 'talks back', pays homage and revises in a 'three-way dialogue with the dramatic canon, social history and contemporary American culture.'[15] In *The Long Christmas Ride Home*, Vogel returns to a family drama through the iconic car-ride to the grandparents' home during the holiday season. However, in Vogel's characteristic non-linear structure, this family journey moves between past and present, as fragments of memories intrude on the lives of the adult children and draw the characters back into the maelstrom of childhood. Here Vogel dialogues with canonical author Thornton Wilder, paying homage to his *The Happy Journey to Trenton and Camden* and *The Long Christmas Dinner*, as well as the tenor of his *Our Town*. With *Christmas Ride*, Vogel broke new ground in her formal experimentation with Japanese theatre techniques, specifically Bunraku puppetry (large puppets represent the siblings as children). Ann Pellegrini interprets this device as 'symbolizing the psychic grip of the past on the present. The characters are literally carrying around earlier "freeze-framed" versions of themselves. In a sense the children have become their own ghosts; the puppets are a haunting theatrical conceit, spectral traces of a past the children cannot let go.'[16]

In her next play, Vogel turned her attention from the family to the nation's history at a time of crisis that also promised change. At least one reviewer noted that *A Civil War Christmas: A Musical Celebration*, premiering at Long Wharf Theatre in December 2008 and restaged at New York Theatre Workshop in December of 2012, evoked the past of a nation divided when many commentators were comparing Obama to Lincoln (Chirico, 630 – see Documents chapter). Vogel's foray into the musical genre presents a pageantry of lives: runaway slaves, soldiers – Black and White – mourning parents, nurses, seamstresses, labourers, famous and anonymous figures. Their stories of grief and hope are woven together in a moving tableau, the narratives interspersed with Christmas carols, spirituals and Civil War songs.

In 2014, Vogel again embarked on new theatrical forms and expanded her collaboration with other theatre practitioners. Her anti-war drama *Don Juan Comes Home From Iraq*, staged at the Wilma Theater in Philadelphia, participates in the genre of theatre of war that has emerged in the context of the wars in Iraq and Afghanistan and armed conflict in Eastern Europe and Africa, as well as debates about American interventions. Revisioning Austro-Hungarian playwright Odon von Horvath's 1936 play *Don Juan Comes Home From the War*, which portrayed his Don Juan figure as a shell-shocked returning soldier from the First World War, Vogel's lost Marine figure comes home from Iraq with PTSD and TBI (traumatic brain injury; again see the Documents chapter).

Vogel's most recent play represents yet another collaborative venture. *Indecent* (2015), conceived with director Rebecca Taichman, pays homage to the potential for theatre to change hearts and minds. The play within the play is the provocative *God of Vengeance* (1907) by writer Sholom Asch, first performed in Yiddish for Warsaw audiences, brought on tour in Europe and performed in English in New York in 1923, only to be shut down by the vice squad and its actors and producer brought to trial. The plot involves a brothel owner and his wife, and the daughter he hopes to keep pure within an arranged marriage. His plan is foiled, however, when his daughter falls in love with one of the prostitutes. Vogel's play re-creates this scene and the efforts of the theatre troupe who dedicated their lives to performing it under the duress of anti-morality charges, rising anti-Semitism and even the playwright's abandonment of his own creation.

In the twenty-first century, Vogel went on to receive an array of honours that indicates the importance of her body of work: the Award for Literature from the American Academy of Arts and Letters; induction into the Academy of Arts and Sciences; the William Inge Festival Distinguished Achievement in the American Theatre Award; the Lifetime Achievement Award from the Dramatists Guild; induction into the Theatre Hall of Fame, among many others. In tribute to her mentoring, three awards in her name have been dedicated to emerging playwrights. In 2003, the Kennedy Center American College Theater Festival launched the Paula Vogel Award in Playwriting for 'the best student-written play that celebrates diversity and encourages tolerance while exploring issues of dis-empowered voices not traditionally considered mainstream'.[17] In 2007, the Vineyard Theatre in New York City established the annual Paula Vogel Award for playwrights. In 2013, the Young Playwrights of Philadelphia inaugurated the Paula Vogel Mentorship Program, curated by Vogel's former student and Pulitzer Prize-winner Quiara Alegría Hudes. The playwright's playwright, Vogel received a Thirtini (2009), the prize given by 13P (13 Playwrights, Inc.), a playwrights collective founded in 2003.

Tony Kushner

Tony Kushner's twenty-first-century career has expanded to include musicals, opera, literature and, especially, screenwriting. He began the century by collaborating with composer Jeanine Tesori on the innovative musical *Caroline, or Change*, notable for its central and atypically unsentimental relationship between an African American housekeeper and a young Jewish boy. *Caroline* opened on Broadway in 2002 and was nominated for six Tonys, including best book by Kushner. In 2007, it won London's Laurence Olivier Award for best musical. Kushner's second collaboration with Tesori, the short opera *A Blizzard on Marblehead Neck*, based on an incident in the life of playwright Eugene O'Neill, premiered at the Glimmerglass Festival in 2011. Although Kushner was not personally involved, a musical incarnation of *Angels* occurred in 2004, when Hungarian composer Péter Eötvös created *Angels in America: The Opera*. The opera was filmed for PBS in 2005 and debuted in the US in 2006. A London production is planned for 2017.

Kushner was represented Off-Broadway in 2006 with a new translation of Bertolt Brecht's anti-war play *Mother Courage and Her Children* with incidental music by Jeanine Tesori, produced by the Public Theater and starring Meryl Streep. In 2009, his *The Intelligent Homosexual's Guide to Capitalism and Socialism with a Key to the Scriptures* premiered at the Guthrie Theatre in Minneapolis before its brief Off-Broadway run. The play features a disillusioned labour leader who has brought his family together to announce his intended suicide and manifests Kushner's distrust of free market capitalism and his love of free speech as a means to achieve social justice and personal happiness. More realistic in form than the typical Kushner play, *The Intelligent Homosexual's Guide* retains, as *New York Times* critic Ben Brantley affirmed, Kushner's trademark 'heady language' and 'visceral commitment to ideas made flesh'.[18]

In 2009, the Guthrie Theatre in Minneapolis devoted two months to celebrating Kushner, producing one of his plays on all three Guthrie stages – in addition to a series of seminars, classes and workshops, and two 'Extreme Kushner Weekends' that involved marathon theatre packages and additional Kushner-related events.

The three featured plays were *Caroline, or Change*, *The Intelligent Homosexual's Guide to Capitalism and Socialism with a Key to the Scriptures* and an evening of his short plays. The 2016–17 season of the Round House Theatre in Bethesda, Maryland, includes a Celebration of Tony Kushner, during which they will produce *Angels in America*, parts 1 and 2, and *Caroline, or Change*. Kushner's literary projects in the twenty-first century include authoring essays, a book about children's author Maurice Sendak, a book about Jewish American responses to the Palestinian–Israeli conflict, and editing the collected plays of Arthur Miller.

Kushner's greatest twenty-first-century successes, however, have come from screenwriting, beginning with his acclaimed adaptation of *Angels in America*, directed by Mike Nichols for HBO in 2003. In 2005, Kushner collaborated with film director Stephen Spielberg on *Munich*, a screenplay adapted from the book *Vengeance* by George Jonas. *Munich* portrays the Israeli retaliation against a Palestinian group who kidnapped and killed 11 Israeli athletes during the 1972 Olympics in Munich. Kushner received an Oscar nomination for best adapted screenplay. He teamed with Spielberg again on the celebrated *Lincoln*, for which Kushner adapted a screenplay based loosely on historian Doris Kearns Goodwin's *Team of Rivals: The Political Genius of Abraham Lincoln*. Kushner received another Oscar nomination and won the Chicago Film Critics' Choice Award for his adapted screenplay. In the twenty-first century, Kushner began work on two screenplays, one adapted from David Kerzer's novel The Kidnapping of Edgardo Mortara, a nineteenth-century story of a Jewish boy who was raised as a Catholic and became a priest, and the other from He Wanted the Moon, a memoir by Mimi Baird and Eve Claxton that recounts the tragic life of Baird's father, medical researcher Dr. Perry Baird, who became a victim himself of the manic depression he investigated. Most recently, Kushner shared screenplay credits with Arthur Laurents for a new film adaptation of West Side Story, directed by Stephen Spielberg and scheduled to open in December 2020.

Kushner has continued to receive prestigious awards, including a 2002 PEN/Laura Pels International Foundation for Theater Award for a playwright in mid-career, an Emmy Award in 2004 and a 2008 Steinberg Distinguished Playwright Award. In 2012, Kushner was awarded the National Medal of Arts, the highest honour given to an individual artist for achievement in the arts, selected by the NEA and presented by the president. He has received honorary doctorates from Columbia College in Chicago (2003), Brandeis University (2008), SUNY Purchase College (2011), CUNY's John Jay College of Criminal Justice (2012) and Ithaca College (2015).[20]

Suzan-Lori Parks

Time magazine's 1999 inclusion of Suzan-Lori Parks in the list of '100 Innovators for the Next New Wave' is an assessment that her subsequent work has indisputably upheld. In addition to those mentioned above, her dramatic works include the second 'Rep and Rev' of Hawthorne's *Scarlet Letter*, *Fucking A* (2000), which continued the focus first manifested in *Venus* and *In the Blood* on gender and the connections between sexual and economic exploitation. Composed of nineteen scenes with songs, and set in a chronologically and geographically displaced patriarchal dystopia, *Fucking A* evokes both Brecht's *Mother Courage* and Margaret Atwood's *The Handmaid's Tale*. The 'A' is for 'Abortionist', the degraded profession of protagonist Hester Smith who struggles to free her son 'Monster', imprisoned since the age of eleven for stealing meat, a role that lured rapper Mos Def to the stage. *Topdog/Underdog* (2001), which earned Parks a Pulitzer and brought Mos Def back onstage for an encore, explores urban 'gangsta' masculinities embodied by two brothers named Lincoln and Booth.[21] Their contest for dominance leads inevitably and compellingly to the play's tragic outcome.

In 2002, Parks decided to write a play a day for a year, ultimately producing 365 dramatic vignettes, some less than a page long, in her typically free-flowing rhythmic idiom, with subjects including an encounter between Mary Todd Lincoln and her Black dressmaker Mrs. Keckley, a conversation between a horse and its rider, and the execution of a king. In 2006, the plays were produced as *365 Days/365 Plays* by 700 theatres around the world in an unprecedented, grassroots collaboration. Her epic *Father Comes Home From the Wars (Parts 1, 2, and 3)* (2014) re-visions the Civil War as Greek myth, with a young Black enslaved man as a hero named Hero, his faithful love Penny and (in Parks's inimitably theatrical fashion) a dog named 'Odd-See' (Odyssey) and a Musican who interjects bluesy accompaniment to Parks's trenchant dialogue. The

Pulitzer-nominated play, like many of Parks's works, excavates and reimagines American history, posing provocative questions about free will and fate, love and loyalty, compassion and cruelty, and presenting freedom, as *Los Angeles Times* writer Charles McNulty suggested, 'as both an existential puzzle and a historical wound'.[22]

In 2011, Parks assumed the role of director for the premiere of her family drama *The Book of Grace*, which portrays a woman's attempt to effect a reconciliation between her husband, a Texas border patrolman, and his estranged son. The following year she adapted the book for one of America's most revered native operas, *Porgy and Bess*, retitled in its revised form as *The Gershwins' Porgy and Bess*. Based on the 1927 play *Porgy*, adapted for the stage by Dubose Heyward and his wife Dorothy from Heyward's 1925 novel of the same name, the folk opera *Porgy and Bess*, with music by George Gershwin and libretto by Heyward and Ira Gershwin, premiered in 1935. The story is set in Catfish Row, a Black enclave in Charleston, South Carolina, and centres on the poignant love story between a disabled Black beggar and a drug-addicted woman. Although the opera enjoyed enormous success, with Gershwin's score, particularly the popular aria 'Summertime', winning iconic status, the work's racial representations (prostitution, drug addiction, gambling, violence) aroused controversy. The 2012 revival, with book adapted by Parks and staging by Diane Paulus, effected changes in the script and performance that increased the humanity and complexity of the characters, especially Bess.

Parks's expanding career included writing a Faulkner-sampling novel, *Getting Mother's Body* (2003), in which a young (poor and pregnant) woman sets out to exhume her mother's body in order to retrieve the cache of jewels allegedly buried with her. In 2005, Parks turned to screenwriting, adapting Zora Neale Hurston's novel *Their Eyes Were Watching God* for Oprah Winfrey's Harpo Productions. Hurston's novel narrates, in flashback, the quest for love and fulfilment by the thrice-married, forty-five-year-old Janie Crawford, who is finally forced to shoot the love of her life, the handsome, sweet-talking Teacake, in self-defence. According to Jennifer Larson, Parks's version significantly reimagined Hurston's text, offering a 'particular emphasis on black female sexuality, specifically sexual autonomy and individual feminine identity'.[23] Since 2001, Parks has been a playwriting teacher at the California

Institute of the Arts, the Yale School of Drama and the Tisch School of the Arts at New York University.

In recent years, Parks has also developed a reputation as a performance artist, touring nationally and internationally with the 'Suzan-Lori Parks Show', which includes music (she is a guitarist), lecture, reading, singing and 'consciousness-raising of the collective unconscious'.[24] In 2011, Parks devised a performance art piece called *Watch Me Work*, carrying on a writing session in the lobby of the Public Theater; the audience is invited to watch and/or get their own writing done, followed by a Q & A/discussion with Parks about her work process or those of the audience. Since 2011, she has performed *Watch Me Work* in various locations.

Parks's achievements in the past two decades have been recognized with numerous prestigious awards, including a Guggenheim Fellowship (2000), a MacArthur Foundation 'Genius' Grant (2001), two Pulitzer finalists (2000 and 2015) and a Pulitzer win (2002). She has also received honorary doctorates from Mount Holyoke College (2001) and Brown University (2004). In 2008, she was named the first 'Master Writer Chair' at the Public Theater, a three-year residency which included a Visiting Arts Professorship at New York University's Tisch School of the Arts. Parks was in residency during the 2016–17 and 2017–18 seasons at New York City's Signature Theatre during which they produced four of her plays: *The Death of the Last Black Man in the Whole Entire World, Venus, In the Blood, and Fucking A.*

DOCUMENTS

Terrence McNally

Nathan Lane, *Playbill*, 2015

Award-winning actor Nathan Lane has originated roles in McNally's The Lisbon Traviata *(1989), Lips Together, Teeth Apart (1991), Love! Valour! Compassion! (1994), the revised* It's Only a Play *(2014) and the film* Frankie and Johnny *(1991). The following quotations are from Lane's tribute to McNally published in* Playbill *in 2015.*[1]

When I first started working with Terrence he had told me about the devastating loss of two of his best collaborators, James 'Jimmy' Coco and Robert Drivas, and that he somehow felt I had been sent to take their place in his theatrical life. He said he wrote better when he knew whom he was writing for and that he wanted to create plays with me in mind. An unbelievably generous and monumental gift for a young actor, especially coming from a writer of his caliber and stature.

I must say there is no better collaborator in the world than Terrence McNally. No one is happier to be in a rehearsal room with a new play and a group of people bringing his story and characters to life. He still has a very pure, genuine, childlike excitement about the whole process. I say childlike, but I mean an extremely sophisticated child with a wicked tongue.

After all these years he's still my favorite writer, and he is very much like his plays: sharply intelligent, witty, heartfelt, passionate and full of surprises. Like a great actor, his writing can turn on a dime. You're laughing hysterically one minute and the next thing you know, tears are running down your face. He has certainly given me some of the best roles of my career, and the plays we have done together are some of my proudest moments in the theatre. He is a unique and original voice in the American theatre, and they come along so rarely they should be celebrated and cherished.

I was also asked to discuss how Terrence's commitment to equality has bettered the gay community. That's a tall order for this amount of space, and I'm not quite sure how something like that can be measured. I would say his influence has been felt by example, personally and professionally, and just by being a visible and viable presence in his field. Oh, and very often being ahead of his time. Who else would write a farce set in a gay bathhouse in the 1970s? *Corpus Christi*, anyone?

Interview by Mervyn Rothstein

The following quotations are drawn from New York Times *writer Mervyn Rothstein's interview with the stars of the Broadway premiere of McNally's* Lips Together, Teeth Apart.[2]

Swoosie Kurtz: The play is at least in part about our responsibility ... specifically the responsibility of heterosexuals to reach out to the gay community in this time of AIDS, to not just turn a blind eye to the situation. But more universally, the play is about whether you can just watch somebody in trouble and think there isn't anything you can do. You can at least try.

Christine Baranski: What was given to us on the first day of rehearsals was the first draft. [The playwright, director and cast] spent the first two weeks just refining and cutting it, drastically reshaping it. Much of the time that would normally be spent as actors working on scenes was spent talking about what the scene would be or what or where or how long a speech should be. In a way, the actors became partly dramaturgs and co-directors.

Anthony Heald: As much as anything else, I think the play is about the difference between our public and private selves, and I think the monologues illustrate that. There are things going on under the surface in other people, and often even in ourselves, that we're not aware of. And it's that struggle to break through, to really connect with each other, to really allow somebody else in, that I find most fascinating. Because it's something in my own life that I have a constant battle with ... It's mentioned in the play that the title refers to a technique of going to sleep without grinding your teeth. But I think it's also something else: We see lips together in a kiss, and behind the lips our teeth are parted ready to tear into flesh.

Interview by Charlie Rose

The following quotations by Terrence McNally are from Charlie Rose's interview with McNally during the Broadway run of the Tony Award-winning Love! Valour! Compassion! *in 1995.*[3]

I think I wanted to write a play about my experience of being a gay man in the last part of the twentieth century ... I wasn't preaching anything. I wanted to take my time and really examine the lives and relationships of these eight men. There's a kind of a leisurely feeling about the play that I exulted in, in writing it. The summer to me is kind of a somnolent time, anyway. And I was very aware of the crickets and mosquitoes when I wrote this play, and I just got into it. I don't know. I wanted to write a play by a lake.

[*On a film version of* Love! Valour! Compassion!]

... there's some real interest in it, and Joe [Director Joe Mantello] and I are talking with some people, and – I hope we can do it. I'd love to capture this on film. I think we can, you know. [But] I'm so stage-struck. You know, my plays are of the theater. I mean, this play has inner monologues, asides to the audience, the way it handles time – back and forth. Who knows? [H]ow do you capture that in the film, and that wonderful moment, to me, when they're in the Swan Lake part of the play – and where they all talk about the rest of their lives, what happens thirty-five years later. That's hard to pull off in a movie. I'm a playwright – and trying to learn how to be a screenwriter – I'm doing a screenplay of *Perfect Ganesh* for Merchant Ivory, and it doesn't come as naturally to me. It's like – I don't know. If you did Shakespeare suddenly, it may not come as easily to you as McNally after all these years, but I know you could do Shakespeare, and I know I can write a good screenplay. But I don't dream in movies. I dream in plays.

Opera and Maria Callas

As John M. Clum affirmed in Chapter 3, opera plays a role in most of Terrence McNally's works, informs his style and has been a crucial part of his life. Opera diva Maria Callas haunts McNally's The Lisbon Traviata *and is the central figure of* Master Class. *The following quote is from an article in the* Philadelphia Inquirer.

I grew up in Corpus Christi ... and when I was a teenager, I heard on the radio from Mexico this magnificent voice. The announcer said it was 'Maria Meneghini Cayas' (pronouncing the last name as the Spanish would). I had no idea who I was listening to, but I knew I loved that voice.

Then when I came to New York to go to Columbia, I heard about her debut at the Met. I went down to 39th Street and stood in line for a couple of days for standing room. She sang only about sixteen times at the Met, but I heard her in thirteen of those performances. I also heard her at La Scala and Covent Garden. When she came back to New York to do those master classes at Juilliard, I made sure I was there.[4]

Director and former classmate Michael Kahn on their mutual fascination for Callas.

[We] waited at the Met box office, sometimes for days at a time, for standing-room tickets to Callas performances ... It was a real obsession. We'd run off to get every pirated Callas record. We went to everything and listened to everything, to every little piece, playing every note, then playing it back to hear this phrase or that again, and then having heated discussions and fights. *Lisbon Traviata* is very much a picture of those times.[5]

On the evolution of *Master Class*

The following quoted passage is from an article in the Washington Post.

I went to four of [Callas's classes]. But if anything gave me the idea, it was watching Leontyne Price give a master class while I was teaching at Juilliard a few years ago. It's a very theatrical setting. The student is the guinea pig. The teacher gets to score points off them ...

I went to a master class taught by Renata Scotto. Either she had read my play, or I got it right. She came out and, after a lot of applause, said, 'No applause.' She said, 'This is not about me,' then reminisced so that the singers didn't do much talking. She flirted with the tenor; then, when he sang, she was reduced to tears. I think these stars who no longer perform at La Scala or the Met need the fix of a New York audience going, 'Bravo!'[6] ...

Zoe Caldwell on McNally

Actress Zoe Caldwell created the role of Maria Callas in the world premiere of Master Class *with the Philadelphia Theatre Company in spring 1995, and won a Tony Award for her performance in its Broadway premiere later that year.*[7] *The following quotations are from an interview with F. Paul Driscoll.*[8]

[Terrence] said, 'I know exactly the play for you. I've got the first line, and it is called *Master Class*. And it is about Maria Callas giving a master class.' Well, I knew it wasn't going to be a load o' laughs if it was to be about Maria Callas ...

After a bit of time, Terrence sent me the first act, a little tiny piece of the tapes of the actual master classes at Juilliard – her farewell to the master class, actually – and a tape of *Tosca* and a tape of *Lady Macbeth* and so on. I thought it was marvelous, but not anything that I could connect with ...

I then read *Master Class* with the other actors, and I suddenly realized [that the play] is about her listening – which I hadn't [understood] in my reading of the text. When Faye [Dunaway] asked me about doing Maria on tour, the first thing I told her was to listen and watch those students. That is key. In my rather stupid reading of the text, I hadn't seen [the play] as funny, either. And it is incredibly funny. Abrasive, often, but funny. So we did the staged reading. And at once I knew the audience really wanted to hear it ...

One of the people I spoke to was Sheila Nadler, who was in the [Juilliard] master classes. She was extraordinarily generous. Sheila gave me wonderful insights about Callas and, just as I was leaving her, she said, 'then of course, there was the walk. Callas had a very special way of sort of ... striding.' This to an actress! I said, 'Show me! Show me!' So she showed me, which was fantastic, because there was no chance for me to see that walk, because as far as I know, Maria never used it – her own stride – in any character. She found the character's walk. Not Maria's walk. I now believe that heavy *lope* Maria had was from propelling her weight forward in the days when she was really stout. No matter how slim she became – Maria always had big legs and that long, heavy stride.

The following quotations are from a Caldwell interview with Charlie Rose.[9]

[Callas's] human frailties were enormous. Her strengths were divine. Her ego was beyond the limit, but you know, if you only know about the really strong, big stuff, as I only knew, then you don't know about the whole person. [W]hat we were talking about before ... what is revealed when people reveal to you something of themselves, their real selves, that's a kind of love when people strip off in front of you – and show you something ...

I love it best of all when I see a man come in from Westchester or New Jersey with his wife – and they think, 'Oh, why do I need this?' And I love it when they're close enough that I can see them eventually – begin to be suckered into Maria. Because if they're open enough to be suckered into Maria, then something will be open in them for life ...

... lots of people say she was very nurturing. Now, Terrence says the word 'nurturing' is wrong. She wasn't a nurturer. [A] lot of people contradict him in that, but ... who knows? ...

Rose: In the end, are you doing history, or are you simply doing your interpretation of the spirit of the woman?

Caldwell: An evocation, the spirit of Maria. You can't do history. It isn't a documentary.

In protest against *Corpus Christi*

McNally's Corpus Christi *(1998), depicting Jesus and his disciples as gay men living in mid-twentieth-century Texas, aroused considerable opposition (including peaceful protests as well as bomb and death threats) from the Catholic League, conservative politicians and others.*

The following quotation is from a campaign called 'America Needs Fatima' sponsored by the American Society for the Defense of Tradition, Family and Property in protest against a planned production of Corpus Christi *in 2009.*[10]

Please join America Needs Fatima in protesting the blasphemous play *Corpus Christi* at the Church of the Foothills in Santa Ana, California. According to the press reports, *Corpus Christi* includes a Christ-like figure who has homosexual relations with his apostles! Besides, the play uses Gospel passages in a contrived way. *The New York Post*, for example, reported: '"Art Thou King of the queers?" McNally's Pontius Pilate character asks. "Thou sayest," Joshua answers.' You now have a unique chance to defend Jesus' honor by peacefully, but loudly raising your voice against this blasphemy.

McNally on *Corpus Christi*

The following quotations by Terrence McNally are from an interview with Larry Murray about Corpus Christi *in 2014.*[11]

The play is a re-telling of Christ's life and passion in a vocabulary that makes it more accessible to gay men and women who had previously been excluded from any place in His story or the Christian religions. All men are divine. That is the simple, Universal meaning of my interpretation of His life …

Why this threatens so many devout Christians is something only they can answer. Fortunately, their numbers are declining. The movement towards more and more freedom for all people has an inevitable momentum. It's a good time for the best kind of human change ...

Rejection makes us feel alone and disenfranchised. Inclusion allows us to express the love within each of us and feel the love of others. I never felt more connected to the world around me than when I was writing *Corpus Christi*. It was my spiritual journey: begun as a Catholic in a South Texas parochial school, sidetracked for many years, and begun again when I traveled in India and saw how profoundly religious day to day life was there. I came home wanting my spiritual life back ...

Paula Vogel

Interview with Arthur Holmberg about *How I Learned to Drive*

Paula Vogel's How I Learned to Drive *was produced at the American Repertory Theater in Cambridge, Massachusetts, from 18 September 1998 to 10 October 1998. The following excerpts are from an interview with Vogel by Arthur Holmberg, Literary Director of A.R.T.*[12]

Holmberg: Your plays frequently deal with taboos. If I had to explain your theatrical signature to someone unfamiliar with your work, I would say that you trespass into forbidden territory with a smile on your face. You disturb the bones of forbidden topics, then make the audience laugh. What is the function of humor in your vision?

Vogel: I actually describe [*How I Learned to*] *Drive* as a comedy. Of course it's not, but the first half very much functions as comedy. At some elemental level, it is who I am. My family had the most inappropriate moments of humor at funerals. Maybe it's a survival strategy. Some people say that this comes from Jewish genes. At the beginning of the *Baltimore Waltz* [a play about her brother's death from AIDS] I used a real letter my brother wrote me with instructions for his funeral that included directions on how to lay him out in the coffin in drag. For me combining sadness and comedy heightens both. The collision of tones makes both more extreme ... It doesn't defuse the terror, it defuses the guarding against the terror. We don't want to be taken by surprise, so we keep our guard up. Comedy defuses that vigilance so in the next moment we are unprepared for the explosion. The comedy dismantles any protective covering ...

Holmberg: Humor is also a form of seduction. In one of the play's funniest speeches, 'A Mother's Guide to Social Drinking,' an older woman tells a young girl how not to get drunk. She advises her never to touch a drink with a sexual position in the name like Dead Man Screw or The Missionary and to learn to drink like a man: straight up. The speech makes the audience laugh, but then you hit hard with an emotionally devastating scene.

Vogel: Li'l Bit's drunk and can't defend herself.

Holmberg: A double seduction, Li'l Bit and the audience.

Vogel: Comedy is complicity. If you make an audience laugh ...

Holmberg: They are your friends.

Vogel: Not only your friends, but also in alliance with the play world. They're on the side of the play now because they laughed.

Holmberg: Many of your plays deal with families. European critics often say American drama does not achieve greatness because our playwrights, obsessed by petty family melodramas, never look through the living room window to see the larger world and the problems outside.

Vogel: Rubbish ... The family remains the structure at the heart of most drama because the family, after all, reflects its community's values and the politics of their time ... The great American playwrights, like the great European playwrights, like the great global playwrights, deal with the family as a unit within a greater body politic.

Holmberg: So how do you see *Drive* as political?

Vogel: A lot of people are trying to turn this into a drama about an individual family. To me it is not. It is a way of looking on a microcosmic level at how this culture sexualizes children. How we are taught at an extremely early age to look at female bodies. One of the tag lines I had in my head when I was writing this play was, it takes a whole village to molest a child. Jon Benet Ramsey was not a fluke. When we Americans saw the video tape of her at the beauty contest when she was five, a chill went up our collective spines. At what age are we sexualizing our children in a consumer culture to sell blue jeans and underwear? ... I would call that political and not specifically the psychopathology of an individual family. I would say that's cultural. And now we are starting to see a sexualized gaze toward young boys ... Wherever there is confusion or double, triple, and quadruple standards, that is the realm of theatre. Drama lives in paradoxes and contradictions. If you look at the structure of my play, all I'm doing is asking how do you feel about this? We see a girl of seventeen and an older man in a car seat. You think you know how you feel about this relationship? Alright, fine. Now, let's go back a year earlier. Do you still think you know what you feel about this situation? Great. Now let's change the situation a little bit more. He's married to her aunt. How do you feel about that? The play allows me this kind of slippage because we have these contradictory feelings about the sexuality of boys and girls. So I tease out those contradictions. The play is a reverse syllogism. It constantly pulls the rug out from under our emotional responses by going back earlier and earlier in time. The play moves in reverse ...

Holmberg: *Drive* dramatizes in a disturbing way how we receive great harm from the people who love us.

Vogel: I would reverse that. I would say that we can receive great love from the people who harm us.

Holmberg: Why is it significant to reverse it?

Vogel: We are now living in a culture of victimization, and great harm can be inflicted by well-intentioned therapists, social workers, and talk show hosts who encourage people to dwell in their identity as victim. Without denying or forgetting the original pain, I wanted to write about the great gifts that can also be inside that box of abuse. My play dramatizes the gifts we receive from the people who hurt us.

Holmberg: So what does Li'l Bit receive?

Vogel: She received the gift of how to survive.

Holmberg: From her Uncle?

Vogel: Absolutely. I am going to teach you to drive like a man, he says. He becomes her mentor and shows her a way of thinking ahead ten steps down the road before anyone else to figure out what the other guy is going to do before he does it. That not only enables her to survive but actually enables her, I think, to reject him and destroy him.

Holmberg: And she does destroy him.

Vogel: He gives her the gifts to do that. He gives her the training. He gives her the ego formation. You, he says, you've got a fire in the head. He gives her gifts in just about every scene. He teaches her the importance of herself as an individual and the ability to strategize to protect that. It's all there in the driving lessons. It's abuse simultaneously with a kind of affirmation and reassurance.

Holmberg: In *Drive*, Li'l Bit looks at her painful memories, processes the experiences, and then moves on. Why is it important to forgive the harm?

Vogel: Many people stay rooted in anger against transgressions that occurred in childhood, and this rage will be directed to other people in their adult lives and toward themselves. Whether we call it forgiveness or understanding, there comes a moment when the past has to be processed, and we have to find some control. There are two forgivenesses in the play. One forgiveness for Peck, but the most crucial forgiveness would be Li'l Bit's forgiving Li'l Bit. Li'l Bit as an adult looking at and understanding her complicity ...

Holmberg: Her destructiveness. You once said that it was important to give the audience a catharsis.

Vogel: Catharsis purges the pity and the terror and enables the audience to transcend them. So you have her memories of the final confrontation with Peck in the hotel room and afterwards the flashback to the first driving lesson. And then the last scene, which brings us up to the present. This is a movement forward. For me, purgation means a forward movement.

Miriam Chirico on *A Civil War Christmas*

Miriam Chirico's performance review of A Civil War Christmas *at the Long Wharf Theatre in Connecticut includes Vogel's reference to herself as a 'historian-playwright' in the post-show symposium, and Chirico notes the multicultural perspective that Vogel brings to her rendering of the nation's history.*[13]

Over the second half of the twentieth century, historians have worked toward writing texts with more inclusive depictions of the varied peoples and cultures that constitute the United States. Rather than provide a linear narrative of conquerors and colonialists, these texts now reveal stories about marginalized groups and peripheral personages, often told in sidebars and box insertions. Portraying the Civil War from this fragmented, multicultural perspective, Paula Vogel's ambitious musical captures a crucial twenty-four-hour period during the nation's divisive war. Referring to herself as a 'historian-playwright' at a post-show symposium, Vogel deliberately portrays the Civil War from a multicultural perspective. *A Civil War Christmas* offers a panoramic view of Washington, DC, and its surroundings at Christmastime, depicting runaway and freed slaves; White, Black, and Native American soldiers; women serving as nurses or as soldiers in disguise; Union and Confederate leaders; and Quakers, Christians, and Jews. It is a synchronistic snapshot of the ordinary people who comprise Civil War history, but who often are overshadowed by historical figures such as Lincoln, Grant, and Lee ...

The balance between historical accuracy and artistic license undergirds this endeavor, and Vogel, as a historian-playwright, resolved the dilemma for herself by focusing on plausible events rather than precise details. As she noted during the post-show talk, she often would question historians and colleagues about whether scenes from her play were credible, even if they were not necessarily true. But when facts proved otherwise she amended them, such as altering a scene in which Walt Whitman visited soldiers at the Armory Hospital in Washington; when documents proved him to be in Brooklyn at Christmas, Vogel had the soldiers dream about him instead. More important than focusing on verifiable details was her desire to acknowledge the period's social diversity, and to that end she presents plausible encounters among historical figures. 'I wanted to know what it was like trying to light the lights [for Hanukkah] in the field,' she explains in the program notes. 'I wanted to find one Native American who was there on this Christmas Eve. So that the children in [my] family who trace back that heritage can point and say, "OK, we were there."' Vogel includes well-known stories such as Grant's letter to Lincoln upon conquering Savannah, as well as ones she mined from archives and biographies: for example, Mary Todd Lincoln's spending sprees, and the two African Americans, Decatur Dorsey and James Bronson, who received Medals of Honor ...

The use of ghosts and flashbacks express Vogel's recurring thematic interest in the tangible confluence between past and present. Elizabeth Keckley talks to her deceased son just before he was killed on the battlefield; later, she relives a beating she received from a slave master. Charles Longfellow, a Union lieutenant, summons in his mind the figure of Henry Wadsworth Longfellow onto the stage to recite his Civil War poem, 'Christmas Bells.' And Decatur Bronson, the African American Union sergeant (a composite of the two actual historical figures, Decatur Dorsey and James Bronson), revisits moments when his wife taught him to read before she was kidnapped into slavery. The play itself serves as a reminder of America's past, particularly in light of the frequent comparisons between Abe Lincoln and Barack Obama in today's media.

On teaching

In an interview with Steven Druckman in Dramatists Guild Quarterly, *Paula Vogel describes her famous 'Bake-Offs' in her 'Bootcamp' playwriting intensives.*[14]

Druckman: I wanted to first ask you about teaching at Brown and your teaching method. You have said in the past that everyone can write a play. What do you do?

I try to create a group dynamic where people start to enjoy the game of writing. To me, plays are really a collective game, and you have to engage the audience to play along. I set up a game-playing situation where everybody participates, and I try to bring back the fun. I think people don't write because there is a lot of inhibition and censorship. I try to create conditions where that censorship really can't play a role.

For example, every year, all the graduate playwrights – and alumni who want to participate – do something called 'The Great American Play Bake-Off.' I make up two or three simple rules and tell everybody they must have these two or three ingredients in their Bake-Off play – but they have to write it in 48 hours. No exceptions ... Then I take everybody to a farmhouse retreat in New Hampshire, and we do our Bake-Off ... They have an entire semester, a year, or the rest of their lives to work on their Bake-Off Plays ...

On collaboration

Don Juan Comes Home from Iraq *is the result of two years of development, beginning with a conversation between Paula Vogel and Artistic Director of the* Wilma Theater in Philadelphia, Blanka Zizka, *during a playwriting 'boot camp' led by Ms Vogel in January 2011, where they discovered a mutual love of the Weimar-era playwright Ödön von Horvath. This led to a decision, months later, to write a new play inspired by Horvath's* Don Juan Comes Home From the War *(1936) following the First World War. Months of conversations between the artistic collaborators followed and expanded to include encounters with veterans of Iraq and Afghanistan in interviews and playwriting workshops led by Ms Vogel in Philadelphia, DC and New York. The following excerpt is from 'A Conversation between Paula Vogel and Blanka Zizka'.*[15]

Vogel: For the first time I feel like a company member. And I'm working for people whose voices I'm hearing. I'm watching your work and your process and listening to the things that you respond with. I think this is the great thing for companies – it's more of a call and response than a synthetic piece of work. You keep the multiple voices alive when you work this way. It's so thrilling.

Zizka: I love also that you challenge the actors to become writers as well, because in that process of writing and the way that you set up the exercises, we reveal so much about ourselves and we get to know each other so quickly …

I think theatre is not the truth.

Vogel: It's not the truth! That's right. It's not the truth. We're not going to be the perfect mirror. Hopefully though, again, what I hope is that there's some lifting of the experience and a vibrancy that we can give back. And the second thing is to say, 'Thank you.' 'I'm sorry, and thank you.' Because I think the veterans we've encountered and I'm thinking about all of the time that these veterans have given us, to go back and revisit their experiences and to tell us is incredible generosity.

Also note Paula Vogel's discussion of her use of 'negative empathy', theorized by early twentieth-century German philosopher Theodore Lipps, in her 2012 Keynote Address to the Comparative Drama Conference. As Vogel explains, 'The purpose of drama is to make us project ourselves into everything that we fear, everything that we resist, and everything that we are revolted by.'[16]

Tony Kushner

Interview with Zeljko Djukic by Cheryl Black regarding the Serbian premiere of *Homebody/Kabul*

In 2009, Zeljko Djukic, founding Artistic Director of the Utopian Theatre Asylum in Chicago, Illinois, directed Tony Kushner's Homebody/Kabul *at the National Theatre in Belgrade, Serbia, as part of a cultural exchange between the two theatres. Supported in part by the MacArthur Foundation, the production ran in repertory for almost three years. Actress Dusanka Stojanovic Glid received Serbia's prestigious 'Milos Zutic Award' for her critically acclaimed performance of the Homebody.*[17] *The following quotations are from Mr Djukic's interview with Cheryl Black, 28 November 2015.*[18]

Black: Tell me how you discovered the play, did you read it or see it ...?

Djukic: I saw the production at Steppenwolf. I believe it was 2007, 2008. When it first came. Frank Galati's staging ... and I loved the play immediately. And then when the opportunity arose [to stage a contemporary American play in Belgrade] ... I thought that *Homebody/Kabul* in Belgrade would make a lot of sense, for a variety of reasons, I mean, it's a beautiful play, but it also touches on subjects and themes that at the time still are very, very relevant. The abundance [of issues] that the play touches on is really related to both the historical and the political and the daily life of people in the Balkans. And although the play's set obviously in London and Afghanistan, the issues are very close to the local culture and society. And at the same time I think that the play reflects universal problems that are above any local issues ... a universal aspect of the world in crisis.

Black: I'm interested in the relationship of the translation of the play to the play in English ...?

Djukic: Doing a lot of translated plays in English, I am aware of how important the quality of the translation is. So I was very anxious to get a good translation. *Homebody/Kabul* is a language play, so it was really important that everything works on that level, and, as soon as I got the translation I was very happy – with its quality, and preciseness, and rhythm, and Marija Stojanovic, the playwright, who did a superb translation, I was safe with that ... I think that a good translation is always an artistic act ... You translate something so it doesn't feel like a translation, that's a piece of art, and that's what Marija did, and I was happy with it, that I would not have issues with the translation through the process ...[19] There was talk about the translation, the language, I mean, as you know, *Homebody/Kabul* [characters] speak several languages, and they don't translate, Farsi, or ...

Black: That has to stay.

Djukic: That has to stay, so that is another aspect of it. I love that Babel-on ... Tower of Babel sort of idea ...

Black: Did anybody on the production team speak pashto?

Djukic: Yes, we found a journalist who spent about fifteen years in Kabul. He was proficient, and he would come to rehearsal and work with actors and with me to get them to learn the sound of the language.

Black: Could you talk a little about working with the Homebody, the actress, and the first act?

Djukic: That's another unique ... That's why you have to prepare yourself to work on a play like this, because it's not like any other play, you actually have two – we referred to it as 'we're building a tunnel from two different sides of the mountain.' On one side you work on Homebody's monologue, and on the other side you work with the ensemble on the second part of the play. And I was extremely lucky to have an actress who was just amazing, with a wonderful technical skill and at the same time very imaginative. And who, not from the very beginning, but slowly through process, merged with the role, and was able to create something very unique and very beautiful that was recognized by both the theatre community and regular audiences in Belgrade. And it is a piece, I believe, that demands everything that an actor can give, and we worked for hours. Rehearsals were long, exhausting, because the amount of the text ... especially the first phase, learning the lines, often repetitive, was not easy.

Black: Can you tell me a little about staging, and directorial choices about how this play should look?

Djukic: My idea was that the first part – well, that's Kushner's idea, really, that the first part is a monologue, and without adding anything artificial to that, or anything external. That doesn't mean that there was no *mise en scène* in it, because it is such a micro situation where any small gesture becomes very visible and very important. And so we did discuss everything on a small scale. And that's how the first part was worked on, very subtle, any shift of her body in the chair was meaningful and reflected some internal disturbance – and so we wanted to keep it very micro, very delicate, without big gestures. But the second part we went for the opposite. We treated it sort of like an action film, where you constantly bring tensions as you narrate the story as it happens. So there are those two very opposite dynamics in terms of staging, in terms of composition, of the whole thing.

Black: You said something earlier about making sure you're in the same world. How did you accomplish that?

Djukic: Yes, in my opinion, it has to do with recognizing the world of the playwright. The unique framework, I mean whether it's London or Kabul or whether it's monologue or action there is a very distinct style in writing a play that is Kushner's own, and trying to identify these elements, and keep them.

Black: What are those elements?

Djukic: Language is one. Whether it's a monologue or a dialogue you always can recognize his sentence, I think ...

Black: And in translation what you're recognizing is the same kind of structure?

Djukic: It's a highly ... what's the word ... it's a highly saturated language. You know Kushner is not shy of making his characters very eloquent and elaborate in expressing themselves – the Homebody is a wonderful example. You have this woman who is so well read ... [and] has such a quantity of useless knowledge ... that it becomes sort of a burden for her. I mean, she is alone, despite all of this ... the realistic convention is that she is talking to nobody, that her confession is her internal journey with herself. Another thing that I found in Kushner that you find in great playwrights is this ability to switch easily to different worlds, to drama, to go from London to Kabul, to go from Wall Street to a street in Kabul. There is direct connection just like in Shakespeare, where one scene is –

Black: Another part of the forest –

Djukic: Yes, not just that, but also the vertical scale of classes. You are now with Falstaff in the, what's the word? Pub ...

Black: Tavern?

Djukic: Tavern, right, and then with the King. I find that fascinating in Kushner, that ability to travel vertically and horizontally ...

Black: And that itself makes a distinct world, that is made up of all the other worlds ...

Djukic: Exactly. Few writers do that ... but then another thing is just simply creating a playground for collision of ideas.

Black: Oh, that's a good phrase ...

Djukic: Which is every Kushner play. And especially *Homebody*, where everything mingles and everything moves like flags in the wind. You know, that's how his sentences are never dead, always moving. And I think an actor needs to recognize that, and be able to play it in such a way ... So yeah, that's what kept the style, I think. Making sure you are staying in a Kushner play.

Black: What about sound?

Djukic: For sound in *Kabul* – I think that the play has an interesting intersection of a certain mysticism with historical dialectics. I know that sounds pretentious, but I'll try to explain. [*laughter*]

Black: Yeah, OK ...

Djukic: But there is a sense of ritual in non-western rhythm, like the music that is coming from the far east. So I went for that trance-like, disturbing rhythm that you find in the folk music of both Afghanistan and [Afghanistan's] many different cultural regions ... so I went for music that is suggesting rhythm, disturbing rhythm, constant change, a lot of percussion.

Black: Was it original?

Djukic: We found most of it. Of course Kushner is also suggesting – like there is a Frank Sinatra song –

Black: Did you use his music suggestions for all the ... ?

Djukic: Yes, yes, and Sinatra comes really in a beautiful moment, as a break from these trance-like rhythms. So yes, we played with sound, I know there were many details related to sound that helped in transitions, in making this shift from London to Kabul. And another interesting thing I thought was how this story about east and west played in the Balkans, in Belgrade. Which is the region that never stops debating that rift between – well, actually east and west literally meet, historically and geographically, and that's probably one of the reasons why I wanted to do the play. It was, although it wasn't, the story is not related directly to the local history, yet it really did, I mean, we had just [come out] of the war in the Balkans, what, a couple of years before, and so it echoed, it really did resonate. And I like that, I like it when theatre is not always explicit about addressing certain problems, when you kind of look and find analogies, find yourself in stories about others. But it is interesting how life also betrays theatre. I mean, we did *Kabul* in 2009 and in 2015 you actually did get refugees from in the Balkans. So, I mean, just to talk about [what a] visionary Kushner [is], and how he sees something that is sort of a question of logic not of vision, but with a certain way of thinking that can tell you this is going to happen politically unless you react or do something. I found that really fascinating.

Black: I think he would like that perception. Because he jokes about how everybody says he's prescient. When I think he would say that he's logical. Rational.

Djukic: Yeah. I think it has to do with how you look at the history and the past, and how you interpret that ...

Black: If you pay attention –

Djukic: Exactly. You're gonna see how it's going to evolve further, it's not a mystery ... he says that very clearly in his play. He maps it out in such a way that, I mean, that's – you should all follow that. It's what you should learn in school.

Black: There's a word that a lot of people use to describe this particular play and Tony Kushner in general, which is meta-theatrical, and I just wondered if it meant anything to you?

Djukic: I don't like that word.

Black: Why?

Djukic: Because I think that theatre is meta-theatrical by nature. Everything in theatre refers to theatre first. And I think I do a lot of meta-theatrical plays, plays that actually talk about theatre, but I think it is a paradox that is often not acknowledged that theatre is meta-theatrical ... it cannot be anything but that. The question is only how far you insist on acknowledging that, or how clearly you want to state to the audience that what they watch is theatre, not an illusion ... and in a play like *Homebody/Kabul*, where the language is so dense, you also have to be careful – to give these words room to kind of become alive.

Black: How about your audiences, how was the play received?

Djukic: I have to tell you I left after opening, but opening night was quite beautiful. And moving in many ways.

Black: And did people feel that connection that you're talking about? That this is relevant to us, too?

Djukic: Yeah, yeah I think they did. Especially I mean, you have imagery of a war, of mass killings ... lingering through *Homebody* ... of horrible misunderstandings between civilizations, with horrible consequences, which this city, Belgrade, experienced, in many ways. And I do think that the audiences recognized that, from what I saw. But it's also a demanding play on the audience. And I know that not just from my experience, I've seen the production here, too, with American audiences. Which I think is good because ...

Black: Tony Kushner says something about that, too, my audience has to come wanting to think ...

Djukic: Yes! And I think that that's – I love that kind of theatre – I personally like to be treated that way as an audience member to come to see a show that doesn't explain problems, but exposes them and makes you figure it out.

Black: Did you address the question of the truth of the mystery?

Djukic: Oh, yeah.

Black: Some actors want to know those things. And some audiences want to know those things. Did you make a decision? Did anybody think yes, I think she's dead, or no, I think she really did marry the guy from Kabul?

Djukic: I think that question lingered all the time.

Black: Right. [*Laughter*]

Djukic: I think what was important to me was that we feel her presence in the second part. That we feel that she is there. Which is kind of leaning toward that she is alive, and we get that through the Priscilla character, of course ... and I loved the absent characters, characters that are not there? Ghost characters, that's what she is, a ghost character. Despite the fact that she is physically not on stage, she impacts everything that happens ... but to me it's more a driving device for Kushner than his primary focus in the play. It's more a trick to make sure everybody is engaged into the ideas that are being debated in the play.

Black: If that's not the primary focus, then what is? For you?

Djukic: I think the act of the disappearance of Homebody opens up a journey for her husband and her daughter, of which we have heard and already know a lot in her monologue, so what that fact does is send two other people on a physical and spiritual journey ... and in a way, she sort of helps them find themselves by searching for her, and for me that becomes the primary focus ...

Kushner takes a family story [and] raises it to a larger scope, makes a larger issue out of it, I think he is kind of an innovator in that sense ... because you follow this family story and it just opens up the world. And you see how matters of family can matter; that it's not a closed social system – the relationship between mother and daughter or [father and daughter] – actually, the consequences of their relationships are global.

Note the similarity of thought expressed in Vogel's interview with Arthur Holmberg on the global implications of 'family' dramas.

Suzan-Lori Parks

Liz Diamond

Liz Diamond is Professor and Chair of Directing, Yale School of Drama and Resident Director of Yale Repertory Theatre. She directed the world premieres of Suzan-Lori Parks's Imperceptible Mutabilities in the Third Kingdom *(1989),* Betting on the Dust Commander *(1991),* The Death of the Last Black Man in the Whole Entire World *(1992) and* The America Play *(1994). The quotations below come from her participation in a symposium organized and moderated by Jonathan Kalb at Hunter College in 2004.*[20]

On casting a White actor as a Black child in Imperceptible Mutabilities:

The audience was deeply troubled at Manhattan Theater Club that Suzan-Lori had depicted a Black family's only son – and the last child in the line – as a White person ... At one point when I talked to her about it she said something very interesting, which I found moving at the time and still do. She said she felt that it made sense because he was the 'dream child' of this family – a statement that she declined to make at Manhattan Theater Club because she had no confidence that they would understand this. When I asked her what she meant she said: a Black family would dream of having a child that they wouldn't have to fear for, and you don't have to fear for a White boy. He'll be okay. The thought that you might have a child that you wouldn't have to protect was critical in her exploration of this play. In some ways the dream comes true, the assimilationist dream of that play comes true in the end, which she sees as a kind of tragicomic fact.

On directing Death of the Last Black Man:

We staged it as, in a sense, a high mass. Suzan-Lori is Roman Catholic. I remember she said to me, 'Whatever it is, it isn't Baptist and I don't want it to be Baptist. Don't give me the eruptions of song and gestures.' She said, 'It's cooler than that.' And she said, 'I promise you, the cast is gonna wanna go there. Don't go there.' And it was very interesting because the cast did want to go there. Many of them were young African American actors from Black Baptist backgrounds, and they were terribly resistant to this cool, cool tone that Suzan-Lori wanted in the play. They finally embraced it because I think they saw what she was after. The end of the play is solemn, not ecstatic.

On scenic space and The America Play:

We had huge issues relating to the design of *The America Play*. At Yale Rep, Ricardo Hernandez designed a beautiful container for this show, which takes place in 'The Great Hole of History': what a suggestive and beautiful phrase from which to imagine a set! But the play also seems to take place in a hall of wonders. And so Ricardo created a conflation of those two images, a sort of mausoleum type space with white formica walls reaching up to the ceiling, very rectilinear, very sterile, shiny black coal on the floor. At the Public it just became the black hole. We started chucking the black coal at the wall, obscuring what we had created at Yale and going for the one metaphor rather than the two or three or four. I continue to debate with myself as to which world I prefer. I loved the strangeness of the former, but I found the latter space really haunting and dark and more psychologically disturbing.

Richard Foreman

Richard Foreman is the founder of the avant-garde Ontological-Hysteric Theater, the recipient of seven OBIE Awards (for directing, playwriting and lifetime achievement), and a MacArthur Fellow. He directed and designed Parks's Venus *at the Public Theater in 1996 (produced by George C. Wolfe). These quotations are from Foreman's participation in the Hunter College symposium.*

I thought that the texture [of the play], which is basically what I respond to first in all writing, seemed provocative and difficult and interesting. So I said, 'Yeah, I'll do the play.' Then I thought, 'God, how do you do something like this?'

Now, I rehearsed the play for, I think, six weeks. And I had Peter Francis James playing the doctor as a sort of bumbling, shy guy, who was falling over things ... After the New Haven opening, George [Wolfe] and Rosemary [Tichler][21] came to me and said, 'Richard, why are you doing that to Peter? He's such a good actor and you're making him into this wormy little schlep.' So my big mistake was bowing to their wishes, and changing Peter's performance. In New York Peter Francis James played it – a very good performance – more as a distinguished English gentleman of that period who was a serious man of medicine, a little disturbed by his feelings for the Hottentot Venus but nevertheless a man of culture and determination. I think my original version served the play and its strangeness much better. I thought there were many fine things about the production but, as often happens in the theater, you compromise and you negotiate. If I had to do it again today I would try to have the courage to make it stranger than it was. Maybe people thought it was strange, but I think it should have been even stranger.

'An Equation for Black People Onstage'[22]

The following is drawn from Parks's essay, first published in 1995.

The use of the White in the dramatic equation is, I think, too often seen as the only way of exploring our Blackness; this equation reduces Blackness to merely a state of 'non-Whiteness.' Blackness in this equation is a people whose lives consist of a series of reactions and responses to the White ruling class. We have for so long been an 'oppressed' people, but are Black people only blue? As African Americans we have a history, a future and a daily reality in which a confrontation with a White ruling class is a central feature. This reality makes life difficult. This reality often traps us in a singular mode of expression. There are many ways of defining Blackness and there are many ways of presenting Blackness onstage ...

Can a White person be present onstage and not be an oppressor? Can a Black person be onstage and be other than oppressed? For the Black writer, are there Dramas other than race dramas? Does Black life consist of issues other than race issues? ...

So. As a Black person writing for theatre, what is theatre good for? What can theatre do for us? We can 'tell it like it is;' 'tell it as it was;' 'tell it as it could be.' In my plays I do all three; and the writing is rich because we are not an impoverished people, but a wealthy people fallen on hard times ...

I write plays because I love Black people. As there is no single 'Black Experience,' there is no single 'Black Aesthetic' and there is no one way to write or think or feel or dream or interpret or be interpreted. As African Americans we should recognize this insidious essentialism for what it is: a fucked-up trap to reduce us to only one way of being. We should endeavor to show the world and ourselves our beautiful and powerfully infinite variety.

Interview with Han Ong

The following quotations are from Parks's interview with playwright and novelist Han Ong in 1993.[23]

I usually don't write sitting down. To me, language is a physical act. I do this with my own writing and I try to get my students to do this when they write – to move around, so that they are focusing on the breath of the characters, on the physical life of the character, and are putting themselves in an approximation of that character's physical experience. That's where the words come from: movement. I dance around, dance around, dance around, and then I know what the character's saying. I act it out, then I get it in my body, and then I take it up and get it in my head ... then I sit down and go, 'Oh yeah, right ...'

I feel [the characters'] bodies, I know what their bodies are going to be doing. Ninety-five percent of the action, in all of my plays, is in the line of text. So you don't get a lot of parenthetical stage direction. I've written, within the text, specific directions to them, to guide their breathing, to guide the way they walk, whether or not they walk, whether or not they walk with a limp, whatever. They know what to do from what they say and how they say it. The specifics of it are left up to the actor and the director. The internals are in the line, the externals are left up to them ...

I've said I write plays because I love Black people. I just figured it out fairly recently. Not that I had any other reason before that, but I realized why I want Black people on stage – because I love them. And it probably sounds very vague, but it's true.

That's poetry, see. I'm a poet. I'm not a journalist. I'm vague but you know exactly what I mean. I write because I love Black people. I don't know, that in itself will take me a long way ...

[Witnessing] is the perfect word. I'm witnessing. I'm not judging. I'm not proclaiming. I'm not messaging. I'm just saying, 'Here it is.' ...

In playwriting, it has to really work night after night and you have to be able to interpret anew every night, every minute, every day. It's like someone who's practiced Yoga for nine million years. They're incredibly strong and incredibly flexible at the same time. That's what a play has to be. I'm talking about a kind of playwriting that really demands something of itself, too. Right now, I'm writing better than I possibly can. I spend three years on a play, and I look at it and can't believe I wrote it. I wonder where it came from. I feel like I'm writing beyond myself.

Commencement Address at Mount Holyoke

The following quotations are from Suzan-Lori Parks's Commencement Address at Mount Holyoke, Sunday, 27 May 2001 (the punctuation and spelling are Parks's).

SUGGESTION #1: CULTIVATE THE ABILITY TO THINK FOR YRSELF. When someone gives you advice, you lay their advice along side yr own thoughts and feelings, and if what they suggest jives with what youve got going on inside, then you follow their suggestion ... THINK for yrself, LISTEN to yr heart, TUNE IN to yr gut.

SUGGESTION #2: EMBRACE DISCIPLINE. Give yrself the opportunity to discover that discipline is just an extension of the love you have for yrself discipline is not, as a lot of people think, some horrid exacting torturous self flagellating activity. Discipline is just an expression of Love like the Disciples they didnt follow Christ because they <u>HAD TO.</u>

SUGGESTION #3: PRACTICE PATIENCE ... Things will come to you when yr ready to handle them not before. Just keep walking yr road.

SUGGESTION #4: And as you walk yr road, as you live yr life, RELISH THE ROAD. And relish the fact that the road of yr life will probably be a windy road.

SUGGESTION #5: DEVELOP THE ART OF MAKING A SILK PURSE FROM A SOW'S EAR. Cause, you know, it aint whatcha got, its how you work it.

SUGGESTION #6: For every 30 min of tv you watch, READ one poem outloud.

SUGGESTION #7: GET OUT OF YOUR WAY. You can spend yr life **tripping on yrself,** you can also spend yr life **tripping yrself up.** Get out of yr own way.

SUGGESTION #8: <u>**SPLURGE**</u> YR LIFE BY DOING SOMETHING YOU LOVE. 'Talent' happens when yr in love with something and you devote yr life to it and its yr love of it that makes you want to keep doing it, its yr love of it which helps you overcome the obstacles along the way, and its yr love of it that <u>begets a talent for it.</u>

SUGGESTIONS #9, 10, 11, 12, & 13: Eat Yr Vegetables, Floss Yr Teeth, Try Meditation, Get Some Exercise, & SHARPEN YR 7 SENSES: the basic 5 Senses + the 6th Sense: ESP & the 7th Sense which is yr sense of HUMOR.

SUGGESTION #14: SAY 'THANK YOU' at least once a week.

SUGGESTION #15: LOVE YRSELF. Why not.

SUGGESTION #16: BE BOLD. ENVISION YRSELF LIVING A LIFE THAT YOU LOVE. Believe, even if you can only muster yr faith for just this moment, believe that the sort of life you wish to live is, at this very moment, just waiting for you to summon it up. And when you wish for it, you begin moving toward it, and it, in turn, begins moving toward you.[24]

NOTES

1 Introduction to the 1990s

1. This sentence was written in January 2016. To maintain consistency throughout this series, the terms "America" and "American" are used in this volume to refer to the United States of America.

2. Kurt Anderson, 'Best Decade Ever? The 1990s, Obviously', *New York Times*, 6 February 2015, http://www.nytimes.com/2015/02/08/opinion/sunday/the-best-decade-ever-the-1990s-obviously.html (accessed 10 December 2015).

3. Haynes Johnson, *The Best of Times: America in the Clinton Years* (New York: Harcourt, Inc., 2001).

4. Wick Allison, 'The Democrats Should Adopt Perot', *New York Times*, 28 April 1992, http://www.nytimes.com/1992/04/28/opinion/the-democrats-should-adopt-perot.html (accessed 12 December 2015).

5. John Dorschner, 'The Hurricane that Changed Everything', *Miami Herald*, 30 August 1992, 1.

6. Rock the Vote was a non-profit organization founded in 1990 to encourage political engagement among eighteen- to twenty-four-year-olds, in partnership with MTV and widely endorsed by celebrities.

7. Although Perot won no electoral votes, he was the most successful third-party presidential candidate since Theodore Roosevelt, who won 27.4 per cent of the popular vote and eighty-eight electoral votes.

8. Kevin Sack, 'The 1992 Campaign: Political Memo; Quayle's Words Show Plan for Attacking Clinton', *New York Times*, 31 July 1992, http://www.nytimes.com/1992/07/31/us/the-1992-campaign-political-memo-quayle-s-words-show-plan-for-attacking-clinton.html (accessed 4 January 2016).

9. Mark White (ed.), *The Presidency of Bill Clinton: The Legacy of a New Domestic and Foreign Policy* (London and New York: I.B.Tauris, 2012), 53.

10 The United States had a budget deficit in 2002, and it has recorded budget deficits every year since. http://politicalticker.blogs.cnn.com/2010/02/03/cnn-fact-check-the-last-president-to-balance-the-budget/ (accessed 14 December 2015).

11 Throughout 2015, the unemployment rate in the US ranged from 5.7 to 5 per cent. Bureau of Labor Statistics, http://www.bls.gov/data/ (accessed 16 December 2015).

12 White (ed.), *The Presidency of Bill Clinton*, 81.

13 Bob Woodward, *Maestro: Alan Greenspan and the American Economy* (New York: Simon and Schuster, 2000), 217.

14 Joseph Stiglitz, *The Roaring 1990s: A New History of the World's Most Prosperous Decade* (New York: W. W. Norton & Co., 2003); David Remnick (ed.), *The New Gilded Age: The New Yorker Looks at the Culture of Affluence* (New York: Modern Library, 2001).

15 See Francis Fukuyama, *The End of History and the Last Man* (New York: Free Press, 1992).

16 Colin Harrison, *American Culture in the 1990s* (Edinburgh: Edinburgh University Press, 2010), 10.

17 Keith B. Richburg, 'Somalia Battle Killed 12 Americans, Wounded 78', *Washington Post*, 5 October 1993, http://www.washingtonpost.com/wp-dyn/content/article/2006/08/07/AR2006080700747.html (accessed 30 December 2015).

18 The US did, however, participate in the controversial NATO air strikes ('Operation Allied Force') against the Federal Republic of Yugoslavia in spring 1999. Steven Erlanger, 'Rights Group Says NATO Bombing in Yugoslavia Violated Law', *New York Times*, 8 June 2000.

19 Scott Macleod, 'In Yemen, a Massacre of Americans is Averted', *Time*, 17 September 2008, http://content.time.com/time/world/article/0,8599,1842045,00.html (accessed 15 December 2015).

20 Erica Pearson, 'Khobar Towers Bombing of 1996', *Encyclopedia Brittanica*, http://www.britannica.com/event/Khobar-Towers-bombing-of-1996 (accessed 15 December 2015).

21 CNN Library, '1998 US Embassies in Africa Bombing', http://www.cnn.com/2013/10/06/world/africa/africa-embassy-bombings-fast-facts/ (accessed 14 December 2015).

22 'Oklahoma City Bombing', History Channel, http://www.history.com/topics/oklahoma-city-bombing (accessed 3 January 2016).

23 Aviva Shen, 'A Timeline of Mass Shootings in the US Since Columbine', *ThinkProgress*, 14 December 2012, http://

thinkprogress.org/justice/2012/12/14/1337221/a-timeline-of-mass-shootings-in-the-us-since-columbine/ (accessed 3 January 2016).

24 Marilyn Manson, 'Columbine: Whose Fault is It?' *Rolling Stone*, 24 June 1999, 23–4.

25 Centers for Disease Control and Prevention (CDC), 'HIV and AIDS – United States, 1981–2000', http://www.cdc.gov/mmwr/preview/mmwrhtml/mm5021a2.htm (accessed 4 January 2016).

26 Ashe died from AIDS-related pneumonia in 1993.

27 amfAR (Foundation for AIDS Research), 'Thirty Years of HIV/AIDS: Snapshots of an Epidemic', http://www.amfar.org/thirty-years-of-hiv/aids-snapshots-of-an-epidemic/ (accessed 4 January 2016).

28 United States Census Bureau, '1990 Census', http://www.census.gov/main/www/cen1990.html (accessed 12 October 2015).

29 United States Census Bureau, 'Demographic Trends in the Twentieth Century', https://www.census.gov/prod/2002pubs/censr-4.pdf (accessed 12 October 2015).

30 Stephen McFarland and Katie Nelson, 'How the 1991 Crown Heights Riots Unfolded', *New York Daily News*, 14 August 2011, http://www.nydailynews.com/new-york/timeline-1991-crown-heights-riots-unfolded-article-1.945012 (accessed 31 January 2016).

31 Marcia D. Greenberger, 'What Anita Hill Did for America', Special to CNN, 22 October 2010, http://www.cnn.com/2010/OPINION/10/21/greenberger.anita.hill/ (accessed 2 February 2016).

32 *Daily Mail*, 'News', http://www.dailymail.co.uk/news/article-2810058/Slashed-wrists-sex-prison-guards-jailhouse-lesbian-lover-Inside-twisted-world-Susan-Smith-20-years-drowned-sons-blamed-black-man.html (accessed 6 January 2016).

33 Editors of Time-Life Books, *The Digital Decade: The 90s* (New York: Bishop Books, 2000), 26.

34 'Robertson Letter Attacks Feminists', *New York Times*, 26 August 1992, http://www.nytimes.com/1992/08/26/us/robertson-letter-attacks-feminists.html (accessed 11 December 2016).

35 YouTube recorded 2,075,612 viewings of this clip as of 4 January 2016.

36 Nina Esperanza Serrianne, *America in the Nineties* (Syracuse, NY: Syracuse University Press, 2015), 220–4.

37 GLAAD is an organization of advocacy and support for the LGBTQ community.

38   Don't Ask, Don't Tell was repealed in 2010. In 2013 the Supreme Court declared that key components of DOMA were unconstitutional. In 2015, the Supreme Court declared same-sex marriage legal in all fifty states. US Government Publishing Office, https://www.gpo.gov/fdsys/pkg/PLAW-104publ199/html/PLAW-104publ199.htm (accessed 4 January 2016).

39   Frank Rich, 'Journal: Summer of Matthew Shepard', *New York Times*, 3 July 1999, http://www.nytimes.com/1999/07/03/opinion/journal-summer-of-matthew-shepard.html?pagewanted=all (accessed 6 January 2016).

40   Johnson, *The Best of Times*, 17.

41   Susannah Fox and Lee Rainie, 'How the Internet has Woven Itself into American Life', Pew Research Center, 27 February 2014, http://www.pewinternet.org/2014/02/27/part-1-how-the-internet-has-woven-itself-into–American-life/ (accessed 11 December 2015).

42   Johnson, *The Best of Times*, 25.

43   Patrick Thibodeau, 'DOJ Goes for Jugular: Break it Up', *Computerworld*, 1 May 2000, 1, 101.

44   Johnson, *The Best of Times*, 78–9. In 2001, Venter, Celera and the NIH/Human Genome Project essentially shared credit for the mapping of the human genome.

45   J. Madeleine Nash, 'This Rice Could Save a Million Kids a Year', *Time*, 31 July 2000, http://content.time.com/time/magazine/article/0,9171,997586,00.html (accessed 3 January 2016).

46   Hubble Space Telescope: New Views of the Universe, http://hubblesite.org/hubble_discoveries/hstexhibit/ (accessed 18 December 2015).

47   United States Census Bureau, '1990 Census', http://www.census.gov/main/www/cen1990.html (accessed 12 October 2015).

48   Ibid.

49   'Demographic Trends in the Twentieth Century', https://www.census.gov/prod/2002pubs/censr-4.pdf (accessed 12 October 2015).

50   'Religion', http://www.gallup.com/poll/1690/religion.aspx (accessed 28 June 2016).

51   'Trends in Attitudes Toward Religion and Social Issues, 1987–2007', http://www.pewresearch.org/2007/10/15/trends-in-attitudes-toward-religion-and-social-issues-19872007/ (accessed 27 June 2016).

52   'Religion', Gallup poll.

53 See http://nces.ed.gov/pubs2004/2004075.pdf (accessed 7 January 2016).
54 'The History of Film: The 1990s', http://www.filmsite.org/90sintro.html (accessed 7 January 2016).
55 Juliet B. Schor, *The Overspent American: Upscaling, Downshifting, and the New Consumer* (New York: Basic Books, 1998), 14.
56 Johnson, *The Best of Times*, 26.
57 '102 Popular Fads and Trends from the 90s', http://star102cleveland.cbslocal.com/2014/03/13/102-popular-trends-and-fads-from-the-90s/ (accessed 15 December 2016).
58 US Department of Education, National Center for Education Statistics (2016), *Digest of Education Statistics, 2014* (NCES 2016–006), https://nces.ed.gov/fastfacts/display.asp?id=65 (accessed 27 June 2016).
59 Ibid., https://nces.ed.gov/Pressrelease/reform/ (accessed 27 June 2016).
60 Gale Group, 'The 1990s: Education, an Overview', http://ic.galegroup.com (accessed 28 June 2016).
61 Mary Ann Zehr, 'Schools Grew More Segregated in the 1990s', *Education Week*, 8 August 2001.
62 Arielle Eiser, 'The Crisis on Campus', *American Psychological Association* 42 (8) (September 2011), http://www.apa.org/monitor/2011/09/crisis-campus.aspx (accessed 27 June 2016).
63 National Center for Eduation Statistics, http://nces.ed.gov/pubs2004/2004075.pdf (accessed 26 June 2016).
64 Frederic A. Emmert, 'U.S. Media in the 90s', http://www.4uth.gov.ua/usa/english/media/files/media1cd.htm (accessed 12 December 2016).
65 Brian Hiatt, 'Best 100 Albums of the 1990s', *Rolling Stone*, 27 April 2011, http://www.rollingstone.com/music/lists/100-best-albums-of-the-nineties-20110427#ixzz3wURg4B9B (accessed 6 January 2016).
66 Jack Endino, quoted in Michael Azerrad, 'NEW MUSIC 1992: For real rockers Seattle is the ultimate wet dream', *Rolling Stone*, 16 April 1992, 43.
67 Douglas A. Blackmon, 'Forget the Stereotype: America is Becoming a Nation of Culture', *Wall Street Journal*, 17 September 1998, http://www.wsj.com/articles/SB905921089919950500 (accessed 20 January 2016).

68 David Edelstein, 'Indie Movies Saved Cinema', *New York Magazine*, 3 February 2013, http://nymag.com/movies/features/david-edelstein-1993-movies/ (accessed 6 January 2016).

69 Ibid.

70 AMC Filmsite, 'Top Box Office Hits: By Decade/Year', http://www.filmsite.org/boxoffice2.html (accessed 20 January 2016). This record reflects unadjusted domestic gross totals.

71 Serrianne, *America in the Nineties*, 143.

72 Candice Bergen famously sang 'You Make Me Feel Like a Natural Woman' to her newborn during the final episode of the show's fourth season.

73 Bill Carter, '*Friends* Finale Audience is the Fourth Biggest Ever', *New York Times*, 8 May 2004, http://www.nytimes.com/2004/05/08/arts/friends-finale-s-audience-is-the-fourth-biggest-ever.html?_r=0 (accessed 3 January 2016).

74 Ibid.

75 A number of sports heroes from the 1990s fell from grace in the twenty-first century. Baseball player Jose Conseco's *Juiced: Wild Times, Rampant 'Roids, Smash Hits & How Baseball Got Big* (New York: Dey Street/HarperCollins, 2006) claimed that most MLB players took performance-enhancing drugs, including McGwire and Sosa. In 2012, Lance Armstrong was banned for life from competing in all sports that follow the World Anti-Doping Agency code for using performance-enhancing drugs, a decision he did not contest.

76 Reference for Business, SIC 2731 Book Publishing, http://www.referenceforbusiness.com/industries/Printing-Publishing-Allied/Book-Publishing.html (accessed 21 January 2016).

77 Ibid.

78 Allex Allenchey, 'How the Upheaval of the 90s Revolutionized the Art World', *Artspace*, 26 February 2013, http://www.artspace.com/magazine/art_101/art_market/the_art_world_in_the_90s-5912 (accessed 23 January 2016).

79 Jerry Saltz, 'On '93 in Art', *New York Magazine*, 3 February 2013, http://nymag.com/arts/art/features/jerry-saltz-1993-art/ (accessed 23 January 2016).

80 Beverly Bundy, *The Century in Food: America's Fads and Favorites* (Portland, OR: Collectors Press, 2002), 174.

81 Gil Troy, *The Age of Clinton: America in the 1990s* (New York: St Martin's Press, 2015), 255.

82 John Quiggin, 'The Y2K Scare: Causes, Costs, Cures', *Australian Journal of Public Administration* 64 (3) (September 2005): 46.
83 Ibid., 47–8.
84 Troy, *The Age of Clinton*, 264–6.

2 American Theatre in the 1990s

1   Jeffrey D. Mason, 'American Stages (Curtain Raiser)', in Jeffrey D. Mason and J. Ellen Gainor (eds), *Performing America: Cultural Nationalism in American Theater* (Ann Arbor: University of Michigan Press, 1999), 1–2.
2   Ibid.
3   Ibid., 2.
4   See, for example, C. W. E. Bigsby, 'Redefining the Centre: Politics, Race, Gender', in C. W. E. Bigsby, *Modern American Drama, 1945–2000* (Cambridge: Cambridge University Press, 2000), 261–362; Brenda Murphy with Laurie J. C. Cella, *Twentieth Century American Drama, Volume IV, 1980–2000* (London: Routledge, 2006), 3; S. E. Wilmer, 'Imaging and Deconstructing the Multicultural Nation in the 1990s', in S. E. Wilmer, *Theatre, Society and the Nation: Staging American Identities* (Cambridge: Cambridge University Press, 2002), 173–202.
5   James Davison Hunter, *Culture Wars: The Struggle to Define America* (New York: HarperCollins, 1991).
6   Kimberle Crenshaw, 'Mapping the Margins: Intersectionality, Identity Politics, and Violence Against Women', *Stanford Law Review* 43 (6) (July 1991): 1241–99.
7   S. E. Wilmer, *Theatre, Society and the Nation: Staging American Identities* (Cambridge: Cambridge University Press, 2002), 181, 186.
8   Ibid., 196, 198.
9   Jeffrey Sweet, 'Broadway and Off Broadway', in Otis L. Guernsey Jr and Jeffrey Sweet (eds), *Theater Yearbook 1990–1991* (New York: Applause Theatre Book Publishers, 1992), 41.
10 Jeffrey Sweet, 'Broadway and Off Broadway', in Otis L. Guernsey Jr and Jeffrey Sweet (eds), *Theater Yearbook 1991–1992* (New York: Applause Theatre Book Publishers, 1992), 49.
11 Jill Dolan, 'Rehearsing Democracy: Advocacy, Public Intellectuals,

and Civic Engagement in Theatre and Performance Studies', *Theatre Topics* 11 (1) (2001): 2.
12. Ibid., 5, 7, 9–10.
13. Gerald M. Berkowitz, Introduction, in *American Drama of the Twentieth Century* (New York: Longman Publishing Group, 1992), 5.
14. Ibid., 7–9.
15. Robert A. Schanke, Introduction, in Robert A. Schanke (ed.), *Angels in the American Theater* (Carbondale: Southern Illinois University Press, 2007), 1, 4–8.
16. Berkowitz, Introduction, 9.
17. June Schlueter, 'American Drama of the 1990s On and Off-Broadway', in David Krasner (ed.), *A Companion to Twentieth-Century American Drama* (Malden, MA: Blackwell Publishing Ltd, 2005), 504.
18. Marshall W. Mason, 'ECTC Keynote Address', presented and printed in the programme of the East Central Theatre Conference (ECTC), Philadelphia, Pennsylvania, 19 February 1993.
19. Schlueter, 'American Drama of the 1990s', 505.
20. Ibid.
21. See Dean Adams, 'Puttin' the Profit in Nonprofit Broadway Theatre Companies', *Theatre Symposium* 22 (2014): 48–61.
22. Robert Viagas, 'How to Tell Broadway from Off-Broadway from …', *Playbill*, 4 January 1998, http://www.playbill.com/article/how-to-tell-broadway-from-off-broadway-from-com-110450 (accessed 17 March 2016).
23. Schlueter, 'American Drama of the 1990s', 516–17.
24. Mason, 'ECTC Keynote Address'.
25. Schanke, Introduction, 6.
26. Ibid., 7. It should be noted that Schanke's account draws on Steven C. Dubin's *Arresting Images: Impolitic Art and Uncivil Actions* (Abingdon: Routledge, 1992).
27. Mason, 'ECTC Keynote Address'.
28. Adams, 'Puttin' the Profit', 50–4.
29. National Endowment for the Arts, 'All America's a Stage: Growth and Challenges in Nonprofit Theater', https://www.arts.gov/publications/all-americas-stage-0 (accessed 17 March 2016).
30. Arnold Aronson, 'American Theatre in Context: 1945–Present', in Don B. Wilmeth and Christopher Bigsby (eds), *The Cambridge*

History of American Theatre, Vol. III, Post-World War II to the 1990s (Cambridge: Cambridge University Press, 2000), 156.

31 Gerald M. Berkowitz, *New Broadways, Theatre Across America: Approaching a New Millennium*, rev. edn (New York: Applause Books, 1997), 204.

32 Aronson, 'American Theatre in Context', 100.

33 Schlueter, 'American Drama of the 1990s', 506.

34 C. W. E. Bigsby, Introduction, in Don B. Wilmeth and Christopher Bigsby (eds), *The Cambridge History of American Theatre, Vol. III, Post-World War II to the 1990s* (Cambridge: Cambridge University Press, 2000), 16.

35 Berkowitz, *New Broadways*, 203.

36 John Kendrick, 'Spectacles and Boardrooms – "As If We Never Said Goodbye"', in *Musical Theatre: A History* (New York: Continuum International Publishing Group, 2008), 362.

37 Nathan Hurwitz, *A History of the American Musical Theatre: No Business Like It* (New York: Routledge, 2014), 216.

38 Sweet, *Theatre Yearbook, 1990–1991*, 40.

39 Aronson, 'American Theatre in Context', 190; The Broadway League: A History, https://www.broadwayleague.com/about (accessed 17 March 2016).

40 Stacy Wolf, Introduction, in *Changed For Good, A Feminist History of the Broadway Musical* (Oxford: Oxford University Press, 2011), 5.

41 Raymond Knapp, *The American Musical and the Formation of National Identity* (Princeton, NJ: Princeton University Press, 2005), 3.

42 John Bush Jones, *Our Musicals, Ourselves: A Social History of the American Musical Theatre* (Waltham, MA: Brandeis University Press, 2003), 270–3.

43 See Miranda Lundskaer-Nielsen's 'Staging the Canon', in *Directors and the New Musical Drama: British and American Musical Theatre in the 1980s and '90s* (New York: Palgrave Macmillan, 2008) for her discussion of revivals of *Nine, Follies, Cabaret* and *Oklahoma!*

44 John Degan, 'Musical Theatre Since World War II', in Don B. Wilmeth and Christopher Bigsby (eds), *The Cambridge History of American Theatre, Vol. III, Post-World War II to the 1990s* (Cambridge: Cambridge University Press, 2000), 459–63.

45 Jessica Sternfeld, Introduction, in *The Megamusical* (Bloomington: Indiana University Press, 2006), 1–4.
46 Ibid., 293–304.
47 Ibid., 313.
48 Michael Feingold, 'Musical Muddlings', *Village Voice*, 6 May 1997, quoted in Sternfeld, Introduction, 319.
49 Sternfeld, Introduction, 324.
50 http://www.thefiscaltimes.com/Articles/2014/09/24/10-Top-Grossing-Broadway-Musicals (accessed 17 March 2016).
51 Bush Jones, *Our Musicals, Ourselves*, 330; http://www.nytimes.com/1994/04/19/theater/review-theater-beauty-and-the-beast-disney-does-broadway-dancing-spoons-and-all.html?pagewanted=all (accessed 17 March 2016).
52 Knapp, *The American Musical*, 163.
53 Bush Jones, *Our Musicals, Ourselves*, 1.
54 Knapp, *The American Musical*, 284.
55 Wolf, Introduction, 12.
56 Bush Jones, *Our Musicals, Ourselves*, 305–8.
57 Ibid., 320–1, 308–12.
58 Knapp, *The American Musical*, 120–2.
59 Ibid., 103.
60 Wolf, Introduction, 169
61 Knapp, *The American Musical*, 9.
62 Bush Jones, *Our Musicals, Ourselves*, 341
63 Ibid.
64 Jeffrey Eric Jenkins, 'Broadway and Off Broadway', in Otis L. Guernsey Jr (ed.), *Theater Yearbook: The Best Plays of 1999–2000* (New York: Limelight Editions, 2000), 10–12.
65 Sweet, *Theatre Yearbook, 1991–1992*, 3.
66 Frank Rich, 'Review/Theater; 200 Years of a Nation's Sorrows, in 9 Chapters', *New York Times*, 15 November 1993, http://www.nytimes.com/1993/11/15/theater/review-theater-200-years-of-a-nation-s-sorrows-in-9-chapters.html?pagewanted=all (accessed 17 March 2016).
67 Annette J. Saddik, Introduction, in *Contemporary American Drama* (Edinburgh: Edinburgh University Press, 2007), 10.
68 C. W. E. Bigsby, 'Arthur Miller: The Moral Imperative', in C. W. E.

Bigsby, *Modern American Drama, 1945–2000* (Cambridge: Cambridge University Press, 2000), 115.
69 Ibid., 120.
70 Steven Price, 'Fifteen-Love, Thirty-Love: Edward Albee', in David Krasner (ed.), *A Companion to Twentieth-Century American Drama* (Malden, MA: Blackwell Publishing Ltd, 2005), 260–1.
71 Saddik, Introduction, 36.
72 Price, 'Fifteen-Love, Thirty-Love', 247.
73 C. W. E. Bigsby, 'Edward Albee: Journey to Apocalypse', in C. W. E. Bigsby, *Modern American Drama, 1945–2000* (Cambridge: Cambridge University Press, 2000), 152.
74 Saddik, Introduction, 139.
75 Brenda Murphy with Laurie J. C. Cella, Introduction, in Brenda Murphy with Laurie J. C. Cella (eds), *Twentieth Century American Drama, Vol. IV, 1980–2000* (London: Routledge, 2006), 1.
76 Leslie A. Wade, '*States of Shock*, *Simpatico*, and *Eyes for Consuela*: Sam Shepard's Plays of the 1990s', in Matthew Roudane (ed.), *The Cambridge Companion to Sam Shepard* (Cambridge: Cambridge University Press, 2002), 262, 258–9.
77 Ibid., 263.
78 Carla J. McDonough, *Staging Masculinity: Male Identity in Contemporary American Drama* (Jefferson, NC: McFarland & Co., 1997), 75.
79 Ibid., 71–2.
80 Lesley Kane (ed.), *David Mamet in Conversation* (Ann Arbor: University of Michigan Press, 2001), 125, quoted in Brenda Murphy, '*Oleanna*: Language and Power', in Christopher Bigsby (ed.), *The Cambridge Companion to David Mamet* (Cambridge: Cambridge University Press, 2004), 125.
81 Gene A. Plunka, 'John Guare and the Popular Culture Hype of Celebrity Status', in David Krasner (ed.), *A Companion to Twentieth-Century American Drama* (Malden, MA: Blackwell Publishing Ltd, 2005), 365. Plunka cites the term 'radical chic' used by Tom Wolfe, *Radical Chic and Mau-Mauing the Flak Catchers* (New York: Farrar, Straus, and Giroux, 1970).
82 David Roman, *Acts of Intervention: Performance, Gay Culture, and AIDS* (Bloomington: Indiana University Press, 1998), 158–60.
83 Saddik, Introduction, 138.

84 Tiffany Ana Lopez, 'Writing Beyond Borders: A Survey of US Latina/o Drama', in David Krasner (ed.), *A Companion to Twentieth-Century American Drama* (Malden, MA: Blackwell Publishing Ltd, 2005), 371.

85 See *Theatre Journal* 52 (1) (March 2000), Special Issue on Latina/o Performance.

86 We recognize that designations for collective identities as well as artistic practices continue to change over time; the designations used in this volume reflect the language of the period.

87 Harvey Young, Introduction, in Harvey Young (ed.), *The Cambridge Companion to African American Theatre* (Cambridge: Cambridge University Press, 2013), 6–7.

88 Ibid., 9.

89 Faedra Chatard Carpenter, 'Spectacles of Whiteness from Adrienne Kennedy to Suzan-Lori Parks', in Harvey Young (ed.), *The Cambridge Companion to African American Theatre* (Cambridge: Cambridge University Press, 2013), 174–5. Also see Suzan-Lori Parks, 'New Black Math', *Theatre Journal* 57 (4) (2005): 580.

90 Young, Introduction, 1–2.

91 August Wilson, 'The Ground on Which I Stand', *Callaloo* 20 (3) (1998): 493–503.

92 http://www.playbill.com/article/the-big-event-wilson-vs-brustein-at-town-hall-com-69419 (accessed 17 March 2016).

93 Ibid. Also see William Grimes, 'Face to Face Encounter on Race in the Theater', *New York Times*, 29 January 1997, http://www.nytimes.com/1997/01/29/theater/face-to-face-encounter-on-race-in-the-theater.html (accessed 17 March 2016).

94 Harry J. Elam, Jr, 'August Wilson', in David Krasner (ed.), *A Companion to Twentieth-Century American Drama* (Malden, MA: Blackwell Publishing Ltd, 2005), 318.

95 Ibid., 321.

96 Sandra G. Shannon, Introduction, in Sandra G. Shannon (ed.), *August Wilson's Pittsburgh Cycle: Critical Perspectives on the Plays* (Jefferson, NC: McFarland & Co., 2016), 5.

97 Sarah Saddler and Paul Bryant-Jackson, '*Two Trains Running*: Bridging Diana Taylor's "rift" and Narrating Manning Marable's Living History', in Sandra G. Shannon (ed.), *August Wilson's Pittsburgh Cycle: Critical Perspectives on the Plays* (Jefferson, NC: McFarland & Co., 2016), 55–6.

98 See Werner Sollors (ed.), *The Adrienne Kennedy Reader* (Minneapolis: University of Minnesota Press, 2001), which includes many of her most well-known plays, such as *A Movie Star Has to*

Star in Black and White, *The Alexander Plays* and *The Ohio State Murders*.

99 Philip C. Kolin, Introduction, in *Understanding Adrienne Kennedy* (Columbia: University of South Carolina Press, 2005), 2; Caroline Jackson Smith, 'From Drama to Literature: The Unparalleled Vision of Adrienne Kennedy', *Black Masks* (August/September 1996): 15, quoted in Kolin.

100 Kolin, Introduction, 161.

101 Anna Deavere Smith, Introduction, in *Fires in the Mirror* (New York: Anchor Books, 1993), xxvi.

102 Joan Wylie Hall, '"Everybody's Talking": Anna Deavere Smith's Documentary Theatre', in Philip C. Kolin (ed.), *Contemporary African American Women Playwrights* (London: Routledge, 2007), 151.

103 Kimberly Rae Connor, 'Negotiating the Differences: Anna Deavere Smith and Liberation Theater', in Ellen J. Goldner and Safiya Henderson-Holmes (eds), *Racing and (E)Racing Language: Living with the Color of Our Words* (Syracuse, NY: Syracuse University Press, 2001), 178, quoted in Wylie Hall, '"Everybody's Talking"', 151.

104 Lisa M. Anderson, *Black Feminism in Contemporary Drama* (Urbana: University of Illinois Press, 2008), 65.

105 Daphne Lei, 'Staging the Binary: Asian American Theatre in the Late Twentieth Century', in David Krasner (ed.), *A Companion to Twentieth-Century American Drama* (Malden, MA: Blackwell Publishing Ltd, 2005), 301–3, 314.

106 Esther Kim Lee, *A History of Asian American Theatre* (Cambridge: Cambridge University Press, 2006), 42. It should be noted that the Asian American Theater Company in San Francisco was originally named the Asian American Theatre Workshop, and that Northwest Asian American Theatre was first called the Theatrical Ensemble of Asians, Seattle.

107 Ibid., 43.

108 Ibid., 1.

109 See Chapter 5, 'The Second Wave Playwrights', in Esther Kim Lee, *A History of Asian American Theatre* (Cambridge: Cambridge University Press, 2006), 124–54.

110 Esther Kim Lee, *The Theatre of David Henry Hwang* (London: Bloomsbury Methuen Drama, 2015), 76, 89, 107.

111 Ibid., 100.

112 Lee, *A History of Asian American Theatre*, 211, 222.
113 Ibid., 202–6.
114 Yvonne Yarbro-Bejaro, 'The Female Subject in Chicano Theatre: Sexuality, "Race", and Class', in Sue-Ellen Case (ed.), *Performing Feminisms: Feminist Critical Theory and Theatre* (Baltimore: Johns Hopkins Press, 1990), 131, 133.
115 Tiffany Ana Lopez, 'Writing Beyond Borders: A Survey of US Latina/o Drama', in David Krasner (ed.), *A Companion to Twentieth-Century American Drama* (Malden, MA: Blackwell Publishing Ltd, 2005), 377.
116 Irma Mayorga, 'Afterword: Homecoming: The Politics of Myth and Location in Cherrie L. Moraga's *The Hungry Woman: A Mexican Medea* and *Heart of the Earth: A Popol Vuh Story*', in *The Hungry Woman* by Cherri L. Moraga (Albuquerque, NM: West End Press, 2001), 158.
117 W. B. Worthen, 'Staging America: The Subject of History in Chicano/a Theatre', *Theatre Journal* 49 (2) (May 1997): 101.
118 Alberto Sandoval-Sanchez, *Jose, Can You See? Latinos On and Off Broadway* (Madison: University of Wisconsin Press, 1999), 116, quoted in Tiffany Ana Lopez, 'Writing Beyond Borders: A Survey of US Latina/o Drama', in David Krasner (ed.), *A Companion to Twentieth-Century American Drama* (Malden, MA: Blackwell Publishing Ltd, 2005), 378.
119 See Joel G. Fink, '*Marisol* (Review)', *Theatre Journal* 48 (1) (March 1996): 101–2.
120 Geraldine Harris, *Staging Femininities: Performance and Performativity* (Manchester, NH: Manchester University Press, 1999), 2. Harris maintains that 'Advances in performance practices may be *influenced by* theories, but are ultimately produced through the process of creating work.'
121 Penny Farfan and Lesley Ferris, Introduction, in *Contemporary Women Playwrights into the Twenty-First Century* (Basingstoke: Palgrave Macmillan, 2013), 2–3.
122 Ibid., 6–7.
123 Kathy A. Perkins and Roberta Uno, Introduction, in *Contemporary Plays by Women of Color: An Anthology* (London: Routledge, 1996), 10.
124 Helene Keyssar, Introduction, in Helene Keyssar (ed.), *Feminist Theatre and Theory: Contemporary Critical Essays* (New York: St Martin's Press, 1996), 1.

125 Susan M. Steadman, *Dramatic Re-Visions: An Annotated Bibliography of Feminism and Theatre, 1972–1988* (Chicago: American Library Association, 1991), 12–16.
126 See Jan Balakian, 'Wendy Wasserstein: A Feminist Voice from the Seventies to the Present', in Brenda Murphy (ed.), *The Cambridge Companion to American Women Playwrights* (Cambridge: Cambridge University Press, 1999), 213–31.
127 Bigsby, *Modern American Drama*, 337.
128 Christine M. Cooper, 'Worry about Vaginas: Feminism and Eve Ensler's *The Vagina Monologues*', *Signs* 32 (3) (Spring 2007): 727–8.
129 Ibid., 732–4.
130 Ann Pellegrini, 'Repercussions and Remainders in the Plays of Paula Vogel: An Essay in Five Moments', in David Krasner (ed.), *A Companion to Twentieth-Century American Drama* (Malden, MA: Blackwell Publishing Ltd, 2005), 474, 478.
131 Grayley Herren, 'Narrating, Witnessing, and Healing Trauma in Paula Vogel's *How I Learned to Drive*', *Modern Drama* 53 (1) (Spring 2010): 44; Arthur Holmberg, quoted in Herren, 44. Arthur Holmberg, 'Through the Eyes of Lolita: Interview with Paula Vogel', *ART News* (September 1998), ARTicles gallery, American Repertory Theater, Cambridge, MA, http://americanrepertorytheater.org/inside/articles/through-eyes-lolita (accessed 16 July 2016).
132 Jeanne Colleran, *Theatre and War, Theatrical Responses since 1991* (Basingstoke: Palgrave Macmillan, 2012), 50.
133 Jill Dolan, Introduction, in Alisa Solomon and Framji Minwalla (eds), *The Queerest Art: Essays on Lesbian and Gay Theater* (New York: New York University Press, 2002), 5.
134 Scott Herring, Introduction, in Scott Herring (ed.), *The Cambridge Companion to American Gay and Lesbian Literature* (Cambridge: Cambridge University Press, 2015), 5.
135 Jill Dolan, 'Lesbian and Gay Drama', in David Krasner (ed.), *A Companion to Twentieth-Century American Drama* (Malden, MA: Blackwell Publishing Ltd, 2005), 488–9.
136 Ibid., 490–1.
137 David Roman, Introduction, in *Acts of Intervention, Performance, Gay Culture, and AIDS* (Bloomington: Indiana University Press, 1998), xiii.
138 Ibid., 58–65.

139 David Savran, 'Queer Theater and the Disarticulation of Identity', in Alisa Solomon and Framji Minwalla (eds), *The Queerest Art: Essays on Lesbian and Gay Theater* (New York: New York University Press, 2002), 153–64.
140 Lenora Champagne, 'Once Upon a Time in Performance Art', in Bruce King (ed.), *Contemporary American Theatre* (New York: St Martin's Press, 1991), 183.
141 Ibid., 180.
142 Dolan, 'Lesbian and Gay Drama', 494.
143 Lee, *A History of Asian American Theatre*, 168–73.
144 Lopez, 'Writing Beyond Borders', 381–2.
145 Ibid., 382–3.
146 Elizabeth C. Ramirez, *Chicanas/Latinas in American Theatre: A History of Performance* (Bloomington: Indiana University Press, 2000), 130–1.
147 Wilmer, *Theatre, Society and the* Nation, 199.
148 Theodore Shank, *Beyond the Boundaries, American Alternative Theatre* (Ann Arbor: University of Michigan Press, 2002), 252.
149 Ibid., 194.
150 Ehren Fordyce, 'Experimental Drama at the End of the Century', in David Krasner (ed.), *A Companion to Twentieth-Century American Drama* (Malden, MA: Blackwell Publishing Ltd, 2005), 536, 541.
151 Ibid., 538.
152 Amy S. Green argues that it is 'contradiction' rather than 'continuity' between a familiar text and its 'all-new theatrical idiom that marks contemporary classical revival as the unique product of our specific theatrical, cultural and historical milieu'. See Amy S. Green, *The Revisionist Stage* (Cambridge: Cambridge University Press, 1994), 2.
153 Sharon Friedman, 'Feminist Revisions of Classic Texts on the American Stage', in Barbara Ozieblo and Maria Dolores Narbona-Carrion (eds), *Codifying the National Self, Spectators, Actors and the American Dramatic Text* (Brussels: P.I.E.-Peter Lang, 2006), 89.
154 Carol Martin, *Theatre of the Real* (Basingstoke: Palgrave Macmillan, 2013), 5.
155 Ryan M. Claycomb, '(Ch)oral History: Documentary Theatre, the Communal Subject and Progressive Politics', *Journal of Dramatic Theory and Criticism* XVII (2) (Spring 2003): 95.

156 Carol Martin, 'Bodies of Evidence', *TDR* 50 (3) (Autumn 2006): 9.

3 Terrence McNally

1 Terrence McNally died in Sarasota, Florida on March 24 2020 of complications from COVID 19. He was 81 years old.
2 Terrence McNally, *The Ritz*, in *Fifteen Short Plays* (Lyme, NH: Smith and Kraus, 1994), 293.
3 Terrence McNally, *Love! Valour! Compassion!*, in *Selected Works: Terrence McNally, A Memoir in Plays* (New York: Grove Press, 2015), 443. Unless otherwise noted, further references to Terrence McNally's plays are to this edition.
4 Terrence McNally, *Andre's Mother*, in *Fifteen Short Plays* (Lyme, NH: Smith and Kraus, 1994), 350.
5 Toby Silverman Zinman, 'Interview with Terrence McNally', in Toby Silverman Zinman (ed.), *Terrence McNally: A Casebook* (New York and London: Garland, 1997), 5.
6 Ibid., 4.
7 Terrence McNally, *The Lisbon Traviata*, in *Three Plays by Terrence McNally* (New York: Plume, 1990), 85. Further references are to this edition.
8 Tennessee Williams, *A Streetcar Named Desire*, in *The Theatre of Tennessee Williams, Volume 1* (New York: New Directions Publishing, 1971), 355.
9 Zinman, 'Interview with Terrence McNally', 4.
10 The same trio from *Cosi fan Tutte* was used prominently in the 1970 British film *Sunday Bloody Sunday*, one of the first serious films to treat bisexuality and gay relationships as normal.
11 One could add to this list Anna, the mother in *The Rink* (1985; book, Terrence McNally; music, John Kander; lyrics, Fred Ebb). Anna's conflict is with a grown daughter, Angel, who ran away from home and became part of 1960s countercultural movements. It is easy to read their conflict as one between a mother and a gay son. After all, here was a musical that starred Broadway diva Chita Rivera and Liza Minnelli, who had a sizeable gay following.
12 David M. Halperin, *How to Be Gay* (Cambridge, MA: Harvard University Press, 2012), 408.
13 Actually, at the time he wrote the play, there was not a recording in circulation of Callas's Lisbon *Traviata*. The title was supposed

to represent 'the mythic, the unobtainable' (McNally in Zinman, 'Interview with Terrence McNally', 158). Later, a recording of this performance became available.

14 John Ardoin, 'Callas and the Juilliard Master Classes', in Zinman, 'Interview with Terrence McNally', 161.

15 Terrence McNally and Wendy Wasserstein, *Kiss Kiss Dahlings* and *The Last Mile*, DVD (W. Long Branch, NJ: Kulturvideo, Broadway Theatre Archive, 2002). Also distributed by Great Performances (WNET Television Station, New York).

16 Terrence McNally, *Corpus Christi* (New York: Grove Press, 1998), 50. Further references to *Corpus Christi* are to this edition.

17 *Corpus Christi: Playing with Redemption*, documentary film directed by Nic Arnzen and James Brandon, DVD (Philadelphia, PA: Breaking Glass Pictures, 2014).

18 Richard D. Mohn analyses these aspects of *Parsifal* in *Gay Ideas: Outing and Other Controversies* (Boston: Beacon Press, 1994).

19 Mrs McElroy is also the name of the diva's favourite teacher in *The Last Mile*.

20 See my discussion in *Still Acting Gay* (New York: St Martins, 2000), 281.

21 The administration of the Manhattan Theatre Club cancelled the production of *Corpus Christi* after they received threats from religious groups of damage to the theatre, its personnel and its audiences. When writers, theatre artists and well-meaning protestors staged protests in favour of free artistic expression and against censorship and the sort of bullying threatened by the so-called Christians, the theatre decided to produce the play after all. This was one of the most publicized examples of the cultural wars waged over gay dramas in many cities in the US at the time.

4 Paula Vogel

1 C. W. E Bigsby, *Contemporary American Playwrights* (New York: Cambridge University Press, 1999), 295.

2 Quoted in Steven Drukman, 'A Playwright on the Edge Turns Toward the Middle', *New York Times*, 16 March 1997, 5.

3 Paula Vogel, email reply to author, 22 July 2011. Defamiliarization is a term developed by Russian formalist Victor Shklovsky, which Bertolt Brecht adapted and renamed *Verfremdungseffekt*.

4   Judith Butler, *Gender Trouble* (New York: Routledge, 1990), 43–4.
5   'Women in Theater: Dialogues with Notable Women in American Theater', Linda Winer, interviewer, CUNY TV, 2002, Billy Rose Theater Collection, New York Public Library.
6   Paula Vogel, *The Baltimore Waltz*, in David Savran (ed.), *Baltimore Waltz and Other Plays* (New York: TCG, 1997), 5 (hereafter cited in text).
7   In 1995, AIDS deaths had reached an all-time high in the United States, but by 1998, the number of new AIDS cases dropped 30 per cent and death rates dropped more than half. See *Health in the Americas 2002*, Vol. II (Washington, DC: Pan American Health Organization and World Health Organization, 2002), 538. Moreover, as well-known figures like actor Robert Reed, dancer Rudolf Nureyev and basketball player Earvin 'Magic' Johnson succumbed to the disease, public attitudes toward AIDS changed considerably by the end of the decade. Even as awareness rises and infection rates slow, AIDS continues to spread globally, especially in parts of Africa and Asia.
8   David Roman, 'Review: *The Baltimore Waltz* by Paula Vogel', *Theatre Journal* 44 (4) (1992): 520.
9   Frank Rich, 'A Play about AIDS Uses Fantasy to Try to Remake the World', *New York Times*, 12 February 1992.
10 'Women in Theatre', CUNY TV.
11 This line was added to the Signature Theatre production; it does not appear in either printed edition of the play.
12 This quote is taken from the 'Author's Note' (229–31) published with the 1997 TCG version, edited by David Savran.
13 Paula Vogel, *Hot 'n' Throbbing* (New York: Dramatists Play Services, 2000), 13 (hereafter cited in the text). Unless otherwise noted, all citations will come from this version of the play.
14 This citation is taken from the 1996 playtext: 'Hot 'n' Throbbing', in David Savran (ed.), *Baltimore Waltz and Other Plays* (New York: TCG, 1997), 294.
15 This ending is unpublished but occurred in the Arena Stage production, which the author accessed at the Theatre and Film on Tape at the New York Performing Arts Library.
16 Lloyd Rose, '"Hot 'n' Throbbing": Double Feature', *Washington Post*, 13 September 1999.
17 Alisa Solomon, 'Bump and Grind', *Village Voice*, 30 March 2005, 69.

18 'Women in Theatre', CUNY TV.
19 Paula Vogel, 'Interview with Alexis Greene', in Alexis Greene (ed.), *Women Who Write Plays: Interviews with American Dramatists* (Hanover, NH: Smith and Kraus, 2001), 430.
20 Robert Hicks, 'Playwright Melds Modern Tension and Ancient Convention', *St. Petersburg Times*, 3 June 2004, 18W.
21 Alex Witchel, 'After the Prize is the Pressure: Now What?', *New York Times*, 7 February 1999.
22 Paula Vogel, 'The Mineola Twins', in *The Mammary Plays* (New York: Theatre Communications Group, 1998), 97, 111 (hereafter cited in the text).
23 Paula Vogel, 'Interview with Arthur Holmberg', http://americanrepertorytheater.org/inside/articles/through-eyes-lolita (accessed 12 January 2017).
24 The play title has been variously translated in English as *The Good Woman of Szechwan* or *The Good Woman of Setzuan*.
25 Vogel, 'Interview with Alexis Greene', 442.
26 Ben Brantley, 'Well, at Least She's Not Triplets', *New York Times*, 19 February 1999.
27 Vincent Canby, 'A Mad History of Women as Told by Twin Barbies', *New York Times*, 28 February 1999.
28 Michael Feingold, 'Double Takes', *Village Voice*, 2 March 1999, 161.
29 'Women in Theatre', CUNY TV.
30 Vogel, 'Interview with Alexis Greene', 441–2.
31 Michael Feingold, 'All for Love', *Village Voice*, 25 March 1997, 97.
32 Bigsby, *Contemporary American Playwrights*, 319.
33 Vogel, 'Interview with Arthur Holmberg'.
34 See Bigsby, *Contemporary American Playwrights*, 318; C. W. E. Bigsby, *Modern American Drama, 1945–2000* (Cambridge: Cambridge University Press, 2000), 233.
35 Drukman, 'Playwright on the Edge'.
36 Andrew Kimbrough, 'The Pedophile in Me: The Ethics of *How I Learned to Drive*', *Journal of Dramatic Theory and Criticism* 16 (2) (2002): 49.
37 Ibid.
38 Paula Vogel, 'How I Learned to Drive', in *The Mammary Plays*

(New York: Theatre Communications Group, 1998), 21 (hereafter cited in the text).

39 Ben Brantley, 'A Pedophile Even a Mother Could Love', *New York Times*, 17 March 1997.
40 Feingold, 'All for Love', 97.
41 Jill Dolan, 'Performance Review: How I Learned to Drive', *Theatre Journal* 50 (1) (1998): 128.
42 Even as it resists many of the conventions of traditional confessional narratives, *Drive* taps into the 1990s discourse around sexual abuse, which was more ubiquitously represented on British stages than American. British plays that revolved around experiences of sexual abuse include Sarah Daniels's *Beside Herself* (1990), David Spencer's *Killing the Cat* (1990), Claire Dowie's *Easy Access* (1997), Mike Cullen's *Anna Weiss* (1997) and Simon Gray's *The Late Middle Classes* (1999). Solo performers in the United States, such as Spalding Gray, Tim Miller, Holly Hughes and Paul Zaloom, also mobilized confessional theatre in the 1990s as a queer performative strategy. These forms coincided with identity politics, as both performance and politics of this decade became centrally concerned with the formation and articulation of individual and group identities based on gender, sexuality, race and ethnicity.
43 Smith writes, 'A play has every right not to answer the questions it raises – most works of art don't. But just how many unknowns is an equation entitled to?' See John Smith, 'When Seduction's All in the Family', *New York Times*, 31 March 1997, 86.
44 John Heilpern, 'Pedophiles, Sock Fetishists … Hey, Kids, It's Oprah-Drama', *New York Observer*, 7 April 1997.
45 Michael Toscano, 'Ambiguous "Drive" Takes Audience on Muddled Ride', *Washington Post*, 5 February 2004.
46 Robert Brustein, 'Review: "How I Learned to Drive"', *New Republic*, 7 July 1997, 28.
47 Vogel's long-overdue Broadway debut garnered three Tony Award nominations, and won Best Direction of a Play for Rebecca Taichman and Lighting Design in a Play for Christopher Akerlind.

5 Tony Kushner

1 Amy Barrett, 'The Way We Live Now: 10-07-01: Questions for Tony Kushner', *New York Times*, 7 October 2001, Section 6, 230.
2 David Savran, 'Tony Kushner', in Philip C. Kolin and Colby H. Kullman (eds), *Speaking on Stage: Interviews with Contemporary*

American Playwrights (Tuscaloosa, AL: University of Alabama Press, 1996), 293.
3 Peter Marks, 'On Stage and Off', *New York Times*, 28 June 1996, C2.
4 Tony Kushner, *Thinking About the Longstanding Problems of Virtue and Happiness* (New York: Theatre Communications Group, Inc., 1995), 10–11.
5 Frank Rich, 'Embracing All Possibilities in Life and Art', *New York Times*, 5 May 1993, C16.
6 Jack Kroll, 'A Seven-Hour Gay Fantasia: A Daring and Dazzling Play for Our Time', *Newsweek*, 23 November 1992, 83.
7 Tony Kushner, *Angels in America: A Gay Fantasia on National Themes. Part One: Millennium Approaches* (New York: Theatre Communications Group, Inc., 1992), 118. Further references are to this edition.
8 Anna Quindlen, 'Happy and Gay', *New York Times*, 6 April 1994, A2, 1.
9 Jordan Mann, 'The Good Person of La Jolla', *Theater Week*, 18–24 July 1994, 22.
10 Tony Kushner, *Homebody/Kabul* (New York: Theatre Communications Group, Inc., 2002), 1.
11 Raymond Williams, 'Walking Backwards Into the Future', in Robin Gale (ed.), *Resources of Hope, Culture, Democracy, Socialism* (London and New York: Verso, 1989), 283.
12 Email from Tony Kushner to James Fisher, 25 March 2002.
13 Marc Peyser, 'Tales from Behind Enemy Lines', *Newsweek*, 17 December 2001, 68.
14 Tony Kushner, 'Fighting the Arts Bullies', *The Nation*, 29 November 1999, 41.
15 James Reston, Jr, 'A Prophet in His Time', *American Theatre*, March 2002, 53.
16 John Heilpern, 'Zounds! Kushner's *Homebody/Kabul* Is Our Best Play in Last 10 Years', *New York Observer*, 5 January 2002, 1.
17 *Angels in America*, DVD, directed by Mike Nichols, HBO Films, 2003. (Kushner and his friend Maurice Sendak also appeared in bit roles as rabbis.)
18 Travis Mader, 'Tony Kushner and Dr. Browne', *Alley Theatre Newsletter*, September 1998, 1.
19 Jane Edwardes, 'Kabul's Eye', *Time Out*, 30 June to 7 July 1999.

20 Octavio Roca, 'Kushner's Next Stage', *San Francisco Chronicle*, 6 September 1998, 32.
21 John Lahr, 'Angels on Broadway', *New Yorker*, 23 May 1993, 137.

6 Suzan-Lori Parks

1 Her birth name was Susan Lori Parks. A misprint on an early flier called her 'Suzan-Lori' and she was told to keep it and it would all work out. She did and it did.
2 All biographical information from 'Chronology' in Kevin J. Wetmore, Jr and Alycia Smith-Howard (eds), *Suzan-Lori Parks: A Casebook* (London: Routledge, 2007), xiii.
3 Philip C. Kolin (ed.), *Suzan-Lori Parks: Essays on the Plays and Other Works* (Jefferson, NC: McFarland & Co., 2010), 9.
4 Suzan-Lori Parks, *365 Days/365 Plays* (New York: Theatre Communications Group, 2006), 401.
5 Kevin J. Wetmore, Jr, 'Perceptible Mutabilities: The Many Plays of Suzan-Lori Parks / The Many Suzan-Lori Parks of Plays', in Kevin J. Wetmore, Jr and Alycia Smith-Howard (eds), *Suzan-Lori Parks: A Casebook* (London: Routledge, 2007), xvii.
6 Monte Williams, 'At Lunch with: Suzan-Lori Parks', *New York Times*, 17 April 1996, C1.
7 Deborah R. Geis, *Suzan-Lori Parks* (Ann Arbor: University of Michigan Press, 2008), 39.
8 Philip C. Kolin and Harvey Young, '"Watch Me Work": Reflections on Suzan-Lori Parks and Her Canon', in Philip C. Kolin and Harvey Young (eds), *Suzan-Lori Parks in Person: Interviews and Commentaries* (London: Routledge, 2014), 1.
9 Suzan-Lori Parks, *The America Play and Other Works* (New York: Theatre Communications Group, 1995).
10 The others are *Betting on the Dust Commander*, *Pickling* and *Devotees in the Garden of Love*.
11 Suzan-Lori Parks, 'From Elements of Style', in *The America Play and Other Works* (New York: Theatre Communications Group, 1995), 8–10.
12 Heidi J. Holder, 'Strange Legacy: The History Plays of Suzan-Lori Parks', in Kevin J. Wetmore, Jr and Alycia Smith-Howard (eds), *Suzan-Lori Parks: A Casebook* (London: Routledge, 2007), 19.

13 Parks, *The America Play*, 9.
14 Quoted in Michele Pearce, 'Alien Nation: An Interview with the Playwright', *American Theatre* 11 (3) (March 1994): 26.
15 Quoted in Faedra Chatard Carpenter, 'A Parks Remix: An Interview with Liz Diamond', in Philip C. Kolin (ed.), *Suzan-Lori Parks: Essays on the Plays and Other Works* (Jefferson, NC: McFarland & Co., 2010), 193.
16 Parks, *The America Play*, 8–9.
17 Ibid., 9.
18 Nicole Hodges Persley, 'Sampling and Remixing: Hip Hop and Parks's History Plays', in Philip C. Kolin (ed.), *Suzan-Lori Parks: Essays on the Plays and Other Works* (Jefferson, NC: McFarland & Co., 2010), 66–7.
19 Ibid., 75.
20 Kevin J. Wetmore, Jr, 'It's an Oberammergau Thing: An Interview with Suzan-Lori Parks', in Kevin J. Wetmore, Jr and Alycia Smith-Howard (eds), *Suzan-Lori Parks: A Casebook* (London: Routledge, 2007), 129.
21 Parks, *The America Play*, 19.
22 Ibid., 21.
23 Ibid.
24 Ibid., 21–2.
25 Kolin and Young, 'Watch Me Work', 4.
26 Quoted in Pearce, 'Alien Nation', 26.
27 Han Ong, 'Suzan-Lori Parks', in Philip C. Kolin and Harvey Young (eds), *Suzan-Lori Parks in Person: Interviews and Commentaries* (London: Routledge, 2014), 39.
28 Quoted in Pearce, 'Alien Nation', 26.
29 Holder, 'Strange Legacy', 19.
30 Parks, *The America Play*, 164.
31 Suzan-Lori Parks, *Venus* (New York: Theatre Communications Group, 1997), 3.
32 Shawn-Marie Garrett, 'The Possession of Suzan-Lori Parks', *American Theatre* 17 (8) (October 2000): 25.
33 See Kevin J. Wetmore, Jr, 'Re-enacting: metatheatre in thuh Plays of Suzan-Lori Parks', in Kevin J. Wetmore, Jr and Alycia Smith-Howard (eds), *Suzan-Lori Parks: A Casebook* (London: Routledge, 2007), 89–105.

34 Harvey Young, 'Choral Compassion: In the Blood and Venus', in Kevin J. Wetmore, Jr and Alycia Smith-Howard (eds), *Suzan-Lori Parks: A Casebook* (London: Routledge, 2007), 30.
35 Wetmore, 'It's an Oberammergau Thing', 132.
36 Mel Gussow, 'Identity Loss in "Imperceptible Mutabilities"', *New York Times*, 20 September 1989, C24.
37 Ibid.
38 Kolin and Young, 'Watch Me Work', 4.
39 Parks, *The America Play*, 43, 52. Subsequent quotations are from this edition.
40 Jennifer Larson, *Understanding Suzan-Lori Parks* (Columbia: University of South Carolina Press, 2012), 11.
41 Amiri Baraka, 'Slave Ship', in William Branch (ed.), *Crosswinds: An Anthology of Black Dramatists in the Diaspora* (Bloomington: University of Indiana Press, 1993), 250–9; August Wilson, *Gem of the Ocean* (New York: Theatre Communications Group, 2006).
42 Larson, *Understanding*, 12.
43 Mel Gussow, 'Dangers of Becoming Lost in a Culture', *New York Times*, 25 September 1990, C15.
44 Ibid.
45 Parks, *The America Play*, 101. Subsequent quotations are from this edition.
46 Note that Parks calls herself a 'recovering Catholic'; Ong, 'Suzan-Lori Parks', 44.
47 Ong, 'Suzan-Lori Parks', 38.
48 Parks, *The America Play*, 158. Subsequent quotations are from this edition.
49 Alvin Klein, 'Yale Rep Offers "America" Premiere', *New York Times*, 30 January 1994, 13CN 17.
50 Quoted in Andrea Stevens, 'A Playwright Who Likes to Bang Words Together', *New York Times*, 6 March 1994, Section 2, p. 5.
51 Pearce, 'Alien Nation', 26.
52 Parks, *The America Play*, 159; Pearce, 'Alien Nation', 26.
53 See T. Denean Sharpley-Whiting, *Black Venus: Sexualized Savages, Primal Fears, and Primitive Narratives in French* (Durham, NC: Duke University Press, 1999).
54 Tom Sellar, 'Making History: Suzan-Lori Parks: The Shape of the Past', in Philip C. Kolin and Harvey Young (eds), *Suzan-Lori Parks*

      in Person: Interviews and Commentaries (London: Routledge, 2014), 49.
55   Kolin and Young, 'Watch Me Work', 13.
56   Alvin Klein, 'About Women, About Pedestals', *New York Times*, 31 March 1996, 13CN 21.
57   Ibid.
58   Williams, 'At Lunch with: Suzan-Lori Parks', C1.
59   Wetmore, 'It's an Oberammergau Thing', 137.
60   Ibid., 138.
61   Ibid., 124.
62   Suzan-Lori Parks, *The Red Letter Plays* (New York: Theatre Communications Group, 2001). The 'almost-twin' plays premiered in November 1999 (*In the Blood*) and February 2000 (*Fucking A*), and thus clearly developed together.
63   Margo Jefferson, '"The Scarlet Letter," Alive and Well in the Bitter City', *New York Times*, 23 November 1999, E1.
64   Nathaniel Hawthorne, *The Scarlet Letter*, ed. Ross C. Murfin (Boston: Bedford/St Martin's, 2006), 58.
65   Shari Benstock, 'The Scarlet Letter (a)dorée, or the Female Body Embroidered', in Nathaniel Hawthorne, *The Scarlet Letter*, ed. Ross C. Murfin (Boston: Bedford/St Martin's, 2006), 397.
66   Parks, *The Red Letter Plays*, 5–7.
67   Franklin Gilliam, 'The "Welfare Queen" Experiment: How Viewers React to Images of African-American Mothers on Welfare', *Nieman Reports* 53 (2) (1999).
68   Ibid.
69   Larson, *Understanding*, 42.
70   John Heilpern, 'And the Heilpern Awards for 1999 Go to …', *New York Observer*, 10 January 2000, D27.
71   Ibid.
72   Jefferson, 'The Scarlet Letter', E1.
73   Quoted in Faedra Chatard Carpenter, 'A Parks Remix', 194.

Afterword

1. Many might consider the surprising political victory of Donald Trump, who became US president-elect in November 2016, a culmination of this 'fallout'.
2. At the time of writing (May 2016), three of the couples remain together; Parks and Oscher divorced in 2013.
3. Gallup poll, http://www.gallup.com/poll/1675/most-important-problem.aspx (accessed 1 June 2016).
4. http://variety.com/2016/legit/news/broadway-sales-2015-16-season-1201781283/ (accessed 28 May 2016).
5. http://broadwayjournal.com/hamilton-sets-price-record-again-with-998-tickets/ (accessed 2 January 2017).
6. These statistics come from the Internet Broadway Database, https://www.ibdb.com/ (accessed 31 May 2016 and 14 November 2020).
7. This list excludes entries in biographical dictionaries.
8. As of 2016, Parks's career spans twenty-two years, Kushner's twenty-four, Vogel's thirty-four and McNally's forty-two.
9. David John Sorrells, 'The Evolution of AIDS as Subject Matter in Select American Dramas', PhD diss., University of North Texas, 2000; Nancy Ann Plooster, 'Performing Loss: Mourning on the American Stage', PhD diss., University of California, Santa Barbara, 2003; Scott Alan Rayer, 'He Who Laughs Last: Comic Representations of AIDS', PhD diss., University of Toronto, 2003; Francisco Costa, '"I Used to be Subversive, but Now I'm Gay": Representations of Queer Identities on the American Stage from the Postwar to the 1990s', PhD diss., University of East Anglia, 2013.
10. Raymond Thomas Schultz, 'When the A-Word Is Never Spoken: The Direct and Subtle Impact of AIDS on Gay Dramatic Literature', PhD diss., Wayne State University, 1999.
11. Yong-Nam Park, 'The Melting Pot Where Nothing Melted: The Politics of Subjectivity in the Plays of Suzan-Lori Parks, Wendy Wasserstein, and Tony Kushner', PhD diss., Indiana University of Pennsylvania, 2008.
12. James W. Frieze, 'The Interpretation of Difference: Staging Identity in the United States, 1986–1992', PhD diss., University of Madison, Wisconsin, 2002; Kathleen Potts, 'The Pulitzer Prize and Women: An Investigation into Three Decades of Winning Plays by Female Dramatists', PhD diss., City University of New York, 2015.

13 'Terrence McNally New Play Award', http://philadelphiatheatrecompany.org/on-stage/new-plays/ (accessed 30 May 2016).

14 'Boot Camp: A History', http://paulavogelplaywright.com/boot-camp/ (accessed 14 July 2016).

15 Joanna Mansbridge, *Paula Vogel* (Ann Arbor: University of Michigan Press, 2014), 1.

16 Ann Pellegrini, 'Repercussions and Remainders in the Plays of Paula Vogel: An Essay in Five Moments', in David Krasner (ed.), *A Companion to Twentieth-Century American Drama* (Malden, MA: Blackwell, 2005), 483.

17 'The Paula Vogel Award in Playwriting', http://web.kennedy-center.org/Education/KCACTF/awards/Playwriting/PaulaVogel (accessed 14 July 2016).

18 Ben Brantley, 'Debating Dialects and Dad's Suicide Plan', *New York Times*, 5 May 2011, http://www.nytimes.com/2011/05/06/theater/reviews/the-intelligent-homosexuals-guide-by-tony-kushner-review.html (accessed 30 May 2016).

19 'The Kidnapping of Edgardo Mortara', http://www.imdb.com/title/tt3675680/ (accessed 30 May 2016).

20 CUNY's board of trustees attempted to prevent the awarding of the degree, citing Kushner's allegedly 'anti-Israeli' political views. After a storm of protest, the board reversed that decision and voted to grant Kushner the degree. John Tarleton, 'Tony Kushner at John Jay: Both Giving and Receiving', 5 January 2012, http://www.psc-cuny.org/tony-kushner-john-jay-both-giving-and-receiving (accessed 28 May 2016).

21 Mos Def replaced actor Don Cheadle, who created the role of Booth.

22 Charles McNulty, '*Father Comes Home from the Wars* is an Entrancingly Intimate Drama', *Los Angeles Times*, 18 April 2016, http://www.latimes.com/entertainment/arts/la-et-cm-father-comes-home-wars-review-20160419-column.html (accessed 31 May 2016).

23 Jennifer Larson, *Understanding Suzan-Lori Parks* (Columbia: University of South Carolina Press, 2012), 116.

24 Suzan-Lori Parks website, http://www.suzanloriparks.com/slp-on-tour/ (accessed 31 May 2016).

Documents

1. Nathan Lane, 'Nathan Lane Reveals How Terrence McNally's Wicked Tongue Changed His Life', *Playbill*, 6 June 2015, http://www.playbill.com/article/nathan-lane-reveals-how-terrence-mcnallys-wicked-tongue-changed-his-life-com-350687 (accessed 24 May 2016).
2. Mervyn Rothstein, 'Terrence McNally's Four Stars Talk Happily of His Lips Together', *New York Times*, 3 July 1991, http://www.nytimes.com/1991/07/03/theater/terrence-mcnally-s-four-stars-talk-happily-of-his-lips-together.html?pagewanted=all (accessed 24 May 2016).
3. Interview with Charlie Rose, 28 March 1995, https://charlierose.com/videos/7790 (accessed 25 May 2016).
4. Daniel Webster, 'Terrence McNally Sets Stage for Fading Diva Maria Callas', *Philadelphia Inquirer*, 26 February 1995, http://articles.philly.com/1995-02-26/entertainment/25707037_1_terrence-mcnally-master-class-manhattan-theater-club (accessed 23 May 2016).
5. Peter Marks, 'Playwright Terrence McNally's Love of Opera Takes Center Stage at Kennedy Center', *Washington Post*, 14 March 2010, http://www.washingtonpost.com/wpdyn/content/article/2010/03/12/AR2010031200148.html (accessed 22 May 2016). In this interview, Kahn reports that he and McNally protested against the infamous 1958 firing of Callas by the Metropolitan Opera Manager Rudolph Bing by painting 'Viva Callas' across the Met's advertising posters.
6. Christine Dolen, 'Theatre's Man of Moment Talks About *Master Class*', *Miami Herald*, 30 March 1997, 3I.
7. Caldwell also performed the role at the Mark Taper Forum (May–June 1995) and the Kennedy Center (September–October 1995). Audra McDonald, who created the role of Sharon Graham in *Master Class*, won her second Tony for best featured performance by an actress in a play.
8. F. Paul Driscoll, 'Going to the Opera with Zoe Caldwell and Robert Whitehead', *Opera News* 62 (3) (September 1997): 28–32.
9. Interview with Charlie Rose, 1 January 1996, https://charlierose.com/videos/15279 (accessed 28 May 2016).
10. Our Lady of Fatima refers to a reported appearance of the Virgin Mary at Fátima in Portugal in 1917. Petition available at https://

gloria.tv/photo/vayBmKSfsWL (accessed 26 May 2016). The same Pennsylvania-based Christian group organized an email petition against the showing of the documentary about the play, *Corpus Christi: Playing with Redemption*, in 2012, which acquired 7,000 signatures; 13 April 2012, http://www.dallasvoice.com/documentary-corpus-christi-controversy-open-10106747.html (accessed 26 May 2016).

11 Larry Murray, 'Terrence McNally on Corpus Christi: Playing With Redemption', 17 September 2014, http://www.broadwayworld.com/article/BWW-Interviews-Terrence-McNally-on-CORPUS-CHRISTI-PLAYING-WITH-REDEMPTION-20140917 (accessed 26 May 2016).

12 Arthur Holmberg, 'Through the Eyes of Lolita: Interview with Paula Vogel', *ART News* (September 1998), ARTicles gallery, American Repertory Theater, Cambridge, Massachusetts, http://americanrepertorytheater.org/inside/articles/through-eyes-lolita (accessed 16 July 2016).

13 '*A Civil War Christmas*' (2008), *Theatre Journal* 61 (4) (December 2009): 629–31.

14 Steven Druckman, 'Playwrights and Their Work: Paula Vogel', *Dramatists Guild Quarterly* 34–35 (Summer 1997): 4–13.

15 'A Conversation Between Paula Vogel and Blanka Zizka', 26 March 2014, https://www.google.com/url?sa=t&rct=j&q=&esrc=s&source=web&cd=1&cad=rja&uact=8&ved=0ahUKEwivsePmhvvNAhXJ2R4KHdEXCmMQFgghMAA&url=http%3A%2F%2Fhowlround.com%2Fa-conversation-between-paula-vogel-and-blanka-zizka&usg=AFQjCNHjy1G82Iup_pBTDFsS0xD8BpE93Q&sig2=Ipedpt5_6AE0kY8rW7Dq0A (accessed 14 July 2016).

16 Comparative Drama Conference Keynote Event – 'Negative Empathy', https://www.youtube.com/watch?v=7iVrFCZ6bY0 (accessed 17 March 2016). This conversation is also published in *Text and Presentation* (2012).

17 In 2012, Ms Stojanovic performed the first act of *Homebody* (the hour-long monologue that begins the play) in a special engagement at the Serbian American Museum of St Sava in Chicago (performed in Serbian with English subtitles).

18 The editors would like to express gratitude to Natasha Djukic, costume designer for the production, who also granted an interview which space prevented us from including.

19 Marija Stojanovic is a journalist and playwright whose play *Ratcatcher* (a retelling of the Pied Piper legend) has been described

as 'in the spirit of Tom Stoppard ... an exercise in style, a game with language, and a parable on the use of youngsters in war'. See Dennis Barnett and Arthur Skelton (eds), *Theatre and Performance in Eastern Europe: The Changing Scene* (Lanham, MD and Plymouth: Scarecrow Press, 2008), 218.

20 'Remarks on Parks: A Symposium on the Work of Suzan-Lori Parks, Part Two: Directors', Hunter College, 30 April 2004. This symposium was organized and moderated by Jonathan Kalb; transcript available at http://www.hotreview.org/articles/remarksparks2_print.htm (accessed 17 May 2016).

21 Rosemary Tichler was then Head of Casting at the New York Shakespeare Festival.

22 Suzan-Lori Parks, 'An Equation for Black People Onstage', in *The America Play and Other Works* (New York: Theatre Communications Group, 1995), 19–21.

23 The interview of Suzan-Lori Parks by Han Ong was commissioned and first published by *Bomb* magazine, issue 47, Spring 1994. © *Bomb* Magazine, New Art Publications, and its Contributors. All rights reserved. The BOMB Digital Archive can be viewed at www.bombmagazine.org (accessed 16 May 2016).

24 Speech available at https://www.mtholyoke.edu/media/commencement-speech#sthash.bT6HzaIy.dpuf (accessed 21 May 2016).

BIBLIOGRAPHY

Key books and websites on the 1990s

Books

Harrison, Colin. *American Culture in the 1990s*. Edinburgh: Edinburgh University Press, 2010.
Johnson, Haynes. *The Best of Times: America in the Clinton Years*. New York: Harcourt, Inc., 2001.
Marks, Craig and Rob Tannenbaum. *I Want My MTV: The Uncensored Story of the Music Video Revolution*. New York: Dutton, 2011.
Schor, Juliet B. *The Overspent American: Upscaling, Downshifting, and the New Consumer*. New York: Basic Books, 1998.
Serrianne, Nina Esperanza. *America in the Nineties*. Syracuse, NY: Syracuse University Press, 2015.
Stiglitz, Joseph E. *The Roaring Nineties: A New History of the World's Most Prosperous Decade*. New York and London: W. W. Norton & Company, 2003.
Time-Life Books. *The Digital Decade: The 90s*. New York: Bishop Books, 2000.
Troy, Gil. *The Age of Clinton: America in the 1990s*. New York: St Martin's Press, 2015.
White, Mark, ed. *The Presidency of Bill Clinton: The Legacy of a New Domestic and Foreign Policy*. London and New York: I.B.Tauris, 2012.

Websites

Pew Research Center (Religion and Public Life), http://www.pewforum.org/.
US Census Bureau, http://www.census.gov.
US Department of Labor, http://www.bls.gov/opub/ted/1999/apr/wk1/art01.htm.

Key books on American theatre in the 1990s

The following books offer chapters pertaining to American theatre in the 1990s within the context of a broader theatre history.

Anderson, Lisa M. *Black Feminism in Contemporary Drama.* Urbana: University of Illinois Press, 2008.
Berkowitz, Gerald M. *American Drama of the Twentieth Century.* New York: Longman, 1992.
Berkowitz, Gerald M. *New Broadways, Theatre Across America: Approaching a New Millennium.* Revised edition. New York: Applause Books, 1997.
Bigsby, C. W. E. *Modern Drama, 1945–2000.* Cambridge: Cambridge University Press, 2000.
Bush Jones, John. *Our Musicals, Ourselves: A Social History of the American Musical Theatre.* Waltham, MA: Brandeis University Press, 2003.
Colleran, Jeanne. *Theatre and War, Theatrical Responses Since 1991.* Basingstoke: Palgrave Macmillan, 2012.
Farfan, Penny and Lesley Ferris, eds. *Contemporary Women Playwrights into the Twenty-First Century.* Basingstoke: Palgrave Macmillan, 2013.
Green, Amy S. *The Revisionist Stage.* Cambridge: Cambridge University Press, 1994.
Hurwitz, Nathan. *A History of the American Musical Theatre: No Business Like It.* New York: Routledge, 2014.
Huxley, Michael and Noel Witts, eds. *The Twentieth-Century Performance Reader.* 2nd edition. London: Routledge, 2002.
Kendrick, John. *Musical Theatre: A History.* New York: Continuum International Publishing Group, 2008.
Keyssar, Helene. *Feminist Theatre and Theory: Contemporary Critical Essays.* New York: St Martin's Press, 1996.
Knapp, Raymond. *The American Musical and the Formation of National Identity.* Princeton, NJ: Princeton University Press, 2005.
Kolin, Philip C., ed. *Contemporary African American Women Playwrights.* London: Routledge, 2007.
Krasner, David, ed. *A Companion to Twentieth-Century American Drama.* Malden, MA: Blackwell Publishing Ltd, 2005.
Lee, Esther Kim. *A History of Asian American Theatre.* Cambridge: Cambridge University Press, 2006.
Lundskaer-Nielsen, Miranda. *Directors and the New Musical Drama:*

British and American Musical Theatre in the 1980s and '90s. New York: Palgrave Macmillan, 2008.

Martin, Carol. *Theatre of the Real*. Basingstoke: Palgrave Macmillan, 2013.

Mason, Jeffrey D. and J. Ellen Gainor, eds. *Performing America: Cultural Nationalism in American Theater*. Ann Arbor: University of Michigan Press, 1999.

McDonough, Carla J. *Staging Masculinity, Male Identity in Contemporary American Drama*. Jefferson, NC: McFarland & Company, 1997.

Murphy, Brenda, ed. *The Cambridge Companion to American Women Playwrights*. Cambridge: Cambridge University Press, 1999.

Murphy, Brenda with Laurie J. C. Cella, *Twentieth Century American Drama*, Volume IV, *1980–2000*. London: Routledge, 2006.

Ozieblo, Barbara and Maria Dolores Narbona-Carrion, eds. *Codifying the National Self, Spectators, Actors and the American Dramatic Text*. Brussels: P.I.E.-Peter Lang, 2006.

Ramírez, Elizabeth C. *Chicanas/Latinas in American Theatre: A History of Performance*. Bloomington: Indiana University Press, 2000.

Roman, David. *Acts of Intervention: Performance, Gay Culture, and AIDS*. Bloomington: Indiana University Press, 1998.

Saddik, Annette J. *Contemporary American Drama*. Edinburgh: Edinburgh University Press, 2007.

Sandoval-Sanchez, Alberto. *Jose, Can You See? Latinos On and Off Broadway*. Madison: University of Wisconsin Press, 1999.

Savran, David, ed. *The Playwright's Voice: American Dramatists on Memory, Writing, and the Politics of Culture*. New York: Theatre Communications Group, 1999.

Shank, Theodore. *Beyond the Boundaries, American Alternative Theatre*. Ann Arbor: University of Michigan Press, 2002.

Shanke, Robert A., ed. *Angels in the American Theater*. Carbondale: Southern Illinois University Press, 2007.

Solomon, Alisa and Framji Minwalla, eds. *The Queerest Art: Essays on Lesbian and Gay Theater*. New York: New York University Press, 2002.

Sternfeld, Jessica. *The Megamusical*. Bloomington: Indiana University Press, 2006.

Wilmer, S. E. *Theatre, Society and the Nation*. Cambridge: Cambridge University Press, 2002.

Wilmeth, Don B. and Christopher Bigsby, eds. *The Cambridge History of American Theatre*, Volume Three, *Post-World War II to the 1990s*. Ann Arbor: University of Michigan Press, 2002

Wolf, Stacy. *Changed For Good: A Feminist History of the Broadway Musical*. Oxford: Oxford University Press, 2011.

Young, Harvey, ed. *The Cambridge Companion to African American Theatre*. Cambridge: Cambridge University Press, 2013.

The playwrights

Terrence McNally

Collections

McNally, Terrence. *Terrence McNally: Fifteen Short Plays*. Lyme, NH: Smith and Kraus, 1994. Includes *The Ritz* and *Bad Habits* in addition to one-act plays.
McNally, Terrence. *Terrence McNally: Volume Two*. Lyme, NH: Smith and Kraus, 1996. Includes original versions of *And Things That Go Bump in the Night* and *Where Has Tommy Flowers Gone*.
McNally, Terrence. *Selected Works: A Memoir in Plays*. New York: Grove Press, 2015. Contains most of the major full-length work with commentary from the playwright.

Single editions of uncollected plays cited

McNally, Terrence. *Corpus Christi*. New York: Grove Press, 1998.
McNally, Terrence. *Some Men and Deuce*. New York: Grove Press, 2007.
McNally, Terrence. *Mothers and Sons*. New York: Dramatists Play Service, 2014.

Film and television cited

McNally, Terrence. *Love! Valour! Compassion!* DVD N4946. New Line Cinema, 1997.
McNally, Terrence. *Common Ground*. VHS. Directed by Donna Deitch, Paramount, 2002.
McNally, Terrence. *Corpus Christi: Playing with Redemption*. Documentary film directed by Nic Arnzen and James Brandon. DVD-QCC 505. Philadelphia, PA: Breaking Glass Pictures, 2014.
McNally, Terrence. *The Last Mile*. Available online: http://www.dailymotion.com/video/xmtgb0_the-last-mile_shortfilms (accessed 30 January 2016).

Recommended texts

Clum, John M. *Still Acting Gay: Male Homosexuality in Modern Drama*. New York: St Martins, 2000.

Clum, John M. *The Drama of Marriage: Gay Playwrights/Straight Unions from Oscar Wilde to the Present*. New York: Palgrave, 2012.

Clum, John M. *Terrence McNally and Fifty Years of American Gay Drama*. Amherst, NY: Cambria Press, 2016.

Frontain, Raymond-Jean. '"All Men Are Divine": Religious Mystery and Homosexual Identity in Terrence McNally's *Corpus Christi*', in Raymond-Jean Frontain (ed.), *Reclaiming the Sacred: The Bible in Gay and Lesbian Culture*, 231–57. New York: Harrington Park Press, 2003.

Frontain, Raymond-Jean. *The Theatre of Terrence McNally: Something About Grace*. Madison, NJ: Fairleigh Dickinson University Press, 2019.

Wolfe, Peter. *The Theater of Terrence McNally*. Jefferson, NC: McFarland, 2013.

Zinman, Toby Silverman. *Terrence McNally: A Casebook*. New York: Garland, 1997.

Paula Vogel

Plays

Vogel, Paula. *Baltimore Waltz and Other Plays*. Edited by David Savran. New York: TCG, 1996.

Vogel, Paula. *The Mammary Plays: The Mineola Twins and How I Learned to Drive*. New York: TCG, 1998.

Vogel, Paula. *The Long Christmas Ride Home: A Puppet Play with Actors*. New York: Dramatist Play Service, 2004.

Vogel, Paula. *A Civil War Christmas: An American Musical Celebration*. New York: Dramatists Play Services, 2010.

Vogel, Paula. *Don Juan Comes Home from Iraq*. New York: TCG, 2016.

Recommended texts

Bigsby, C. W. E. *Contemporary American Playwrights*. New York: Cambridge University Press, 1999.

Graley, Herren. 'Narrating, Witnessing, and Healing Trauma in Paula Vogel's *How I Learned to Drive*', *Modern Drama* 53 (1) (2010): 103–14.

Greene, Alexis, ed. *Women Who Write Plays: Interviews With American Dramatists*. Hanover, NH: Smith and Kraus, 2001.

Kimbrough, Andrew. 'The Pedophile in Me: The Ethics of *How I*

Learned to Drive', *Journal of Dramatic Theory and Criticism* 16 (2) (2002): 47–65.

Mansbridge, Joanna. 'Popular Bodies, Canonical Voices: Paula Vogel's *Hot 'n' Throbbing* as Performative Burlesque', *Voice and Performance*, special issue of *Modern Drama*, ed. Allan Pero, 52 (4) (2009): 469–89.

Mansbridge, Joanna. 'Memory's Dramas, Modernity's Ghosts: Thornton Wilder, Japanese Theater, and Paula Vogel's *The Long Christmas Ride Home*', *Comparative Drama* 46 (2) (2012): 209–35.

Mansbridge, Joanna. *Paula Vogel*. Ann Arbor: University of Michigan Press, 2014.

Pellegrini, Ann. 'Repercussions and Remainders in the Plays of Paula Vogel: An Essay in Five Moments', in *A Companion to Twentieth-Century American Drama*, 473–85. Malden, MA: Blackwell, 2005.

Savran, David, ed. *The Playwright's Voice: American Dramatists on Memory, Writing, and the Politics of Culture*. New York: Theatre Communications Group, 1999.

Savran, David, ed. *A Queer Sort of Materialism: Recontextualizing American Theater*. Ann Arbor: University of Michigan Press, 2003.

Tony Kushner

Plays

Kushner, Tony. *A Bright Room Called Day*. New York: Theatre Communications Group, Inc., 1994.

Kushner, Tony. *The Illusion*. Adapted from Pierre Corneille's play. New York: Theatre Communications Group, Inc., 1994.

Kushner, Tony. *Thinking About the Longstanding Problems of Virtue and Happiness: Essays, A Play, Two Poems, and A Prayer*. New York: Theatre Communications Group, Inc., 1995.

Kushner, Tony. *Slavs! Thinking About the Longstanding Problems of Virtue and Happiness*. New York: Broadway Play Publishing, 1996.

Kushner, Tony. *A Dybbuk and Other Tales of the Supernatural*. New York: Theatre Communications Group, Inc., 1997.

Kushner, Tony. *Death and Taxes: Hydriotaphia and Other Plays*. New York: Theatre Communications Group, Inc., 1998.

Kushner, Tony. *Caroline, or Change*. New York: Theatre Communications Group, Inc., 2004.

Kushner, Tony. *Homebody/Kabul*. Revised edition. New York: Theatre Communications Group, Inc., 2005.

Kushner, Tony. *Angels in America: A Gay Fantasia on National Themes:*

Revised and Complete Edition. 20th Anniversary Edition. New York: Theatre Communications Group, Inc., 2013.

Kushner, Tony. *The Intelligent Homosexual's Guide to Capitalism and Socialism with a Key to the Scriptures*. New York: Theatre Communications Group, Inc., 2016.

Recommended texts

Bloom, Harold, ed. *Tony Kushner: Bloom's Modern Critical Views*. New York: Chelsea House, 2005.

Brask, Per, ed. *Essay on Kushner's Angels*. Winnipeg: Blizzard, 1996.

Fisher, James. *The Theater of Tony Kushner: Living Past Hope*. Revised edition. New York: Routledge, 2002.

Fisher, James, ed. *Tony Kushner: New Essays on the Art and Politics of the Plays*. Jefferson, NC: McFarland, 2006.

Fisher, James. *Understanding Tony Kushner*. Columbia: University of South Carolina Press, 2008.

Geis, Deborah R. and Steven F. Kruger, eds. *Approaching the Millennium: Essays on Angels in America*. Ann Arbor: University of Michigan Press, 1997.

Kekki, Lasse. *From Gay to Queer: Gay Male Identity in Selected Fiction by David Leavitt and in Tony Kushner's Play Angels in America I–II*. New York: Peter Lang, 2003.

Nielsen, Ken. *Tony Kushner's Angels in America: Modern Theatre Guides*. New York: Continuum, 2013.

Suzan-Lori Parks

Plays

Parks, Suzan-Lori. 'The America Play', *American Theatre* 11 (3) (March 1994): 25–39.

Parks, Suzan-Lori. *The America Play and Other Works*. New York: Theatre Communications Group, 1995. Contains *Imperceptible Mutabilities in the Third Kingdom, Betting on the Dust Commander, Pickling, The Death of the Last Black Man in the Whole Entire World, Devotees in the Garden of Love* and *The America Play*.

Parks, Suzan-Lori. *Venus*. New York: Theatre Communications Group, 1997.

Parks, Suzan-Lori. *The Red Letter Plays*. New York: Theatre Communications Group, 2001. Contains *In the Blood* and *Fucking A*.

Books about Parks

Geis, Deborah R. *Suzan-Lori Parks*. Ann Arbor: University of Michigan Press, 2008.

Kolin, Philip, ed. *Suzan-Lori Parks: Essays on the Plays and Other Works*. Jefferson, NC: McFarland and Company, 2010.

Kolin, Philip and Harvey Young, eds. *Suzan-Lori Parks in Person: Interviews and Commentaries*. London: Routledge, 2013.

Larson, Jennifer. *Understanding Suzan-Lori Parks*. Columbia: University of South Carolina Press, 2012.

Wetmore, Jr, Kevin J. and Alycia Smith-Howard, eds. *Suzan-Lori Parks: A Casebook*. London: Routledge, 200

INDEX

36 Views (Iizuka, Naomi) 78
365 Days/365 Plays (Parks, Suzan-Lori) 176–7, 184, 197, 213
365 Festival 197
1990s 1–2, 123, 199–205
  AIDS 6–7, 199–200
  America 33–4
  Clinton presidency 2–4
  culture 18–30 *see also* theatre
  culture wars 34–5
  domestic economy 16
  domestic terrorism 5–6
  education 17
  fads 16–17
  identity politics 7–13, 33–4
  international relations 4–5
  media 18
  millennium, the 20–1, 199
  music 18–21
  politics 2–5
  population and demographics 15
  race 7–10, 200–1
  religion 15–16
  science and technology 13–15
  society 5–13
1992 Blood (Colorado, Hortensia/Colorado, Elvira) 83

Abagnale, Frank, Jr 206
ABC network 22
'Achy Breaky Heart' (Cyrus, Billy Ray) 19
ACT, San Francisco 41
ACT II conference 43
actors, casting 36–7, 51, 70–1, 77
Actors Equity 37
Actors Theatre of Louisville 41
actos 79
Acts of Intervention (Roman, David) 88
adaptation 93–4 *see also* cross-over artistry
African American theatre 69–75 *see also* race
Agamemnon (Mee, Charles) 94
Ahrens, Lynn/Flaherty, Stephen
  Anastasia 206
  Ragtime 50, 52–3, 56, 58
Aida (John, Elton/Rice, Tim) 54, 59
AIDS 6–7, 88–9, 90, 125, 149–50, 199–200
  Kushner, Tony 150, 158–9
  McNally, Terrence 97, 100–2, 114, 118
  Parks, Suzan-Lori 195
  Vogel, Paula 126
al-Qaeda 1, 4–5
Aladdin (film) 22
Aladdin (musical) 203
Albee, Edward 48, 63–4, 121
  American Dream, The 63, 64
  Delicate Balance, A 63

Play about the Baby, The 64
Sandbox, The 63
Three Tall Women 63, 64
Who's Afraid of Virginia Woolf 63, 64, 156, 159
Zoo Story, The 63
Albright, Madeleine 11
Alexander Plays (Kennedy, Adrienne) 73
Alfaro, Luis 79, 91–2
  Bitter Homes and Gardens 92
  Downtown 92
  Straight as a Line 92
Alice in Chains 20
All America's a Stage: Growth and Challenges in Nonprofit Theatre (National Endowment of the Arts) 43–4
All My Sons (Miller, Arthur) 61
All Saints 29
All the Rules: Time-Tested Secrets for Capturing the Heart of Mr. Right (Fein, Ellen/ Schneider, Sherrie) 28
Allen, Paul 13
Allenchey, Allex 28
Alley Theatre, Houston 41
Allison, Wick 2
Ally McBeal (TV show) 23
alternative theatre 38, 93
Amazon 26
America 33–4, 36, 190–1
America Needs Fatima campaign 223
America Play, The (Parks, Suzan-Lori) 175, 178, 185, 188–91
  design 240
  history 75, 179–80
  metatheatre 183
  violence 182

American Beauty (film) 21, 22
American Daughter, An (Wasserstein, Wendy) 84
'American Drama of the 1990s On and Off-Broadway' (Schlueter, June) 39, 40–1
American Dream 33–4
  marginalized groups 68
  Miller, Arthur, critique of 61
  Rogers, Will, realization of 56
American Dream, The (Albee, Edward) 63, 64
American Dreams (Houston, Velina Hasu) 76–7
American Girl Dolls 16
American identity 55–60
America Play and Other Plays, The (Parks, Suzan-Lori) 178, 179
American Repertory Theatre, Cambridge 41
American Television and Communications Corp 24
Americans with Disabilities Act 6
Anastasia (musical) 206
And Away We Go (McNally, Terrence) 206
And Baby Makes Seven (Vogel, Paula) 121, 124
And Things That Go Bump in the Night (McNally, Terrence) 98, 107
Anderson, Kurt 1
Andre's Mother (McNally, Terrence) 97, 98, 100, 108
Anemone Me (Parks, Suzan-Lori) 175
Angelos, Moe 90
Angels in America (Nichols, Mike) 212
Angels in America: A Gay Fantasia on National Themes (Kushner, Tony)

35, 36, 149, 151, 153–61, 205, 212
AIDS 35, 125, 154–5, 158–9, 161
Broadway 45
HBO miniseries 172–3, 205, 212, 161
homosexuality 35, 200, 161
White supremacy 201
Angels in America: the Opera (Eötvös, Péter) 211
Angels in the American Theater (Schanke, Robert A.) 39
Angelus Novus (Klee, Paul) 159–60
animation 22, 23
Anita Hill vs Clarence Thomas 8–9
Annie Get Your Gun (musical) 56
Ansky, S. 163
 Dybbuk; or, Between Two Worlds, A 151, 165–7
Apple Inc. 14
Approaching Zanzibar (Howe, Tina) 84
Armey, Richard 3
Armstrong, Lance 26, 250 n.75
Arnzen, Nic: *Corpus Christi: Playing with Redemption* 115
Aronson, Arnold 44, 45
art 28
As I Lay Dying (Faulkner, William) 197
As Is (Hoffman, William) 89, 159
Asa Ga Kimashita (Houston, Velina Hasu) 76–7
Asch, Sholem: *God of Vengeance* 147, 201, 210
Ashe, Arthur 6
Ashman, Howard/Rice, Tim/Menken, Alan: *Beauty and the Beast* 46, 49, 53

Asian American Theater Company 76
Asian American theatre 75–8, 91
Aspects of Love (Lloyd Webber, Andrew) 51
Assassins (Sondheim, Stephen) 54
astrophysics 15
Atkinson, Jean 145
Atwood, Margaret: *Handmaid's Tale, The* 213
audience attendance 44
Auel, Jean: *Plains of Passage, The* 27
Avenue Q (musical) 203

Backlash: The Undeclared War Against American Women (Faludi, Susan) 10
Backstage Pass to Hell, A (Kushner, Tony) 162
Bad Habits (McNally, Terrence) 99
Baird, Mimi/Claxton, Eve: *He Wanted the Moon* 212
Baird, Perry 212
Baird, Zoe 84
Baitz, Jon Robin 89
Baldwin, James 176, 177
Baltimore Waltz (Vogel, Paula) 35, 43, 122, 124–8, 208
 AIDS 35, 224, 124–8
 homosexuality 35, 200
 Mantello, Joe 134
Baraka, Amiri 69
 Slave Ship 185
Baranski, Christine 104, 218
Barkley, Charles 25
Barney, Matthew 28
Barr, Roseanne 23
Bartmaan, Sartjie 191
baseball 25
basketball 25
Beaser, Robert/McNally, Terrence

Food of Love, The 206–7
Beauty and the Beast (film) 22
Beauty and the Beast (Menken, Alan/Ashman, Howard/Rice, Tim) 46, 49, 53
Beauty Myth, The (Wolf, Naomi) 28
Beavis and Butthead (animated TV show) 23
Beckett, Samuel 177
   Waiting for Godot 206
Before it Hits Home (West, Cheryl L.) 125
Belasco, David: *Madame Butterfly* 51
Bell Curve, The: Herrnstein, Richard/Murray, Charles 28
Bellini, Vincenzo: *Puritani, I* 100, 206
Benjamin, Walter 153
   'Theses on the Philosophy of History' 159–60
Benstock, Shari 193
Bent (Sherman, Martin) 159
Bergen, Candice 23
Berkowitz, Gerald M. 38–9, 45
Berlin Wall 1
Bertelsmann AG 27
Best Little Whorehouse Goes Public, The (musical) 49
Best Plays of 1999–2000, The (Jenkins, Jeffrey Eric) 59
Betting on the Dust Commander (Parks, Suzan-Lori) 176
Bhabha, Homi: *Location of Culture, The* 28
Bigsby, C. W. E. 46, 62, 64, 84, 122
Bird, Larry 25
Bitter Homes and Gardens (Alfaro, Luis) 92
Black, Cheryl 231–9
Black Power movement 69, 72

Black theatre *see* African American theatre
Blessing, Lee 48
Blizzard on Marblehead Neck, A (Kushner, Tony) 173, 211
Bloolips 90–1
Bobbitt, Lorena 11–12
Bock, Adam 208
Bogart, Anne 124, 127, 129, 132
Boheme, La (Puccini, Giacomo) 55
Bond, Edward 153
Bondage (Hwang, David Henry) 77, 177
Book of Grace, The (Parks, Suzan-Lori) 197, 214
Book of Mormon, The (musical) 203
Bopp, Thomas 15
Borderlands Theater Company 35
Borders 26
Bourne Identity, The (Ludlum, Robert) 27
Boy Gets Girl (Gilman, Rebecca) 85–6
Boys in the Band (Crowley, Mart) 88
Branch Davidians 5
Brantley, Ben 137, 145–6, 211
Brecht, Bertolt 152, 153, 163
   Good Person of Setzuan, The 136, 151, 163–4, 168
   Mother Courage and Her Children 168, 211, 213
   Seven Deadly Sins 136
Breuer, Lee 92
   Lear 94
Bricusse, Frank/Wildhorne, Frank
   Bridges of Madison County, The (Waller, Robert James) 27
   Jekyll and Hyde 52
Bright Room Called Day, A

(Kushner, Tony) 151, 167, 169
Bring in 'Da Noise, Bring in 'Da Funk (musical) 58
British Musical Invasion 39
Broadway 39–40, 43, 44–8, 203
  Disney on Broadway 53–4
  Kushner, Tony 204
  McNally, Terrence 204
  Parks, Suzan-Lori 204
  Vogel, Paula 204
Broadway Alliance 47
Broadway on Broadway 47
Brokaw, Mark 143, 145
Broken Glass (Miller, Arthur) 62–3
Bronson, James 229
Brooks, Garth 19
Brooks, Terry: *Star Wars Episode I: The Phantom Menace* 27
Brown, Jason Robert/Uhry, Alfred
  Parade 57–8
Browne, Sir Thomas 173
Brustein, Robert 37, 70, 146
Bublil, Alain/Schönberg, Claude-Michel
  Les Misérables 51, 203
  Miss Saigon 36, 51, 56, 59
Buckley, Betty 51
Buried Child (Shepard, Sam) 65
Bush, Barbara 30
Bush, George H. W. 2–3, 4, 55
Bush Jones, John 54, 55, 56, 58, 59
But Still, Like Air, I'll Rise (Houston, Velina Hasu) 77
Butler, Judith 123
  Gender Trouble 27
Byrd, James, Jr 12–13

Café La Mama 88

Caffe Cino 88
Caldwell, Zoe 221–3
Callas, Maria 100, 113–14, 220–3
Calvin Klein 29
Canby, Vincent: 'Mad History of Women as Told by Twin Barbies' 137–8
Carey, Mariah 19
Carlos, Laurie 176
Caroline, or Change (Kushner, Tony) 151, 167, 201, 202, 211, 212
Carroll, Lewis 143
Cartoon Network 24
Carville, James 3
Cat on a Hot Tin Roof (Williams, Tennessee) 63
Catch Me if You Can (movical) 206
Cato, Gavin 8
Cats (Lloyd Webber, Andrew) 51, 59
Celera Genomics 14
censorship 38
  Corpus Christi 262 n.20
  National Endowment for the Arts 41–2
  NEA Four 42, 90, 129
Chambers, Jane: *Last Summer at Bluefish Cove* 88
Champagne, Lenora 90
Chapman, Tracy 19
Chastain, Brandi 26
Chekhov, Anton: *Seagull, The* 48, 206
Chicano Secret Service 92
Chirico, Miriam 228–9
Chita Rivera: The Dancer's Life (movical) 206
Chong, Ping 92
Chow, Tina 6
Christian Coalition 12

'Christmas Bells' (Longfellow, Henry Wadsworth) 229
Churchill, Caryl 153
Circle in the Square 40
Circle Repertory Theater 40
Civil Rights Act 72
Civil War, The (Wildhorne, Frank) 52
Civil War Christmas: A Musical Celebration, A (Vogel, Paula) 209, 228–9
Clancy, Tom: *Sum of All Fears, The* 27
Clark, Larry 21
Clarke, Breena 83
class 67, 202–3
classical music 20–1
Claxton, Eve/Baird, Mimi: *He Wanted the Moon* 212
Claycomb, Ryan M. 94–5
Clerks (film) 21
Cleveland Raining (Rno, Sung) 77–8
Client, The (Grisham, John) 27
Clinton, Bill 1, 2–4, 7, 11, 31, 123, 200
Clinton, Hillary 10, 30, 138
Clit Notes (Hughes, Holly) 90
cloning 14
Close, Glenn 51
CMT (music video series) 19
Cobain, Kurt 20
Coco, James 'Jimmy' 218
Cohn, Roy 154–6, 158, 160, 162
Cold Mountain (Frazier, Charles) 27
Cold War 1
Coleman, Cy/Green, Adolph/Comden, Betty: *Will Rogers Follies, The* 55–6
collaboration 92
Colleran, Jean 86
Colorado, Elvira/Colorado, Hortensia: *1992 Blood* 83
Columbine High School Massacre 6, 35, 55, 123
Combs, Sean (Puff Daddy) 20, 205
Comden, Betty/Coleman, Cy/Green, Adolph: *Will Rogers Follies, The* 55–6
Come Down Burning (Corthron, Kia) 83
comets 15
Company (Sondheim, Stephen) 203
confessional theatre 265 n.42
Confessions of a Black Working Class Woman (McCauley, Robbie) 91
Connor, Kimberly Rae 74
Conseco, Jose: *Juiced: Wild Times, Rampant 'Roids, Smash Hits & How Baseball Got Big* 250 n.75
Contact (Stroman, Susan/Weidman, John) 49
Contemporary Plays by Women of Color (Perkins, Kathy A./Uno, Roberta) 82, 83
Cooper, Christine M. 85
Corneille, Pierre: *L'illusion comique* 151
Cornerstone Theater 35
corporate musicals 46–7
Corpus Christi (McNally, Terrence) 98, 99, 114–18, 119, 218, 223–4
Corpus Christi: Playing with Redemption (film) 115
Corthron, Kia: *Come Down Burning* 83
Cosby, Bill 20
Cosby Show, The (TV show) 20
Cosi Fan Tutte (Mozart, Wolfgang Amadeus) 103

Coughlin, Paula 11
country music 19
Country Weekly (magazine) 19
Crazy for You (musical) 49
creationism 17
Crenshaw, Kimberle: 'Mapping the Margins' 35
Crichton, Michael: *Lost World, The* 27
Crimes of the Heart (Henley, Beth) 83
cross-over artistry 205
Crow, Sheryl 19
Crowley, Mart: *Boys in the Band* 88
Crown Heights 8
Crucible, The (Miller, Arthur) 48, 61
Cruz, Migdalia 79, 80, 81
  Have-Little, The 80
  Miriam's Flowers 80
Cruz, Nilo 79, 122, 208
culture 18–30
Culture Clash 92
culture wars 34–5, 38
Culture Wars: The Struggle to Define America (Hunter, James Davison) 34
Cuomo, Mario 46
Curse of the Starving Class, The (Shepard, Sam) 65
Cyrus, Billy Ray: 'Achy Breaky Heart' 19

D.O.C. 20
Daly, Tyne 48
Damn Yankees (musical) 56
Dancenoise 90
Dances With Wolves (film) 22
Dangerous (Jackson, Michael) 20
Daniels, Jeff 205
David, Larry 205
Davison, Bruce 145

Davy, Babs 90
Day, Doris 137
Day Standing on its Head (Gotanda, Philip Kan) 76
Dazed and Confused (film) 21
Dead Man Walking (McNally, Terrence) 100
death 182–3
Death and the Maiden (Dorfman, Ariel) 37
Death of a Salesman (Miller, Arthur) 61, 62
Death of the Last Black Man in the Whole Entire World (Parks, Suzan-Lori) 75, 175, 177, 178, 185–8, 215
death 182–3
Diamond, Liz 240
  history 75, 180, 181, 187–8
  sampling 180
  stereotypes 181, 186
Death Row Records 20
Deep End of the Ocean, The (Mitchard, Jacquelyn) 27
defamiliarization 123
Defense of Marriage Act 12
Degen, John 49–50
DeGeneres, Ellen 12
Delicate Balance, A (Albee, Edward) 63
demographics 15
Dennehy, Brian 62
Desdemona (Vogel, Paula) 94, 121, 124, 201
Devotees in the Garden of Love (Parks, Suzan-Lori) 175, 177–8, 182, 183
Diamond, Liz 175, 179, 184, 197–8, 239–40
Dibbell, Dominique 90
Dick Tracy (film) 22
Dickerson, Glenda 83
Dietz, Steven: *Lonely Planet* 125

Dinkins, David 46
Dion, Celine 19
Dirty Blonde (Shear, Claudia) 49
Disney 22, 46, 49
  Disney on Broadway 53–4, 203
Dixie Chicks 19
Djukic, Zeljko 231–9
Doctorow, E. L.: *Ragtime* 52, 207
docudramas 94–5
Doggystyle (Snoop Doggy Dogg) 20
Dolan, Jill 37–8, 88, 95, 146
Dolly the sheep 14
Dolores Claiborne (King, Stephen) 27
domestic economy 16
domestic terrorism 5–6
domestic violence 128–34
Don Juan Comes Home From Iraq (Vogel, Paula) 147, 209–10, 230–1
Don Juan Comes Home From the War (Horváth, Ödön von) 147, 109–10, 230
Dorfman, Ariel 163
  Death and the Maiden 37
Dorsey, Decatur 229
Downtown (Alfaro, Luis) 92
Dr. Dre 20
Drabinsky, Garth 46
Drattell, Deborah 206
Dreams from My Father (Obama, Barack) 28
DreamWorks 21, 203
Driscoll, F. Paul 221
Drivas, Robert 218
Druckman, Steven 229–30
D'Souza, Dinesh: *Illiberal Education: The Politics of Race and Sex on Campus* 28
Du Bois, W. E. B. 69

Dunaway, Faye 221
Dürrenmatt, Friedrich: *Visit, The* 206
Dybbuk; or, Between Two Worlds, A (Ansky, S.) 151
Dybbuk; or, Between Two Worlds, A (Kushner, Tony) 151, 165–8

Earth in the Balance (Gore, Al) 28
East Coast Ode to Howard Jarvis (Kushner, Tony) 151, 154, 172
East West Players 76
eBay 13
Ebb, Fred/Kander, John
  Kiss of the Spider Woman, The 59
  Rink, The 261 n.10
EBN 19
ecology, literature 28
economy 2, 3–4, 16, 36, 38–41, 55
  financial crisis 2, 55, 202
Edelstein, David 21
education 17
El Teatro Campesino (ETC) 78–9
Elam, Harry J. 71
'Elements of Style' (Parks, Suzan-Lori) 180
Ellen (TV show) 12, 24
Eminem: *Slim Shady LP* 20
End of History and the Last Man, The (Fukuyama, Francis) 4
English Patient, The (film) 22
Ensler, Eve: *Vagina Monologues, The* 85
Eötvös, Péter: *Angels in America: the Opera* 211
Epistemology of the Closet, The (Sedgwick, Eve Kosofsky) 27

'Equation for Black People on Stage, An' (Parks, Suzan-Lori) 180, 241–2
ER (TV show) 24
Esquevel, Laura: *Like Water for Chocolate* 27
ETC *see* El Teatro Campesino
Eureka Theatre Company, San Francisco 41
Eustis, Oscar 208
Ewing, Patrick 25
Eyes for Consuela (Shepard, Sam) 65, 66

Face Value (Hwang, David Henry) 77
fads 16–17
Fair Housing Act 72
Falsettos, The (Finn, William) 59
Faludi, Susan: *Backlash: The Undeclared War Against American Women* 10
Family Guy (animated TV show) 23
Farfan, Penny 81
fashion 29
Father Comes Home from the Wars (Parts 1, 2, 3) (Parks, Suzan-Lori) 176, 184, 197, 201, 202, 213–14
Faulkner, William 177
  As I Lay Dying 197
Fausto-Sterling, Anne 122, 200
Fefu and Her Friends (Fornés, Maria Irene) 79
Fein, Ellen/Schneider, Sherrie: *All the Rules: Time-tested Secrets for Capturing the Heart of Mr. Right* 28
Feingold, Michael 138, 146
feminism 8, 10–12 *see also* gender relations
  art 28

Cruz, Migdalia 80
Houston, Velina Hasu 76
literature 27–8
Moraga, Cherríe 79–80
music 19
Oleanna 35
Parade 58
patriarchy 94
pornography 128
television 23–4
Vogel, Paula 122
feminist theatre 81–6
Fences (Wilson, August) 203
Ferris, Lesley 81
Fey, Tina 138
Fierstein, Harvey 150
  Torch Song Trilogy 88
film 21–2
Fin de la Baleine: An Opera for the Apocalypse, La (Kushner, Tony) 151
fin de millénaire anxiety 30–1
Finley, Karen 42, 129
  Shock Treatment 90
  We Keep our Victims Ready 90
Finn, William
  Falsettos, The 59
  March of the Falsettos 59
Finney, Albert 206
Fires in the Mirror (Smith, Anna Deavere) 35–6, 74
Firm, The (Grisham, John) 27
Fischer, Ernst: *Necessity of Art: A Marxist Approach, The* 152
Five Lesbian Brothers 90, 91
Flaherty, Stephen/Ahrens, Lynn
  Anastasia 206
  Ragtime 50, 52–3, 56, 58
Fleck, John 42, 90, 129
Flowers, Gennifer 11
food 29–30

Food of Love, The (McNally, Terrence/Beaser, Robert) 206–7
football 25
Foote, Horton 48
'For All My Niggaz and Bitches' (Snoop Doggy Dogg) 20
Ford, Henry 56
Ford Center for the Performing Arts 46
Fordyce, Ehren 93
Foreman, Richard 92, 153, 178, 191–2, 241
Forever Plaid (musical) 56
Fornés, Maria Irene 48, 79, 81, 153
  Fefu and Her Friends 79
Forrest Gump (film) 22
Fox News Channel 24
Frank, Leo 57
Frankie and Johnny (film) 207
Frankie and Johnny in the Clair de Lune (film) 97
Frankie and Johnny in the Clair de Lune (McNally, Terrence) 97, 98, 119, 207
Frasier (TV show) 24, 30
Frazier, Charles: *Cold Mountain* 27
Freak (Leguizamo, John) 92
Fresh Prince of Bel-Air, The (TV show) 24
Friends (TV show) 24, 29, 30
Frohnmayer, John 129
Fucking A (Parks, Suzan-Lori) 179, 180, 193, 202, 213, 215
Fukuyama, Francis: *End of History and the Last Man, The* 4
Full Monty, The (movical) 97, 203, 206
funding 38–42, 47

Funnyhouse of a Negro (Kennedy, Adrienne) 72–3
furbies 16
Fusco, Coco 28, 92
Fusco, Coco/Gómez-Peña, Guillermo: *Two Undiscovered Amerindians Visit New York* 92
Futurama (animated TV show) 23

G. David Schine in Hell (Kushner, Tony) 162
Gaines, Ernest J.: *Lesson Before Dying, A* 27
Gainor, J. Ellen/Mason, Jeffrey D.: *Performing America* 33–4
Gal (Parks, Suzan-Lori) 175
Galati, Frank 169, 232
gangsta rap 19, 20
Garrett, Shawn-Marie 183
Gates, Bill 13
gay theatre 87–9 *see also* homosexuality; LGBTQ rights
Geffen, David 21
Gehrig, Lou 25
Geis, Deborah 178
Gem of the Ocean (Wilson, August) 185
gender relations 8–9, 10–12, 34, 66–7 *see also* feminism; sexuality
  art 28
  fashion 29
  feminist theatre 81–6
  Kushner, Tony 161
  literature 27–8
  masculinity 24, 66–7
  Mineola Twins, The 134–9
  music 19
  Parks, Suzan-Lori 75, 181–2, 191–6
  playwrights 81–6

sexuality 130–2, 140–3,
   193–4, 201–2
television 23–4,
Vogel, Paula 123–4, 130–2,
   135
WOW Café 90–1
Gender Trouble (Butler, Judith)
   27
genetics 14
Gershwin, George/Gershwin, Ira/
   Heyward, Dubose
   Porgy and Bess 197, 214
   'Summertime' 214
Gershwins' Porgy and Bess, The
   (Parks, Suzan-Lori) 197,
   201, 203, 214
Getting Mother's Body (Parks,
   Suzan-Lori) 197, 214
Gilliam, Franklin 194–5
Gilman, Rebecca 85
   Boy Gets Girl 85–6
   Glory of Living, The 85
Gingrich, Newt 3
Ginsberg, Ruth Bader 11
Gionfriddo, Gina 208
Girl 6 (Parks, Suzan-Lori) 175, 178
Gladiator (film) 21
Glaser, Elizabeth 6
Glass Menagerie, The (Williams,
   Tennessee) 63
Glid, Dusanka Stojanovic 232
Glory of Living, The (Gilman,
   Rebecca) 85
Glover, Savion 58
GMO (genetically modified
   organism) foods 14
God of Vengeance (Asch, Sholem)
   147, 201, 210
God's Country (Parks,
   Suzan-Lori) 175
Goethe, Johann Wolfgang von:
   Stella: A Play for Lovers
   151

Golden Age (McNally, Terrence)
   100, 206, 207
Golden Child (Hwang, David
   Henry) 77
Goldman, Emma 56
Goldman, Ron 9–10
Gomez, Marga: *Marga Gomez is
   Pretty Witty & Gay* 83
Gómez-Peña, Guillermo 36
Gómez-Peña, Guillermo/Fusco,
   Coco: *Two Undiscovered
   Amerindians Visit New
   York* 92
*Gone, An Historical Romance of
   a Civil War as It Occurred
   Between the Dusky Thighs
   of One Young Negress and
   Her Heart* (Walker, Kara)
   28
Good Person of Setzuan, The
   (Brecht, Bertolt) 136, 151,
   163–4
Good Person of Setzuan, The
   (Kushner, Tony) 151,
   163–5
Goodbye Girl, The (Simon, Neil)
   50
Goodman Theatre, Chicago 41
Goodwin, Doris Kearns: *Team of
   Rivals: The Political Genius
   of Abraham Lincoln* 212
Google 13
Goosebumps series (Stein, R. L.)
   27
Gore, Al 3
   Earth in the Balance 28
Gotanda, Philip Kan 76
   Day Standing on its Head 76
   Sisters Matsumoto 76
   Wash, The 76
   Yohen 76
government 37–8
Gozzi, Carlo: *Green Bird, The* 49

Grammer, Kelsey 24
Green, Adolph/Comden, Betty/Coleman, Cy: *Will Rogers Follies, The* 55–6
Green, Amy S. 260 n.151
Green Bay Packers 25
Green Bird, The (Gozzi, Carlo) 49
Greenspan, Alan 3–4
Greenwich Village *see* Stonewall riots
Gretzsky, Wayne 26
Grimm, Jacob/Grimm, Wilhelm: *Two Journeymen* 172
Grim(m) (Kushner, Tony) 151, 154, 172
Grisham, John
  Client, The 27
  Firm, The 27
  Pelican Brief, The 27
'Ground on Which I Stand, The' (Wilson, August) 70
Group Theatre 63
grunge 19–20
Guare, John 48, 152, 153
  Six Degrees of Separation 67
Guide to Casual Businesswear, A (Levi Strauss & Co.) 29
Gulf War 55, 86, 94
Gurney, A. R. 206
Gussow, Mel 184, 185, 186
Guthrie Theatre, Minneapolis 41
Guys and Dolls (musical) 56

Hair (musical) 55
Hale, Alan 15
Hall, Joan Wylie 74
Halperin, David M.: *How to Be Gay* 113
Halston 6
Hamilton (musical) 203
Hamilton, Alexander 203

Hamilton, Jane: *Map of the World, A* 27
Hammerstein, Oscar/Rodgers, Richard: *State Fair* 49
Handmaid's Tale, The (Atwood, Margaret) 213
Hanks, Tom 7, 22, 205
Hannibal (Harris, Thomas) 27
Happy Journey to Trenton and Camden, The (Wilder, Thornton) 208
Harding, Tonya 26
Hare, David 153
Haring, Keith 6
Harris, Julie 48
Harris, Mark 200
Harris, Thomas
Harrison, Colin 4
  Hannibal 27
  Silence of the Lambs 27
Harry Potter and the Sorcerer's Stone (Rowling, J. K.) 27
Hart, Lynda: *Making a Spectacle: Feminist Essays on Contemporary Women's Theatre* 81
Have-Little, The (Cruz, Migdalia) 80
Having Our Say: The Delany Sisters' First Hundred Years (Mann, Emily) 84–5
Hawthorne, Nathaniel: *Scarlet Letter, The* 75, 180, 193–6, 213
Hayakutake, Yuji 15
Hayes, Sean 205
He Wanted the Moon (Baird, Mimi/Claxton, Eve) 212
Headley, Heather 54
Heald, Anthony 104, 218–19
Healey, Peg 90
Hearst Corporation 27
Heartbreak House: A Fantasia

in the Russian Manner on English Themes (Shaw, George Bernard) 157
Heavenly Theatre, The (Kushner, Tony) 151
Heggie, Jake 207
  Dead Man Walking 100
Heidi Chronicles, The (Wasserstein, Wendy) 83, 138
Heilpern, John 146, 171–2, 196
Hellman, Lillian 45
Hello (Sex) Kitty (Uyehara, Denise) 91
Helms, Jesse 42
Henley, Beth 83
  Crimes of the Heart 83
Henry V (Shakespeare, William) 105
Hernandez, Ricardo 240
Heroes and Saints (Moraga, Cherríe) 79–80
Herring, Scott 88
Herrnstein, Richard/Murray, Charles: *Bell Curve, The* 28
Heyward, Dubose/Gershwin, George/Gershwin, Ira
  Porgy and Bess 197, 214
  'Summertime' 214
Heyward, Dubose/Heyward, Dorothy: *Porgy* 214
Hezbollah al-Hejaz 4, 5
Hiatt, Brian 18
Hill, Anita 8–9, 34–5, 67, 85, 123
Hill, Faith 19
  'This Kiss' 19
Hill, Lauryn 19
Hispanic Organization of Latin Actors 37
Hispanic Playwrights Lab 79
history 181, 188–91, 228–9
Hoffman, Dustin 172

Hoffman, William 150
  As Is 89, 159
Holder, Heidi J. 179, 182
Holes (Sachar, Louis) 27
Holiday, George 7
Holmberg, Arthur 224, 239
Holyfield, Evander 26
Home Alone (film) 22
Homebody (Kushner, Tony) 151, 168
Homebody/Kabul (Kushner, Tony) 151, 167, 168–72, 201, 231–9
Homeland Security, Department of 199
homophobia 12, 35, 88, 98, 104–5, 115
homosexuality 12–13, 34, 87–9
  Callas, Maria 100, 113–14
  homophobia 12, 35, 88, 98, 104–5, 115
  Kushner, Tony 159, 161, 199–200
  Laramie Project, The 35
  laws 12, 117–18, 200
  literature 27
  McNally, Terrence 35, 98, 117–19, 199–200
  Miller, Tim 90
  musicals 58–9
  religion 223–4
  same-sex marriage 12, 118, 200
  television 24
  Vogel, Paula 35, 199–200
Horváth, Ödön von: *Don Juan Comes Home From the War* 147, 209–10, 230
Hot 'n' Throbbing (Vogel, Paula) 121, 124, 128–34, 208
Hottentot Venus 191
Houghton, James 48
Houston, Velina Hasu 76, 81

American Dreams 76–7
Asa Ga Kimashita 76–7
But Still, Like Air, I'll Rise 77
Politics of Life 77
Tea 76–7
Houston, Whitney 19
How I Learned to Drive (Vogel, Paula) 86, 122, 134, 138–46, 201–2, 224–8
  Broadway 204
  success 86, 124, 137, 139, 145–6
How to Be Gay (Halperin, David M.) 113
Howe, Tina 84
  Approaching Zanzibar 84
  Pride's Crossing 84
Hubble Space Telescope 15
Hudes, Quiara Alegría 210
Hughes, Holly 42, 90, 129
  Clit Notes 90
  Preaching to the Converted 90
Human Genome Project 14
Hungry Woman: A Mexican Medea, The (Moraga, Cherríe) 80
Hunter, James Davison: *Culture Wars: The Struggle to Define America* 34
Huntington Theatre Company, Boston 41
Hurricane Andrew 3
Hurricane Katrina 202
Hurston, Zora Neale: *Their Eyes Were Watching God* 205, 214
Hurwitz, Nathan 47
Hwang, David Henry 76, 77
  Bondage 77, 177
  Face Value 77
  Golden Child 77
  M. Butterfly 76, 77
  Yellow Face 77
Hydriotaphia, or The Death of Dr. Browne (Kushner, Tony) 151, 173
Hyman, Earl 48

I Know This Much is True (Lamb, Wally) 27
Ibsen, Henrik: *Master Builder, The* 48
identity 55–60 *see also* American identity
identity politics 7–13, 33–7 *see also* homosexuality; gender relations; race
  confessional theatre 265 n.42
  masculinity 24, 64–7
  musical theatre 55–60
Iizuka, Naomi 78
  36 Views 78
Illiberal Education: The Politics of Race and Sex on Campus (D'Souza, Dinesh) 28
Illusion, The (Kushner, Tony) 151, 172
L'illusion comique (Corneille, Pierre) 151
Immigration and Nationality Act 17
Imperceptible Mutabilities in the Third Kingdom (Parks, Suzan-Lori) 175, 177, 178, 181, 182, 184–6
  casting 239–40
  sampling 180
In Great Eliza's Golden Time (Kushner, Tony) 151
In the Blood (Parks, Suzan-Lori) 175, 176, 178, 180, 193–6, 202, 215
  gender exploitation 193–4, 195, 213

objectification 182, 183, 193, 195
In the Heart of America (Wallace, Naomi) 36
Incident at Vichy, The (Miller, Arthur) 61
Indecent (Vogel, Paula) 147, 201
Independence Day (film) 22
Independent Film Channel 21
Indigo Girls 19
Intelligent Homosexual's Guide to Capitalism and Socialism with a Key to the Scriptures, The (Kushner, Tony) 152, 173, 202, 211, 212
international relations 4–5
internet 13
Internet Explorer 13
intersectionality 35
Intiman Theatre, Seattle 41
Ionesco, Eugène 177
Iphigenia and Other Daughters (McLaughlin, Ellen) 94
It's Only a Play (McNally, Terrence) 99

Jackman, Hugh 205
Jackson, Alan 19
Jackson, Jesse 35
Jackson, Michael: *Dangerous* 20
Jagged Little Pill (Morissette, Alanis) 19
James, Peter Francis 241
Jarvis, Howard 172
Jefferson, Margot 193
Jekyll and Hyde (Stevenson, Robert Louis) 52
Jekyll and Hyde (Wildhorne, Frank/Bricusse, Frank) 52
Jelly's Last Jam (musical) 58
Jenkins, Jeffrey Eric: *Best Plays of 1999–2000, The* 59

Jersey Boys (musical) 203
Jitney (Wilson, August) 71
Jobs, Steve 14
Johansson, Scarlet 205
John, Elton/Rice, Tim
   Aida 54, 59
   Lion King, The 46, 50, 53, 203
Johnson, Earvin 'Magic' 6, 25, 263 n.7
Jonas, George: *Vengeance* 212
Jones, Paula 11
Jordan, Michael 25
Joseph Papp Public Theater 40
Joyce, James: *Ulysses* 132
Judds, The 19
Judson Poets Theatre 88
Juiced: Wild Times, Rampant 'Roids, Smash Hits & How Baseball Got Big (Conseco, Jose) 250 n.75
Jujamcyn Theaters 46–7
juke box musicals 203
June and Jean in Concert (Kennedy, Adrienne) 73
Jurassic Park (film) 22

Kaczynski, Theodore 5
Kahn, Michael 220–1
Kalb, Jonathan 239
Kander, John/Ebb, Fred
   Kiss of the Spider Woman, The 59
   Rink, The 261 n.10
Katzenberg, Jeffrey 21
Kaufman, Moisés/Tectonic Theater Project 94
   Laramie Project, The 35
Keith, Toby 19
Kendrick, John 46
Kennedy, Adrienne 48, 72–3, 81, 177
   Alexander Plays 73

Funnyhouse of a Negro 72–3
June and Jean in Concert 73
Motherhood 93
Ohio State Murders, The 73
Kennedy, Adrienne/Kennedy,
    Adam: *Sleep Deprivation
    Chamber* 73
Kennedy, John F. 42
Kennedy, John F., Jr 30
Kentucky Cycle, the (Schenkkan,
    Robert) 60–1
Kerrigan, Nancy 26
Kerzer, David: *Kidnapping of
    Edgardo Mortara, The* 211
Keyssar, Helene 82
*Kidnapping of Edgardo Mortara,
    The* (Kerzer, David) 211
Kids (film) 21
Kimbrough, Andrew 140, 141
King, Martin Luther 72, 85
King, Rodney 7–8, 35, 73, 74,
    123
King, Stephen
    Dolores Claiborne 27
    Stand, The 27
King of the Hill (animated TV
    show) 23
Kirdahy, Tom 200
Kirk, Justin 173
Kiss of the Spider Woman, The
    (Kander, John/Ebb, Fred)
    59
Kiss of the Spider Woman, The
    (McNally, Terrence) 59, 97
Klee, Paul: *Angelus Novus*
    159–60
Klein, Alvin 189, 191–2
Kleist, Heinrich von 163
Knapp, Raymond 54, 55, 56, 58
Kolin, Philip 73, 176, 181, 184
Koskinen, John 31
Kramer, Larry 150, 174
    Normal Heart, The 89, 159

Kroll, Jack 156
Kron, Lisa 90
Kunitz, Stanley 153
Kurtz, Swoozie 104, 135, 138,
    218
Kushner, Tony 89, 149–54,
    172–4, 211–13 *see also
    individual plays*
    Angels in America: the Opera
    211
    Backstage Pass to Hell, A 162
    *Blizzard on Marblehead Neck,
    A* 173, 211
    Bright Room Called Day, A
    151, 167, 169
    Broadway 204
    Caroline, or Change 151, 167,
    201, 202, 211, 212
    class 202–3
    *Dybbuk; or, Between Two
    Worlds, A* 151, 165–8
    *East Coast Ode to Howard
    Jarvis* 151, 154, 172
    Fences 203
    G. David Schine in Hell 162
    Good Person of Setzuan, The
    151, 163–5
    Grim(m) 151, 154, 172
    He Wanted the Moon 212
    Heavenly Theatre, The 151
    Homebody 151, 168
    Homebody/Kabul 151, 167,
    168–72, 201, 231–9
    *Hydriotaphia, or The Death of
    Dr. Browne* 151, 173
    Illusion, The 151, 172
    In Great Eliza's Golden Time
    151
    *Intelligent Homosexual's
    Guide to Capitalism and
    Socialism with a Key to the
    Scriptures, The* 152, 173,
    202, 211, 212

Kidnapping of Edgardo Mortara, The 212
La Fin de la Baleine: An Opera for the Apocalypse 151
Lincoln 201, 212
Mayor of Castro Street, The 172
metatheatre 237
Millennium Approaches 154–5, 156, 160
Mother Courage and Her Children 168, 202, 211
Munich 201, 212
Perestroika 154, 155–6, 158, 160–1
Protozoa Review, The 151
race 201
regional theatre 204
scholarly works about 204–5
Slavs! Thinking About the Longstanding Problems of Virtue and Happiness 151, 154, 162, 167
St. Cecilia; or, The Power of Music 151
Stella: A Play for Lovers 151
television 205
Yes, Yes, No, No 151
Kwong, Dan 91

Lahr, John 174
Lamb, Wally: *I Know This Much is True* 27
Lane, Nathan 99, 104, 217–18
Lange, Jessica 205
Language of their Own, A (Yew, Chay) 78
Lapine, James: *Falsettos, The* 59
Laramie Project, The (Kaufman, Moisés/Tectonic Theater Project) 35
Larson, Jennifer 185, 214

Larson, Jonathan: *Rent* 54–5, 58, 203
Last Mile, The (McNally, Terrence) 97, 114
Last Summer at Bluefish Cove (Chambers, Jane) 88
Last Yankee, The (Miller, Arthur) 62
Latina/o theatre 78–80, 91–2
Lauro, Shirley: *Piece of My Heart, A* 36
Law, Jude 205
Law and Order (TV show) 24
League of American Theatres and Producers 47
League of Resident Theaters (LORT) 45, 70
Lear (Mabou Mines production) 94
LeCompte, Elizabeth 92
Lee, Esther Kim 76, 77, 78
Lee, Spike 20
 Girl 6 175, 178
Leguizamo, John 92
 Freak 92
 Mambo Mouth 92
 Spic-O-Rama 92
Lei, Daphne 75
Leiber, Jerry 56
Les Misérables (Bublil, Alain/Schönberg, Claude-Michel) 51, 203
Lesbian and Gay Studies Reader (Abelove, Henry) 87
lesbian theatre 87–9, 90–1
 see also homosexuality; LGBTQ rights
Lesson Before Dying, A (Gaines, Ernest J.) 27
Levi Strauss & Co.: *Guide to Casual Businesswear, A* 29
Lewinsky, Monica 11, 123, 138
LGBTQ (lesbian, gay, bi-sexual,

transgender, queer)
rights 12–13 *see also*
homosexuality; queer theatre
Liddell, Alice 143
Like Water for Chocolate
(Esquevel, Laura) 27
Lil' Kim 19, 20
Lincoln (Kushner, Tony/Spielberg,
Stephen) 201, 212
Lincoln, Abraham 180, 188–9,
190, 229
Lincoln, Mary Todd 229
Lincoln Center 40, 43
Linklater, Richard 21
Linney, Laura 205
Linney, Romulus 48
Lion King, The (film) 22
Lion King, The (John, Elton/Rice,
Tim) 46, 50, 53, 203
Lipps, Theodore 231
Lips Together, Teeth Apart
(McNally, Terrence) 100–5,
107, 108, 116, 200, 208,
218–19
  AIDS 97, 100–2, 125, 200
  homophobia 98, 101, 104–5,
118
Lisbon Traviata, The (McNally,
Terrence) 100, 107, 113,
118, 207–8, 220
literature 26–8
Little Mermaid, The (film) 22
Liu, Lucy 205
Livent 46
Living Colour 19
Lloyd Webber, Andrew 51
  Aspects of Love 51
  Cats 51, 59
  Phantom of the Opera, The
51, 203
  Sunset Boulevard 51–2
Location of Culture, The
(Bhabha, Homi) 28

Locke, John 190
Locomotive (Parks, Suzan-Lori)
175, 178
Lolita (Nabokov, Vladimir) 140
Lollapalooza 19
Lonely Planet (Dietz, Steven) 125
Long Christmas Dinner, The
(Wilder, Thornton) 208
Long Christmas Ride Home, The
(Vogel, Paula) 121, 208
Long Day's Journey into Night
(O'Neill, Eugene) 159
Long Walk to Freedom (Mandela,
Nelson) 28
Long Wharf Theatre, New Haven
41
Longfellow, Henry Wadsworth:
'Christmas Bells' 229
LORT *see* League of Resident
Theaters
Lost World, The (Crichton,
Michael) 27
Love! Valour! Compassion!
(McNally, Terrence) 102,
107, 108–12, 115, 116,
159, 208
  AIDS 35, 97, 111–12, 118, 200
  film version 219–20
  homophobia 35, 98, 118
  success 47, 97
Lucas, Craig 89
Ludlum, Robert: *Bourne Identity,
The* 27

M. Butterfly (Hwang, David
Henry) 76, 77
Mabou Mines 92
  Lear 94
McCarter Theatre, Princeton 41
McCauley, Robbie
  *Confessions of a Black
Working Class Woman* 91
  Sally's Rape 91

McDonough, Carla J. 66
McEntire, Reba 19
McGraw, Tim; *Not a Moment too Soon* 19
McGwire, Mark 25
Mackintosh, Cameron 51
McLaughlin, Ellen: *Iphigenia and Other Daughters* 94
McMillan, Terry: *Waiting to Exhale* 27
McNally, Terrence 89, 97–101, 150, 205–8 see also individual plays
  Anastasia 206
  And Away We Go 206
  And Things That Go Bump in the Night 98, 107
  Andre's Mother 97, 98, 100, 108
  Bad Habits 99
  Broadway 204
  Callas, Maria 100, 113–14, 220–3
  Catch Me if You Can 206
  Chita Rivera: The Dancer's Life 206
  class 203
  comedy 99
  Common Ground 205
  Corpus Christi 98, 99, 114–18, 119, 218, 223–4
  Dead Man Walking 100
  Food of Love, The 206–7
  Frankie and Johnny 207
  Frankie and Johnny in the Clair de Lune 97, 98, 119, 207
  Full Monty, The 97, 203, 206
  Golden Age 100, 206, 207
  It's Only a Play 99
  Kiss of the Spider Woman, The 59, 97
  Lane, Nathan 217–18
  Last Mile, The 97, 114
  Lisbon Traviata, The 100, 107, 113, 118, 207–8, 220
  Man of No Importance, A 206
  metatheatre 206
  'Mr Roberts' 97
  Mothers and Sons 98, 99, 107, 108, 119
  Nights at the Opera 207
  opera 99–100, 103, 206–7, 220–3
  race 57, 201
  Ragtime 52, 97, 201, 203, 207
  regional theatre 204
  Rink, The 261 n.10
  Ritz, The 98, 99, 207
  scholarly works about 204–5
  Selected Works: A Memoir in Plays 208
  Some Men 98, 99
  television 205
  Terrence McNally New Play Award 207–8
  Visit, The 206
McNulty, Charles 214
McVeigh, Timothy 6
'Mad History of Women as Told by Twin Barbies' (Canby, Vincent) 137–8
Madama Butterfly (Puccini, Giacomo) 36, 51
Madame Butterfly (Belasco, David) 51
Making a Spectacle: Feminist Essays on Contemporary Women's Theatre (Hart, Lynda) 81
Malby, Richard, Jr 51
Maleczech, Ruth: *Lear* 94
Mambo Mouth (Leguizamo, John) 92
Mamet, David 64, 66–7, 121, 174
  Oleanna 35, 66–7, 133, 139

Mamma Mia (musical) 203
Mammary Plays, The (Vogel, Paula) 138–9
Man of No Importance, A (movical) 206
Mancina, Mark 53
Mancini, Henry: *Victor/Victoria* 49
Mandela, Nelson: *Long Walk to Freedom* 28
Manhattan Theatre Club 40, 43, 98
Mann, Emily 84, 94
  Having Our Say: The Delany Sisters' First Hundred Years 84–5
Manson, Marilyn 6
Mantello, Joe 134
Map of the World, A (Hamilton, Jane) 27
'Mapping the Margins' (Crenshaw, Kimberle) 35
Mapplethorpe, Robert 42
March of the Falsettos (Finn, William) 59
Marga Gomez is Pretty Witty & Gay (Gomez, Marga) 83
Margolin, Deb 90
Marino, Dan 25
Maris, Roger 25
Marisol (Rivera, José) 80
Mark Taper Forum, Los Angeles 41
Markham, Kika 168
Mars Pathfinder 15
Martin, Carol 94, 95
Martin, Mary 122
Martinez, Daniel J. 29
Marx, Karl 153
masculinity 24, 66–7
Mason, Jeffrey D./Gainor, J. Ellen: *Performing America* 33–4

Mason, Marshall W. 41, 43
Master Builder, The (Ibsen, Henrik) 48
Master Class (McNally, Terrence) 100, 112–14, 204, 207, 208, 220–2
  success 47, 97, 204, 207, 208
Matalin, Mary 3
Matrix, The (film) 30
Matsushita Industrial, Inc. 22
Matthew Shepard and James Byrd, Jr. Hate Crimes Prevention Act 13
Mayer, Oliver 79
Mayor of Castro Street, The (Kushner, Tony) 172
MC Hammer 20
MCA/Universal 33
Me Against the World (Shakur, Tupac) 20
media 2, 18
Mee, Charles
  Agamemnon 94
  Orestes 94
  Trojan Women: A Love Story, The 94
Meese Commission on Pornography 128
megamusicals 46, 49, 50–3, 203
Men in Black (film) 22
Mendes, Sam 21
Menken, Alan/Ashman, Howard/Rice, Tim: *Beauty and the Beast* 46, 49, 53
mental health 17
Mercury, Freddie 6
Merrick, David 47
metatheatre 183, 206, 237
metrosexuals 24
MGM 22
Microsoft 13–14
military 11, 12
Milk, Harvey 172

millennium 20–1, 199
Millennium Approaches (Kushner, Tony) 154–5, 156, 160
Miller, Arthur 45, 48, 61–3, 152, 174
  All My Sons 61
  Broken Glass 62–3
  Crucible, The 48, 61
  Death of a Salesman 61, 62
  Incident at Vichy, The 61
  Last Yankee, The 62
  Mr. Peters' Connections 62
  Price, The 61
  Ride Down Mt. Morgan, The 62
  View From the Bridge, A 61, 152
Miller, Tim 42, 129
  Naked Breath 90
Mineola Twins, The (Vogel, Paula) 134–9, 201–2
Minnesota Twins 25
Miriam's Flowers (Cruz, Migdalia) 80
Miss Saigon (Bublil, Alain/ Schönberg, Claude-Michel) 36, 40, 51, 56, 59
  Hwang, David Henry 77
Mr. Peters' Connections (Miller, Arthur) 62
'Mr Roberts' (McNally, Terrence) 97
Mitchard, Jacquelyn: *Deep End of the Ocean, The* 27
Mixed Blood Theatre 35
Monk, Meredith 92
Monsanto 14
Monty Python: *Spamalot* 203
Moraga, Cherríe 79, 81
  Heroes and Saints 79–80
  Hungry Woman: A Mexican Medea, The 80
  Shadow of a Man 79

Morgan, J. P. 56
Morissette, Alanis: *Jagged Little Pill* 19
Morrison, Toni: *Paradise* 27
Morse, David 145
Morton, Jelly Roll 58
Mos Def 205, 213
Mosaic 13
Mother Courage and Her Children (Brecht, Bertolt) 168, 211, 213
Mother Courage and Her Children (Kushner, Tony) 168, 202, 211
Motherhood (Kennedy, Adrienne) 93
Mothers and Sons (McNally, Terrence) 98, 99, 107, 108, 119
movicals 203, 206
Mozart, Wolfgang Amadeus: *Cosi Fan Tutte* 103
MTV 23
multiculturalism 35–6, 228
Munich (Kushner, Tony/Spielberg, Steven) 201, 212
Murder She Wrote (TV show) 24
Murphy, Brenda 65
Murphy Brown (TV show) 23
Murray, Charles/Herrnstein, Richard: *Bell Curve, The* 28
Murray, Larry 223
music 18–21, 135
  Parks, Suzan-Lori 179–80
musical theatre 46–7, 48–50, 203
  American identity 55–60
  book shows 49
  concept musicals 49
  Disney on Broadway 53–4, 203
  homosexuality 58–9
  juke box musicals 203
  marriage trope 58

megamusicals 46, 49, 50–3, 203
movicals 203, 206
national identity 56–8
non-profit theatre 54–5
nostalgia 55–6
race 57–8, 203
trends 49
Mutual of Omaha's Wild Kingdom (TV show) 180, 184

Nabokov, Vladimir: *Lolita* 140
Nadler, Sheila 222
Naked Breath (Miller, Tim) 90
Napier, John 51
Napster 16
National Actors Theatre 48
National Endowment for the Arts (NEA) 41–2
  All America's a Stage: Growth and Challenges in Nonprofit Theatre 43–4
national identity 56–8
Native Son (Wright, Richard) 186
NEA *see* National Endowment for the Arts
NEA Four 42, 90, 129
Necessity of Art: A Marxist Approach, The (Fischer, Ernst) 152
Nesbit, Evelyn 56
Netscape 13
Neugroschel, Joachim 165
Nevermind (Nirvana) 20
New 42nd Street 46
New York Giants 25
New York Yankees 25
News Corporation 27
NeXT 14
Nichols, Mike 172
Nichols, Terry 6
'night Mother (Norman, Marsha) 83

Nights at the Opera (McNally, Terrence) 207
Nintendo 16
Nirvana
  Nevermind 20
  'Smells Like Teen Spirit' 20
non-profit theatre 37, 39, 43–4
  musical theatre 54–5
Normal Heart, The (Kramer, Larry) 89, 159
Norman, Marsha 50, 83
  'night Mother 83
Northwest Asian American Theatre 76
nostalgia 55–6
Not a Moment too Soon (McGraw, Tim) 19
Not About Nightingales (Williams, Tennessee) 63
Nottage, Lynn 122, 208
Nunn, Trevor 51
Nureyev, Rudolf 6, 263 n.7
Nyong'o, Lupito 205

Obama, Barack: *Dreams from My Father* 28
obscene art 41, 42, 90, 129
O'Connor, Sinead 19
Odets, Clifford 63, 152
Off-Broadway 37, 38–9, 40, 60–1, 98
Off-Off-Broadway 37, 38–9, 40, 60–1, 88
Offshore (San Francisco Mime Troupe) 36
OG: Original Gangster (Body Count) 20
Ohio State Murders, The (Kennedy, Adrienne) 73
Oklahoma City bombing 5–6, 35, 55
Old Globe Theatre, San Diego 41

Oldest Profession, The (Vogel, Paula) 121, 124, 08
Oleanna (Mamet, David) 35, 66–7, 133, 138
Olympic Games 5
'On Cultural Power' (debate) 70–1
Onassis, Aristotle 113
O'Neill, Eugene 153, 173, 211
    Strange Interlude 103
Ong, Han 242–3
Ontological Theatre 92
opera 99–100, 103, 220–3
'Operation Desert Storm' 4
'Operation Restore Hope' 4
Oprah Winfrey's Book Club 27
Oprah Winfrey Show, The 12
Orestes (Mee, Charles) 94
Orion 22
Orlandersmith, Dael 91
Oscher, Paul 200
Ostrow, Stuart 47
Our American Cousin (Taylor, Tom) 180, 189
Our Town (Wilder, Thornton) 159, 209

PACE theatrical group 46–7
Pacino, Al 173, 207
paedophilia 140–1, 226
Paglia, Camille: *Sexual Personae* 27
Paige, Elaine 51
Palin, Sarah 138
Pan Asian Repertory Theatre 76
Papp, Joseph 47, 60
Parade (Uhry, Alfred/Brown, Jason Robert) 57–8
Paradise (Morrison, Toni) 27
Paramount (UPN) 24
Paramount Pictures 22
Parker, Mary-Louise 145, 173
Parks, Suzan-Lori 74–5, 81, 175–84, 196–8, 213–15, 239–44 *see also individual plays*
    365 Days/365 Plays 176–7, 184, 197, 213
    America Play and Other Plays, The 178, 179
    Anemone Me 175
    Betting on the Dust Commander 176
    Black body 181–2, 191–2, 195–6, 202
    Book of Grace, The 197, 214
    Broadway 204
    class 202
    Commencement Address, Mount Holyoke 243–4
    death 182–3
    Devotees in the Garden of Love 175, 177–8, 182, 183
    'Elements of Style' 180
    'Equation for Black People on Stage, An' 180, 241–2
    Father Comes Home from the Wars (Parts 1, 2, 3) 176, 184, 197, 201, 202, 213–14
    Fucking A 179, 180, 193, 202, 213, 215
    Gal 175
    Gershwins' Porgy and Bess, The 197, 201, 214
    Getting Mother's Body 197, 214
    Girl 6 175, 178
    God's Country 175
    hip-hop theory 180
    history 181, 188–91
    Locomotive 175, 178
    metatheatre 183
    music 179–80
    Pickling 175
    race 180–2, 184–92, 195, 201, 239–40, 241–2
    Ray Charles Live! 197, 201

regional theatre 204
Rep and Rev 179, 197
scholarly works about 204–5
Sinner's Place, The 176
spirituality 183–4
'Suzan-Lori Parks Show' 215
television 205
Their Eyes Were Watching God 205, 214
Third Kingdom, The 175, 178
time 183
Watch Me Work 215
working 242–3
patriarchy 94
Patriot Act 199
Paula Vogel Award 210
Paula Vogel Award in Playwriting 210
Paula Vogel Mentorship Program 210
Paulus, Diane 214
Pearl Jam 20
Pelican Brief, The (Grisham, John) 27
Pellegrini, Ann 209
Perestroika (Kushner, Tony) 154, 155–6, 158, 160–1
Perfect Ganesh, A (McNally, Terrence) 97, 98, 104–8, 118, 208
screenplay 219
white supremacy 201
performance art 89–93
Performing America (Mason, Jeffrey D./Gainor, J. Ellen) 33–4
Perkins, Anthony 6
Perkins, Kathy A./Uno, Roberta: *Contemporary Plays by Women of Color* 82, 83
Perkins, Marlin 180
Perot, Ross 2, 3
Persley, Nicole Hodges 179–80

Peters, Bernadette 114
Pfeiffer, Michelle 207
Phagan, Mary 57
Phair, Liz 19
Phantom of the Opera, The (Lloyd Webber, Andrew) 51, 203
Philadelphia (film) 7
Piano Lesson, The (Wilson, August) 43, 45, 71, 72
Pickling (Parks, Suzan-Lori) 175
Piece of My Heart, A (Lauro, Shirley) 36
Pierce, David Hyde 24
Piñero, Miguel: *Short Eyes* 79
Pippen, Scottie 25
Pirandello, Luigi 177
'Piss Christ' (Serrano, Andres) 42
Pixar 14
Plains of Passage, The (Auel, Jean) 27
Play about the Baby, The (Albee, Edward) 64
Playboy (magazine) 143
playwrights 61–4
women 81–6
Playwrights Horizons 40
Plunka, Gene A. 67
Poehler, Amy 138
politics 2–5, 37–8, 134–5
Kushner, Tony 151–3, 157–9, 164, 173
Politics of Life (Houston, Velina Hasu) 77
population and demographics 15
Porgy (Heyward, Dubose/Heyward, Dorothy) 214
Porgy and Bess (Gershwin, George/Gershwin, Ira/Heyward, Dubose) 197, 214
pornography 128, 130

postfeminism 9
postliterate 26
Preaching to the Converted (Hughes, Holly) 90
Price, Leontyne 221
Price, Steven 64
Price, The (Miller, Arthur) 61
Pride's Crossing (Howe, Tina) 84
Prince, Harold: *Parade* 57–8
producers 47
Protozoa Review, The (Kushner, Tony) 151
Pryce, Jonathan 36, 51
Public Theater 43
Puccini, Giacomo
    La Boheme 55
    Madama Butterfly 51
Puff Daddy *see* Combs, Sean
Puig, Manuel 59
Pulp Fiction (film) 21, 123, 133
Puritani, I (Bellini, Vincenzo) 100, 206

Quayle, Dan 3
Queen Latifah 19, 20
Queer Nation 12
Queer Theater Conference 87
queer theatre 87–9
Quindlen, Anna 161

Rabe, David 64
race 7–10, 34, 64–7, 200–1
    African American theatre 69–75
    art 28
    Asian American theatre 75–8, 91
    casting actors 36–7, 51, 70–1, 77
    Contemporary Plays by Women of Color 82, 83
    education 17
    gangsta rap 19, 20

Kushner, Tony 201
Latina/o theatre 78–80, 91–2
McNally, Terrence 57, 201
multiculturalism 35–6, 228
musical theatre 57–8, 203
Parade 57–8
Parks, Suzan-Lori 180–2, 184–92, 195, 201, 239–40, 241–2
performance art 91
Twilight in Los Angeles 35
Vogel, Paula 201
white male privilege/supremacy 66–7, 68, 200–1
Race Matters (West, Cornel) 28
radical theatre 81
Ragtime (Doctorow, E. L.) 52, 207
Ragtime (Flaherty, Stephen/ Ahrens, Lynn) 50, 52–3, 56, 58
Ragtime (McNally, Terrence) 52, 97, 201, 203, 207
Raisin in the Sun, A (Hansberry, Lorraine) 159
Ramsey, Jon Benet 226
Randall, Tony 48
Randle, Theresa 178
Random House 27
Rappoport, Solomon *see* Ansky, S.
Ray Charles Live! (Parks, Suzan Lori) 197, 201
Reagan, Ronald 2, 125, 149, 159
Real World, The (TV Show) 23
Reality Bites (film) 21
Red Shoes, The (Styne, Jule) 49–50
Redgrave, Corin 63
Redgrave, Lynn 48
Redgrave, Vanessa 63
Reed, Robert 263 n.7
regional theatre 38, 40–1, 204
religion 15–16, 17

Reno, Janet 11
Rent (Larson, Jonathan) 54–5, 58, 203
Reservoir Dogs (Tarantino, Quentin) 21
Reston, James, Jr 171
Revlon 135
Rice, Jerry 35
Rice, Tim/John, Elton
  Aida 54, 59
  Lion King, The 46, 50, 53, 203
Rice, Tim/Menken, Alan/Ashman, Howard: *Beauty and the Beast* 46, 49, 53
Rich, Frank 12, 54, 61, 128, 156
Richards, David 54
Richards, Lloyd 71
Ride Down Mt. Morgan, The (Miller, Arthur) 62
Rifkin, Jay 53
Rilke, Rainer Maria 153
Ring Pops 17
Ringwald, Molly 145
Rink, The (McNally, Terrence) 261 n.10
Ripken, Cal, Jr 25
Ritz, The (McNally, Terrence) 98, 99, 207
Rivera, Chita 206
Rivera, José 80
  Marisol 80
Rno, Sung: *Cleveland Raining* 77–8
Robertson, Pat 10–11, 12
Rodgers, Richard/Hammerstein, Oscar: *State Fair* 49
Rodman, Dennis 25
Rodriguez, Diane 91
rollerblading 17
Rollins Band 19
Roman, David 67, 127–8
  Acts of Intervention 88

Rose, Charlie 219–20, 222–3
Rose, Lloyd 133
Roseanne (TV show) 23
Rosenbaum, Yankel 8
Rosenberg, Ethel 155
Rosenberg, Julius 155
Rothstein, Mervyn 218–19
Roundabout Theatre 40, 43
Rowling, J. K.: *Harry Potter and the Sorcerer's Stone* 27
Rudnick, Paul 89
Rudolph, Eric Robert 5
Ruhl, Sarah 122, 153, 208
Russell, Ken: *Tommy* 50

Sachar, Louis: *Holes* 27
Saddik, Annette J. 61, 65, 68
St. Cecilia; or, The Power of Music (Kushner, Tony) 151
Saint Joan (Shaw, George Bernard) 48
Sally's Rape (McCauley, Robbie) 91
Salome (Wilde, Oscar) 206
Saltz, Jerry 28
same-sex marriage 12, 118, 200
Sampras, Pete 26
San Francisco Mime Troupe: *Offshore* 36
Sandbox, The (Albee, Edward) 63
Sandoval-Sanchez, Alberto 80
Sartre, Jean-Paul 177
Saturday Night Live (TV show) 138
Saudi Arabia 5
Savran, David 89
Scarlet Letter, The (Hawthorne, Nathaniel) 75, 180, 193–6, 213
Scarlet Pimpernel, The (Wildhorne, Frank) 52
Schanke, Robert A. 42

Angels in the American Theater 39
Schenkkan, Robert: *Kentucky Cycle, The* 60–1
Schindler's List (film) 22
Schine, G. David 162
Schlesinger, Arthur 42
Schlueter, June 45
    'American Drama of the 1990s On and Off-Broadway' 39, 40–1
Schneerson, Menachem 8
Schneider, Sherrie/Fein, Ellen:
    All the Rules: Time-Tested Secrets for Capturing the Heart of Mr. Right 28
Schönberg, Claude-Michel/Bublil, Alain
    Les Misérables 51, 203
    Miss Saigon 36, 51, 56, 59
Schor, Juliet B. 16
science and technology 13–15
Scott, Ridley 21
Scotto, Renata 221
Scottsboro Boys, The (musical) 203
Seagram 22
Seagull, The (Chekhov, Anton) 48, 206
Seattle Repertory Theatre 41
Second Shepherds' Play (mystery play) 117
Sedgwick, Eve Kosofsky:
    Epistemology of the Closet, The 27
Sega 16
Seinfeld (TV show) 24, 30
Seinfeld, Jerry 24
Selected Works: A Memoir in Plays (McNally, Terrence) 208
Seles, Monica 26
September 11 2001 attack on the World Trade Center 1, 168–9, 199
Serrano, Andres: 'Piss Christ' 42
Seven Deadly Sins (Brecht, Bertolt) 136
Seven Guitars (Wilson, August) 71, 72
Sex and the City (TV show) 23–4
Sex, Lies, and Videotape (film) 21
Sex Pictures series (Sherman, Cindy) 28
sexual abuse 85–6, 90, 201–2
    British plays 265 n.42
    How I Learned to Drive 139–46, 226
    Sally's Rape 91
sexual harassment 8–9, 34–5, 67, 85
Sexual Personae (Paglia, Camille) 27
sexual politics 66–7, 87
sexuality 130–2, 140–3, 193–4, 201–2
Shadow of a Man (Moraga, Cherríe) 79
Shakespeare, William 94, 121, 177
    Henry V 105
Shakespeare in Love (film) 22
Shakur, Tupac: *Me Against the World* 20
Shange, Ntozake 177
Shank, Theodore 93
Shannon, Sandra 71–2
Shaw, George Bernard 152
    Heartbreak House: A Fantasia in the Russian Manner on English Themes 157
    Saint Joan 48
Shaw, Peggy 90–1
Shear, Claudia: *Dirty Blonde* 49
Shepard, Matthew 12–13, 35

Shepard, Sam 48, 64, 65–6, 121, 174
  Buried Child 65
  Curse of the Starving Class, The 65
  Eyes for Consuela 65, 66
  Simpatico 65, 66
  States of Shock 36, 65–6
  True West 65
Sherman, Cindy: *Sex Pictures* series 28
Sherman, Martin: *Bent* 159
Shock Treatment (Finley, Karen) 90
Short Eyes (Piñero, Miguel) 79
Shrek: The Musical (musical) 203
Shubert Foundation 46
Shubert Organization 44, 46
Shuffle Along: The Making of the Musical Sensation of 1921 (musical) 203
Shula, Don 25
Signature Theatre 48
Silence of the Lambs (Harris, Thomas) 27
Silence of the Lambs, The (film) 22
Silicon Valley 13–14
Simon, Neil: *Goodbye Girl, The* 50
Simpatico (Shepard, Sam) 65, 66
Simpson, Nicole 9–10
Simpson, O. J. 9–10, 123, 133
Simpsons, The (animated TV show) 23
Sinatra, Frank 236
Sinese, Gary 22
Sinner's Place, The (Parks, Suzan-Lori) 176
Sister Soulijah 19
Sisters Matsumoto (Gotanda, Philip Kan) 76

Sisters Rosensweig, The (Wasserstein, Wendy) 83–4
Six Degrees of Separation (Guare, John) 67
Sixth Sense, The (film) 22
Slave Ship (Baraka, Amiri) 185
Slavs! Thinking About the Longstanding Problems of Virtue and Happiness (Kushner, Tony) 151, 154, 162, 167
Sleep Deprivation Chamber (Kennedy, Adrienne/ Kennedy, Adam) 73
Slim Shady LP (Eminem) 20
Smashing Pumpkins 20
'Smells Like Teen Spirit' (Nirvana) 20
Smith, Anna Deavere 70, 73–4, 94
  Fires in the Mirror 35–6, 74
  Twilight in Los Angeles 35, 36, 74
Smith, Caroline Jackson 73
Smith, Emmitt 25
Smith, John 146
Smith, Kevin 21
Smith, Molly 124, 133
Smith, Sharon Jane 90
Smith, Susan 9
Smith, Will 20, 24
Smokey Joe's Café (musical) 49, 56
Snoop Doggy Dogg
  Doggystyle 20
  'For All My Niggaz and Bitches' 20
soccer 26
society 5–13
Soderbergh, Steven 21
Solis, Octavio 79
Solomon, Alisa 134
Somalia 4

Some Men (McNally, Terrence) 98, 99
Sommers, Christina Hoff: *Who Stole Feminism? How Women Have Betrayed Women* 27–8
Son, Diana: *Stop Kiss* 78
Sondheim, Stephen 54
   Assassins 54
   Company 203
   Sweeney Todd 203
Sosa, Sammy 25
Soundgarden 20
South Coast Repertory, Costa Mesa 41
South Park (animated TV show) 23
space 15
Spamalot (musical) 203
Spears, Britney 19
Spic-O-Rama (Leguizamo, John) 92
Spice Girls 19
Spielberg, Steven 21, 212
spirituality 183–4
Split Britches collective 90
sport 25–6
Stand, The (King, Stephen) 27
Star Wars Episode I: The Phantom Menace (Brooks, Terry) 27
Star Wars Episode 1: The Phantom Menace (film) 22
Starbucks 30
Starr, Kenneth 11
State Fair (Rodgers, Richard/ Hammerstein, Oscar) 49
States of Shock (Shepard, Sam) 36, 65–6
Steadman, Susan 83
Stein, Gertrude 177
Stein, R. L.: *Goosebumps* series 27

Stella: A Play for Lovers (Goethe, Johann Wolfgang von) 151
Stella: A Play for Lovers (Kushner, Tony) 151
Sternfeld, Jessica 50, 52
Stevens, David: *Sum of Us, The* 43
Stevenson, Robert Louis: *Jekyll and Hyde* 52
Stewart, Martha 10, 30
Stiller, Ben 21
Stojanovic, Marija 232
Stoller, Mike 56
Stone, Peter: *Will Rogers Follies, The* 55–6
Stonewall riots 58, 87
Stop Kiss (Son, Diana) 78
Straight as a Line (Alfaro, Luis) 92
Strange Interlude (O'Neill, Eugene) 103
Streep, Meryl 172–3, 211
Streetcar Named Desire, A (Williams, Tennessee) 63, 91, 101, 159
Stroman, Susan/Weidman, John: *Contact* 49
Strug, Kerri 25
Styne, Jule: *Red Shoes, The* 49–50
Suge Knight 20
Sum of All Fears, The (Clancy, Tom) 27
Sum of Us, The (Stevens, David) 43
'Summertime' (Gershwin, George/ Heyward, Dubose) 214
Sundance Channel 21
Sunday Bloody Sunday (film) 261 n.9
Sunset Boulevard (Lloyd Webber, Andrew) 51–2
'Suzan-Lori Parks Show' (Parks, Suzan-Lori) 215

Svich, Caridad 79
Sweeney Todd (Sondheim, Stephen) 203
Sweet, Jeffrey 60
Sweet Bird of Youth (Williams, Tennessee) 63

Taichman, Rebecca: *Indecent* 147, 210
Tailhook convention assaults 11
Tamagotchi pets 16
Tarantino, Quentin
  Pulp Fiction 21, 123
  Reservoir Dogs 21
Taymor, Julie 49, 53
TBS (Turner Broadcasting System) 22
Tea (Houston, Velina Hasu) 76–7
Team of Rivals: The Political Genius of Abraham Lincoln (Goodwin, Doris Kearns) 212
technology 1–2, 13–14, 16, 93
  competition with theatre 39–40
  film 22
  Y2K 30–1
Tectonic Theater Project/ Kaufman, Moisés 94
  Laramie Project, The 35
television 23–4, 205
tennis 26
Terrence McNally New Play Award 207–8
terrorism 1, 4–6, 55, 168–9, 199
Tesori, Jeanine 151, 173, 211
The Who: *The Who's Tommy* 50
theatre 93–5 *see also* playwrights
  1990s 33–8
  actos 79
  adaptation 93–4
  African American theatre 69–75

alternative theatre 38, 93
America 33–4
Asian American theatre 75–8, 91
attendance 44
business models 43–4
confessional theatre 265 n.42
docudramas 94–5
feminist 81–6
funding 38–42, 47
gay theatre 87–9
identity politics 33–7
Latina/o theatre 78–80, 91–2
Mason, Marshall W. 43
most produced plays 204
non-profit 37, 39, 43–4
Off-Broadway 37, 38–9, 40, 60–1, 98
Off-Off-Broadway 37, 38–9, 40, 60–1, 88
performance art 89–93
politics 37–8
queer 87–9
radical 82
regional theatre 38, 40–1, 204
structure 37, 38–9
Theatre Communications Group 42
Theatre Congress 43
Theatre Genesis 88
Their Eyes Were Watching God (Hurston, Zora Neale) 205, 214
'Theses on the Philosophy of History' (Benjamin, Walter) 159–60
Third Kingdom, The (Parks, Suzan-Lori) 175, 178
Third Man, The (film) 126
'This Kiss' (Hill, Faith) 19
Thomas, Clarence 8–9, 34–5, 67, 85, 123
Thompson, Emma 173

Three Tall Women (Albee, Edward) 63, 64
Tichler, Rosemary 241
ticket prices/sales 40, 47, 203
Tickle-Me Elmo 16
Time Inc. 22
Time/Warner 22
Time Warner Cable 24
Times Square Alliance 47
Titanic (film) 22
Titanic (Yeston, Maury) 50, 52
Tommy (Russell, Ken) 50
Tommy (Townshend, Pete) 50
Topdog/Underdog (Parks, Suzan-Lori) 175, 204, 213
  class 202
  sampling 180
Torch Song Trilogy (Fierstein, Harvey) 88
Torke, Michael 206
Toscano, Michael 146
Townshend, Pete: *Tommy* 50
Toy Story (film) 22
Toy Story 2 (film) 22
Trinity Repertory Company, Providence 41
Trojan Women: A Love Story, The (Mee, Charles) 94
troll dolls 16
Tropicana, Carmelita *see* Troyano, Alina
Trotsky, Leon 153
Troyano, Alina 90, 91
  Milk of Magnesia 91
True West (Shepard, Sam) 65
Turner Broadcasting System *see* TBS
Turner, Ted 24
Twain, Shania 19
Twilight: Los Angeles, 1992 (Smith, Anna Deavere) 35, 36, 74
Twister (film) 22

Two Journeymen (Grimm, Jacob/Grimm, Wilhelm) 172
Two Trains Running (Wilson, August) 45, 71, 72
Two Undiscovered Amerindians Visit New York (Fusco, Coco/Gómez-Peña, Guillermo) 92
Tyson, Mike 26

Uhry, Alfred/Brown, Jason Robert: *Parade* 57–8
Ulysses (Joyce, James) 132
'Unabomber' 5
Unforgiven (film) 22
Universal Studios 22
Uno, Roberta/Perkins, Kathy A.: *Contemporary Plays by Women of Color* 82, 83
Urinetown; the Musical (musical) 203
USA *see* America
Uyehara, Denise 91
  Hello (Sex) Kitty 91

V-day 85
Vagina Monologues, The (Ensler, Eve) 85
Valdez, Luis 78–9
  Zoot Suit 79
Vengeance (Jonas, George) 212
Venter, J. Craig 14
Venus (Parks, Suzan-Lori) 75, 175, 181–2, 191–2, 196, 213
  Foreman, Richard 178, 241
  metatheatre 183
  sampling 179–80
Verdi, Guiseppe: *Aida* 54
Viacom 22
Victor/Victoria (musical) 49
Vietnam War 56, 86
View From the Bridge, A (Miller, Arthur) 61, 152

Vineyard Theatre 40
violence 17, 85–6, 123 *see also* sexual abuse; terrorism
domestic violence 128–34
Violent Femmes 19
Visit, The (Dürrenmatt, Friedrich) 206
Vogel, Carl 124, 125
Vogel, Paula 86, 89, 121–4, 147, 150, 208–10 *see also individual plays*
  And Baby Makes Seven 121, 124
  Broadway 204
  Civil War Christmas: A Musical Celebration, A 209, 228–9
  collaboration 230–1
  comedy 134, 224–5
  Common Ground 205
  defamiliarization 123
  Desdemona 94, 121, 124, 201
  Don Juan Comes Home From Iraq 147, 209–10, 230–1
  family, the 225
  history 228–9
  Hot 'n' Throbbing 121, 124, 128–34, 208
  Indecent 147, 201, 210
  Long Christmas Ride Home, The 121, 208
  Mammary Plays, The 138–9
  Mineola Twins, The 134–9, 201–2
  negative empathy 231
  Oldest Profession, The 121, 124, 208
  Paula Vogel Award 210
  Paula Vogel Award in Playwriting 210
  Paula Vogel Mentorship Program 210
  race 201
  regional theatre 204
  scholarly works about 204–5
  sexual abuse 139–46, 201, 226–7
  teaching 229–30
  television 205
Voight, Jon 48

Waco, Texas 5
Wade, Leslie A. 65
Waiting for Godot (Beckett, Samuel) 206
Waiting to Exhale (McMillan, Terry) 27
Walker, Kara: *Gone, An Historical Romance of a Civil War as It Occurred Between the Dusky Thighs of One Young Negress and Her Heart* 28
'Walking Backwards into the Future' (Williams, Raymond) 157
Wallace, Naomi: *In the Heart of America* 36, 86
Waller, Robert James: *Bridges of Madison County, The* 27
war 4–5, 36, 55, 56, 123, 199
  Gulf War (first) 55, 86, 94
  In the Heart of America 36, 86
  States of Shock 36, 65–6
  Vogel, Paula 209–10, 228
Ward, Nari 28
Warner Brothers (WB) 24
Warner Cable 24
Warner Communications 22
Wash, The (Gotanda, Philip Kan) 76
Washington, Denzel 202–3, 205
Wasserstein, Wendy 83, 206
  American Daughter, An 84
  Heidi Chronicles, The 83, 138

Sisters Rosensweig, The 83–4
Watch Me Work (Parks, Suzan-Lori) 215
Waters, Les 133
We Keep our Victims Ready (Finley, Karen) 90
Weaver, Lois 90–1
Weaver, Randy 5
Weber, Carl 151
Weidman, John 54
Weidman, John/Stroman, Susan: *Contact* 49
welfare 194–5
West, Cheryl L.: *Before it Hits Home* 125
West, Cornel: *Race Matters* 28
White, Mark 3
White, Ryan 6
White, Stanford 56
White male privilege/supremacy 66–7, 68, 200–1
Whitman, Walt 229
Whitney Biennial 28
Who Stole Feminism? How Women Have Betrayed Women (Sommers, Christina Hoff) 27–8
Who's Afraid of Virginia Woolf (Albee, Edward) 63, 64, 156, 159
Wilde, Oscar: *Salome* 206
Wilder, Thornton 121
  Happy Journey to Trenton and Camden, The 208
  Long Christmas Dinner, The 208
  Our Town 159, 208
Wildhorne, Frank
  Civil War, The 52
  Scarlet Pimpernel, The 52
Wildhorne, Frank/Bricusse, Frank: *Jekyll and Hyde* 52
Will and Grace (TV show) 12, 24

Will Rogers Follies, The (Comden, Betty/Green, Adolph/Coleman, Cy) 55–6
Will Rogers Follies, The (Stone, Peter) 55–6
Willey, Kathleen 11
William Morrow 27
Williams, Monte 177
Williams, Raymond 171
  'Walking Backwards into the Future' 157
Williams, Tennessee 45, 63, 152, 153, 161, 173
  Cat on a Hot Tin Roof 63
  Glass Menagerie, The 63
  Not About Nightingales 63
  Streetcar Named Desire, A 63, 91, 101, 159
  Sweet Bird of Youth 63
Williamstown Theatre Festival 41
Wilmer, S. E. 35–6
Wilson, August 37, 69–72
  Fences 203
  Gem of the Ocean 185
  'Ground on Which I Stand, The' 70
  Jitney 71
  Piano Lesson, The 43, 45, 71, 72
  Seven Guitars 71, 72
  Two Trains Running 45, 71, 72
Wilson, Lanford 89
Wilson, Robert 92
Winfrey, Oprah 10, 27, 205
Wolf, Naomi: *Beauty Myth, The* 28
Wolf, Stacy 48–9, 55, 57–8
Wolfe, George C. 58, 188, 241
women 8–9, 10–12, 34 *see also* feminism
  status of in the 1990s 10–12
  underrepresentation of women playwrights 81–2

Women's Project and Productions 82
Woodard, Charlayne 196
Woods, Tiger 25
Woolverton, Linda 53
Wooster Group 92
World Trade Center attack (1993) 5, 55
World Trade Center attack (2001) *see* September 11
World Wide Web 13
Worthen, W. B. 80
WOW Café 90–1
Wozniak, Steve 14
Wright, Jeffrey 173
Wright, Richard: *Native Son* 186

X Files, The (TV show) 24

Y2K 30–1

Yale Repertory Theatre, New Haven 41
Yarbro-Bejarano, Yvonne 78
Yellow Face (Hwang, David Henry) 77
Yemen 4–5
Yes, Yes, No, No (Kushner, Tony) 151
Yeston, Maury: *Titanic* 50, 52
Yew, Chay: *Language of their Own, A* 78
Yohen (Gotanda, Philip Kan) 76
Young, Harvey 69, 70, 181, 183, 184

Zimmer, Hans 53
Zizka, Blanka 230–1
Zoo Story, The (Albee, Edward) 63
Zoot Suit (Valdez, Luis) 79